D1276748

Microsoft®

ACTIVE DIRECTORY®
for Microsoft®
WINDOWS®
SERVER 2003
Technical Reference

Stan Reimer
Mike Mulcare

PUBLISHED BY
Microsoft Press
A Division of Microsoft Corporation
One Microsoft Way
Redmond, Washington 98052-6399

Copyright © 2003 by Microsoft Corporation

All rights reserved. No part of the contents of this book may be reproduced or transmitted in any form or by any means without the written permission of the publisher.

Library of Congress Cataloging-in-Publication Data
Reimer, Stan, 1958-
    Active Directory for Microsoft Windows Server 2003 Technical Reference / Stan Reimer,
    Mike Mulcare.
        p. cm.
    Includes index.
    ISBN 0-7356-1577-2
    1. Directory services (Computer network technology)   2. Microsoft
software--Examinations--Study guides. 3. Microsoft Windows (Computer file)   I. Mulcare,
Mike II. Title.

    TK5105.595.M85   2003
    005.7'13769--dc21   2003042113

Printed and bound in the United States of America.

1 2 3 4 5 6 7 8 9   QWT   8 7 6 5 4 3

Distributed in Canada by H.B. Fenn and Company Ltd.

A CIP catalogue record for this book is available from the British Library.

Microsoft Press books are available through booksellers and distributors worldwide. For further information about international editions, contact your local Microsoft Corporation office or contact Microsoft Press International directly at fax (425) 936-7329. Visit our Web site at www.microsoft.com/mspress. Send comments to *mspinput@microsoft.com*.

Active Directory, Authenticode, FrontPage, IntelliMirror, Microsoft, Microsoft Press, MS-DOS, NetMeeting, Outlook, Visio, Windows, Windows Media, and Windows NT are either registered trademarks or trademarks of Microsoft Corporation in the United States and/or other countries. Other product and company names mentioned herein may be the trademarks of their respective owners.

The example companies, organizations, products, domain names, e-mail addresses, logos, people, places, and events depicted herein are fictitious. No association with any real company, organization, product, domain name, e-mail address, logo, person, place, or event is intended or should be inferred.

Acquisitions Editor: Jeff Koch
Project Editor: Julie Miller

Body Part No. X08-73299

Contents

7   Migrating to Active Directory   185

Part III   Administering Windows Server 2003 Active Directory

Tables

Dedications

I dedicate this book to my parents for their continued interest and support, even when they don't understand what the book is about. And to Rhonda, Angela, and Amanda, who light up my life.

—S.R.

One benefit of an extended book-writing project is the opportunity to have more kids to dedicate it to! I would like to dedicate this book to my three sons: James, Sean, and our latest edition, Patrick, and of course my wife, Nancy. I owe you guys a whole bunch of Saturdays.

—M.M.

Acknowledgments

Stan Reimer

This book has been an interesting exercise in patience and persistence. Mike and I started working on the book in the fall of 2001. After writing a couple of chapters each, work on the book was put on hold while the product delivery dates slipped (and the product went through several name changes). When we finally *did* get back to work on the book, it seemed like the deadlines were tight—making me almost wish that I had spent the summer working on the book rather than riding my motorcycle. But in the end, it all came together rather well.

Many thanks to my cowriter, Mike Mulcare, for getting this project off the ground and getting me involved. Mike and I have worked together on projects for several years, and it is always a pleasure.

And thanks to the team at Microsoft Press for putting this book together. Thanks to David Clark for providing me with the opportunity to do this book, and to Jeff Koch for picking up the book in midstream. And speaking of picking up the book in midstream, Julie Miller did a great job pulling the book together across product versions and months of writing and editing. Thanks to Jim Johnson, Uma Kukathas, Linda Robinson, and the team at Microsoft Press. It has been a pleasure working with you—we must do this again some time.

Mike Mulcare

In addition to the team at Microsoft Press, I would like to acknowledge the support and assistance of several individuals within Microsoft Training & Certification. Foremost, thanks to Greg Weber for your technical expertise and for being my sounding board and reality check throughout this entire project. Thanks also to Julie Truax, Keith Loeber, and Mark Johnson for your continued mentoring and opening doors.

Finally, many thanks to my partner, Stan Reimer. You have been a tremendous source of support, information, and humor during this undertaking. I have enjoyed this project as much as anything we have done together, and I look forward to much future collaboration.

Introduction

Welcome to *Active Directory for Microsoft Windows Server 2003 Technical Reference*, your complete source for the information you need to design and implement Active Directory directory service in Windows Server 2003. Active Directory was first released with Microsoft Windows 2000. Most of the Active Directory concepts from Windows 2000 have been retained in Windows Server 2003, and there are many additional enhancements. This book includes everything you need to know about Active Directory, including detailed technical information about Active Directory in Windows 2003 and guidance to plan, implement, and manage Active Directory in your organization. In short, this book is your one-stop reference for everything you need to make Active Directory work for you.

How This Book Is Structured

Active Directory for Microsoft Windows Server 2003 Technical Reference is structured to describe and explain Active Directory technology as clearly as possible. Many companies have not implemented Windows 2000 Active Directory, so this book does not assume an in-depth knowledge of Active Directory. Rather, this book starts by describing the basics of directory services and explaining how a directory service is implemented in Active Directory. It then describes how Active Directory works and how to implement and manage Active Directory in your environment.

This book is divided into four parts, progressing in a manner that follows a process in which you learn about, and learn how to deploy, Active Directory. Part I provides an overview of Active Directory terms and concepts. Part II explains the planning, design, and implementation required to get Active Directory deployed in your environment. After you deploy Active Directory, you will need to administer it, and Part III provides details on administering Active Directory with a strong focus on Active Directory security and group policies. Part IV, the final section of the book, covers the maintenance of Active Directory.

Part I, "Windows Server 2003 Active Directory Overview," provides an introduction to the concepts and components of Active Directory in Windows Server 2003. This version of Active Directory is the latest iteration of directory services available from Microsoft. Active Directory provides a powerful directory service to manage users, groups, and computers, and it offers secure access to network resources. To use this directory service most efficiently, you must understand Active Directory concepts and how Active Directory works. This background is provided in Part I, which includes the following chapters:

- Chapter 1, "Active Directory Concepts," offers a brief history of the directory services that Microsoft has provided as a part of Windows NT and Windows 2000. It also elaborates on the benefits of Active Directory over the previous directory services. This chapter is also where you will find an overview of what is new in Windows Server 2003 and what has been enhanced since Windows 2000.

- Chapter 2, "Active Directory Components," provides a detailed description of the concepts and components that make up Active Directory. In this chapter, you will find a description of the physical components that make up Active Directory, such as domain controllers and the Active Directory schema. This chapter also introduces the logical components that make up Active Directory, such as domains, trees, and forests.

- Chapter 3, "Active Directory and Domain Name System," begins to dig deeper into what makes Active Directory tick. Active Directory is so tightly integrated with Domain Name System (DNS) that if you don't implement your DNS infrastructure correctly, you will never create a stable Active Directory implementation. This chapter begins by providing a brief overview of DNS concepts, then focuses on the integration between Active Directory and DNS, and then goes on to explain how you can best implement DNS to provide the name resolution service required for Active Directory.

- Chapter 4, "Active Directory Replication and Sites," continues to detail how Active Directory works. To understand how Active Directory works, you must understand how Active Directory domain controllers replicate information with each other. By default, Active Directory creates a stable and redundant replication topology. However, Active Directory also provides several options for you to create the optimum replication configuration for your company.

Once you understand the basic concepts and components of Active Directory, the next step is to implement Active Directory in your organization. Part II, "Implementing Windows Server 2003 Active Directory," provides you with the information you need to implement Active Directory. The first step in implementing Active Directory is to create the architecture and design for your organization. The forest, domain, site, and organizational unit (OU) structures are unique in almost every company, and it takes a significant amount of knowledge and effort to create the right design for your particular environment. Once you have created your Windows Server 2003 Active Directory design, you are ready to start installing Active Directory. Many companies that implement Windows Server 2003 Active Directory migrate from a previous version of a directory service, particularly Microsoft Windows NT 4. Because Windows Server 2003 Active Directory is very different from the Windows NT directory service, this migration can be complex. Part II deals with each of these topics in the following chapters:

- Chapter 5, "Designing the Active Directory Structure," presents an overview of the design process for preparing your Active Directory implementation. This chapter takes you through the process you will go through as you create your own design by starting with a top-down approach to designing your Active Directory structure. This chapter deals with all the components of your design—from deciding how many forests you need to deploy to how you will create your OU structure.

- Chapter 6, "Installing Active Directory," provides you with the concepts and procedures to complete the installation of Active Directory. This chapter looks primarily at the process of installing Active Directory domain controllers and includes a discussion of some of the new options for completing this installation.

- Chapter 7, "Migrating to Active Directory," details the information you need to complete an upgrade from a previous Microsoft directory service to Windows Server 2003 Active Directory. This upgrade is much more complex if you are upgrading from Windows NT than if you are upgrading from Windows 2000 Active Directory. For this reason, this chapter focuses on the upgrade from Windows NT to Windows 2003 Active Directory while still providing the information you need to upgrade from Windows 2000 Active Directory.

After you deploy Active Directory, you must administer it to provide the maximum benefit for your company. Part III, "Administering Windows Server 2003 Active Directory," details many of the administrative processes that you will use. Part III has two primary topics: security and administering your domain using group policies. You will learn how security works in Active Directory and how you can take advantage of the security infrastructure to delegate administrative control within your Active Directory structure. Next comes a discussion of group policies. One of the biggest advantages of Active Directory over previous directory services is that it contains powerful tools to help you manage workstations in your company. The option to centralize the administration of workstations can greatly simplify the management of your network and lead to significant cost savings. Group policies are the primary tools that you will use to manage the workstations on your network. Part III includes the following chapters:

- Chapter 8, "Active Directory Security," begins by describing the concepts behind Windows Server 2003 Active Directory security. The primary focus of this chapter is Kerberos, which is the default authentication protocol in Windows Server 2003 Active Directory.

- Chapter 9, "Delegating the Administration of Active Directory," expands on the Active Directory security discussion by describing ways that you can delegate administrative permissions within your domain. One of the big changes introduced with Active Directory is that it provides administrators with many levels of administrative permissions as well as being able to grant administrative permissions in only part of a domain. This chapter describes how to implement this feature in Active Directory.

- Chapter 10, "Managing Active Directory Objects," introduces you to the management of Active Directory objects. These objects include the user accounts and group accounts that have always been part of a directory service. But Windows Server 2003 Active Directory also includes other objects, such as *inetOrgPerson* objects, universal groups, printer objects, and shared folder objects. This chapter explains how to manage all of these objects.

- Chapter 11, "Introduction to Group Policies," provides an overview of group policies. This chapter details how to create and configure group policies as well as how to apply group policies within Active Directory. This chapter provides background information that you will need to understand the next two chapters, which provide concrete examples of what you can do with group policies.

- Chapter 12, "Using Group Policies to Manage Software," details one way you can use group policies. You can use group policies to install and manage software on client computers. In many companies, the management of software is a complex and time-consuming task. Group policies can automate many of those management tasks. This chapter shows you how.

- Chapter 13, "Using Group Policies to Manage Computers," focuses on how you can use group policies to manage client computers. Group policies provide many options for managing desktops, including locking down some desktop components, configuring security for workstations, and restricting what types of applications a user can run. This chapter shows you how to implement each of these options.

The last part of the book provides you with the information you need to maintain your Active Directory infrastructure after you deploy it. To maintain your Active Directory infrastructure, you must proactively monitor the Active Directory components. Often during monitoring, you see the first warnings that something is starting to go wrong. And because things sometimes go wrong regardless of how carefully you manage the environment, you must also have a disaster recovery plan in place for Active Directory. Part IV, "Maintaining Windows Server 2003 Active Directory," includes the following chapters:

- Chapter 14, "Monitoring and Maintaining Active Directory," details how to monitor Active Directory and includes information on monitoring the performance of the Active Directory directory service and Active Directory replication. This chapter also includes information on how to maintain the Active Directory database.

- Chapter 15, "Disaster Recovery," provides you with the information you need to back up and restore Active Directory. Active Directory is a critical service on your network, and you must be able to recover from any kind of disaster that might impact your implementation.

Each of the sections in this book builds on the process of designing, deploying, administering, and maintaining Active Directory. However, *Active Directory for Microsoft Windows Server 2003 Technical Reference* is primarily a reference book. If you need to learn about a particular topic, you can go right to the chapter that deals with that topic without reading previous chapters. In some cases, you might need background information to understand a topic. For example, Chapter 5's discussion on forests, domains, OUs, and sites assumes that you understand these concepts as introduced in Chapter 2. To understand how to use group policies to deploy software (as discussed in Chapter 12) you will need to understand the group policy components discussed in Chapter 11.

Conventions Used in This Book

Throughout the book, you will find special sections set aside from the main text. These sections draw your attention to topics of special interest and importance or to problems implementers invariably face during the course of a deployment. These features include the following:

Note This feature is used to underscore the importance of a specific concept or to highlight a special case that might apply only to certain situations.

More Info When additional material is available on a subject, whether in other sections in the book or from outside sources such as Web sites or white papers, the links to these extra sources are provided in the More Info sections.

Caution The Caution feature points out the places where you can get yourself into trouble if you do something or fail to do something. Pay close attention to these sections because they could save you a great deal of aggravation.

Best Practices Getting the most stable performance and the highest quality deployment often means knowing a few ins and outs. The Best Practices sections are where you'll find such pieces of knowledge.

Planning There are times when an ounce of prevention through planning is worth many hours of troubleshooting and downtime. Such times merit the Planning feature.

Tip This feature directs your attention to advice on timesaving or strategic moves.

Real World Many common problems that occur during deployment in the field can be solved easily, if you know how to do so. The Real World discussions and scenarios show you workarounds and solutions to deployment problems without you having to learn the hard way. The Real World sections also provide a more accessible context for the discussion of various issues. In some cases, the discussion of a particular technology can be very abstract. The Real World sections often describe a scenario in which a real business problem can be solved with the technology under discussion.

Part I
Windows Server 2003 Active Directory Overview

Microsoft Windows Server 2003 Active Directory is the latest iteration of directory services available from Microsoft. Active Directory provides a powerful directory service to manage users, groups, and computers and offers secure access to network resources. To use this directory service most efficiently, you need to understand the underlying Active Directory concepts and how Active Directory works. That is the goal of Part I of this book. In Chapter 1, "Active Directory Concepts," you are introduced to what Windows Server 2003 Active Directory can do for you. Chapter 1 and Chapter 2, "Active Directory Components," provide a detailed description of the concepts and components that constitute Active Directory. Active Directory is tightly integrated with Domain Name System (DNS), so Chapter 3, "Active Directory and Domain Name System," explains that integration and why it is so critical that you design your DNS implementation correctly before beginning your Active Directory implementation. Finally, to understand how Active Directory works, you must also understand how Active Directory domain controllers replicate information with each other. Chapter 4, "Active Directory Replication and Sites," focuses on how replication works and how you can optimize it.

Chapter 1
Active Directory Concepts

The Microsoft Windows Server 2003 operating system hosts the latest implementation of Microsoft directory services, Active Directory. Originally released with Microsoft Windows 2000, Active Directory directory service has been refined and improved for release with Windows Server 2003.

Note In this book, the use of "Windows Server 2003" refers to those members of the family of Microsoft Windows Server 2003 products that provide and support Active Directory: Windows Server 2003, Standard Edition; Windows Server 2003, Enterprise Edition; and Windows Server 2003, Datacenter Edition.

If you find yourself reading this chapter at your local bookstore, wondering about the new features in Windows Server 2003 Active Directory, this chapter will tell you what they are. This chapter also provides an overview of the key features of Active Directory and explains why you implement these features in a Windows Server 2003 enterprise environment. If you have already decided to implement Active Directory, or if you are already supporting an Active Directory infrastructure, the rest of this book will provide answers to many (hopefully most) of your questions about this product. It will present essential information for planning, implementing, and maintaining your Active Directory infrastructure. Let's begin at the beginning...

The Evolution of Microsoft Directory Services

Active Directory is the latest version of a directory service for the Microsoft Windows operating system. Active Directory first appeared in Windows 2000 Server and is also a component of Windows Server 2003. The need for directory services in the Microsoft workstation computing environment grew out of the proliferation of personal computers in the workplace. As more and more computers entered the corporate work environment, so the need grew to interconnect them to share resources and to enable users to communicate in near-real time. But when a company has shared resources available on a network, it also needs a catalog, or directory, of users and a system for assigning user permissions to the resources.

LAN Manager for OS/2 and MS-DOS

In 1987, the first directory service developed to support a Microsoft workstation computing environment (OS/2 and MS-DOS) was found in the Microsoft LAN Manager network operating system. The LAN Manager's "directory service" provided basic functionality for sharing file and print resources and for user security, but it was not suitable for large-enterprise environments. It did not scale well, and it did not support trust relationships. Instead, network users had to log on to each domain separately to access shared resources.

Windows NT and SAM

Enter Microsoft Windows NT 3.1 Advanced Server. This Windows NT Server platform offered a robust 32-bit computing environment with the familiar look and feel of the popular Microsoft Windows for Workgroups desktop operating system. At the heart of the Windows NT NOS is the security accounts management (SAM) accounts database. It provides a central database of accounts, including all user and group accounts in the domain. These accounts are used to control access to shared resources on any server in the Windows NT domain.

The SAM database remained the primary directory service for several revisions of the Microsoft Windows NT NOS, including Windows NT 3.5 and, most recently, Windows NT Server 4. The SAM scaled much better than previous directory service architectures because of the introduction of interdomain trusts. Trust relationships in Windows NT were essential to overcoming other limitations of the Windows NT directory service.

However, there were several limitations to the SAM, including lack of capacity and poor accessibility. The SAM database had a practical size limitation of 40 megabytes (MB). In terms of user, group, and computer objects, this limitation manifested itself in an account object limit of approximately 40,000 objects. In order for a computing environment to scale beyond this 40,000-object limitation, network administrators had to add more domains to their environments. Organizations were also split into multiple domains to achieve administrative autonomy, so that every administrator could have complete control over his or her own domain. Since all Windows NT 4 domain administrators have essentially unbounded administrative privileges, creating separate domains was the only method to define the boundaries of administration. Within the domain, however, all administrators had complete control over the servers and the services that ran on them. But creating additional domains was not an appealing method, as each new domain required additional server hardware and a resultant increase in administrative overhead. As the number of domains in an organization grew, so did the reliance on trust relationships to enable user authentication for resource access on external domains. To deal with this growing complexity of domains and trusts, network administrators implemented one of four different domain models: single domain, master domain, multiple master domain (or multimaster), and complete trust. These domain models are illustrated in Figure 1-1.

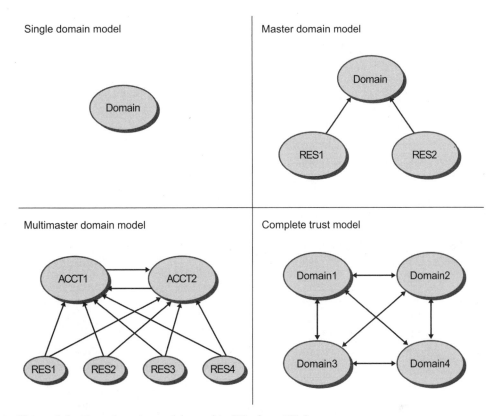

Figure 1-1. *Four domain models used in Windows NT 4.*

The greatest administrative concern in supporting these domain models was creating and maintaining the large number of trusts that were needed. This was a burdensome task, because all interdomain trusts in Windows NT 4 must be created bilaterally—in the domains on both ends of the trust relationship. In scenarios with different domain administrators, this required coordination and communication—not necessarily the hallmark trait of network administrators. Additionally, trusts in a Windows NT domain were not particularly stable. Due to the unique computer-to-computer authentication method that was used to maintain trusts in Windows NT, these trusts were often unavailable.

The second limitation to the SAM database was accessibility. The single access method for interacting with the SAM was the NOS itself. It had limited programmatic accessibility, and it was not easily searchable by the end user. All calls to read, create, or modify objects in the SAM had to be initiated using one of several tools included with the Windows NT 4 user interface (UI), such as User Manager For Domains or Server Manager. This limited the utility of the SAM as a directory service, and it contributed to the need to find a replacement for the Windows NT directory service for future versions of the Windows NOS. That directory service was starting to take form on, of all places, the drawing boards of the Microsoft Exchange Server development team.

Windows 2000 and Active Directory

Since the SAM was not very accessible outside of the NOS itself, it was not suitable for supporting network applications such as Exchange Server. When Exchange Server version 4 was released, it hosted its own directory service, the Exchange Directory. The Exchange Directory was designed to support large enterprise environments, and in later versions, it was based on open Internet standards. Open standard support meant that the Exchange Directory was exposed to the Lightweight Directory Access Protocol (LDAP) Transmission Control Protocol/Internet Protocol (TCP/IP) specification and could be readily accessed programmatically.

When it developed the next version of the Windows NOS, Microsoft looked at the Exchange Server directory service as a model for future directory service implementations. An added benefit of developing the network directory service around the existing Exchange Server directory service was that in future releases of Exchange Server, there could be a common directory service platform that served both the network environment and the Exchange Server environment. This goal would become a reality with the release of Windows 2000.

The robust directory service that began humbly as the Exchange Server version 4 directory service was ultimately released with Windows 2000: Active Directory. Active Directory replaced the SAM as the directory service for Microsoft networking environments. This new directory service implementation addressed the limitations of the Windows NT 4 SAM and provided additional benefits to network administrators.

The main benefit of Active Directory as implemented in Windows 2000 is that it is scalable. The new accounts database file can scale up to 70 terabytes, a dramatic capacity advance over the SAM's limitation of 40 MB. The number of objects that can be stored in Active Directory is greater than 1 million. In fact, Active Directory has been implemented in a test environment with a single domain model containing over 100 million objects. As a scalability demonstration, Compaq Computer Corporation, now part of Hewlett-Packard Corporation, successfully combined into a single domain model the consolidated residential telephone directories for all fifty states in the United States of America. Listings for two of the largest states were loaded twice to push the capacity to over 100 million objects. If Active Directory can store, manage, and quickly respond to queries for every residential telephone number in the United States, it can certainly scale to the size of large enterprise organizations.

Such a tremendous capacity advance means that network administrators no longer need to partition their environments into multiple domains to work around the directory service size limitation. The result is fewer domains, less server hardware, and less network administration—three compelling reasons to implement Active Directory. The complex domain models that prevailed in Windows NT 4 can now be consolidated into fewer domains, using organizational units (OUs) to group the contents of the resource or regional Windows NT 4 domains. Figure 1-2 illustrates a typical Windows 2000 single-domain model.

Figure 1-2. *A Windows 2000 single-domain model.*

Another major benefit of Active Directory is that it is accessible. Active Directory architecture is designed around open Internet standards, such as LDAP and the X.500 namespace. Not only is Active Directory based on open standards, it is exposed to these open standards programmatically. Administrators can manage their Active Directory implementations using LDAP-compliant tools, such as Active Directory Service Interface (ADSI) Edit and Ldp.exe (the LDAP-compliant Active Directory administration tool). Since Active Directory is exposed to LDAP, it can be managed programmatically. As a result, network administrators can script management tasks, such as batch imports of user objects, which are time consuming when performed through the graphical user interface (GUI).

Windows Server 2003 Domains and Active Directory

The latest version of Active Directory, an improved and refined version of the stalwart directory service introduced with Windows 2000, is a component of all members of the Windows Server 2003 family except the Web Edition, which neither needs nor implements the Active Directory component. Windows Server 2003 Active Directory offers network administrators the scalability, accessibility, and functionality necessary to manage the directory services infrastructure of today's enterprise computing environments. What we have come to expect of a directory services implementation has grown significantly since the days of MS-DOS workstations connected to a LAN Manager network, and Active Directory is the ideal tool to meet these expectations. The rest of this chapter explains how Active Directory fulfills its role at the center of the Windows Server 2003 universe and what features are new to this release.

Active Directory Open Standards

To meet the growing demands of a directory service in the ever-pluralistic environment of modern enterprise computing, Microsoft had to incorporate open computing standards in its NOS and its directory services implementation. It is increasingly likely that, eventually, server rooms of medium to large organizations will house a variety of NOSs running on a variety of types of server hardware. This could include Windows and Novell NetWare servers running on Intel-based platforms, UNIX platforms running on RISC (Reduced Instruction Set Computing)-based hardware, and Linux-based workgroup servers running on any platform administrators can get their hands on. In order for these systems to coexist, the NOSs must communicate using a common language or languages. This need for common languages is the basis for open standard computing. Rather than struggling under the old paradigm of homogenous server environments using proprietary directory service implementations, today's enterprise computing environment strives to be an integrated network service.

The following two sections look at a couple of the open standards on which Active Directory is based: the X.500 namespace hierarchy and LDAP.

X.500 Hierarchies

The *X.500 namespace* defines how objects are stored in Active Directory. The X.500 namespace is a hierarchical naming structure that identifies the unique path to the directory services container. It also provides a unique identifier for each object in that container. Using the X.500 name, or Object Identifier (OID), every object in every directory services structure can be uniquely identified. Active Directory is an X.500-based directory service, and Microsoft has included all of the base (or original) specified classes.

This namespace can be represented either in dotted notation (numeric) or in string notation. For example, the X.500 OID is 2.5.4.10, which is the equivalent of the attribute *Organization-Name* (with an LDAP display name of "o"). The numeric representation of this object class uniquely identifies this object within the X.500 hierarchy, and so the object becomes unique. Active Directory objects can also be uniquely identified using the X.500 string notation, also known as the Open Systems Interconnection (OSI) directory. In string notation, a user object can be represented as:

```
cn=Karen Friske, cn=Users, dc=Contoso, dc=com
```

To satisfy the requirement of uniqueness in the X.500 namespace, there can only be one Karen Friske in the Users container in the Contoso.com domain. There may, however, be other Karen Friske user accounts in the Contoso organization. The X.500 name includes the name of the container in which the user account is found (such as an organizational unit) and enables the user account name to be unique. The string representation of the X.500 namespace is defined in Request for Comments (RFC) 1779, which is available at *http://www.faqs.org/rfcs/rfc1779.html.*

To view the X.500 OID, you can use either the Active Directory Schema snap-in or the ADSI Edit snap-in. To view the X.500 OID for the *Organization-Name* attribute, use ADSI Edit to open the schema container and scroll down to the distinguished name of the attribute: CN=Organization-Name. Figure 1-3 shows the attributeID (X.500 name) of the *http://Organization-Name* attribute.

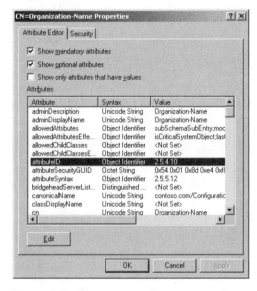

Figure 1-3. *The* Organization-Name *attribute properties as displayed with ADSI Edit.*

Heterogeneous Network Environments

If properly designed and engineered, a heterogeneous network environment is invisible to end users. In other words, users need not notice that the network services that they rely on to do their jobs are being run on a variety of server platforms. They should be able to use a common set of tools and applications to interact on both a private network and the public network (the Internet). One key to achieving an invisible heterogeneous network environment is to choose a central directory service that supports single sign-on, such as Windows Server 2003 Active Directory. Otherwise, users must provide account credentials for every operating system they want to access. A typical manifestation of a heterogeneous computing environment might consist of:

- A Windows-based desktop operating system, running a variety of compatible applications that all possess the same look and feel and require little or no retraining to use.

- A Windows- or Novell-based NOS running on Intel-based server hardware, or a hybrid environment with one vendor NOS for the directory service and another for application and member servers. For the traditional client–server computing model popular in today's corporate Information Technology (IT) departments, mainstream NOSs are preferred. By choosing a version of these operating systems that is open-standard compliant, a successful heterogeneous computing environment can be achieved. Windows 2000 Active Directory, Windows Server 2003 Active Directory, and the Novell Directory Services in Novel NetWare 5 and later are all based on open-standard architecture for their directory services infrastructures.

- A UNIX-based Domain Name System (DNS), Dynamic Host Configuration Protocol (DHCP), firewall/proxy, or a Network Address Translation (NAT) server running on RISC-based server hardware. Some or all of the Internet connectivity in the enterprise may be supported on UNIX servers. Since Internet services are by definition open standard, there is no requirement that the services supporting Internet access be of a certain type.

- A Linux-based file or application server running on a low-end Intel or RISC-based server. The Linux environment, often deployed in a development or test capacity, offers an affordable route to provide non-mission-critical network services. Such a Linux environment would be accessible to those using Windows-based applications through the Server Message Block (SMB) protocol. The end user would be unaware that these resources were hosted on a non-Windows-based server.

Lightweight Directory Access Protocol (LDAP)

LDAP is both an access protocol and a directory service model in Windows Server 2003 Active Directory. As an information model, the LDAP naming hierarchy is similar to the X.500/OSI Directory naming hierarchy. As an application programming interface (API),

LDAP is implemented in Windows Server 2003 Active Directory in the Wldap32.dll. Active Directory fully supports directory access by using native LDAP queries or by using the ADSI Component Object Model (COM) interface. As an access protocol, LDAP is defined in the TCP/IP suite for accessing data on LDAP-compliant directories. As an open standard, LDAP facilitates the exchange of data among different directory service platforms, as explained in the section "Key Features and Benefits of Active Directory" later in this chapter.

The LDAP naming hierarchy representation of the fictitious user account mentioned earlier is represented as:

```
LDAP://cn=Karen Friske, cn=Users, dc=Contoso, dc=com
```

Using this naming convention, administrators can specifically reference and access objects within an LDAP-compliant directory service. The LDAP protocol and directory model (but not the naming syntax) are defined by RFC 1777, which is available at *http://www.faqs.org/rfcs/rfc1777.html*.

To administer Active Directory using LDAP, use an LDAP-compliant administration tool, such as Ldp.exe, which is available as part of the Suptools.msi package in the Support\Tools folder of the Windows Server 2003 product compact disc. Using Ldp.exe, you can bind, or connect, to Active Directory by its User Datagram Protocol (UDP) port number and display the LDAP display name of each attribute, class, and object. To connect to Active Directory using Ldp.exe and display the attributes of a user object, connect to Active Directory using UDP port 389, expand the container or organizational unit, and then double-click the distinguished name of the user account. Figure 1-4 shows the Karen Friske user account as viewed through Ldp.exe.

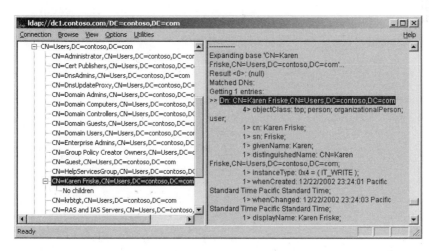

Figure 1-4. *The Karen Friske user account as displayed in Ldp.exe.*

Key Features and Benefits of Active Directory

"Why do I need Active Directory?" you might ask. If you are interested in running the most tightly integrated directory service for Windows Server 2003, Active Directory is a logical choice. Another very popular reason for implementing Active Directory is to support Microsoft Exchange 2000 Server. Exchange 2000 Server relies upon Active Directory for its directory service, so many administrators implement Active Directory to upgrade to Exchange 2000 Server. This section will describe several of the key features and benefits of Active Directory for Windows Server 2003.

Centralized Directory

Active Directory serves as a single, centralized directory service that can be implemented across an enterprise. This simplifies network administration, as administrators do not need to connect to multiple directories to perform account management. Another benefit of a centralized directory is that it can also be used by other applications, such as Exchange 2000 Server. This simplifies overall network administration by having a single directory service for each of the applications as well as for Active Directory.

Single Sign-On

Users anywhere in the Windows Server 2003 forest (a logical component of an Active Directory implementation) can log on to the network using their user principal name (UPN) identity (for example, mike@contoso.com). Upon successful authentication, they will then be granted access to all of the network resources for which they have been given permission, without having to sign on again for different servers or domains. The UPN is a mandatory attribute of the user account object in Active Directory, and is defined by default in Active Directory when a new user account is created.

Delegated Administration

One of the limitations to the Windows NT 4 SAM was that administrative rights were only available in an all-or-nothing fashion. To give a user any degree of administrative rights required that you make the user a member of the Domain Admins group. This level of administrative rights gave the user essentially limitless power within the domain, including the right to remove other users from the Domain Admins group. This was not a particularly secure method for delegating administration. Active Directory, on the other hand, offers administrators the ability to delegate administrative rights. Using the Delegation Of Control Wizard, or by setting specific permissions on Active Directory objects, administrators can offer finely-tuned administrative rights. For example, you can assign to a particular user account the administrative right to reset passwords in a domain, but not to create, delete, or otherwise modify the user object.

Common Management Interface

There are several ways that you will benefit from the integration between Active Directory and the operating system. One is the use of a common management interface: the Microsoft Management Console (MMC). When interacting with Active Directory through the MMC's GUI, all of the management tools have a consistent look and feel. For Active Directory, these include Active Directory Users And Computers, Active Directory Domains And Trusts, and Active Directory Sites And Services. Furthermore, these MMC snap-ins perform the same as all other Windows Server 2003 administrative tools, such as the DNS and DHCP snap-ins.

Integrated Security

Active Directory works hand in hand with the Windows Server 2003 security subsystem to authenticate security principals and to protect the security of shared network resources. Network security in a Windows Server 2003 network starts with authentication during sign-on. The Windows Server 2003 operating system supports two protocols for network authentication within and between Windows Server 2003 domains, including the Kerberos v5 protocol and the NT LAN Manager (NTLM) protocol. Kerberos is the default authentication protocol for clients logging on from client computers running either Windows 2000 Professional or Microsoft Windows XP Professional. Users logging on from down-level client computers (Windows NT 4, Microsoft Windows 98, or earlier operating systems) use the NTLM protocol for network authentication. The NTLM protocol is also used by Windows XP Professional and Windows 2000 clients when they are logging on to servers running Windows NT 4 or to stand-alone computers running Windows 2000 or Windows Server 2003.

Active Directory is also integral to the Windows Server 2003 access control model. When a security principal logs on to a Windows Server 2003 domain, the security subsystem, in conjunction with Active Directory, creates an access token which contains the security identifier (SID) of the user account, as well as the SIDs of all the groups of which the user is a member. The SID is an attribute of the user object in Active Directory. The access token is then compared to the security descriptor on the resource, and the requested level of access is granted to the user if a match is found.

Scalability

As an organization grows, whether gradually through the course of business or quickly through a series of mergers and acquisitions, Active Directory is designed to be scalable in order to keep up with this growth. You can choose to expand the size of the domain model or you can simply add more servers to accommodate the need for increased capacity.

Any changes to Active Directory infrastructure should be carefully implemented in accordance with an Active Directory design plan that anticipates such growth. A single domain, the smallest partition of Active Directory infrastructure that can be replicated on a single domain controller, can support in excess of 1 million objects, so the single domain model will support even large organizations.

What's New in Windows Server 2003 Active Directory

In addition to the key features of Active Directory mentioned above, there are several features that are new to Windows Server 2003 Active Directory. The following section provides an overview of what's new in the Windows Server 2003 operating system release. These features are more fully explained in subsequent chapters, in the context in which they are implemented.

Active Directory Users And Computers Improvements

There are two welcome changes to the Active Directory Users And Computers snap-in. In Windows Server 2003, the Active Directory Users And Computers snap-in allows an administrator to save queries. Administrators can search the directory on a particular attribute, save the query, and then run it again in the future for analysis or troubleshooting. For example, an administrator can save a search for any user object that has a non-expiring password (Account Options: Password Never Expires) and then reuse that search periodically to track this potential security risk.

The Active Directory Users And Computers snap-in also allows an administrator to edit multiple user objects at the same time. In the example mentioned earlier, after the administrator has searched for the user accounts with non-expiring passwords, they can all be opened, and this attribute can be changed for all of the accounts at the same time.

Levels of Functionality

Windows Server 2003 Active Directory introduces levels of domain and forest functionality, which provide backward compatibility for domains that contain down-level domain controllers. (Be aware that you will have to raise the domain or forest functional level to implement many of the other changes in Active Directory for Windows Server 2003. Many of the new features require a network environment with all domain controllers running the Windows Server 2003 operating system.)

Note A down-level domain controller is any domain controller in a Windows Server 2003 domain that is running any earlier version of a NOS, such as Windows NT 4 or Windows 2000.

The default domain and forest level of functionality is "Windows 2000" ("Windows 2000 mixed" in the case of domains). This means that when installed, Active Directory is configured to use only such new features as can be supported by a combination of Windows Server 2003 and Windows 2000 domain controllers. To achieve the benefits of all of the new Active Directory features, the level of functionality must be raised to that for Windows Server 2003 domain controllers as soon as possible (the condition in which there are no Windows 2000 or Windows NT 4 domain controllers remaining in the domain). Otherwise, only features that are supported in previous environments are available.

Note   Functional levels in Windows Server 2003 Active Directory are closely related to the mixed-mode and native-mode domain settings from Windows 2000. With the release of the Windows Server 2003 operating system, there is now the opportunity to have another Microsoft Active Directory directory service platform in the enterprise. Therefore, the domain mode feature had to evolve to accommodate the additional new Active Directory features. The concepts of domain functionality and domain mode are essentially the same. For more information on functionality levels, see Tables 2-1 and 2-2.

Domain Rename

Windows Server 2003 Active Directory now supports the renaming of existing domains within a forest, while preserving the globally unique identifier (GUID) and the SID of the domain. There are several scenarios in which this feature is useful, including the merger of two organizations with separate Active Directory infrastructures that want to consolidate under a single domain name reflecting their external registered namespace. Renaming domains is not a trivial IT procedure. It is somewhat disruptive of the accessibility of the network, in that every domain controller and every member server in the domain must be rebooted to complete the operation.

Application Directory Partitions

In addition to the domain and configuration directory partitions (including the schema directory partition), Windows Server 2003 Active Directory now supports application directory partitions. Application directory partitions can be used to store application-specific information in a separate partition that only replicates with other domain controllers that require updates on this data. This reduces the overall Active Directory replication traffic. A default implementation of application directory partitions is Active Directory integrated DNS zones. The application directory partition is now the default storage partition for Active Directory integrated DNS zones. This configuration results in DNS zone data that is only replicated to the set of domain controllers that are also DNS servers, including DNS servers in different domains in the forest. Application developers can write distributed applications to take advantage of the feature so that their applications store their data in the application directory partition.

Additional Domain Controller Installed from Backup Media

This new feature is an improvement to the Active Directory installation process. In Windows 2000, when installing an additional domain controller, it could take a very long time (several hours to several days) to complete the initial replication of the directory partitions, especially for large directory partitions or for domain controllers separated by slow network links. The Active Directory installation process for Windows Server 2003 now supports creating the directory partitions from a recent backup of the System State data from another Windows Server 2003 domain controller. Since the directory data is accessed from a local drive, rather than across the network through replication, this process is greatly accelerated.

Deactivation of Schema Objects

In Windows Server 2003, network administrators are able to "deactivate," or turn off, schema classes and attributes. As a result, you can redefine attributes and classes, rather than having to create a new attribute or class in the event of an error in defining an immutable property. For example, suppose that an administrator finds it necessary to extend the schema to include the *shoe size* attribute of the object of class User, and inadvertently sets the attribute definition to Integer. Upon reflection, the administrator decides that it should be a string value to include both size and width. By deactivating schema attributes, the original attribute can be turned off and a new attribute, also titled "*Shoe Size*," can be created with the appropriate definition. In the absence of this capability, the administrator would have to create a new, uniquely named attribute and abandon the *Shoe Size* attribute altogether. As a safety net, the changes made by deactivating schema objects are reversible to prevent an accidental deactivation.

Disabling Compression of Replication Traffic Between Different Sites

In Windows Server 2003 Active Directory, as well as Windows 2000, intersite replication traffic is, by default, compressed. While this optimizes network bandwidth between sites, it puts additional load on the domain controller processors to handle compression and decompression. Because they can now turn off compression of replication traffic (between different sites only), administrators can reduce central processing unit (CPU) load. This is at the cost of increased net utilization of bandwidth, but in high-network-bandwidth environments, this may well be a worthwhile tradeoff.

Global Catalog Not Required for Logon

When logging on to a Windows 2000 native-mode domain, a global catalog (GC) server has to be contacted to process the user's universal group membership. This group information is required to create the user's access token. To avoid situations where user logons fail because the connection to the GC is down, a common Active Directory design practice is to place GCs in any location connected by less reliable network links. Windows Server 2003 domain controllers can now be configured to cache universal group membership information, so that user logons can be processed without having to contact a GC. As a result, it is no longer the case that every remote location should have a GC. Additionally, without GCs in each remote site, replication traffic over the network links connecting those sites is reduced.

Group Membership Replication Improvements

In Windows 2000, when a single change was made to the membership of a group, the entire group membership had to be replicated to synchronize the change to other domain controllers. For very large groups, this used a lot of network bandwidth and had the potential of losing group membership data if the group membership happened to change on more than one domain controller. In a Windows Server 2003 functional level forest, group membership changes are now replicated on a per-member basis.

Object Picker UI Improvements

The object picker is the UI feature that you use to select account objects for administration across Active Directory. For example, when adding user accounts to a global group, you use the object picker UI to select the user account you want to include. In past releases, this interface provided a flat view of the directory that was either impractical or impossible to scroll through. The current release of this interface includes advanced querying features that allow searching of the directory at the attribute level and that are scoped down to the specific organizational unit. The results of this improvement are better searching performance as well as reduced directory service network impact. Further, the object picker UI is available to any new MMC snap-in that requires you to select objects from Active Directory.

Lingering Object Removal Mechanism

Lingering object removal is the process by which tombstoned objects are deleted from those domain controllers that were unavailable for replication following the garbage collection process. *Tombstones* are markers that indicate that an object has been deleted. *Garbage collection* is the process by which tombstoned objects are removed from all replicas of the Active Directory database throughout the domain. The process of removing such lingering objects is used for situations in which a domain controller is offline or otherwise unavailable following the removal of the tombstones in the domain directory partition. With no removal of lingering objects, there was formerly no process for cleaning up these "lost" tombstones, and as a result the directory database could grow to such a size that replication performance was affected. It also meant that there were inconsistent copies of the directory partitions among the domain controllers.

inetOrgPerson Support

Windows Server 2003 Active Directory now supports the inetOrgPerson class as defined in RFC 2798, which is available at *http://www.faqs.org/rfcs/rfc2798.html*. This addition to the base schema enables the Active Directory administrator to migrate *inetOrgPerson* objects from other LDAP directories, as well as to create *inetOrgPerson* objects in a Windows Server 2003 Active Directory environment.

Summary

In this chapter you learned how Microsoft directory services implementations have evolved over the years. As network computing environments have evolved, so have the directory services they rely on. Since the release of Windows 2000, the directory service at the core of the Windows NOS has been Active Directory. This chapter provided a brief introduction to this directory service platform and explained how it is designed to meet the demands of today's network computing environment. Key features were discussed to highlight the benefits of Active Directory, and a brief review of new features concluded this chapter.

Chapter 2
Active Directory Components

Microsoft Windows Server 2003 Active Directory directory service exists on two levels: the physical and the logical. In terms of its physical structure, Active Directory is a single file on the server's hard disk and the hard disk of each of the domain controllers that host the service. The logical structure of Active Directory consists of the containers that are used to store the directory service objects (such as directory partitions, domains, and forests) in the enterprise. These directory partitions, domains, and forests ultimately are reduced to bytes that are stored in the physical components of the directory service. In this chapter, you will learn about the physical manifestation of the Active Directory directory service. Then, you will look at the logical structure of an Active Directory implementation. A solid understanding of the physical structure of the directory service is important, but your understanding of the logical structure is vital to successful implementation and management of your directory service infrastructure. It is this logical structure of the directory service that you will interact with on a daily basis.

Active Directory Physical Structure

The physical manifestation of Active Directory consists primarily of a single data file located on every domain controller in the domain. The physical implementation of Active Directory is described by the location of the domain controllers on which the service is hosted. In implementing Active Directory you can add as many domain controllers as are needed to support the directory services needs of the organization. There are five specific roles that each of these domain controllers can serve. These roles are known as *operations master roles*. Another role that any single domain controller in the domain can serve is that of a global catalog (GC). In this section you will look at both the Active Directory data store and the domain controllers that host it.

The Directory Data Store

All the data in an Active Directory database is stored in a single file on the domain controller—Ntds.dit. This data file is stored by default in the %SystemRoot%\NTDS folder on the domain controller. This file stores all the directory information for the domain, as well as some information that is shared by all domain controllers in a given organization.

A second copy of the Ntds.dit file can also be found in the %SystemRoot%\System32 folder structure. This version of the file is the distribution copy (default copy) of the directory database, and is used to install Active Directory. This file is copied to the server when Microsoft Windows Server 2003 is installed so that the server can be promoted to a domain controller without having to access the installation media. When the Active Directory Installation Wizard (Dcpromo.exe) is run, the Ntds.dit file is copied from the System32 folder to the NTDS folder. The copy stored in the NTDS folder then becomes the live copy of the directory data store. If this is not the first domain controller in the domain, this file will be updated from other domain controllers in the domain through the replication process.

Domain Controllers

By definition, any computer running Windows Server 2003 that maintains a copy of the Active Directory database is a *domain controller*. With several exceptions, which are detailed later in this chapter, all domain controllers are created equal. Using the multimaster replication process described in Chapter 4, "Active Directory Replication and Sites," every domain controller in the domain maintains an up-to-date copy of the domain database and is capable of making changes to the database.

In addition to the domain controllers that host Active Directory, there are several special-purpose domain controllers that Active Directory requires to perform certain functions. These are the *global catalog* (GC) servers and the *operations masters*.

Global Catalog Servers

A global catalog server is used to host the global catalog. The GC is a partial, read-only copy of all the domain naming contexts (NCs) in a forest. The GC contains a base set of attributes for every object in the forest (in every domain NC), but it is not a complete set. The GC data is derived from all domain directory partitions in the forest. The data is replicated to every GC using the normal Active Directory replication process.

Tip Whether or not an attribute is replicated to the GC is determined by the schema. Administrators can configure additional attributes to be replicated to the GC by using the Active Directory Schema snap-in on the Microsoft Management Console (MMC). To add an attribute to the GC, select the Replicate This Attribute To The Global Catalog option on the attribute itself. This will set the value of the *isMemberOfPartialAttributeSet* parameter on the attribute to *true*. You may choose to add an attribute to the GC if you anticipate that users will need to search for an object across the forest. Infrequently referenced attributes are not typically added to the GC.

The first domain controller installed in the domain is automatically a GC. Additional domain controllers can be designated as GCs by selecting the Global Catalog Server option in the Active Directory Sites And Services administrative tool. You may choose to designate additional domain controllers as GCs to optimize the logon process. How GCs are used by the logon process is described later in this section. Chapter 5, "Designing the Active Directory Structure," provides more detail about the number of GC servers you will need to deploy and where to locate them.

You may wonder why GC servers are needed at all. One reason is that they are used for searching Active Directory. Without a GC, search requests received by a domain controller that did not possess the sought-after object would result in that domain controller referring the query to another domain's domain controller. Because the GC contains a complete list of every object in the forest (though not every attribute of each object), the GC server can respond to any query using an attribute that has been replicated to the GC without needing to refer to another domain controller. The query that is sent to a GC server is a Lightweight Directory Access Protocol (LDAP) query using port 3268 (the default GC port).

The second, more complicated, reason for configuring GC servers is to process user logons. Ordinarily, every time a user logs on to a domain a GC is contacted. This is because non-GC domain controllers do not contain any information about universal group membership. (Universal groups are only available in domains with a functional level of Microsoft Windows 2000 native or Windows Server 2003. Functional levels are used in Windows Server 2003 to enable Active Directory features for all domain controllers that can support them.) Universal groups can contain user and group accounts from any domain in a particular forest. Since universal group membership is forest wide, group membership can only be resolved by a domain controller that has forest-wide directory information—the GC. In order for an accurate security token to be generated for the user seeking authentication, the GC must be contacted to determine the user's universal group membership.

Note Windows Server 2003 supports a new feature known as *universal group membership caching* that makes it possible to log on to a Windows Server 2003 network without contacting a GC. Universal group membership is cached on non-GC domain controllers once this option is enabled and a user attempts to log on for the first time. Once this information is obtained from a GC, it is cached on the domain controller for the site indefinitely and is periodically updated (by default every 8 hours). Enabling this feature results in faster logon times for users in remote sites, as the authenticating domain controllers do not have to access a GC. To enable the universal group membership option in a site, open the Active Directory Sites And Services snap-in and select the desired site in the console tree. In the details pane, right-click NTDS Site Settings and then click Properties. On the Properties sheet, select the Enable Universal Group Membership Caching option and then select a site from which this site will refresh its cache. The <Default> option will refresh the site from the nearest site that has a GC.

Functional Levels

In Windows Server 2003, each forest, and each domain within a forest, can be assigned a specific functional level. These functional levels are used to enable features that are compatible on the combinations of operating systems supported by the various functional levels. When a functional level is set for a domain, that level of functionality applies only to that domain. Unless specified otherwise, domains are created at the *Windows 2000 mixed* functional level; forests are created at the *Windows 2000* functional level.

Table 2-1 lists the domain functional levels and the operating systems supported on the domain controllers in that domain.

Table 2-1. Domain Functional Levels

Domain functional level	Operating systems supported on the domain controllers in the domain
Windows 2000 mixed (default)	Windows NT 4 Windows 2000 Windows Server 2003
Windows 2000 native	Windows 2000 Windows Server 2003
Windows Server 2003 interim	Windows NT 4 Windows Server 2003
Windows Server 2003	Windows Server 2003

Table 2-2 lists the forest functional levels and the operating systems supported on the domain controllers in that forest:

Table 2-2. Forest Functional Levels

Forest functional level	Operating systems supported on the domain controllers in the forest
Windows 2000 (default)	Windows NT 4 Windows 2000 Windows Server 2003
Windows Server 2003 interim	Windows NT 4 Windows Server 2003
Windows Server 2003	Windows Server 2003

Before raising the forest's functional level to Windows Server 2003, verify that all domains in the forest are set to the domain functional level of Windows 2000 native or Windows Server 2003. Domains that are set to the functional level of Windows 2000 native will automatically be raised to the functional level of Windows Server 2003 at the same time the forest level is raised to Windows Server 2003.

Once the functional level, either domain or forest, has been raised, only domain controllers running those levels of operating system can be added to the domain or forest. Also, once a functional level, either domain or forest, has been raised, it cannot be reset to a lower level.

Finally, the GC is used to facilitate user logon by enabling the use of user principal names (for example, *username*@contoso.com). User principal names (UPNs) are resolved by the GC, because the GC has information about every user in every domain in the forest. The non-GC domain controllers do not possess this data, and they are unable to authenticate user logon in this format.

Operations Masters

Active Directory is designed as a multimaster replication system. This requires that all domain controllers have Write permissions for the directory database. This system works quite well for most directory operations, but for certain directory operations a single authoritative server is required. The domain controllers that perform specific roles are known as operations masters, and each has a flexible single-master operations (FSMO, pronounced *fizz-mo*) role. The five operations master roles in Active Directory are:

- Schema master
- Domain naming master
- RID master
- PDC emulator
- Infrastructure master

The first two roles, schema master and domain naming master, are *per-forest* roles. This means that there is only one schema master and only one domain naming master for every forest. The other three roles are *per-domain* roles; there is only one of these operations master roles for each domain in the forest. When you install Active Directory and create the first domain controller in the forest, it will possess all five of these roles. Similarly, as you add domains to the forest, the first domain controller in each new domain will also acquire these last three operations master roles. As you add domain controllers to a domain, you will transfer certain of these roles to other domain controllers. How you transfer these roles to other domain controllers is covered later in this chapter.

Schema Master

The schema master is the only domain controller that has Write permissions to the directory schema. To make any change to the directory schema, the administrator (who must be a member of the Schema Admins security group) must be connected to the schema master. If a modification to the schema is attempted on a domain controller other than the schema master, it will fail. After a change has been made, schema updates are replicated to all other domain controllers in the forest.

By default, the first domain controller installed in a forest (the domain controller for the forest root domain) assumes the schema master role. This role can be transferred at any time using the Active Directory Schema snap-in or by using the Ntdsutil command-line utility. The schema master is identified by the value of the *fSMORoleOwner* attribute on the schema container.

Domain Naming Master

The domain naming master is the domain controller on which new domains can be added to a forest or from which existing domains can be removed. Administrators must be connected to the domain naming master to add or remove a domain. If the domain naming master is unavailable, any attempt to add a domain to, or remove a domain from, the forest will fail.

Domains are added to a forest in one of two ways, both of which require a remote procedure call (RPC) connection to the domain naming master role holder. The most common method for creating a new domain is running Dcpromo.exe at the command line, which starts the Active Directory Installation Wizard. During this process, you have the option to install the first domain controller in a new domain. Dcpromo.exe will contact the domain naming master to make this change. When using Dcpromo.exe, if the domain naming operations master is not available, domain creation will fail. Alternatively, a new domain can be *precreated* using Ntdsutil. This utility creates a cross-reference object in the partitions container of the configuration directory partition, which is then replicated to every domain controller in the forest. Once the domain has been precreated, Dcpromo.exe can be run to create the new domain without having to contact the domain naming master.

RID Master

The RID master is a per-domain operations master role. It is used to manage the RID pool to create new security principals throughout the domain, such as users, groups, and computers. Every domain controller is issued a block of relative identifiers (RIDs) that are used to build the security identifier (SID), which uniquely identifies security principals in a domain. This block of available RIDs is called the RID pool. When the number of available RIDs in the RID pool on any domain controller in the domain begins to run low, a request is made for another block of RIDs from the RID master. It is the job of the RID master to fulfill these requests, as well as to ensure that no RID is allocated more than once. This process guarantees the unique security identity of every account in the domain.

If the RID master is unavailable for a period of time, the process of creating new accounts on specific domain controllers may be interrupted. The mechanism for requesting a new block of RIDs is designed so that this should not happen, because the request is made before all of the available RIDs in the RID pool are exhausted. However, if the RID master is offline and the requesting domain controller depletes the remainder of its RIDs, account creation will fail. To re-enable account creation, either the RID master role holder must be brought back online or the role must be transferred to another domain controller in the domain.

PDC Emulator

The PDC emulator role is required for Windows Server 2003 to coexist with pre-Windows 2000 domain controllers. In a Windows 2000 mixed functional level domain, the Windows

Server 2003 domain controller acts as the primary domain controller (PDC) for all down-level (Microsoft Windows NT versions 4 or 3.51) backup domain controllers (BDCs). In such an environment, the PDC emulator is required for processing password changes, replicating domain changes to the BDCs, and running the domain master browser service. If the PDC emulator is unavailable, all events related to these services that were initiated from down-level clients will fail.

In a Windows 2000 native or a Windows Server 2003 functional level domain, the PDC emulator still plays a role. It is used primarily to maintain password updates. All password changes made on other domain controllers in the domain are sent to the PDC emulator. If a user authentication fails on a domain controller other than the PDC emulator, authentication is retried on the PDC emulator. If the PDC emulator has accepted a recent password change for this account, authentication will succeed.

Infrastructure Master

The infrastructure master is responsible for updating the cross-domain group-to-user references. This operations master role ensures that changes made to user account names (changes to the common name attribute, *cn*) are reflected in the group membership information for groups located on a different domain. The infrastructure master maintains an up-to-date list of these references, and it then replicates this information to all other domain controllers in the domain. If the infrastructure master is unavailable, the cross-domain group-to-user references will be out of date.

Transferring Operations Master Roles

Operations master roles can be transferred either to better optimize domain controller performance or to substitute a domain controller if a role holder has become unavailable. The process for doing this will depend on the role being transferred. The following tools are used to transfer the five operations master roles:

- **Schema master** Active Directory Schema snap-in
- **Domain naming master** Active Directory Domains And Trusts administrative tool
- **RID master, PDC emulator, and infrastructure master** Active Directory Users And Computers administrative tool

To transfer an operations master role, there must be connectivity to both the current and proposed role holder domain controllers. In the event of server failure, the current role holder may not be available to effect a role transfer. In this case, the role can be seized. Seizing operations master roles is not a preferred option and should be done only if absolutely necessary. You should only seize an operations master role if it is indicated that the domain controller hosting this role will be unavailable for an extended period. More information on seizing operations master roles is provided in Chapter 15, "Disaster Recovery."

The Schema

The schema defines every type of object that can be stored in Active Directory. Before an object can be created in Active Directory, it must first be defined in the schema. The schema also enforces a number of rules regarding the creation of objects in the database. These rules define the information that can be stored with each object and the data type of that information.

Schema Components

The schema is made up of class objects and attribute objects. The *class object* defines what new objects can be created in the directory. There must first be a class for every new object created in the directory. An example of a class object is the User class. All new user objects created in Active Directory are instances of the class "User."

The schema also defines what information can be stored for each object class. This information is defined in the schema as the *attribute object*. An object of a certain class can contain values for all of the attributes defined for that class, as well as for all of the parent classes of which this class is a child. For example, a user account can have defined attribute values for all of the objects in the User class, as well as for the User class's parent class, organizationalPerson. When creating a new user object, you can include information for that user that is defined in the schema as an attribute of all of the classes to which this new user object will belong.

Finally, the type of data that can be stored in Active Directory for each attribute is defined in the schema as the attribute's *syntax*. If the User class contains an attribute titled *displayName*, the syntax for this attribute can be defined as a string value, which accepts any alphanumeric character. The value for each attribute included with an instance of a class must meet the syntax requirements for that attribute.

The Active Directory schema supports inheritance of class objects. All schema objects are organized hierarchically in the schema naming context. Because of this hierarchical structure, any class object is able to inherit all of the characteristics of its parent class object. For example, the Computer class is actually a child of the User class. As such, the Computer class inherits all of the attributes associated with the User class. The Computer class is then associated with the attributes specific to the User class. Using the Active Directory Schema snap-in, you can see the organization of class object inheritance and the hierarchy of the object classes. Figure 2-1 illustrates the Computer class. Notice that it is a child of the User class, which is a child of the organizationalPerson class, and so on. This system of inheritance makes it much easier for administrators to create new object classes, because they do not have to define every attribute that is associated with a new class but can simply inherit all the attribute associations of a suitable parent class.

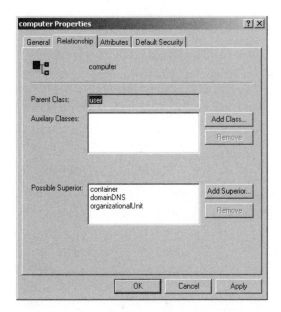

Figure 2-1. *The Computer class object in the schema, as displayed by the Active Directory Schema snap-in.*

Modifying the Schema

The Active Directory schema contains the most commonly used classes and attributes to support an enterprise directory services implementation. These attributes and classes are defined as *Category 1* objects, or *base schema* objects. In anticipation of the need to support customer-specific classes and attributes, the Active Directory schema was designed to be extensible. In other words, it can be modified, or *extended*, to include new class and attribute objects that an organization might need. Schema objects that are subsequently created are defined as *Category 2* objects. The schema is most often extended to meet the needs of an Active Directory-enabled application. A good example of this is Microsoft Exchange 2000 Server, which makes over a thousand additions to the schema to configure Active Directory to support Exchange.

Apart from using Active Directory-enabled applications, administrators can extend the schema using a variety of other methods. The schema can be extended in a batch mode using command-line administrative tools, including the LDAP Data Interchange Format Directory Exchange (LDIFDE) tool and the Comma Separated Value Directory Exchange (CSVDE) tool. The schema can also be extended programmatically, using Active Directory Service Interfaces (ADSI) and Microsoft Visual Basic scripts.

> **More Info** For more information on either LDIFDE or CSVDE, type the command name at the command line for online help. For more information on ADSI and ADSI Edit, see the Microsoft Windows Platform software development kit (SDK), which can be downloaded or ordered on compact disc at *http://www.microsoft.com /msdownload/platformsdk/sdkupdate*. The ADSI portion of the Platform SDK can be viewed online at *http://msdn.microsoft.com/library/default.asp?url=/library /en-us/netdir/adsi /directory_services.asp*.

Finally, the schema can be modified from the Windows Server 2003 user interface (UI) using the Active Directory Schema snap-in. To use the Active Directory Schema snap-in, you must first register the snap-in by executing the *Regsvr32 Schmmgmt.dll* command from the command line. You must be a member of the Schema Admins global group to modify the schema using this interface.

To understand how modifying the schema works, imagine that an organization needed to keep records of employee start dates. It would have to maintain the employee start date as an attribute of the user object in Active Directory. To have this attribute available when each new user object is to be created, the attribute would first be defined in the schema.

➲ **To use the Active Directory Schema snap-in to add a new attribute to the schema and associate it with the User class object, perform the following steps:**

1. Open the Active Directory Schema snap-in.
2. Select the Attributes folder in the tree pane.
3. From the Action menu, click Create Attribute.
4. At the Schema Object Creation warning dialog, click Continue.
5. In the Create New Attribute dialog box, supply information for the Identification section:
   - Common Name
   - LDAP Display Name
   - Unique X500 Object ID
   - Description
6. In the Syntax And Range section, supply information for:
   - Syntax
   - Minimum
   - Maximum
7. Select whether or not the new attribute is a Multi-Valued attribute.

Further information regarding the content of each field is available by selecting the field's text box, then pressing the F1 function key.

Obtaining an X500 Object ID

One of the concerns about modifying the schema is the possibility that two applications will make incompatible modifications to the schema. Each object in the schema must be unique. To manage this concern, every class and attribute in Active Directory can be identified by a unique object identifier (OID). The goals of the OID are to be able to uniquely identify any object or attribute in Active Directory and to ensure that no other schema object uses the same OID.

To accomplish this identification, organizations planning to create new OIDs should register with the International Standards Organization (ISO) or the American National Standards Institute (ANSI). When you register, the standards organization assigns you part of the OID space, which you can then extend to suit your needs. For example, your company may be granted a number such as 1.2.840.*xxxx*. This number is arranged hierarchically and can be broken down into:

1–ISO

2–ANSI

840–United States

xxxx–A unique number identifying your company

Once you have been granted the number, you can manage your own part of the hierarchy. For example, if you create a new attribute called *Employee Start Date*, you could assign it a number like 1.2.840.*xxxx*.12.

To understand how this works, imagine for example that the OID for a contact in Active Directory is 1.2.840.113556.1.5.15. The first three parts of the number have been assigned to ISO, ANSI, and the United States, respectively. ANSI then assigned 113556 to Microsoft, who assigned 1 to Active Directory, 5 to Active Directory classes, and 15 to the Contact class.

The *Microsoft Windows 2000 Server Resource Kit*, available from Microsoft Press, includes a tool called OIDGen that can be used to create a unique OID for object classes or attributes without registering the OIDs. This tool should not be used if you are making changes to a schema that will ever be deployed outside of your organization. For external deployment, Microsoft offers to generate and register your new OIDs. See *http://msdn.microsoft.com /certification/ad-registration.asp* for further details.

Figure 2-2 shows the creation of a new attribute using the Active Directory Schema snap-in.

Note Adding a new attribute to the schema does not mean that the attribute will automatically be accessible from any of the administrative tools. The administrative tools like Active Directory Users And Computers only show some of the attributes for each class and do not show any attributes you add. If you want the new attribute to appear in an administrative tool, you must either modify the existing tool or create your own. For information on how to modify and create administrative tools, see the Directory Services section of the Platform SDK at *http://msdn.microsoft.com/library/default.asp?url=/library/en-us/netdir/ad /extending_the_user_interface_for_directory_objects.asp.*

Figure 2-2. *Creating a new schema attribute.*

Deactivating Schema Objects

While extending the schema is a straightforward operation, careful planning should be done before implementing such changes. Once the schema has been extended, or an existing class or attribute has been modified, these changes are not reversible. Objects in the schema cannot be deleted. If you do make an error when extending the schema, you may choose to disable (deactivate) the object. In Windows Server 2003, schema objects that are deactivated can be used again if necessary, and new schema objects can be created with the same name as a deactivated object.

There are several points to keep in mind regarding deactivating schema class and attribute objects. First, you can only deactivate classes and attributes that you have specifically created—that is, *Category 2* objects. You cannot deactivate a *Category 1*, or *base schema*, object. Second, you cannot deactivate an attribute that is a member of a class that is not also deactivated. This restriction prevents errors in creating new instances of the non-deactivated class if the deactivated attribute is a required attribute.

To deactivate either a *Category 2* class or an attribute object, set the Boolean value of the *isDefunct* attribute of the schema object to *true*. This can be accomplished by using a tool such as ADSI Edit or by using the Active Directory Schema snap-in. Figure 2-3 illustrates the setting that must be unchecked to deactivate the *EmployeeStartDate* attribute created in the example given earlier.

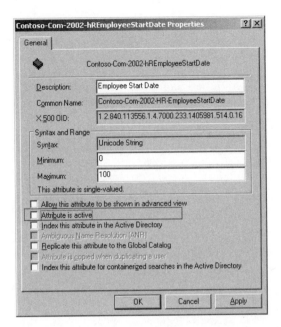

Figure 2-3. *Using the Active Directory Schema snap-in to deactivate a schema attribute.*

After a schema object has been deactivated, it is treated in all respects as if it does not exist. The error messages that are returned if an attempt is made to create a new instance of a defunct class or attribute are the same as when there is no existing class or attribute in the schema. Additionally, the only modification that can be made to a deactivated schema object is to reactivate it. To reactivate the defunct schema object, simply set the *isDefunct* attribute to *false*. After a defunct schema object has been reactivated, it can be used again to create new instances of the class or attribute. There are no adverse effects of this deactivation/reactivation process.

Active Directory Logical Structure

After you install Active Directory in your network environment and begin to implement the appropriate Active Directory design for your business purposes, you will be working with the logical structure of Active Directory. (This logical structure is the directory services model that defines every security principal in the enterprise as well as the organization of these security principals.) The Active Directory database contains the following structural objects:

- Partitions
- Domains
- Domain trees

- Forests
- Sites
- Organizational units

This section provides an introduction to these components. It will also discuss the concept of trusts, which are used to enable access to resources for security principals that are stored in different domains. In Chapter 5 you will learn how and why these structural components are used to achieve specific business goals (such as secured access to resources) and optimize network performance. Security principals themselves, such as users, groups, and computers, are not discussed in this chapter.

Active Directory Partitions

As described earlier, the Active Directory database is stored in one database file on the hard disk of each domain controller. The directory database is divided into multiple logical partitions, with each partition storing different types of information. Active Directory partitions are also called *naming contexts* (NCs). Active Directory partitions are visible through use of a tool such as Ldp.exe or ADSI Edit, as shown in Figure 2-4.

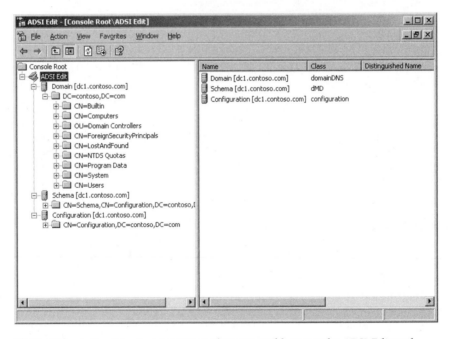

Figure 2-4. *Active Directory partitions that are visible using the ADSI Edit tool.*

Domain Directory Partition

The domain directory partition is the partition where most of the action takes place. This partition contains all of the domain information, including information about users, groups, computers, and contacts. Essentially, anything that can be viewed through the Active Directory Users And Computers administrative tool is stored in the domain directory partition.

The domain directory partition is automatically replicated to all domain controllers in the domain. The partition contains the information that each domain controller needs to authenticate users.

Configuration Directory Partition

The configuration directory partition contains the information about the configuration of the entire forest. For example, all of the information about sites, site links, and replication connections are stored in the configuration directory partition. Many application programs also store information in the configuration partition. Exchange 2000 Server stores all of its configuration information in the Active Directory configuration directory partition rather than in its own directory service, as did previous versions of Exchange. Other applications, like Microsoft Internet Security And Acceleration (ISA) Server, can also store configuration information in the configuration directory partition. When you install the first ISA server in your organization, you can configure an array that will store all of the ISA configuration information in Active Directory. Additional ISA servers can then easily be installed to use exactly the same configuration. The server configuration is read from Active Directory.

Because the configuration directory partition contains information about the entire forest, it is also replicated throughout the entire forest. Each domain controller contains a writable copy of the configuration directory partition, and changes to this directory partition can be made on any domain controller in the organization. This means that the configuration information is then replicated to all the other domain controllers. When the replication is fully synchronized, every domain controller in the forest will have the same configuration information.

Schema Directory Partition

The schema directory partition contains the schema for the entire forest. As described earlier in this chapter, the schema is a set of rules detailing what types of objects can be created in Active Directory as well as rules about each type of object.

The schema directory partition is replicated to all domain controllers in the entire forest. However, only one domain controller, the schema master, has a writable copy of the schema directory partition. All changes to the schema must be made on the schema master; the changes are then replicated to all other domain controllers.

Global Catalog Partition

The GC partition is not a partition in the same sense as the other partitions. The GC partition is stored in the database like the other partitions, but administrators cannot enter information directly into this partition. The GC is a read-only partition on all GC servers, and it is built from the contents of the domain databases. Each attribute in the schema has a Boolean value named *isMemberOfPartialAttributeSet*. If this value is set to *true*, the attribute is replicated to the GC.

Application Directory Partitions

The last type of partition in Windows Server 2003 Active Directory is the application directory partition. Only one type of application directory partition is created by default in Active Directory—for the Domain Name System (DNS) server service. Installing the first Active Directory integrated zone creates the ForestDnsZones and the DomainDnsZones application directory partitions. Application directory partitions can store any type of Active Directory object except security principals. Also, because application directory partitions are created to control where the data is replicated, none of the objects in the application directory partition can be replicated to the GC partition.

Application directory partitions are used to store application-specific information. The advantage of application directory partitions is that replication of the information in the partition can be controlled. Often the information might be fairly dynamic, so you want to control the replicas on the network to limit the amount of replication traffic that is created on the network. When the application directory partition is created, you can configure which domain controllers will receive a replica of the partition. The domain controllers that receive a replica of the application directory partition can be in any domain or site in the forest.

The naming scheme for application directory partitions is identical to other Active Directory directory partitions. For example, the DNS name for the configuration directory partition in the Contoso.com forest is dc=Configuration, dc=Contoso, dc=com. If you create an application directory partition called AppPartition1 in the Contoso.com domain, its DNS name is dc=AppPartition1, dc=Contoso, dc=com. Application directory partitions are quite flexible in regard to where you can create the partition, or more accurately, what the naming context for the partition will be. For example, you can create an additional application directory partition in the AppPartition1 partition resulting in a partition with a name of dc=AppPartition2, dc=AppPartition1, dc=Contoso, dc=com. You can even create an application directory partition with a DNS name that is not contiguous with any domain in the forest. You can create an application directory partition in the Contoso.com domain that has a DNS name of dc=AppPartition. In effect, this creates a new tree in the forest.

Note Choosing the DNS name for the application namespace does not affect the functionality of the application directory partition in any way. The only difference will be in the configuration of the LDAP client that is accessing the partition. Application directory partitions are designed for LDAP access, so the client must be configured to search the right namespace on the server.

One of the complicating factors when creating an application directory partition is maintaining permissions to the objects in the partition. With the default partitions in Active Directory, the permissions are automatically assigned. When an object is created in the domain directory partition, the Domain Admins group is automatically assigned full permissions to the object. When an object is created in the configuration directory partition or schema directory partition, user and group accounts from the forest root domain are assigned permissions. Because an application directory partition can be created in any domain directory partition or even as a separate tree in the forest, this default way of assigning permissions does not apply. While it is easy to assign a group like Domain Admins full control of the objects in the partition, what is not clear is which domain is the default domain. To deal with this issue, application directory partitions are always created with a security descriptor reference domain. This domain becomes the default domain that is used to assign permissions to objects in the application directory partition. If an application directory partition is created in a domain directory partition, the parent domain is used as the security descriptor reference domain, in effect creating an inheritance of permissions. If the application directory partition creates a new tree in the forest, the forest root domain is used as the reference domain.

Tip Normally, the application directory partitions will be created by the installation of an application that requires the use of an application directory partition. Also, the application installation procedure should allow for the creation of additional replicas on other domain controllers. While you can create application directory partitions using Ntdsutil, you would normally not expect to do this in a production environment. The procedures for managing application directory partitions are described in the Windows Server 2003 Help And Support Center. For detailed information on application directory partitions, including how to access them programmatically, search for "Using application directory partitions" on *msdn.microsoft.com*.

Once an application directory partition has been created with multiple replicas, the replication management of the partition is handled in exactly the same way that replication is handled for all other partitions. For more information on Active Directory replication, see Chapter 4.

Domains

The domain is the most basic building block in the Active Directory model. When you install Active Directory on your first computer running Windows Server 2003, you create a domain. A domain serves as an administrative boundary, and it also defines the boundary of certain security policies. Each domain has at least one domain controller; optimally it will have two or more.

Active Directory domains can be hierarchically organized. The first domain in the enterprise is known as the *forest root domain*—commonly referred to as either the *root domain* or the *forest domain*—and it is the starting point for an Active Directory namespace. For example, the first domain in the Contoso organization is Contoso.com. This first domain can either be a *dedicated* or a *non-dedicated* root domain. A dedicated root, also known as an *empty root*, is one that is used as an empty placeholder to start Active Directory. This domain will contain no live user or group accounts, and it will not be used to assign access to resources. The only accounts that are contained in the dedicated root domain are the default domain user and group accounts, such as the Administrator account and the Domain Admins global group. A non-dedicated root domain is one in which actual user and group accounts are created. The reasons for selecting either a dedicated or non-dedicated forest root are discussed in Chapter 5.

All other domains in the enterprise exist either as *peers* to the root domain or as *child* domains. Peer domains exist at the same hierarchical level as the root domain. Figure 2-5 illustrates the peer domain model.

Figure 2-5. *Active Directory domains organized as peers.*

Alternatively, and more commonly, domains installed subsequent to the root domain are installed as child domains. *Child domains* share the same Active Directory namespace as the parent domain (the root domain). For example, if the first domain in the Contoso organization is named Contoso.com, a child domain in this structure might be named NAmerica.Contoso.com. The NAmerica.Contoso.com domain would be created to manage all of the security principals for the North American locations of the Contoso organization. If the organization is sufficiently large or complex, additional child domains, such as Sales.NAmerica.Contoso.com, might be required. Figure 2-6 illustrates the parent-child domain hierarchy for the Contoso organization.

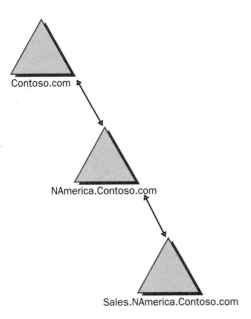

Contoso.com

NAmerica.Contoso.com

Sales.NAmerica.Contoso.com

Figure 2-6. *Parent-child domain model for Contoso Corp.*

Domain Trees

As subsequent domains are created in the Active Directory infrastructure, they can either share the existing Active Directory namespace or they can have a separate namespace. To create a separate namespace for the new domain, a new domain tree is created. Regardless of whether a single namespace or multiple namespaces are used, additional domains in the same forest function in exactly the same way. The creation of additional domain trees is purely an organizational and naming decision, not one that affects functionality. A domain tree contains at least one domain. Even a single-domain organization has a domain tree. Using multiple trees rather than child domains does have an impact on the DNS configuration (as discussed in Chapter 3, "Active Directory and Domain Name System").

A domain tree results when an organization creates a domain subsequent to the forest root domain but does not want to use an existing namespace. In the Contoso example, if the existing domain tree is using the namespace of Contoso.com, a new domain can be created that uses a completely different namespace, such as Fabrikam.com. If further domains are required to satisfy the Fabrikam business unit, they can be created as children of the Fabrikam domain tree. See Figure 2-7 for an illustration of the Contoso organization with multiple domain trees.

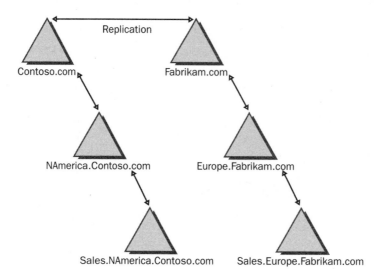

Figure 2-7. *Contoso Corp. with multiple domain trees.*

Forests

The *forest* is the ultimate security boundary for the enterprise. All domains and domain trees exist within one or more Active Directory forests. A forest is the outermost replication and security boundary for the organization.

An Active Directory forest can be defined by what is shared by all domain controllers in the forest. The shared components include:

- **A common schema** All domain controllers in the forest will have the same schema. The only way to deploy two different schemas in your organization is to deploy two separate forests.

- **A common configuration directory partition** All domain controllers in the forest have the same configuration container, which is useful for Active Directory operations like replication within the forest. The configuration directory partition is also used extensively by Active Directory-enabled applications like Exchange 2000 Server and ISA.

- **A common GC** The GC contains information about all of the objects in the entire forest. This makes searching for any object in the forest efficient and enables users to log on in any domain in the forest using their UPN.

- **A common set of forest-wide administrators** Two security groups are created in the root domain for the forest, and these groups have permissions not granted to any other users. The Schema Admins group is the only group that has the right to modify the schema, and the Enterprise Admins group is the only group that has the right to perform forest-level actions such as adding or removing domains from the forest. The Enterprise Admins group is also automatically added to each local Administrators group on the domain controllers in every domain in the forest.
- **A shared trust configuration** All the domains in the forest are automatically configured to trust all the other domains in the forest. There is more on trusts in the next section.

Figure 2-8 shows the Contoso forest.

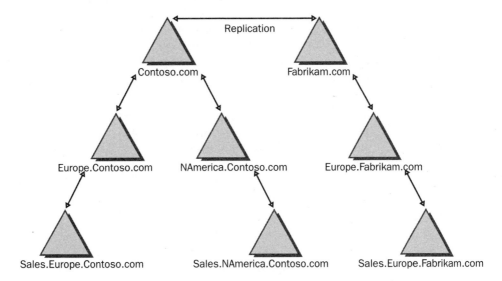

Figure 2-8. *The Contoso forest.*

Trusts

By default, the domain is the boundary of resource access in an organization. With sufficient permissions, any security principal (for example, a user or group account) can access any shared resource in the same domain. In order for security principals to access shared resources that exist outside of their domain, Active Directory trust relationships are utilized. A *trust* is an authentication connection between two domains by which security principals can be authorized to access resources on the other domain. There are several types of trust relationships, including:

- Transitive trusts
- One-way trusts
- Forest trusts
- Realm trusts

Transitive Trusts

All domains in a tree maintain transitive, two-way trust relationships with every other domain in that tree. In the example provided earlier, when the NAmerica.Contoso.com domain is created as a child domain of the root domain Contoso.com, an automatic two-way trust is created between the NAmerica.Contoso.com and the Contoso.com domains. Through this trust, any user in the NAmerica.Contoso.com domain can access any resource in the Contoso.com domain to which permission has been granted. Likewise, if any security principals exist in the Contoso.com domain (as in a non-dedicated root domain), they can be given access to resources in the NAmerica.Contoso.com domain.

Within a forest, the trusts are set up as either parent-child trusts or as tree root trusts. An example of a parent-child trust is the trust between the NAmerica.Contoso.com domain and the Contoso.com domain. A *tree root trust* is the trust between two trees in the forest, for example, between Contoso.com and Fabrikam.com.

However, all of the trusts between domains in a forest are also *transitive*. The transitive nature of the trust means that all the domains in the forest trust each other. If the Contoso.com domain trusts the NAmerica.Contoso.com domain, and the Europe.Contoso.com domain trusts the Contoso.com domain, then transitivity indicates that the Europe.Contoso.com domain also trusts the NAmerica.Contoso.com domain. Therefore, users in the NAmerica.Contoso.com domain can access resources in the Europe.Contoso.com domain and vice versa. The transitive trusts also apply to the tree root trusts. The NAmerica.Contoso.com domain trusts the Contoso.com domain, and the Contoso.com domain trusts the Fabrikam.com domain. Therefore, the NAmerica.Contoso.com domain and the Fabrikam.com domain also share a transitive-trust relationship.

One-Way Trusts

In addition to the automatic, two-way transitive trusts that are created when a new child domain is created, one-way trusts can be created between domains in the forest. One-way trusts might be created to enable resource access between domains that are not in a direct trust relationship. One-way trusts might also be used to optimize performance for domains that are connected through transitive trusts. These one-way trusts are called *shortcut trusts*. A shortcut trust is desirable when there is frequent resource access between domains that are remotely connected through the domain tree or forest. As an example, imagine the Contoso forest as illustrated as Figure 2-9.

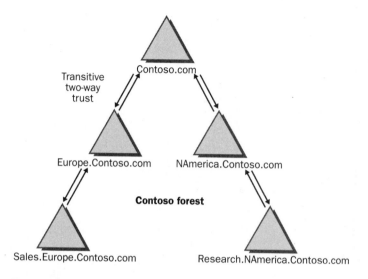

Transitive
two-way
trust

Contoso.com

Europe.Contoso.com   NAmerica.Contoso.com

Contoso forest

Sales.Europe.Contoso.com   Research.NAmerica.Contoso.com

Figure 2-9. *Trusts in the Contoso forest.*

If a security group in the Sales.Europe.Contoso.com domain has a frequent need to access a shared resource in the Research.NAmerica.Contoso.com domain, and with only transitive trusts established between the domains, users in the Sales.Europe.Contoso.com domain must authenticate through every domain in the tree between them and the domain that contains the resource. This is not efficient if the need is frequent. A shortcut trust is a direct, one-way trust that will efficiently enable users in the Sales.Europe.Contoso.com domain to authenticate in the Research.NAmerica.Contoso.com domain—without traversing the entire directory tree to get there. Figure 2-10 illustrates this shortcut trust. If it is determined that there is need to provide this same trust, but in the other direction, another shortcut trust can be created between the two domains, with their two roles reversed. (Such a double shortcut trust has the appearance of a transitive trust, but this unique trust relationship does not extend beyond these two domains.)

Forest Trusts

Forest trusts are a new feature in Windows Server 2003. A *forest trust* is a two-way transitive trust between two separate forests. With a forest trust, security principals in one forest can be given access to resources in any domain in a completely different forest. Also, users can log on to any domain in either forest using the same UPN.

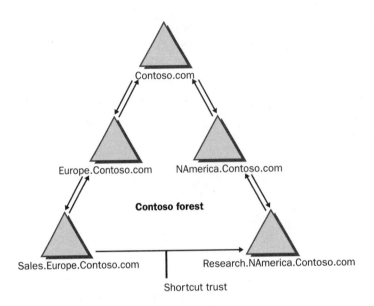

Figure 2-10. *A shortcut trust from the Sales.Europe.Contoso.com domain to the Research.NAmerica.Contoso.com domain.*

Forest trusts can be very useful in a Windows Server 2003 environment. If an organization requires more than one forest for political or technical reasons, the use of a forest trust means that it is easy to assign access to resources across all the domains, regardless of which forest the user or resource is in. If two companies that have deployed Windows Server 2003 forests merge, the two forests can be logically joined by using the trust.

While forest trusts do provide some excellent functionality, they are also subject to some limitations:

- Forest trusts are not transitive to other forests. For example, if Forest1 has a forest trust with Forest2, and Forest2 has a forest trust with Forest3, Forest1 does not automatically have a forest trust with Forest3.

- Forest trusts only make authentication possible between forests; they do not provide any other functionality. For example, each forest will still have a unique GC, schema, and configuration directory partition. No information is replicated between the two forests—the forest trust just makes it possible to assign access to resources between forests.

- In some cases, you may not want to have all the domains in one forest trust all the domains in another forest. If this is the case, you can set up one-way, non-transitive trusts between individual domains in two separate forests.

Figure 2-11 illustrates a forest trust in the Contoso enterprise.

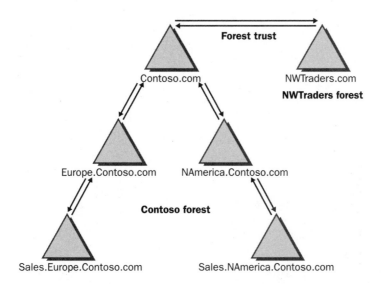

Figure 2-11. *A forest trust in the Contoso enterprise connects the Contoso.com and NWTraders.com domains, each residing in a different forest.*

Realm Trusts

The last type of trust is a *realm trust*. A realm trust is configured between a Windows Server 2003 domain or forest and a non-Windows implementation of a Kerberos v5 realm. Kerberos security is based on an open standard, and there are several other implementations of Kerberos-based network security systems available. Realm trusts can be created between any Kerberos realms that support the Kerberos v5 standard. Realm trusts can be either one-way or two-way, and they can also be configured to be transitive or non-transitive.

Sites

All of the Active Directory logical components discussed so far are almost completely independent of the physical infrastructure for your network. For example, when you design the domain structure for a corporation, where the users are located is not the most important question you need to ask. All the users in a domain may be located in a single office building, or they may be located in offices around the world. This independence of the logical components from the network infrastructure comes about largely as a result of the use of sites in Active Directory.

Sites provide the connection between the logical Active Directory components and the physical network infrastructure. A *site* is defined as an area of the network where all domain controllers are connected by a fast, inexpensive, and reliable network connection. In most cases, a site contains one or more Internet Protocol (IP) subnets connected on a local area network (LAN) or very high-speed wide area network (WAN) and connected to the rest of the network with slower WAN connections.

The primary reason for creating sites is to be able to manage any network traffic that must use slow network connections. Sites are used to control network traffic within the Windows Server 2003 network in three different ways:

- **Replication** One of the most important ways that sites are used to optimize network traffic is in the management of replication traffic between domain controllers and GC servers. For example, within a site, any change made to the directory will be replicated within about 5 minutes. The replication schedule between sites can be managed so that the replication traffic will occur during non-working hours. By default, replication traffic between sites is compressed to conserve bandwidth, while replication traffic within a site is not compressed. (Chapter 4 goes into much more detail on the differences between intersite and intrasite replication.)

- **Authentication** When a user logs on to a Windows Server 2003 domain from a Windows 2000 or Microsoft Windows XP Professional client, the client computer will always try to connect a domain controller in the same site as the client. As discussed in Chapter 3, every domain controller registers site-specific service locator (SRV) records—when the client computer tries to locate a domain controller, it will always query the DNS servers for these site records. This means that the client logon traffic will remain within the site. If the domain is operating at the Windows 2000 native functional level or the Windows Server 2003 functional level, the client will also try to locate a GC during logon. If there is a GC server in the site, the client will also connect to that server. (The role of sites in locating domain controllers is discussed in detail in Chapter 3.)

Note   Client computers running Windows NT 4 SP6a can log onto Active Directory domain controllers if they have installed the Directory Services Client, which is available for download at *http://www.microsoft.com/windows2000/server /evaluation/news/bulletins/adextension.asp*. For those clients that have not been upgraded from Windows 95 or Windows 98, the Directory Services Client software is available on the Windows 2000 Server compact disc.

- **Site-aware network services** The third way that sites can preserve network bandwidth is by limiting client connections to site-aware applications and services on the site. For example, by using Distributed File System (DFS), you can create multiple replicas of a folder in different sites on the network. Because DFS is designed to be aware of the site configuration, client computers always try to access a DFS replica in their own site before crossing a WAN link to access the information in another site.

Every computer on a Windows Server 2003 network will be assigned to a site. When Active Directory is installed in a Windows Server 2003 environment, a default site called Default-

First-Site-Name is created, and all computers in the forest will be assigned to that site unless additional sites are created. When additional sites are created, the sites are linked to IP subnets. When a server running Windows Server 2003 is promoted to become a domain controller, the domain controller is automatically assigned to a site that corresponds to the computer's IP address. If needed, domain controllers can also be moved between sites using the Active Directory Sites And Services administrative tool.

Client computers determine their sites the first time they start up and log on to the domain. Because the client computer does not know which site it belongs to, it will connect to any domain controller in the domain. As part of this initial logon process, the domain controller will inform the client which site it belongs to, and the client will cache that information for the next logon.

Note If a domain controller or a client computer has an IP address that is not linked to a specific site, that computer will be placed in the Default-First-Site-Name site. Every computer that is part of a Windows Server 2003 domain must belong to a site.

As mentioned earlier in this chapter, there is no direct connection between sites and the other logical concepts in Active Directory. One site can contain more than one domain, and one domain can cross multiple sites. For example, as shown in Figure 2-12, the Seattle site contains both the Contoso.com domain and the NAmerica.Contoso.com domain. The NWTraders.com domain is spread across multiple sites.

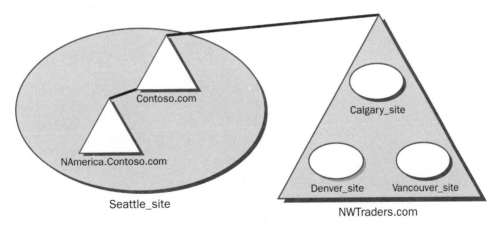

Figure 2-12. *Sites and domains within an Active Directory forest.*

Note Sites are discussed in more detail in several other chapters in this book. Chapter 3 details the role of DNS and sites for client logons. Chapter 4 addresses the role of sites in replication and how to create and configure sites. Chapter 5 goes into detail on designing an optimal site configuration for an Active Directory forest.

Organizational Units

By implementing multiple domains in a forest, either in a single tree or in multiple trees, Windows Server 2003 Active Directory can scale to provide directory services for almost any size network. Many of the components of Active Directory, such as the global catalog and automatic transitive trusts, are designed to make the use and management of this enterprise directory efficient regardless of how big the directory gets.

Organizational units (OUs), however, are designed to make Active Directory easier to administer. Rather than dealing with how to manage multiple Active Directory domains, OUs are used to make the management of single domains more efficient. OUs are used to create a hierarchical structure within a domain. A domain might contain thousands of objects (or even hundreds of thousands). Managing this many objects without some means of organizing the objects into logical groupings is very difficult. OUs provide exactly this functionality. Figure 2-13 shows an example of what the OU structure might look like at Contoso.

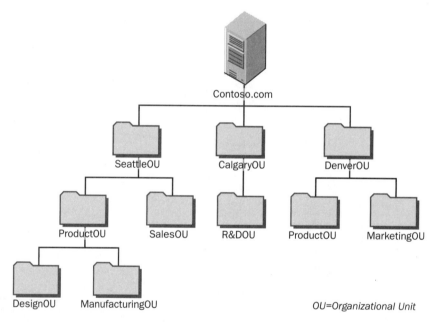

Figure 2-13. *A sample OU structure*

OUs are container objects that can contain several types of directory service objects, including:

- Computers
- Contacts
- Groups

- inetOrgPerson
- Printers
- Users
- Shared folders
- Organizational units

OUs are used to group objects together for administrative purposes. There are two ways that OUs can be used as administrative units: to delegate administrative rights and to manage a group of objects as a single unit.

Using OUs to Delegate Administrative Rights

OUs can be used to delegate administrative rights. For example, a user can be given the rights to perform administrative tasks for a specific OU. These rights could be high-level rights where the user has full control of the OU and can do anything in that OU, or the rights can be very limited and specific (such as only being able to reset passwords for users in that OU). The user that has been given administrative rights to an OU does not by default have any administrative rights outside the OU.

The OU structure is very flexible for assigning rights (also called permissions in many Windows dialog boxes and Properties sheets, and in other portions of this book) to objects inside the OU. The OU itself has an access control list (ACL) where you can assign rights for that OU. Each object in an OU and, in fact, each attribute for each object, also has an ACL. This means that you can have extremely precise control of the administrative rights anyone can have in the OU. For example, you can give a Help Desk group the right to change passwords for users in an OU but not to change any other properties for the user accounts. Or you can give the Human Resources department the right to modify any personal information on all user accounts in all OUs, but not give them any other rights to any other objects.

Using OUs to Administer Groups of Objects

Another reason for using OUs is to group objects together so that the objects can all be administered the same way. For example, if you want to administer all of the workstations in a department the same way (such as limiting which users have the right to log on to the workstations) you can group all the workstations into an OU and configure the Logon Locally permission at the OU level. This permission is applied to all workstations in that OU. As another example of grouping objects for administrative purposes, if a collection of users needs the same standard desktop configuration and the same set of applications, the users can be put into an OU and group policies can then be used to configure the desktop and to manage the installation of applications.

In many cases, objects in an OU will be managed through group policies. The Group Policy Object Editor is a management tool that can be used to manage each user's working environment. Group policies can be used to lock down user desktops, to give them a standardized desktop, to provide logon and logoff scripts, and to provide folder redirection. Table 2-3 provides a brief list of the types of settings available in the Group Policy Object Editor.

Table 2-3. Group Policy Setting Types

Setting types	Explanation
Administrative templates	Used to manage registry-based parameters for configuring application settings and user desktop settings, including access to the operating system components, access to control panel, and configuration of offline files.
Security	Used to manage the local computer, domain, and network security settings, including controlling user access to the network, configuring account policies, and controlling user rights.
Software installation	Used to centralize the management of software installations and maintenance.
Scripts	Used to specify scripts that can be run when a computer starts or shuts down, or when a user logs on or off.
Folder redirection	Used to store certain user profile folders on a network server. These folders, such as the My Documents folder, appear to be stored locally but are actually stored on a server where they can be accessed from any computer on the network.

Group policies will be most commonly assigned at the OU level. This eases the task of administering the users in the OU because you can assign one Group Policy Object (GPO)—for example, a software installation policy—to the OU, which is then enforced on all the users or computers in the OU.

Caution OUs are not security principals. This means that you cannot use an OU to assign permissions to a resource and then have all of the users in the OU automatically inherit those permissions. OUs are used for administrative purposes and to grant access to resources, so you will still need to use groups.

Summary

This chapter introduced the basic physical and logical components of Active Directory in Windows Server 2003. While having an understanding of the physical components is important (especially when dealing with database management, domain controller placement, and schema management), most of the work you will do in Active Directory will be with the logical components. Most of the rest of this book deals with the logical structure of Active Directory.

Chapter 3
Active Directory and Domain Name System

Microsoft Windows Server 2003 Active Directory directory service relies entirely on Domain Name System (DNS) to locate resources on a network. Without a reliable DNS infrastructure, domain controllers on your network will not be able to replicate with each other, your Microsoft Windows 2000 and Microsoft Windows XP Professional clients will not be able to log on to the network, and your servers running Microsoft Exchange 2000 Server will not be able to send e-mail. Essentially, if your DNS implementation is not stable, your Windows Server 2003 network will fail. This means you must have a thorough knowledge of DNS concepts and the Windows Server 2003 implementation of DNS if you are going to manage a Windows Server 2003 Active Directory environment.

This chapter begins by providing a brief overview of DNS as a service. This section is not specific to Windows Server 2003 environments, but is necessary for understanding DNS. The chapter then goes into detail about why Active Directory depends so heavily on DNS and how the name resolution process works. The final section of the chapter focuses on the DNS service in Windows Server 2003, Standard Edition; Windows Server 2003, Enterprise Edition; and Windows Server 2003, Datacenter Edition. The Windows Server 2003 operating system brings several excellent features to DNS that can greatly enhance the deployment of Active Directory.

> **Note**   Windows Server 2003, Web Edition, does not require, nor does it support, Active Directory.

DNS Overview

DNS is a name resolution service. If you are trying to find a server on the Internet, you are much more likely to remember a name like www.microsoft.com than an Internet Protocol (IP) address like 207.46.230.219. However, in order for your computer to connect to the Microsoft Web site, it needs to know the IP address. DNS performs that translation— you provide your browser with the name of the computer that you would like to connect to, and DNS resolves that name to the correct IP address.

Note Because DNS is essential for Active Directory, you must become familiar with DNS concepts and know how DNS is implemented. If you are not familiar with DNS, you should consult some of the excellent resources available on the Microsoft Web site, such as *http://msdn.microsoft.com/library/en-us/dns /dns_concepts.asp.*

Hierarchical Namespace

DNS uses a hierarchical namespace to locate computers. Figure 3-1 shows an example of how the namespace is organized. The root domain is represented by a period ("."). The root domain is the beginning of the DNS namespace, and the entire namespace is located underneath the root. At the next layer under the root domain are the first-level domains, including seven generic domain names (such as com, edu, mil, net, org); about 200 country abbreviations (such as ca, uk, fr, br); plus seven new domains, such as biz, info, and pro, some of which were introduced in 2001.

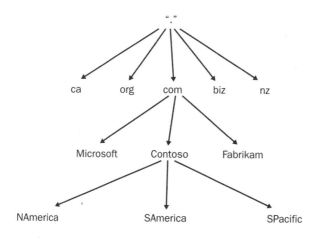

Figure 3-1. *The DNS hierarchical namespace.*

Under the top-level domains are the second-level domains, which usually refer to company names that must be registered with the Internet authority. Under the second-level domains are subdomains. Subdomains usually refer to departments or divisions within a company. These subdomains are registered and managed on the DNS servers that contain the information about the second-level domain.

Another way to think about the hierarchical namespace is to consider a fully qualified domain name (FQDN) such as www.NAmerica.Contoso.com. An FQDN is a complete name that can be used to identify a specific computer within the entire DNS namespace.

To understand how the FQDN identifies the computer in the DNS namespace, read it from right to left. At the far right is the period (".") that identifies the root domain; this is the period that precedes the first-level domain name. This is followed by the first-level com domain, the second-level Contoso domain, and the NAmerica subdomain. At the far left of the FQDN is "www," the host name of the specific computer.

Distributed Database

Because DNS uses a hierarchical namespace, it is also easy to configure it as a *distributed database*. Before DNS was implemented on the Internet, all of the name resolution information for the Internet was stored in a single file. However, as the number of hosts on the Internet increased to thousands of computers, managing the one file became impractical. To deal with this, DNS was designed to use a distributed database.

Using a distributed database means that the DNS information is stored on many computers throughout the world (in the case of the Internet) and throughout your network (in the case of an internal network). Each DNS server maintains only one small part of the DNS database. The entire database is divided into zone files based on domain names. The zone files are distributed across multiple servers. For example, there are approximately a dozen servers that contain the zone files for the root domain. These servers contain information about the DNS servers that have the zone information for the top-level domains. The root servers do not contain all the information about the top-level domains, but they do know which servers maintain that information.

The DNS servers that contain the information about the top-level domains also contain the information about which servers contain the zone files for the next level domains. For example, a server may contain the zone files for the com domain. This means that this server knows about all of the second-level domains that are registered with the com domain, but it might not know all of the details about the second-level domain. Again, the top-level domain server knows which computers at the next level contain the details about the second-level domain. This continues all the way down the DNS namespace. The server responsible for the com domain would have Contoso registered as a valid second-level domain. This server would refer any requests for information about the Contoso domain to the server that contains the zone files for Contoso.com.

Using this method of distributing the database means that no one server on the Internet needs to contain all of the DNS information. Most servers will have information about some part of the tree, but when they receive a request they cannot fulfill, they know which DNS server has the required information. The DNS servers use delegation records, forwarders, and root hints to determine which DNS server has the required information. These topics will be discussed later in this chapter.

Name Resolution Process

The DNS hierarchical namespace and distributed database are used when a client tries to locate the IP address of an Internet resource. To use the example from the previous section (and illustrated in Figure 3-1), a DNS client (also called a resolver) anywhere in the world might want to connect to the Web server at *www.NAmerica.Contoso.com*.

To acquire the IP address, perform the following steps:

1. The client resolver begins by sending a recursive query to its configured DNS server (usually the DNS server of an Internet Service Provider [ISP]) asking for the IP address. A *recursive query* is a query that can have only two possible answers: the IP address that the client is looking for or an error message indicating that the information cannot be found.

2. If the ISP's DNS server has the requested information in its cache, it returns the IP address to the user. If it does not, the DNS server tries to find the information by sending an iterative query to another server that might have the information. The response to an iterative query can be either the name resolution that the client requested or a referral to another DNS server that might be able to fulfill the request. In our example, the ISP's DNS server sends an iterative query to a root server asking for the IP address for www.NAmerica.Contoso.com.

3. The root server cannot supply the answer to the query, but it does reply with a list of servers responsible for the top-level com domain. This process of providing alternate DNS servers to contact is called a *referral*. The ISP's DNS server sends an iterative query to one of these servers, asking for the IP address.

4. The com server replies with a list of servers that are responsible for the Contoso.com domain. The ISP's DNS server then queries the Contoso.com DNS server, which responds with the names of the DNS servers that manage the NAmerica.Contoso.com domain.

5. The NAmerica.Contoso.com DNS server contains all of the information about this domain, so it responds to the ISP's DNS server with the IP address for the requested host.

6. The ISP's DNS server responds to the recursive query it received from the client resolver and sends the IP address for the requested Web server.

7. The client computer connects to www.NAmerica.Contoso.com.

This whole process can happen very quickly, but usually not all the steps are needed. When a DNS server resolves any type of name, it saves that information in a cache for a specified period. In our example, if someone had located the same site earlier in the day and the ISP's DNS server had resolved the name, the DNS server would have looked in its cache and provided the answer immediately.

Resource Records

The actual records that are stored in the DNS zone files are called *resource records* (RRs). Resource records contain the actual information about the domain. You can create twenty-two different types of resource records on a Windows Server 2003 DNS server. The most common resource records are listed in Table 3-1.

Table 3-1. Common Resource Records in Windows Server 2003 DNS

Name	Explanation
Start of Authority (SOA)	Identifies the primary name server for the zone. Also sets parameters for the zone such as the default settings for zone transfers, expiration times on zone information, and the Time to Live (TTL). (See Figure 3-2 for an example of an SOA record.)
Host (A)	Identifies the IP address for a specific host name. This is the record that the DNS server returns during name resolution.
Mail Exchanger (MX)	Identifies Internet messaging servers. This record is used by other messaging servers on the Internet to locate the messaging servers in a domain.
Name Server (NS)	Identifies all of the name servers for the domain.
Pointer (PTR)	Identifies the host names mapped to a specific IP address. These records are stored in the reverse lookup zone.
Canonical Name (CNAME)	Identifies an alias for another host in the domain. This is used when more than one host name uses the same IP address.
Service Locator (SRV)	Identifies a service that is available in the domain. Active Directory makes extensive use of SRV records to locate domain controllers.

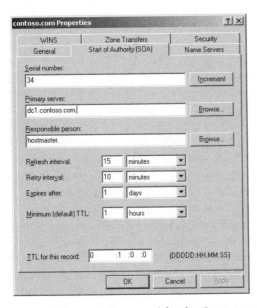

Figure 3-2. *An SOA record for the Contoso.com domain.*

> **Tip** Figure 3-2 shows the SOA record in the DNS administrative tool. The DNS records can also be written in a standard text format. For example, a standard host record for a server called Web1.Contoso.com can be written as Web1.Contoso.com IN A 192.168.1.100.

DNS Domains, Zones, and Servers

One of the important aspects of learning how DNS works is understanding the terminology used to describe the DNS components.

Domains Versus Zones

One of the terminology issues that can be confusing is the difference between domains and zones. One way to understand the difference is to think of a domain as part of the DNS namespace, and a zone as being information about that part of the namespace. For example, a company may own a second-level domain name such as Contoso.com. This means that the company owns one part of the entire DNS namespace—this is their domain. When the company implements the DNS servers for the domain, all of the information about the DNS domain is stored on one or more DNS servers. This information includes all of the resource records for all of the computers in the DNS domain. This information about each domain is the *zone information*, and is stored in zone files on the DNS servers.

There are two different types of zone files in DNS: *forward lookup zones* and *reverse lookup zones*. A forward lookup zone is used primarily to resolve host names to IP addresses. The Host (A) records provide this functionality. The forward lookup zone also includes the SOA and NS records and may also include MX records, CNAME records, and SRV records. The forward lookup zone is used whenever a client resolver queries the DNS server to locate the IP address of a server on the network.

Reverse lookup zones perform the opposite function. A reverse lookup zone is used when a host's IP address is known, but the host name is not. The reverse lookup zone also has SOA and NS records, but the rest of the records are PTR records. A PTR record format is similar to a host record, but it provides the answer for a reverse lookup. (For more information on these records, see Table 3-1.)

A forward lookup zone name is the domain name. A reverse lookup zone name is more difficult to determine because it uses an IP subnet, not a domain name, as the boundary for the zone. When you create the reverse lookup zone, you must give the zone a name based on an IP subnet. For example, if you create a reverse lookup zone for the subnet 192.168.1.0, the zone name would be 1.168.192.in-addr.arpa. The in-addr.arpa is a special name reserved in the DNS namespace to refer to reverse lookup zones. The first part of the zone name is the network address, but in reverse. If you were creating a reverse lookup zone for a Class B subnet (150.38.0.0), the reverse lookup zone name would be 38.150.in-addr.arpa.

Primary Name Servers

A primary name server is the only server with a writable copy of the zone files (the zone on the primary name server is called the *primary zone*). This means that the DNS administrator must have access to the primary name server whenever any changes need to be made to the zone information. After changes have been made to the zone files, the data is automatically replicated to the secondary name servers using a process called a *zone transfer*.

Secondary Name Servers

A secondary name server has a read-only copy of the zone files. The only way the zone information on a secondary name server can be updated is through a zone transfer from the primary name server. In the early iterations of DNS, every zone transfer was a complete zone transfer, that is, the entire contents of the DNS zone file were transferred from the primary name server to the secondary server. Request for Comment (RFC) 1995 introduced a more efficient zone transfer mechanism called an *incremental zone transfer* in which only the changes made to the zone files since the last transfer are replicated to the secondary server. Another improvement to the zone transfer process is described in RFC 1996, which describes a notification mechanism that enables the primary server to alert the secondary name servers when changes have been made to the zone files. Without the notification option, the secondary name server will only contact the primary name server at the refresh intervals defined on the SOA record for each zone.

Note   The Windows Server 2003 DNS server supports both incremental zone transfers and notifications. The Windows Server 2003 DNS server also supports Active Directory integrated zones where the regular zone transfer is replaced by Active Directory replication.

Caching-Only Name Servers

A third type of name server is a caching-only server. This server does not manage any zone files; rather, it only caches any name resolutions that it has completed. A caching-only server is frequently used in remote offices with a limited bandwidth connection to a larger office. Because the caching-only server does not have any zone files, there is no DNS zone transfer traffic across a slow network connection. The caching-only server should be configured to forward all DNS requests to a server at the company's main office. As the caching-only server resolves DNS requests, it caches the information for a certain period (the default is 1 hour). This means that any local DNS requests for the same information can be resolved locally.

Note   All Windows Server 2003 DNS servers, including primary and secondary name servers, are caching servers, but not caching-only servers. The difference between those servers and caching-only servers is that the latter do not have any zone information.

Zones of Authority

To fully understand DNS, you must be familiar with zones of authority, or authoritative name servers. Each primary and secondary name server is authoritative for its domain. For example, if a DNS server contains the zone files for the Contoso.com domain, that server is the authoritative name server for that domain. As the authoritative name server, the server will not forward any queries about hosts in that zone to any other DNS server. Many companies set up a DNS server configuration similar to that shown in Figure 3-3. In this scenario, there are two primary DNS servers configured for the Contoso.com domain. DNS1 contains a host record for a server called Web1.Contoso.com, but DNS2 does not have this record. When a client connects to DNS1, it will be able to resolve the IP address for Web1. When a client connects to DNS2 and requests the IP address for Web1, the server will respond that the host cannot be found. Because DNS2 is authoritative for the Contoso.com domain, it will never forward the request to DNS1. Even if DNS2 has DNS1 configured as a forwarder or root hint, it will never forward requests to the other server because it is the authoritative server for the Contoso.com domain. This behavior is by design and, as the following real-world discussion shows, offers a specific security advantage.

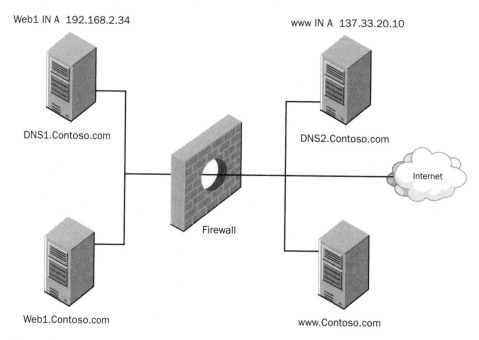

Figure 3-3. *Multiple authoritative DNS servers.*

Real World   Using Multiple Authoritative Servers for the Same Zone

The most common scenario in which a company may have two DNS servers that are both authoritative for the same domain is when the company's Internet DNS name and the internal DNS name are identical (as illustrated in Figure 3-3). The DNS1 server is inside the firewall, and the DNS2 server is outside it. DNS2 is used to resolve DNS requests for Internet clients, while DNS1 is used for internal clients and for Active Directory SRV records. Because both servers are authoritative for the same zone (Contoso.com), they will never forward requests for this domain to each other.

In such a scenario, you should maintain unique zone information on each DNS server. The external DNS server is likely to have a relatively small zone file consisting of the Web servers and MX records that need to be accessible to the Internet. The internal DNS server will likely have a much larger zone file that includes all of the domain controller records, all internal server records, and possibly the host records for all the client computers on the network. The only duplication between the two zone files might be some of the external DNS records. For example, when the internal clients connect to www.Contoso.com, you might want them to connect to the same external Web server as that accessed by Internet clients. In this case, you must include the host record for the Web server in the zone file on DNS1. If you don't, the internal clients will not be able to connect to the Web server.

Delegated Zones

Since DNS uses a hierarchical namespace, there must be some way of connecting the layers of the hierarchy together. For example, if a client connects to a server that is authoritative for the com first-level domain, and requests a server in the Contoso.com domain, the com server must have some way of determining which name servers are authoritative for the Contoso.com domain. This is made possible by the use of *delegation records*.

A delegation record is a pointer to a lower-level domain that identifies the name servers for the lower-level domain. For example, as shown in Figure 3-4, DNS1.Contoso.com is an authoritative name server for the Contoso.com domain. DNS2 and DNS3 are authoritative name servers for the NAmerica.Contoso.com domain. DNS1 is considered authoritative for the NAmerica.Contoso.com domain but does not have all of the resource records for the child domain. However, DNS1 uses a delegation record pointing to DNS2 and DNS3 as the name servers for the child domain. When a client connects to DNS1 requesting information about NAmerica.Contoso.com, the server will refer the client to the name servers for the child domain.

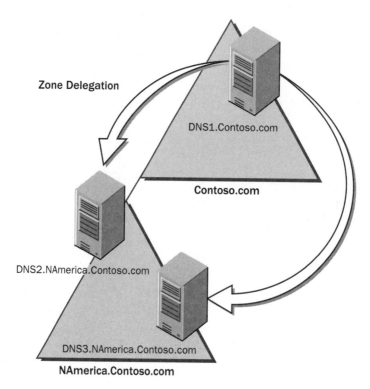

Figure 3-4. *Delegated zones.*

Forwarders and Root Hints

The second method for connecting the different layers of the DNS hierarchy together is by using forwarders and root hints. In most cases, forwarders and root hints are used by those DNS servers lower in the DNS namespace to locate information from DNS servers higher up in the hierarchy. Both forwarders and root hints are used by the DNS server to locate information that is not in its zone files. For example, a DNS server may be authoritative for only the Contoso.com domain. When this DNS server receives a query from a client requesting a name resolution in the Fabrikam.com domain (see Figure 3-1), the Contoso.com DNS server must have some way of locating this information.

One way to configure this is to use *forwarders*. A forwarder is simply another DNS server that a particular DNS server uses when it cannot resolve a query. For example, the authoritative name server for Contoso.com might receive a recursive query for the Fabrikam.com domain. If the Contoso DNS server has been configured with a forwarder, it will send a recursive query to the forwarder requesting this information. Forwarders are often used on an organization's internal network. An organization may have several DNS servers with the primary task of internal name resolution. However, users inside the organization are also likely to need to resolve Internet IP addresses. One way to enable this is to configure all the internal DNS servers to try to resolve the Internet addresses. A more common configuration has all the internal DNS servers configured with a forwarder pointing to one DNS server that is responsible for Internet name resolution. This latter configuration is shown in Figure 3-5. All the internal DNS servers forward any query for a non-authoritative zone to one DNS server, which then tries to resolve the Internet addresses. If a DNS server is configured with more than one forwarder, that DNS server will try all of the forwarders, in order, before trying any other way of resolving the IP addresses.

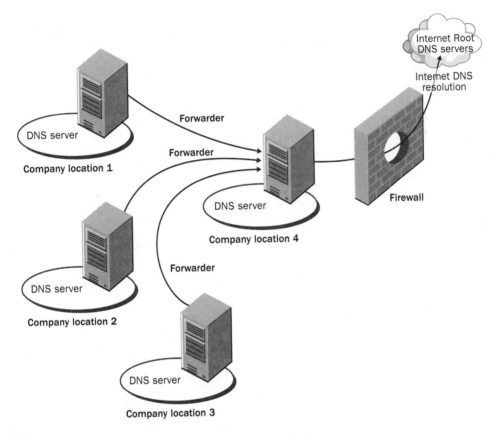

Figure 3-5. *Using forwarders for Internet name resolution.*

The second method available to a DNS server for resolving queries for zones for which it is not authoritative is the use of *root hints*. When you install a Windows Server 2003 DNS server that has access to the Internet, the server is automatically configured with a standard list of root servers. These servers are the servers that are authoritative for the root of the Internet namespace. If a DNS server receives a query for a DNS zone for which it is not authoritative, the server will send an iterative query to one of the root servers, initiating a series of iterative queries until the name is resolved or until the server has confirmed that the name cannot be resolved.

Note The root servers that are automatically configured on the DNS server are copied from the Cache.dns file that is included with the DNS server setup files. You can add additional DNS servers to the root hint list, including the DNS servers on your internal network.

By default, Windows Server 2003 DNS servers use both forwarders and root hints to try to resolve names. If the server is configured with forwarders, it will send recursive queries to all of the configured forwarders first. If none of the forwarders can provide the required information, the DNS server will then begin sending iterative queries to the servers configured as root hints. In some cases, however, you may want to have the DNS server use the forwarders only, and not use the root hints. To configure the DNS server to use the forwarders only, you must select the Do Not Use Recursion For This Domain option on the Forwarders tab of the DNS server's Properties sheet. If you select this option, the DNS server will first try to resolve any queries from its local zone information or its cached information. It will then try to resolve the queries by sending recursive queries to each of its forwarders. However, if the forwarders cannot provide the requested information, the DNS server will not use any other means to locate the information. If the DNS server cannot resolve the query using forwarders, it will inform the client that the host cannot be found.

Note Windows Server 2003 DNS has added greater functionality to the traditional forwarders by implementing conditional forwarders. This topic is covered in detail in "Conditional Forwarding," later in this chapter.

Dynamic DNS

In the past, one difficult aspect of working with DNS was that all the zone information had to be manually entered into the DNS server. Until RFC 2136, there was no way to update the DNS server zone information automatically. However, as described in RFC 2136, DNS servers can now be configured to accept automatic updates to the resource records in the zone files. This option is called dynamic DNS (DDNS).

Windows Server 2003 DNS servers support dynamic DNS. By default, all Windows 2000 and Windows XP Professional clients as well as Windows 2000 Server; Windows 2000 Advanced Server; Windows 2000 Datacenter Server; Windows Server 2003, Standard Edition; Windows Server 2003, Enterprise Edition; and Windows Server 2003, Datacenter Edition automatically update their resource records in DNS. In addition, Windows 2000 and Windows Server 2003 domain controllers automatically register SRV records with the DNS servers that are used to locate domain controllers. Windows Server 2003 DNS servers will also accept dynamic record registration from Dynamic Host Configuration Protocol (DHCP) servers. The Windows Server 2003 DHCP server can be configured to automatically update the DNS records for any of its clients, including Microsoft Windows 95, Microsoft Windows 98, Microsoft Windows Me, or Microsoft Windows NT clients.

One of the concerns with dynamic DNS is security. Without some control over who can update the DNS resource records, anyone with access to your network can potentially create a resource record in your DNS zone files and then use the record to redirect network traffic. To deal with this, Windows Server 2003 DNS provides for *secure updates*. Secure updates are only available in Active Directory integrated zones. With secure updates, you can control who has the right to register and update the DNS records. By default, the members of the Authenticated Users group have the right to update their records in DNS. However, you can change this by modifying the access control list (ACL) for the DNS zone.

Dynamic DNS greatly reduces the amount of work that the DNS administrator needs to do. As will be seen in the next section, Active Directory in Windows Server 2003 requires that the SRV records for each domain controller are listed in the zone information, so enabling dynamic updates is an important feature in Windows Server 2003 DNS.

DNS and Windows Server 2003 Active Directory

Active Directory cannot function without a reliable DNS configuration. Without DNS, the domain controllers cannot locate each other to replicate domain information, and the Windows 2000 and Windows XP Professional clients will be very slow in locating the domain controllers to log on. In addition, without a reliable DNS, any other services that require Active Directory will fail. For example, Exchange 2000 Server stores all of its configuration information in Active Directory, so if the servers running Exchange 2000 Server cannot locate a domain controller when the servers start, they will not be able to start most of the Exchange 2000 Server services.

Tip   Windows 95, Windows 98, Windows ME, and Windows NT clients do not rely on DNS to locate the Windows Server 2003 domain controllers. These clients must use NetBIOS names to locate the domain controllers and usually use Windows Internet Naming Service (WINS) to resolve the NetBIOS names to IP addresses. By default, Windows Server 2003 supports these down-level clients by registering the required NetBIOS names with WINS.

DNS Locator Service

DNS is so important in Active Directory because DNS provides the information that clients need to locate the domain controllers on the network. This section takes a detailed look at the process that a client uses to locate the domain controllers.

Note   In Windows NT, domain logon was based on NetBIOS names. Every domain controller registered the NetBIOS name *Domainname* with a *<1C>* as the sixteenth character in the name on the network and in WINS. When a client tried to log on to the network, the client would try to locate the servers that had the domain controller name registered. If the client could not locate one of these servers, the logon would fail. The SRV records in Windows Server 2003 are used by

Windows 2000 and Windows XP Professional clients to locate domain controllers. Without the SRV records, these clients will also not be able to log on to the Windows Server 2003 domain.

DNS Resource Records Registered by the Active Directory Domain Controller

To facilitate the location of domain controllers, Active Directory uses service locator, or SRV, records. An SRV record is a new type of DNS record described in RFC 2782, and is used to identify services located on a Transmission Control Protocol/Internet Protocol (TCP/IP) network. Every SRV record uses a standard format, as shown in the following example of one of the records used by Active Directory and explained in Table 3-2.

```
_ldap._tcp.contoso.com. 600 IN SRV 0 100 389 dc2.contoso.com
```

Table 3-2. The SRV Record Components

Component	Example	Explanation
Service	_ldap	The service that this record identifies. Additional services include _kerberos, _kpassword, and _gc.
Protocol	_tcp	The protocol used for this service. Can be either TCP or user datagram protocol (UDP).
Name	contoso.com	The domain name that this record refers to.
TTL	600	The default Time to Live for this record (in seconds).
Class	IN	The standard DNS Internet class.
Resource Record	SRV	Identifies the record as an SRV record.
Priority	0	Identifies the priority of this record for the client. If multiple SRV records exist for the same service, the clients will try to connect first to the server with the lowest priority value.
Weight	100	A load balancing mechanism. If multiple SRV records exist for the same service and the priority is identical for all the records, clients will choose the records with the higher weights more often.
Port	389	The port used by this service.
Target	dc2.contoso.com	The host that provides the service identified by this record.

Essentially, the information in this record says that if a client is looking for a Lightweight Directory Access Protocol (LDAP) server in the Contoso.com domain, the client should connect to dc2.contoso.com.

The domain controllers in a Windows Server 2003 domain register many SRV records in DNS. The following list includes all of the records registered by the first server in a forest.

```
contoso.com. 600 IN A 192.168.1.201
_ldap._tcp.contoso.com. 600 IN SRV 0 100 389 dc2.contoso.com.
_ldap._tcp.Default-First-Site-Name._sites.contoso.com. 600 IN SRV 0 100 389
    dc2.contoso.com.
_ldap._tcp.pdc._msdcs.contoso.com. 600 IN SRV 0 100 389 dc2.contoso.com.
_ldap._tcp.gc._msdcs.contoso.com. 600 IN SRV 0 100 3268 dc2.contoso.com.
_ldap._tcp.Default-First-Site-Name._sites.gc._msdcs.contoso.com. 600 IN SRV 0
    100 3268 dc2.contoso.com.
_ldap._tcp.64c228cd-5f07-4606-b843-d4fd114264b7.domains._msdcs.contoso.com.
    600 IN SRV 0 100 389 dc2.contoso.com.
gc._msdcs.contoso.com. 600 IN A 192.168.1.201
    175170ad-0263-439f-bb4c-89eacc410ab1._msdcs.contoso.com. 600 IN CNAME
    dc2.contoso.com.
_kerberos._tcp.dc._msdcs.contoso.com. 600 IN SRV 0 100 88 dc2.contoso.com.
_kerberos._tcp.Default-First-Site-Name._sites.dc._msdcs.contoso.com. 600 IN
    SRV 0 100 88 dc2.contoso.com.
_ldap._tcp.dc._msdcs.contoso.com. 600 IN SRV 0 100 389 dc2.contoso.com.
_ldap._tcp.Default-First-Site-Name._sites.dc._msdcs.contoso.com. 600 IN SRV 0
    100 389 dc2.contoso.com.
_kerberos._tcp.contoso.com. 600 IN SRV 0 100 88 dc2.contoso.com.
_kerberos._tcp.Default-First-Site-Name._sites.contoso.com. 600 IN SRV 0 100 88
    dc2.contoso.com.
_gc._tcp.contoso.com. 600 IN SRV 0 100 3268 dc2.contoso.com.
_gc._tcp.Default-First-Site-Name._sites.contoso.com. 600 IN SRV 0 100 3268
    dc2.contoso.com.
_kerberos._udp.contoso.com. 600 IN SRV 0 100 88 dc2.contoso.com.
_kpasswd._tcp.contoso.com. 600 IN SRV 0 100 464 dc2.contoso.com.
_kpasswd._udp.contoso.com. 600 IN SRV 0 100 464 dc2.contoso.com.
DomainDnsZones.contoso.com. 600 IN A 192.168.1.201
_ldap._tcp.DomainDnsZones.contoso.com. 600 IN SRV 0 100 389 dc2.contoso.com.
_ldap._tcp.Default-First-Site-Name._sites.DomainDnsZones.contoso.com. 600 IN
    SRV 0 100 389 dc2.contoso.com.
ForestDnsZones.contoso.com. 600 IN A 192.168.1.201
_ldap._tcp.ForestDnsZones.contoso.com. 600 IN SRV 0 100 389 dc2.contoso.com.
_ldap._tcp.Default-First-Site-Name._sites.ForestDnsZones.contoso.com. 600 IN
    SRV 0 100 389 dc2.contoso.com.
```

Note When one of the Windows Server 2003 servers is promoted to a domain controller, all of these records are written to a file called Netlogon.dns, which is located in the %systemroot%\system32\config folder. If you do not want to enable dynamic updates on the DNS servers, you can import these records into the DNS zone files.

The first part of the SRV record identifies the service that the SRV record points to. The possible services are:

- **_ldap** Active Directory is an LDAP-compliant directory service, with the domain controllers operating as LDAP servers. The _ldap SRV records identify the available LDAP servers on the network. These servers could be Windows Server 2003 domain controllers or other LDAP servers.

- **_kerberos** The primary authentication protocol for all Windows 2000 and Windows XP Professional clients. The _kerberos SRV records identify all the Key Distribution Centers (KDCs) on the network. These could be Windows Server 2003 domain controllers or other KDC servers.

- **_kpassword** The _kpassword SRV record identifies the kerberos password-change servers on the network (again either Windows Server 2003 domain controllers or other kerberos password-change servers).

- **_gc** The _gc SRV record is specific to the global catalog function in Active Directory. The global catalog server serves a number of important functions in Active Directory.

Many of the SRV records also contain a site identifier in addition to the components listed in Table 3-2. A site is used in Active Directory to identify one or more IP subnets that are connected with fast network connections. One of the advantages of using sites is that the network clients will always try to log on to a domain controller that resides in the same site as the client. The site records are essential for the computers to locate domain controllers in the same site as the client. The exact process that a client uses to locate the site information is discussed in the next section.

Another essential component of the SRV records is the _msdcs_ value that appears in many of the records. Some of the services provided by the SRV records are non–Microsoft specific. For example, there could be non-Microsoft implementations of LDAP or kerberos servers on the network. These servers could also register an SRV record with the DNS server. Windows Server 2003 domain controllers register the generic records (for example, _ldap._tcp.contoso.com), but the domain controllers also register records containing the _msdcs reference. These records refer only to Microsoft-specific roles, that is, to Windows Server 2003 or Windows 2000 domain controllers. The records identify the primary function of each server as gc (global catalog), dc (domain controller) or pdc (primary domain controller emulator).

Another record that is registered contains the domain's globally unique identifier (GUID). The domain GUID record is used to locate domain controllers in the event of a domain rename.

Note There are also several records included under the ForestDnsZones and the DomainDnsZones subdomains. These records are discussed in more detail in "Application Directory Partitions," later in this chapter.

Active Directory Domain Controller Location Process

The domain controllers running Windows Server 2003 register some or all of the records, described earlier, in DNS. These records then play an essential role when a client like Windows 2000 or Windows XP Professional tries to log on to the domain. The following steps describe the process that these clients use to log on to the domain.

1. When the user logs on, the client computer sends a remote procedure call (RPC) to the local Net Logon service initiating a logon session. As part of the RPC, the client sends information such as the computer name, domain name, and site name to the Net Logon service.

2. The Net Logon service uses the domain locator service to call the DsGetDcName() API, passing one of the flag parameter values listed in Table 3-3.

Table 3-3. A Subset of the DsGetDcName Flag Parameter Values

DsGetDcName flag values	DNS record requested
DS_PDC_REQUIRED	_ldap._tcp.pdc._msdcs.*domainname*
DS_GC_SERVER_REQUIRED	_ldap._tcp.*sitename*._sites.gc._msdcs.*forestrootdomainname*
DS_KDC_REQUIRED	_kdc._tcp.*sitename*._sites.dc._msdcs.*domainname*
DS_ONLY_LDAP_NEEDED	_ldap._tcp.*sitename*._sites._msdcs.*domainname*

Note   In almost all cases, the DsGetDcName function also includes the *sitename* parameter. For all of the requests except the DS_PDC_REQUIRED request, the client always makes an initial request using the site parameter. If the DNS server does not respond to the request, the client will send the same request without the site parameter. For example, if the DS_KDC_REQUIRED request is not fulfilled, the client will send a request for the _kdc._tcp.dc._msdcs.*forestrootdomain* record. This can happen when the client is in a site that is not recognized by the DNS servers.

The client may also pass the *DomainGUID* parameter rather than the domain name to DsGetDcName(). In this case, the client is requesting the _ldap._tcp.*domainGUID*.domains._msdcs.*forestname* record. This will only happen when a domain has been renamed.

3. The DNS server returns the requested list of servers, sorted according to priority and weight. The client then sends an LDAP query using UDP port 389 to each of the addresses in the order they were returned. After each packet is sent, the client waits for 0.1 second and if no response is received, it sends a packet to the next domain controller. The client continues this process until it receives a valid response or has tried all of the domain controllers.

4. When a domain controller responds to the client, the client checks the response to make sure that it contains the requested information. If it does, the client begins the logon process with the domain controller.

5. The client caches the domain controller information so that the next time it needs to access Active Directory it does not have to go through the discovery process again.

How the Client Determines Which Site It Belongs To

Having site-specific records is important in order for Active Directory to operate efficiently, because a lot of client activity is limited to a particular site. For example, the client logon process always tries to connect to a domain controller in the client site before connecting to any other sites. So how does the client know which site it belongs to?

The site information for the forest is stored in the configuration directory partition in Active Directory, and this information is replicated to all domain controllers in the forest. Included with the configuration information is a list of IP subnets that are associated with a particular site. When the client logs on to Active Directory for the first time, the first domain controller to respond compares the client's IP address with the site IP addresses. Part of the domain controller's response to the client is the site information, which the client then caches. Any future logon attempts will include the client site information.

If the client is moved between sites (for example, a portable computer may be connected to a network in a different city), the client still sends the site information as part of the logon. The DNS server will respond with the record of a domain controller that is in the requested site. However, if the domain controller determines that the client is not in the original site based on the client's new IP address, it will send the new site information to the client. The client then caches this information and tries to locate a domain controller on the correct subnet.

If the client is not in any site that is defined in Active Directory, it cannot make site-specific requests for domain controllers.

Active Directory Integrated Zones

One of the greatest advantages of running DNS in a Windows Server 2003 operating system is the option to use Active Directory integrated zones. Active Directory integrated zones provide a number of advantages:

- The zone information is no longer stored in zone files on the DNS server hard disk, but is stored in the Active Directory database. This provides additional security.
- The zone transfer process is replaced by Active Directory replication. Because the zone information is stored in Active Directory, the data is replicated through the normal Active Directory replication process. This means that the replication occurs at a per-attribute level so that only the changes to the zone information are replicated. Between sites, the replication traffic can also be highly compressed, saving additional bandwidth. Using an Active Directory integrated zone also enables the use of application partitions that can be used to fine-tune the replication of DNS information.
- Integrated zones offer the possibility of a multimaster DNS server configuration. Without Active Directory, DNS can support only one primary name server for each domain. That means that all changes to the zone information must be made on the primary name server and then transferred to the secondary name servers.

With Active Directory integrated zones, each DNS server has a writable copy of the domain information, so that changes to the zone information can be made anywhere in the organization. The information is then replicated to all other DNS servers.

- Integrated zones offer the option to enable secure updates. If a zone is configured as an Active Directory integrated zone, you can configure the zone to use secure updates only. This means that you have more control over which users and computers can update the resource records in Active Directory.

The greatest disadvantage of Active Directory integrated zones is the fact that DNS must be installed on a Windows Server 2003 domain controller. This can create an additional load on that domain controller.

Tip You can combine Active Directory integrated zones with secondary zones. For example, you might have three domain controllers in a central location with several remote offices where you do not have a domain controller. If you want to install a DNS server into a remote office, you can install DNS on a member server running Windows Server 2003 and then configure a secondary zone on the DNS server. The secondary server will then accept zone transfers from the Active Directory integrated zone.

When the zone is configured as an Active Directory integrated zone, you can view the DNS information in Active Directory (see Figure 3-6). To do this, start the Microsoft Management Console (MMC) and ensure the Active Directory Users And Computers snap-in has been added to the console. Select the Active Directory Users And Computers folder and, from the View menu, select Advanced Features. Open the folder bearing the domain name, open the System folder, and then open the MicrosoftDNS folder. The zone information for all Active Directory integrated zones is listed in each zone folder.

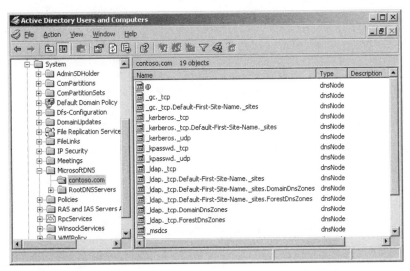

Figure 3-6. *Viewing Active Directory integrated zone information.*

Real World **DNS Resolution Without the Windows Server 2003 DNS Enhancements**
A corporation consisting of four distinct companies, all of which had been independent companies before a series of acquisitions and mergers created one large corporation, was planning and deploying Active Directory in Windows 2000 Advanced Server. Each company insisted on maintaining a distinct namespace within one forest, which meant that a forest with a dedicated root domain and four company domains had to be deployed (see Figure 3-7 for an illustration of the forest plan). Each company was located in a different city in Canada.

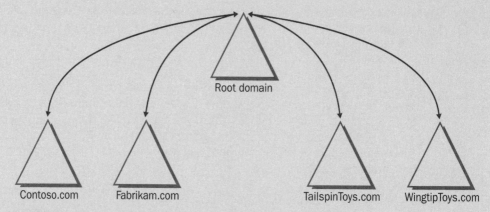

Figure 3-7. *A multiple-tree Active Directory forest design.*

 Because there was no contiguous namespace for the company, the normal process of delegating child domains did not apply. The normal process of configuring forwarders and root hints was also not efficient because the forwarder and root hint configuration was not robust enough. For example, if someone from Contoso.com had needed to locate a resource in Fabrikam.com's domain, the client would have queried Contoso's DNS server. Because the server was not authoritative for the Fabrikam domain, it would have had to try to resolve the name by using a forwarder or root hint. If the Contoso DNS server was configured with a forwarder to the DNS server in the Fabrikam domain, the name could have been resolved. However, that forwarder record could not have been used to resolve computer names in the TailspinToys.com domain, or on the Internet. Using Windows 2000 DNS provides some answers to this problem, as described in the following list, but none of them are particularly satisfying.

- Creating a secondary zone on each DNS server for each of the other domains would result in too much zone transfer traffic.

- Creating a secondary zone for each company domain on the DNS servers in the root domain and configuring all of the domain DNS servers to forward requests to the root domain DNS servers would have created a significant load on the root domain DNS servers. Also, because all of the root domain DNS servers were located in one datacenter, name resolution would result in significant network traffic from other offices.

Neither of these solutions is ideal. The Windows Server 2003 operating system provides three better ways to deal with this scenario. They are *conditional forwarding*, *stub zones*, and *application directory partitions*.

DNS Enhancements

Most of the DNS options that have been discussed up to this point are available in Windows 2000. However, the Windows Server 2003 operating system has added at least three significant enhancements to DNS. The real-world scenario on the previous page illustrates one of the common difficulties in configuring DNS in a large corporation before the development of the Windows Server 2003 operating system.

Conditional Forwarding

Conditional forwarding is designed to add intelligence to the forwarding process. Until the introduction of the Windows Server 2003 operating system, the forwarding process could not make any distinctions based on domain names. When a client resolver made a request that the server could not answer from its cache or zone files, the server would send a recursive query to the list of configured forwarders. There was no option to configure the forwarder to be domain-specific. Conditional forwarding provides exactly this type of intelligence: the DNS server can now forward domain requests to different DNS servers based on domain names.

For example, the company in the scenario described earlier has five trees in a single forest. To replicate, the domain controllers must be able to locate domain controllers in the other domains. Users also frequently travel between companies. They must be able to log on to their home domain regardless of which network they are physically connected to. There is also a significant amount of resource-sharing configured between the companies. These requirements mean that the DNS information must be shared across the domains.

With Windows Server 2003, the DNS servers in each domain can be configured with a conditional forwarder to one or more DNS servers in the other domains. This means that when one of the DNS servers needs to resolve a name in a different domain, it can use just the forwarder that is configured for that domain. For example, when a client in the Contoso.com domain needs to locate a resource in the Fabrikam.com domain, it queries the DNS server in the Contoso.com domain. The DNS server checks its zone files to determine if it is authoritative for the domain and then checks its cache. If it cannot resolve the name from these sources, it will check the forwarder list. One of the forwarders is specific for the Fabrikam.com domain, so the Contoso.com DNS server will send the recursive query only to that DNS server. If there are no conditional forwarders for the Fabrikam.com domain configured on the Contoso.com DNS server, it will forward the request to any forwarder that is configured without any specific domain settings and then try the root hints.

Caution Notice that the DNS server still checks its own zone files first before checking for forwarders. If a DNS server is authoritative for the domain, it will not forward the request to a conditional forwarder.

Conditional forwarding is configured on the server's Properties sheet in the DNS administrative tool (shown in Figure 3-8). Using this interface, you can configure one or more domain controllers as forwarders for each domain name. If you configure multiple DNS servers for a domain name, the DNS server will try the first DNS server on the list. If this server does not respond within the time-out value set on the Forwarders tab, the server will try the next DNS server on the list, until all of the DNS servers have been tried. If there is no conditional forwarder configured for a domain name, the server will try the DNS servers represented by All Other DNS Domains.

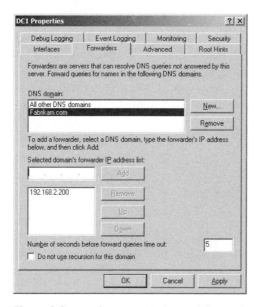

Figure 3-8. *Configuring conditional forwarders.*

The DNS server will always try to match the most qualified domain name when using conditional forwarding. For example, if you have a conditional forwarder configured for Fabrikam.com and for Europe.Fabrikam.com, and a client makes a request for a server such as Web1.Europe.Fabrikam.com, the DNS server will forward the request to the DNS server for Europe.Fabrikam.com.

Stub Zones

Stub zones are the second enhancement to DNS in Windows Server 2003, and are designed to simplify the configuration of name resolution across multiple namespaces. A stub zone is similar to a secondary zone. When you set up a stub zone, you must specify the IP address of a primary name server for the zone. The server holding the stub zone then requests a zone transfer from the primary name server. What is different, however, is that the stub zone contains only the SOA records, the NS records, and the host (A) records for the name servers for the domain, rather than all of the records in the zone.

This enhances name resolution across namespaces without secondary name servers having to be used. When a DNS server is configured with a stub zone, it is not authoritative for the domain. Rather, it is just much more efficient at locating the authoritative name server for the specified zone. With stub zones, the DNS server can locate the authoritative name servers for a zone without having to contact the root hint servers. Consider how a stub zone would work in a forest with a single tree, that is, with a contiguous namespace (see Figure 3-9). Without stub zones, if a client from NAmerica.Contoso.com requests an IP address for a host in the SAmerica.Contoso.com domain, the DNS server at NAmerica.Contoso.com checks its zone files, cache, and forwarders, and if none of these sources provides the information, it sends an iterative query to a root-hint server. In this case, a DNS server in the Contoso.com root domain should be configured as a root server, so the NAmerica.Contoso.com DNS server would send the query to this root server. This root server checks its delegation records and forwards the IP address of the authoritative name servers in the SAmerica.Contoso.com domain to the NAmerica.Contoso.com name server. The NAmerica.Contoso.com name server then queries one of the SAmerica.Contoso.com DNS servers for the IP address of the server that the client requested.

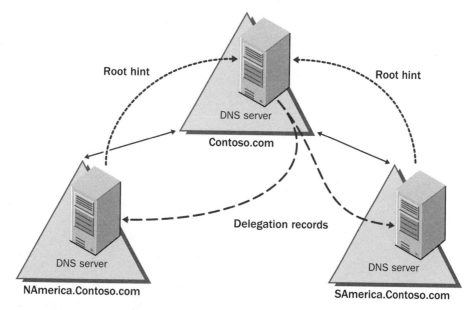

Figure 3-9. *A single forest DNS configuration without using stub zones.*

With a stub zone, the DNS server in the NAmerica.Contoso.com domain does not need to connect to the DNS server in the root domain. That is, it does not need to use its root hints to locate the name servers for the SAmerica.Contoso.com domain. Rather, when the client makes the query, the server checks its zone files, locates the stub zone, and sends an iterative query to any of the name servers in the SAmerica.Contoso.com domain.

While using stub zones in a single-tree forest may by useful (especially if there are many levels in the tree), they are even more useful in a multiple-tree scenario. Consider the previous example in which there are five trees in the forest. Using delegation records in the root zone does not work in this case because the domains do not share a common namespace. In this scenario, you can configure a stub zone for each domain on the DNS servers in the other domains. Then when any DNS query needs information from a different domain, the DNS server can use the stub zone information to immediately connect to the correct name server in the other domain.

Another useful function for stub zones is to maintain the name server list for delegated zones. When you set up a delegated subdomain, you must enter the IP address of all the name servers in the delegated domain. If that list of name servers changes—for example, if one of the name servers is removed from the network—you must manually update the delegation record. You can use a stub zone to automate the process of keeping the name server list updated. To configure this in the Contoso.com domain, you would configure a stub zone for the NAmerica.Contoso.com domain on the DNS servers in the Contoso.com domain. You would also configure a delegation record in the Contoso.com zone pointing to the stub zone. As name server records are modified in the child domain, they will be updated automatically in the stub zone. When the Contoso.com DNS servers use the delegation record, they will be referred to the stub zone, so they will always have access to the updated name server information.

To configure a stub zone, use the New Zone Wizard in the DNS administrative tool. Right-click Forward Lookup Zones (or Reverse Lookup Zones) and select New Zone. You are given the option to create a stub zone (see Figure 3-10).

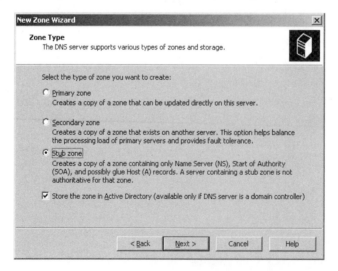

Figure 3-10. *Creating a new stub zone.*

Application Directory Partitions

A third enhancement to DNS that helps with resolving host names across multiple domains is the use of application directory partitions.

DNS in Windows Server 2003 Active Directory makes use of application directory partitions to facilitate the replication of DNS information throughout a forest. When you install DNS while you are promoting the first server in the forest to be a domain controller, two new directory partitions are created in Active Directory. These partitions are the DomainDnsZones partition and the ForestDnsZones partition. (These partitions are not visible in any of the regular Active Directory management tools but can be seen when using ADSI Edit or Ldp.exe; the use of ADSI Edit is shown in Figure 3-11.) Each of these partitions has a different replication configuration. The DomainDnsZones partition is replicated to all DNS servers running on domain controllers in a domain. The ForestDnsZones is replicated to all DNS servers running on domain controllers in the forest. You can also store the DNS information in the domain directory partition, which means that the DNS information will be replicated to all domain controllers in the domain.

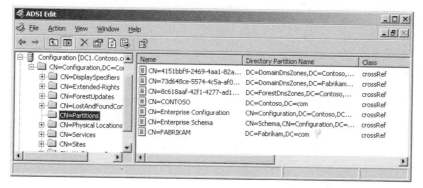

Figure 3-11. *The DNS application directory partitions in ADSI Edit.*

You are given a choice about where to store the DNS information when you create a new zone (see Figure 3-12) or through the Zone Properties sheet in the DNS administrative tool. You are given the following four choices of where to store the DNS information:

- **To All DNS Servers In The Active Directory Forest *domainname*** The information is stored in the ForestDnsZones partition, where it is replicated to all DNS servers running on domain controllers in the forest. This is the default configuration for the _msdcs zone in an Active Directory integrated zone.

- **To All DNS Servers In The Active Directory Domain *domainname*** The information is stored in the DomainDnsZones partition, to all the DNS servers running on domain controllers in the domain. This is the default configuration for the Active Directory integrated zones created during the domain controller upgrade process.

- **To All Domain Controllers In The Active Directory Domain** *domainname* The information is stored in the domain directory partition, where it is replicated to all domain controllers in the domain. The difference between this option and the option to store the information in the DomainDnsZones partition is that, in this case, all domain controllers will receive the information while the DomainDnsZones partition is only replicated to domain controllers that are also DNS servers.

- **To All Domain Controllers Specified In The Scope Of The Following Application Directory Partition** This option is only available if you create an additional application directory partition with its own replication configuration. The DNS information will be replicated to all domain controllers that have a replica of this partition.

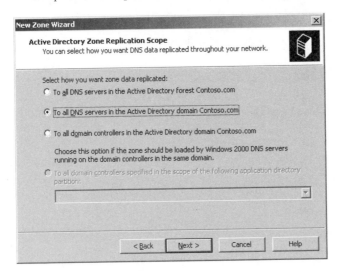

Figure 3-12. *Configuring the replication scope for DNS zones.*

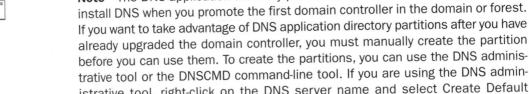

Note The DNS application directory partitions are created only if you choose to install DNS when you promote the first domain controller in the domain or forest. If you want to take advantage of DNS application directory partitions after you have already upgraded the domain controller, you must manually create the partition before you can use them. To create the partitions, you can use the DNS administrative tool or the DNSCMD command-line tool. If you are using the DNS administrative tool, right-click on the DNS server name and select Create Default Application Directory Partitions. If you are using DNSCMD, open a command line and type *dnscmd **DNSservername** /CreateBuiltinDirectoryPartitions /forest*. This will create the ForestDnsZones partition. To create the DomainDnsZones partition, use *"/domain"* as the last parameter in the command, instead of *"/forest"*. Because this command modifies the configuration directory partition in Active Directory, you must be logged in as a member of the Enterprise Admins group.

Normally, you should not change the default configuration for the zones. If you have multiple domain controllers in a domain but only some of them are DNS servers, using the DomainDnsZones partition reduces the amount of replication to the domain controllers that are not DNS servers. The _msdcs zone for each domain, which includes only information about the Active Directory servers in the domain, is stored in the ForestDnsZones partition. This information is replicated throughout the forest, so the DNS information needed to locate all the domain controllers in the forest is replicated to all DNS servers in the forest.

Summary

DNS is an essential network service for Windows Server 2003 networks. Without a stable DNS infrastructure, almost all logon and resource location efforts will fail on a Windows Server 2003 network. As a network administrator for a Windows Server 2003 network, you must become a DNS expert. This chapter provided an overview of how DNS works as a network service in any environment. It then discussed specifically the integration of DNS with Active Directory. The most important component of the integration is the domain controller locator process where the domain controllers in Active Directory register SRV records in DNS, and then the clients use these records to locate the domain controllers. Also covered were some of the DNS enhancements that Windows Server 2003 provides.

Chapter 4
Active Directory Replication and Sites

Virtually every company that implements Active Directory directory service in Microsoft Windows Server 2003 will be deploying more than one domain controller. These domain controllers might all be located in one datacenter at the company head office where they are connected by very fast network connections. Or they might be spread across many locations around the world, with a variety of wide area network (WAN) connections linking the company locations. Some companies might have a single domain in a forest, and other companies might have many domains in several domain trees in the corporate forest.

Regardless of how many domain controllers a company has or where those domain controllers are located, they must replicate information with each other. If they cannot replicate the information, the directories on the domain controllers might become inconsistent. For example, if a user is created on one domain controller and that information is not replicated to all the other domain controllers, the user will be able to log on to only the one domain controller.

Active Directory uses a multimaster replication model, where changes can be made to the directory on any domain controller and the changes are replicated to all other domain controllers. This chapter describes the process of replication in Active Directory. The focus of this chapter is on how replication works, that is, on how the replication topology is created and how domain controllers replicate with each other.

Active Directory Replication Model

As described in Chapter 2, "Active Directory Components," Active Directory is made up of multiple logical partitions. However, the replication of information between domain controllers, with replicas of each partition, is handled in exactly the same way for all partitions. When an attribute is changed in the configuration directory partition, it is replicated using the same model and processes as when an attribute is changed in any other partition. The only thing that changes is the list of domain controllers that will receive a copy of the replicated change. Also, replication between domain controllers in the same site is handled differently than it is between domain controllers in different sites, but the essential model does not change. This section describes the replication model used by Active Directory.

In contrast to the single-master replication model used by Microsoft Windows NT domain controllers, Active Directory uses a multimaster replication model. In Windows NT, the primary domain controller (PDC) is the only domain controller that can accept changes to the domain information. After the change is made, the change is replicated to all of the backup domain controllers (BDCs). The problem with the single-master replication model is that it is not scalable to a large distributed environment. Because changes (which include user password changes) can only be made on the PDC, the PDC can become a bottleneck if thousands of changes are made at once. Further, the PDC can be in only one company location and any changes made to the domain information in a remote location must still be made on that one PDC. Another problem with a single-master replication model is that the PDC is a single point of failure. If the PDC is not available, no changes can be made to the directory information until the PDC is brought back online or until a BDC is promoted to be the PDC.

In Active Directory, changes to the domain information can be made on any domain controller. That is, every domain controller has a writable copy of the directory and there is no PDC. Once a change has been made, it is then replicated to all the other domain controllers. This multimaster replication model addresses many important reliability and scalability issues. In this model, changes to the directory can now be made on any domain controller, regardless of where the domain controller is located. Because all of the domain controllers provide the same services, no domain controller represents a single point of failure.

Note As discussed in Chapter 2, Active Directory has specific operations master roles that can be held by only one domain controller. These roles represent a single point of failure, but the roles can also be easily moved or seized to another domain controller.

The replication model used by Active Directory can be described as being loosely consistent, but with convergence. The replication is *loosely consistent* because not all domain controllers with a replica of a partition will always have identical information. For example, if a new user is created on one of the domain controllers, the other domain controllers will not receive that information until the next replication cycle. The replication always moves towards *convergence*, however. This means that if the system is maintained in a steady state, with no new changes made to the directory for a period of time, all domain controllers will reach a state of convergence, that is, they will all have identical information.

The replication model also uses a *store and forward* replication process. This means that a domain controller can receive a change to the directory and then forward the change to other domain controllers. This is advantageous in a scenario in which multiple domain controllers in a number of company locations are separated by slow WAN links. A change to the directory can be replicated from one domain controller in one site to a single domain controller in another site. The domain controller that receives the update can then forward the changes to other domain controllers in the second site. The domain controller where the directory change is made does not have to replicate directly with all other domain controllers, as is the case in a single-master replication model.

Replication Enhancements in Windows Server 2003 Active Directory

The replication model for Windows Server 2003 Active Directory is essentially the same as that for Microsoft Windows 2000. However, the Windows Server 2003 Active Directory replication model also provides some significant enhancements over that provided in Windows 2000, including the following:

- **Partial replication of multivalued attributes** In Windows 2000, the smallest unit of replication is an attribute. This means that in some cases, changing one value in a multivalued attribute can create a significant amount of replication traffic. The most common example of this is what happens with universal group membership. Because the entire membership list for the universal group is one attribute, adding a single user to the universal group results in significant replication, especially when the group already had several thousand members. In Windows Server 2003 Active Directory, multivalued attributes like group membership can be updated by replicating only the attribute's updated value.

- **Support for groups of more than 5,000 members** In Windows 2000, groups cannot contain more than 5,000 members because of the attribute-level updates and replication. The practical limit for committing a change to the directory database in one transaction is 5,000. This also defines the maximum number of updates that can be replicated in one update during replication. This means that the maximum group size in Windows 2000 is 5,000 members. In Windows Server 2003 Active Directory, support for modifications of only one value on a multivalued object removes these restrictions.

Note   These enhancements are only available when the domain is running in the Windows Server 2003 functional level or the Windows Server 2003 interim functional level. The Windows Server 2003 functional level is available only when all the domain controllers in the forest are servers running Windows Server 2003. The Windows Server 2003 interim functional level is available when the forest contains only Windows Server 2003 and Windows NT domain controllers. For more information on functional levels, see Chapter 7, "Migrating to Active Directory."

- **Ability to turn off compression for intersite replication** By default, all replication traffic between sites is compressed for both Windows 2000 Active Directory and Windows Server 2003 Active Directory. However, compressing the traffic places an extra load on the domain controller's processor. If you have sufficient bandwidth between the Active Directory sites, you can disable the compression in Windows Server 2003 Active Directory.

- **Ability to enable notification for intersite replication** By default, replication between sites is based on the schedule and replication frequency configured on the site link. In Windows Server 2003 Active Directory, you have the option to enable notification for intersite replication. If notification is enabled, the bridgehead server in a site where a change has occurred notifies the bridgehead server in the destination site, and the changes are pulled across the site link. This can greatly reduce replication latency between sites, but will also increase the network traffic between sites.

Note To turn off compression or to turn on notification for intersite replication, you must use a tool such as ADSI Edit to modify the Options attribute on either the site link object or the connection object. To turn off compression, set the value of the Options attribute to *4*; to turn on notification, set the value to *1*.

- **Improved intersite topology generation** In Windows 2000, organizations are limited to a maximum of about 100 sites in a forest. This is primarily due to the amount of time it takes for Knowledge Consistency Checker (KCC) to calculate a routing topology for this many sites. The process KCC uses to calculate the routing topology has been improved in Windows Server 2003 Active Directory, effectively removing this limitation.

Intrasite and Intersite Replication

One of the main reasons to create additional sites in Active Directory is to manage replication traffic. Because all of the domain controllers within a site are assumed to be connected with fast network connections, the replication between these domain controllers is optimized for maximum speed and reduced latency. However, if the replication traffic has to cross a slow network link, conserving network bandwidth is a much more significant issue. Creating multiple sites allows for this conservation of network bandwidth.

Tip If you have worked with Microsoft Exchange Server 5.5 or earlier, the differences between intersite and intrasite replication will be familiar to you. Active Directory uses many of the same principles for managing replication that are used in Exchange Server 5.5.

Intrasite Replication

The primary goal for replication within a site is to reduce replication latency, that is, to make sure that all domain controllers in a site are updated as quickly as possible. This means that intrasite replication traffic has the following characteristics:

- Replication occurs almost immediately after a change has been made to the Active Directory information. By default, a domain controller will wait for 15 seconds after a change has been made and then begin replicating the changes to other domain controllers in the same site. The domain controller will complete replication with one partner, wait 3 seconds, and then initiate replication with another partner. The reason the domain controller waits 15 seconds after a change is to increase the efficiency of the replication in case additional changes are made to the partition information. The actual duration of this waiting period can be modified through the registry on Windows 2000 or Windows Server 2003 domain controllers (refer to the respective Resource Kits for details on this specific modification to the registry). If your forest is running in Windows Server 2003 functional level, you can also modify this value for each directory partition using ADSI Edit.

- The replication traffic is not compressed. Because all the computers within a site are connected with fast network connections, the data is sent without compression. Compressing the replication data adds an additional load on the domain controller server. By not compressing the replication traffic, server performance is preserved at the expense of network utilization.

- The replication process is initiated by a notification from the sending domain controller. When a change is made to the database, the sending computer notifies a destination domain controller that changes are available. The changes are then pulled from the sending domain controller by the destination domain controller using a remote procedure call (RPC) connection. After this replication is complete, the sending domain controller notifies another destination domain controller, which then pulls the changes. This process continues until all the replication partners have been updated.

- Replication traffic is sent to multiple replication partners during each replication cycle. Whenever a change is made to the directory, the domain controller will replicate the information to all direct replication partners, which might be all or some of the other domain controllers in the site.

- There is very little that needs to be done to modify the replication traffic within a site. You can configure manual connection objects through the Active Directory Sites And Services administrative tool and modify some of the values such as the initial replication partner notification through the registry (refer to the respective Resource Kits for details on this specific modification to the registry) or on the *Partition* object if your forest is running in Windows Server 2003 functional level. However, in most cases, you should not have to modify any intrasite replication configurations.

Intersite Replication

The primary goal of replication between sites is to reduce the amount of bandwidth used for replication traffic. This means that intersite replication traffic has the following characteristics:

- Replication is initiated according to a schedule rather than when changes are made. To manage replication between sites, you must configure a site link connecting the two sites. One of the configuration options on the site link is a schedule for when replication will occur. Another is the replication interval setting for how often replication will occur during the scheduled time. If the bandwidth between company locations is limited, the replication can be scheduled to happen during non-working hours.

- Replication traffic is compressed down to about 10 to 15 percent of the non-compressed size when replication traffic is more than 32 KB in size. To save bandwidth on the network connection, the bridgehead servers in each site compress the traffic at the expense of additional CPU usage.

- Notifications are not used to alert a domain controller in another site that changes to the directory are available. Instead, the schedule determines when to replicate.

- Intersite replication connections can use either an Internet Protocol (IP) or a Simple Mail Transfer Protocol (SMTP) transport. The connection protocol you use is determined by the available bandwidth and the reliability of the network that connects company locations.

- Replication traffic is sent through bridgehead servers rather than to multiple replication partners. When changes are made to the directory in one site, the changes are replicated to a single bridgehead server (per directory partition) in that site, and the changes are then replicated to a bridgehead server in the other site. The changes are replicated from the bridgehead server in the second site to all the domain controllers in that site.

- You can easily modify the flow of replication between sites. Almost every component of the intersite replication can be changed.

Planning One of the key elements in designing Active Directory is site design. Site design includes planning the number and location of sites plus the configuration of intersite connections to optimize the use of network bandwidth while minimizing the replication latency. Configuration options for the intersite connections are discussed later in this chapter, while site design issues are discussed in Chapter 5, "Designing the Active Directory Structure."

Replication Latency

Because of the way replication works in Windows Server 2003 Active Directory, it can take some time for a change made on one domain controller to be replicated to all the other domain controllers in an organization. This time lag is called the *replication latency*. In most cases, the replication latency is easy to calculate, especially within a site. As mentioned earlier, any change made to the directory database on one domain controller will be replicated to that domain controller's replication partners in about 15 seconds. The destination domain controller will hold that change for 15 seconds and then pass it on to its replication partners. So the replication latency within a site is about 15 seconds times the number of hops the change has to take before reaching all domain controllers. As explained in the next section, the replication topology within a site never requires more than three hops, so the maximum replication latency within a site will be about 45 seconds.

Determining the replication latency between sites is more difficult. First of all, you must calculate the replication latency within the source site. This replication latency is the amount of time it takes for a change made on a domain controller in the site to be replicated to the source site's bridgehead server. Once the information arrives at the originating site's bridgehead server, the site link schedule and replication interval determine the amount of time it takes for the information to get to the destination site. The default configuration for site links is to replicate every 3 hours throughout the day. If this configuration is not changed, a maximum of 3 hours might be added to the replication latency. When the information arrives at the bridgehead server in the destination site, the intrasite replication latency for the destination site must be added. In some cases, this replication latency might be unacceptable. To minimize this, you can shorten the replication interval to a minimum of 15 minutes for intersite replication.

Managing replication latency is a matter of balancing the need for a short latency period and bandwidth limitations. If you want the shortest possible latency period, you should put all the domain controllers in the same site, and the replication latency will be about 45 seconds for all domain controllers. However, if your company locations are separated by WAN connections with limited bandwidth, you will require multiple sites, but replication latency will be longer.

Urgent Replication

In some cases the replication latency described in the previous section is too long. In particular, this is the case when a security-related attribute has been modified in the directory. For these situations, Active Directory uses *urgent replication,* in which a domain controller forwards the changes immediately to its replication partners. Any domain controller receiving an urgent update will also immediately forward the change. In this way, all domain controllers in the site are updated within seconds. The following types of changes trigger an urgent replication.

- Modifying the account lockout policy for the domain
- Modifying the domain password policies
- Moving the relative identifier (RID) master to a new domain controller
- Changing a Local Security Authority (LSA) secret, such as when the domain controller machine password is modified

By default, urgent updates apply only to intrasite replication and not to intersite replication. This default handling of urgent updates can be modified by enabling notification for replication between sites.

User password changes are not replicated using the same urgent replication model. Instead, when a user changes his or her password on a domain controller, the password change is immediately replicated directly to the PDC emulator. This replication crosses site boundaries and does not make use of the bridgehead servers in each site. Instead, the domain controller where the change was made uses an RPC connection to the PDC emulator to update the password. The PDC emulator then updates all the other domain controllers through the normal process of replication. If the user tries to log on to a domain controller that has not yet received the new password, the domain controller will check with the PDC emulator to see if there are any updated password changes for the user before denying the logon.

Replication Topology Generation

One of the keys to understanding Active Directory replication is understanding how the replication topology is created. By default, the process of creating the replication topology is handled automatically by Active Directory. While the replication topology can be manually configured, in most cases the default configuration by the system is the best option.

Knowledge Consistency Checker

KCC is the process that runs on every domain controller and is responsible for creating the replication topology within a site and between sites. As soon as a second domain controller is added to the Active Directory forest, KCC begins creating a replication topology that is both efficient and fault tolerant. As additional domain controllers are added to a site, or as additional sites are added, KCC uses the information about servers, sites, site links, and schedules to create the optimal replication topology. KCC also dynamically deals with changes or failures within the replication topology. If one of the domain controllers is offline for a period of time, KCC revises the replication topology to work around the down domain controller. By default, KCC on every domain controller recalculates the replication topology every 15 minutes. You can force KCC to recalculate the replication topology at any time through the Active Directory Sites And Services administrative tool by locating the server where you want to check the replication topology, right-clicking the NTDS Settings container in the server container, selecting All Tasks, and then selecting Check Replication Topology.

Connection Objects

When KCC creates the replication topology, it creates a series of connection objects that are stored in the configuration directory partition of Active Directory. The connection objects are direct logical connections between domain controllers that are used to replicate directory information. As mentioned earlier, KCC tries to create a replication topology that is both efficient and fault tolerant. KCC builds as many connection objects as are required to achieve these goals.

Connection objects are always created as one-way pull connections between two domain controllers. This is because the normal process of replication is always a pull operation where the destination domain controller requests the information from a sending domain controller. In most cases, KCC will build two one-way connections between domain controllers so that information can be replicated either way.

> **Note**   You can force a push replication for a directory partition using Replication Monitor. However, the normal replication process is always a pull operation. (See the section "Monitoring and Troubleshooting Replication" later in this chapter, for details of installing and using the Replication Monitor.)

In most cases, the connection objects automatically created by KCC are optimized and you do not need to make any changes. However, in some cases you might want to modify the connection objects. For example, you might want to ensure that the operations master domain controllers in your domain are always direct replication partners with the domain controllers that you have designated as your fallback operations masters in the case of an operations master failure. By creating a connection agreement, you can ensure the optimal replication topology for that particular set of domain controllers.

You can modify the default connection objects in two ways: by modifying some settings on connection objects created by KCC and by adding new connection objects.

Modifying a Connection Object Created by KCC

You can modify the schedule and the source domain controller for a connection object within a site, and you can also modify the transport protocol for connection objects between sites. By default, domain controllers within a site will check all their replication partners for missed updates every hour. You can change that schedule to never check or to check every half hour or every 15 minutes. (The connection interface is shown in Figure 4-1.) When you modify the connection object, it is renamed from <*automatically generated*> to the object's globally unique identifier (GUID). You can rename the object after modifying it.

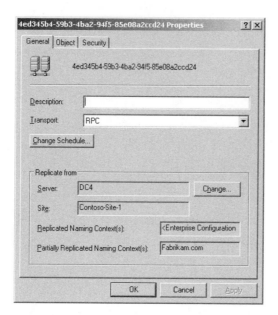

Figure 4-1. *Configuring an existing connection object.*

Creating a New Connection Object

You can also create an entirely new connection object to force a particular replication topology. When you create a connection object, you are given a choice as to which domain controller to pull changes from. You can also modify any of the other settings on the connection agreement.

KCC will not delete or modify any connections that have been manually modified or created. However, KCC will use the manual connection objects as it would use any other connection, and KCC might reconfigure the connection objects in the site to compensate for the manually created connections.

Intrasite Replication Topology

Theoretically, there are two ways that replication might be configured between domain controllers in Active Directory. One option would be to use a spanning tree model where a replication topology is created that includes only one path for replication to flow between domain controllers. If the spanning tree algorithm were used, the replication topology would be created so that every domain controller that hosts a directory partition would have only one sending replication partner for that partition. This ensures that connections are never created that could send information to a particular domain controller by more than one path. The advantage of using a spanning tree algorithm to create the replication topology is that the domain controllers never receive the same update twice, because the updates can come from only one source. The primary disadvantage of using a spanning tree algorithm is the lack of redundancy: If one of the domain controllers fails, it might take some time to recalculate a replication path around the failed domain controller.

The second option for creating a replication topology is to create a replication topology that includes redundant links. This is the model used for Active Directory replication. The primary goal for designing Active Directory replication is availability and fault tolerance. If a single domain controller is not available for replication, Active Directory replication should not fail. The disadvantage of using redundant links is that a domain controller might receive the same update several times because each domain controller will have multiple replication partners. Active Directory replication uses propagation dampening to avoid multiple updates of the same information.

As domain controllers with replicas of particular Active Directory partitions are added to the organization, KCC automatically begins creating the replication topology. This topology forms a replication ring. Figure 4-2 shows an example of a simple network structure with three domain controllers in the same domain and in a single site.

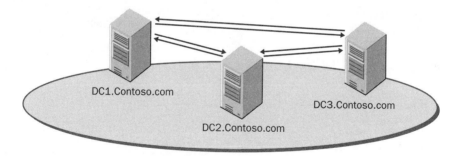

Figure 4-2. *A simple replication ring.*

As shown in Figure 4-2, KCC creates a replication ring in which every domain controller is configured with two incoming replication connections. If one of the connections is not available, updates can still arrive on the other connection. Also, each domain controller is configured as the source domain controller for two other domain controllers. This creates a redundant ring for each domain controller.

As the number of domain controllers with a replica of a particular partition increases, a second principle for creating connections becomes important. KCC will always create a replication topology in which each domain controller in a site is no more than three replication hops away from any other domain controller. As the number of domain controllers in a site increases beyond seven, extra connection objects are created to decrease the potential number of hops to three or fewer. For example, the site shown in Figure 4-3 has nine domain controllers. It would have a replication topology that would include at least one additional connection.

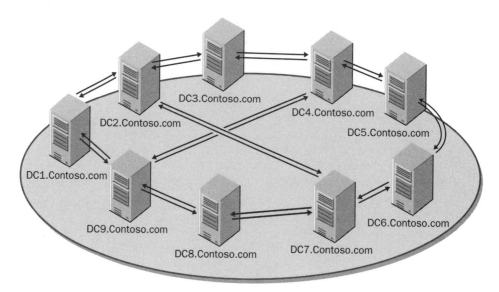

Figure 4-3. *A replication ring with more than seven domain controllers.*

Replication rings are based on directory partitions. This means that KCC calculates a replication ring for each directory partition. For example, an organization might have multiple domains in a single site and an application directory partition that is replicated to several domain controllers in the site. The configuration could be set up as shown in Figure 4-4.

In the scenario illustrated in Figure 4-4, the replication rings shown in Table 4-1 would be created.

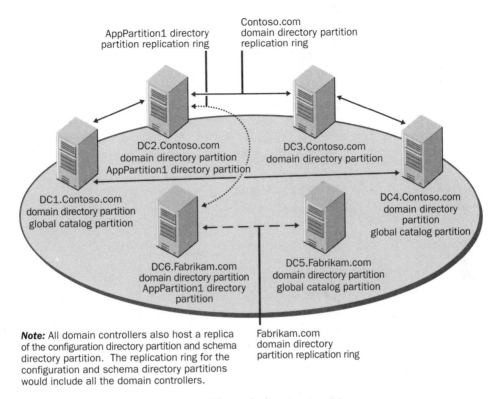

Note: All domain controllers also host a replica of the configuration directory partition and schema directory partition. The replication ring for the configuration and schema directory partitions would include all the domain controllers.

Figure 4-4. *Replication rings created for each directory partition.*

Table 4-1. Replication Rings in a Complex Site

Directory partition	Replication partners
Configuration directory partition, schema directory partition	All the domain controllers would be included in the replication ring for both the configuration directory partition and the schema directory partition because they are replicated to all domain controllers in the forest.
Contoso.com domain directory partition	DC1.Contoso.com, DC2.Contoso.com, DC3.Contoso.com, DC4.Contoso.com.
Fabrikam.com domain directory partition	DC5.Fabrikam.com, DC6.Fabrikam.com.
Global catalog (GC) partition[1]	DC1.Contoso.com, DC4.Contoso.com, DC5.Fabrikam.com.
AppPartition1 application directory partition	DC2.Contoso.com, DC6.Fabrikam.com.

[1]For more information, see the following Note.

Note The Domain Name System (DNS) application directory partitions (ForestDnsZones and DomainDnsZones) are also included in the replication topology. To keep the Figure 4-4 scenario from getting too complicated, these partitions are not included in that figure nor in the associated table. As discussed in Chapter 3, "Active Directory and Domain Name System," these partitions are treated exactly like other domain directory partitions. Also, the GC replication topology is not shown in Figure 4-4. The process of creating a GC replication ring is slightly different than for other partitions and will be described in the next section.

The replication partitions and the topology can be viewed through Replication Monitor. Replication Monitor is one of the support tools included on the Windows Server 2003 compact disc. To install the support tools, install the Suptools.msi file from the Support\Tools directory on the Windows Server 2003 compact disc. To start the Replication Monitor, open the Run command and type *replmon*. Figure 4-5 shows the configuration just discussed using Replication Monitor for four of the servers in the forest.

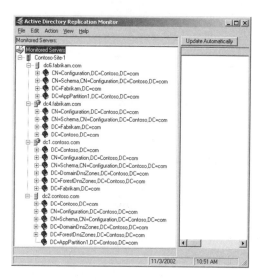

Figure 4-5. *Using Replication Monitor to view the replication partitions.*

The replication ring is a logical concept; the actual replication topology as implemented with the connection objects does not duplicate the replication rings exactly. While a separate replication ring is created for each directory partition, KCC will not create additional connection objects for each replication ring. Instead, KCC reuses connection objects for as many replication rings as possible. In the example illustrated in Figure 4-5, DC1.Contoso.com has a connection object with DC4.Fabrikam.com.

One of the ways to view the properties of this connection object is by using Replication Monitor. To view the properties of a server's inbound connections, add the server to the monitored servers list. Then right-click the server name and click Show Replication Topologies. Click View, then Connection Objects Only, and then right-click the server and select Properties. The Inbound Replication Connections tab shows all the inbound connections for the domain controller as well as the partitions replicated through each connection. As shown in Figure 4-6, this connection object is being used to replicate the GC (shown as the Fabrikam.com partition), the schema directory partition, and the configuration directory partition. Whenever possible, KCC will create a connection object to replicate more than one directory partition.

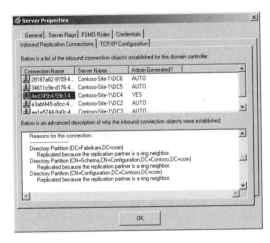

Figure 4-6. *A single connection object used to replicate multiple directory partitions.*

Global Catalog Replication

The GC is a different partition than the other partitions in that it is built from all the domain databases in the entire forest. The GC itself is read-only on all domain controllers, which means that the information in the GC cannot be directly modified by the administrator.

Rather, the GC is just a list of all the attributes that are moved into the GC because their *isMemberOfPartialAttributeSet* attribute is set to *true*.

The fact that the GC is created from the domain databases also affects the replication ring for the GC. Each GC server must get the GC information from the domain controllers in all domains. For a simple example, see Figure 4-7, which shows a company with two domains and one domain controller in each domain, in the same site. Only the DC1.Contoso.com domain is configured as a GC server. The GC server is also the only domain controller for the Contoso.com domain, so it will extract the GC information for Contoso.com from its own domain database. The domain controller in the Fabrikam.com domain has the only copy of that domain directory partition, so DC1.Contoso.com collects the GC information for the Fabrikam.com domain from DC2.Fabrikam.com. To extract the information from the Fabrikam.com domain, a connection object is created from DC2.Fabrikam.com to DC1.Contoso.com. This connection is then used to replicate the GC information to DC1.Contoso.com.

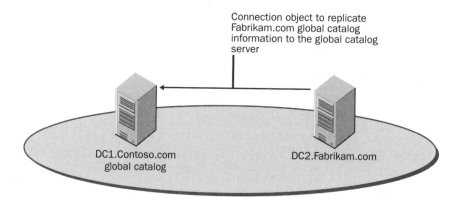

Connection object to replicate Fabrikam.com global catalog information to the global catalog server

DC1.Contoso.com global catalog

DC2.Fabrikam.com

Figure 4-7. *An example of simple GC replication.*

Figure 4-8 shows a more complicated example of how the GC is created and replicated. In this scenario, a connection object is configured from a domain controller in every domain to each GC server. For example, DC1.Contoso.com will have an inbound connection object from DC2.Contoso.com, DC4.Fabrikam.com, and DC6.NWTraders.com. This connection object is used to build the GC on DC1.Contoso.com. Each of the other GC servers will have a similar set of connection objects created. Also, a separate replication ring is created for the GC partition with all of the GC servers.

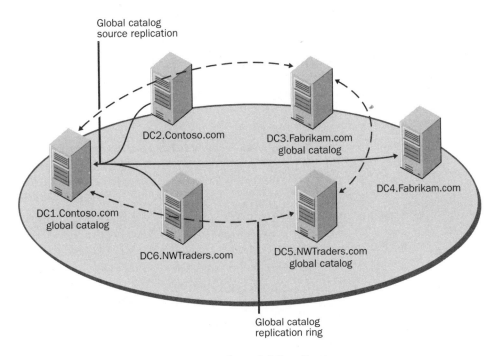

Figure 4-8. *An example of a more complicated GC replication.*

Intersite Replication Topology

When additional sites are added to a forest, the replication topology becomes increasingly complex. In a multisite scenario, a replication topology must be created for each site, and a replication topology must be created for replication between sites. To deal with this complexity, the process for creating connection objects changes for the intrasite replication. Within a site, KCC on each domain controller is responsible for creating the connection objects that it needs to ensure that it has the required replication redundancy for all of its partitions, and it then replicates the information about the connection objects to the other domain controllers. Also, the domain controller receives information about the connection objects that have been created by other domain controllers. The next time KCC runs, connection objects might be added, modified, or deleted based on the information the domain controller has received about other connection objects in the site. Eventually, KCCs on all the domain controllers in a site determine the optimal replication configuration.

A similar approach is used when determining the replication topology between sites, except that one domain controller in each site is responsible for developing the intersite topology. KCC on one domain controller in the site is designated as the Inter-Site Topology Generator (ISTG) for the site. There is only one ISTG per site regardless of how many domains or other directory partitions there are in the site. ISTG is responsible for calculating the ideal replication topology for the entire site. This process consists of the following two actions:

- **Identifying the bridgehead servers for each directory partition that is present in the site** Replication between sites is always sent from a bridgehead server in one site to a bridgehead server in another site. This means that information is replicated only once across the network connection between the sites.

- **Creating the connection objects between the bridgehead servers to ensure that the information is replicated between the sites** Because the replication is configured between bridgehead servers, there are no redundant connection objects configured as there are within a site.

When a new site is added to the forest, ISTG in each site determines which directory partitions are present in the new site. ISTG then calculates the new connection objects that will be needed to replicate the required information from the new site. Also, ISTG designates one domain controller to be the bridgehead server for each directory partition. ISTG creates the required connection agreement in its directory, and this information is replicated to the bridgehead server. The bridgehead server then creates a replication connection with the bridgehead server in the remote site, and replication begins.

To see how the replication topology is created between sites, see Figure 4-9. In this example, the forest contains two sites and two domains with domain controllers for each domain in each site. There is also at least one GC server in each site. This means that each site contains a directory partition for each of the domains, a GC partition, as well as the schema directory partition and the configuration directory partition. Two bridgehead servers would be designated in each site, because each of these partitions must be replicated between the sites. One of the bridgehead servers in each site will be a domain controller in the Contoso.com domain. Another bridgehead server in each site must be a domain controller in the Fabrikam.com domain. In the Figure 4-9 example, DC1.Contoso.com and DC6.Fabrikam.com are also GC servers. This means that they will become bridgehead servers to replicate GC information between sites. Because the schema directory partition and the configuration directory partition are shared by all domain controllers, one of the existing connection objects can be used to replicate these partitions.

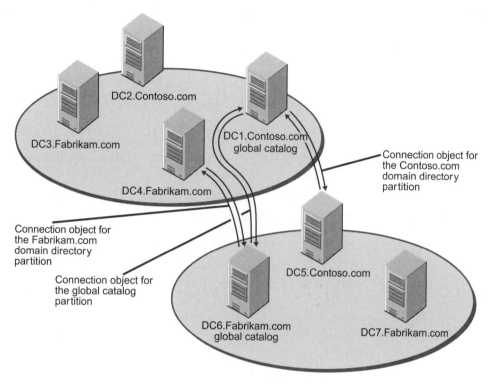

Figure 4-9. *Intersite connection objects.*

Note This discussion of the replication topology is based on the default behavior for Active Directory domain controllers. Administrators can modify the default behavior, especially for replication between sites. These modifications and the effect of these changes are discussed later in this chapter.

Replication Process

The discussion up to this point has dealt with the details of how the replication topology is created in Active Directory. This section approaches replication from a completely different perspective. The focus now switches from how replication information flows through the organization to how the updated information is actually transmitted between domain controllers. In other words, the focus now is on how the domain controllers know what information they must replicate between KCC-determined replication partners.

Update Types

There are two types of changes that can be made to the Active Directory information on a particular domain controller. The first type of update is an *originating update*. An originating update is performed when an object is added, modified, or deleted on a domain controller. The second type of update is a *replicated update*. A replicated update is performed when a change that was made on one domain controller is replicated to another domain controller. By definition, there can be only one originating update performed for any particular change, and this occurs on the domain controller where the change is made. This originating update is then replicated to all the domain controllers that have a replica of the affected Active Directory partition.

Originating updates occur in Active Directory under any of the following circumstances:

- A new object is added to Active Directory.
- An existing object is deleted from Active Directory.
- The attributes for an existing object are modified. This modification can include adding a new value to an attribute, deleting a value for an attribute, or modifying an existing value.
- An object in Active Directory is moved to a new parent container. If the parent container is renamed, each object in the container is also moved to the renamed container.

All originating updates to Active Directory are *atomic operations*, which means that when an update is committed to Active Directory, either the entire transaction is committed and permanent, or no part of the update will be committed.

Replicating Changes

After an originating update has been committed to Active Directory, the change must be replicated to other domain controllers that host a replica of that partition. Within a site, the domain controller where the originating update occurred waits 15 seconds before replicating the changes to its direct replication partners. The 15-second wait occurs so that if multiple updates are committed to the database, they can all be replicated at the same time. This increases the efficiency of the replication. Between sites, the originating update will be replicated to replication partners based on the schedule configured on the site link.

When replicating changes to the directory information, the domain controllers require a mechanism for managing the flow of replication. To optimize Active Directory replication, only those changes that need to be replicated between two domain controllers should be sent. To accomplish this, the domain controllers should be able to determine what, if any, changes have not yet been replicated, and then replicate only those changes that are required. Active Directory uses a combination of update sequence numbers (USNs), high-watermark values, up-to-dateness vectors, and change stamps to manage directory replication. These components are discussed in the following sections.

Update Sequence Numbers

When an object is updated in the database, an *update sequence number* is assigned to the update. The USN is specific to the database on the server. For example, if a telephone number update for one user was assigned USN 5555, the next change to the database, regardless of which object was modified, would be USN 5556. One USN is assigned for each committed change. If multiple attributes are changed with one update (for example, a user's address, telephone number, and office location are all modified at once), only one USN is assigned during the update.

There are actually three ways that the USN is used when an update is committed. First, the local USN value is stored with the attribute that was updated. The local USN value identifies the USN of the changed attribute. The second way the USN is used is for the object's *uSNChanged* attribute. This attribute is stored with each object and identifies the highest USN for any attribute for the object. To understand how these USNs are related, consider this example. Suppose a user's telephone number was changed and the USN applied to that change was 5556. Both the local USN and the *uSNChanged* attribute will be set to 5556. If the next update applied to the directory on that server were an address change for the same user, the local USN on the address attribute and the *uSNChanged* attribute for the user object would both be changed to 5557. However, the local USN for the telephone number attribute would remain at 5556, because that was the USN for the last update that changed that particular attribute.

The local USN and the *uSNChanged* attribute are applied for both originating and replicated updates. The last way the USN is used is as the *originating USN* for the attribute. This value is set only for originating updates and is replicated to all other domain controllers as part of the attribute replication. When the telephone number for a user is changed on a server, the USN for the change is assigned to the originating USN value. When the modified telephone number is replicated to another domain controller, the originating USN is sent along with the update and this value is not modified on the destination domain controller. The local USN and the *uSNChanged* attribute will be modified on the destination domain controller, but the originating USN is not changed until the attribute itself is updated again. The originating USN is used for propagation dampening, which is described later in this chapter.

High-Watermark Values

The high-watermark values are used to manage what information is replicated between domain controllers. Each domain controller maintains its own set of high-watermark values for each of its direct replication partners. The high-watermark is just the latest *uSNChanged* value that the domain controller has received from a specific replication partner. When a domain controller sends an update to a replication partner, the *uSNChanged* value is sent along with the update. The destination domain controller retains this *uSNChanged* as the high-watermark value for the replication partner.

The high-watermark values are used during the process of replication. When one domain controller requests updates from another domain controller, the destination domain controller sends its high-watermark value for use by the sending domain controller. The sending domain controller uses the destination domain controller's high-watermark to filter all of the potential directory updates and sends only the changes with a higher *uSNChanged* value.

> **Note** A separate high-watermark value is maintained for each directory partition on the domain controller and for each direct replication partner.

Up-To-Dateness Vectors and Propagation Dampening

The up-to-dateness vectors are also used to control what information is replicated between domain controllers. The up-to-dateness vectors are used to keep track of all of the originating updates that a domain controller has received from any domain controller. For example, suppose the telephone number for a user is changed on DC1 and the attribute is given the originating USN of 5556. When this attribute is replicated to DC2, the originating USN is replicated with the updated attribute. Also, the GUID for DC1 is replicated with the attribute. When DC2 receives this update, it would modify its up-to-dateness vector to show that the latest originating update it received from DC1 is now 5556.

The up-to-dateness vector is used to limit replication traffic between domain controllers. When a destination domain controller requests updates from a sending domain controller, it includes its up-to-dateness vectors with the request. The sending computer then uses this information to filter the list of all possible updates it could send to the destination domain controller. This option is important when there are more than two domain controllers for a directory partition. For example, if DC3 is added to the scenario described in the preceding paragraph, the telephone number change made on DC1 will be replicated to both DC2 and DC3. Now both DC3 and DC2 will have the updated telephone number, and they will modify their up-to-dateness vector to show that the latest update both of them received from DC1 had an originating USN of 5556. About 15 seconds after receiving this update, DC2 will notify DC3 that it has updated information. When DC3 requests the directory updates from DC2, it will include its up-to-dateness vector with the request. In this case, DC2 determines that DC3's up-to-dateness vector for DC1 already has the most recent originating USN. If this telephone number update were the only change made to the directory during this time period, no information would be replicated between the DC2 and the DC3 domain controllers.

This process of limiting the updates sent during replication by using the up-to-dateness vector is called *propagation dampening*. As described earlier, KCC creates redundant replication connections between domain controllers. One of the problems with creating the redundant links is that the same updates might be sent to a domain controller from multiple replication partners. This could create a significant amount of unnecessary replication traffic, as well as potentially leading to a situation where the same update is sent repeatedly to all domain controllers (resulting in a replication loop). Propagation dampening using the up-to-dateness vector eliminates this possibility.

Viewing USN Information

The USNs for any object can be viewed through several different administrative tools included with the Windows Server 2003 support tools. One way to view the local USN, originating domain controller, originating USN, and time stamp for any attribute is by using the Repadmin command-line tool. (See the section "Monitoring and Troubleshooting Replication" later in this chapter, for complete instructions on installing Repadmin.) Type *repadmin /showmeta* ***object distinguished name*** at a command prompt. The *uSNCreated* value and the *uSNChanged* value are also visible through the object properties in ADSI Edit. To access the replication information through Ldp.exe, locate the object and then right-click the object, select Advanced, and then select Replication Metadata. The USN values are also visible through Replication Monitor (see Figure 4-10). To view this information, add the server to the monitored list and then right-click the server and select Show Attribute Meta-Data For Active Directory Object. Provide the credentials for an account with access to Active Directory, and then type the distinguished name for the object.

Some USN information is also accessible from the regular administrative tools. To see the USN current and original values for an object in the Active Directory Users And Computers administrative tool, turn on Advanced Features under the View menu and then access the Object tab in the object's Properties sheet.

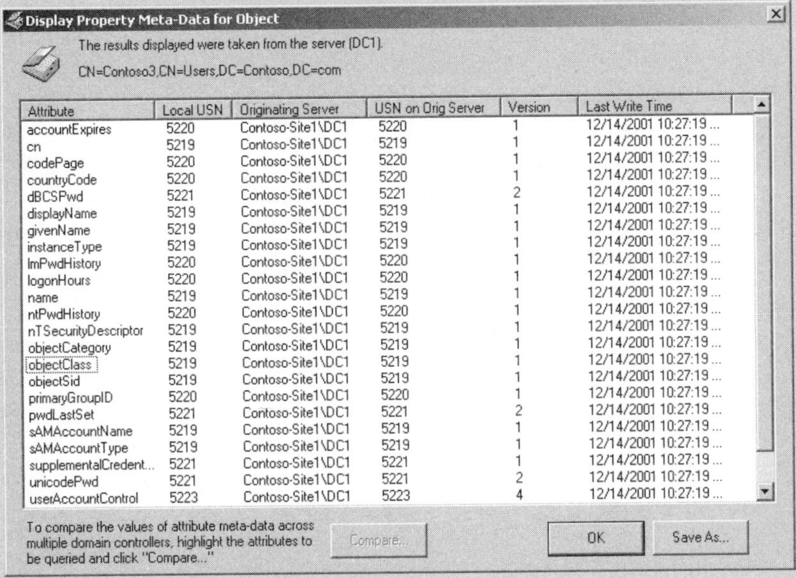

Attribute	Local USN	Originating Server	USN on Orig Server	Version	Last Write Time
accountExpires	5220	Contoso-Site1\DC1	5220	1	12/14/2001 10:27:19 ...
cn	5219	Contoso-Site1\DC1	5219	1	12/14/2001 10:27:19 ...
codePage	5220	Contoso-Site1\DC1	5220	1	12/14/2001 10:27:19 ...
countryCode	5220	Contoso-Site1\DC1	5220	1	12/14/2001 10:27:19 ...
dBCSPwd	5221	Contoso-Site1\DC1	5221	2	12/14/2001 10:27:19 ...
displayName	5219	Contoso-Site1\DC1	5219	1	12/14/2001 10:27:19 ...
givenName	5219	Contoso-Site1\DC1	5219	1	12/14/2001 10:27:19 ...
instanceType	5219	Contoso-Site1\DC1	5219	1	12/14/2001 10:27:19 ...
lmPwdHistory	5220	Contoso-Site1\DC1	5220	1	12/14/2001 10:27:19 ...
logonHours	5220	Contoso-Site1\DC1	5220	1	12/14/2001 10:27:19 ...
name	5219	Contoso-Site1\DC1	5219	1	12/14/2001 10:27:19 ...
ntPwdHistory	5220	Contoso-Site1\DC1	5220	1	12/14/2001 10:27:19 ...
nTSecurityDescriptor	5219	Contoso-Site1\DC1	5219	1	12/14/2001 10:27:19 ...
objectCategory	5219	Contoso-Site1\DC1	5219	1	12/14/2001 10:27:19 ...
objectClass	5219	Contoso-Site1\DC1	5219	1	12/14/2001 10:27:19 ...
objectSid	5219	Contoso-Site1\DC1	5219	1	12/14/2001 10:27:19 ...
primaryGroupID	5220	Contoso-Site1\DC1	5220	1	12/14/2001 10:27:19 ...
pwdLastSet	5221	Contoso-Site1\DC1	5221	2	12/14/2001 10:27:19 ...
sAMAccountName	5219	Contoso-Site1\DC1	5219	1	12/14/2001 10:27:19 ...
sAMAccountType	5219	Contoso-Site1\DC1	5219	1	12/14/2001 10:27:19 ...
supplementalCredent...	5221	Contoso-Site1\DC1	5221	1	12/14/2001 10:27:19 ...
unicodePwd	5221	Contoso-Site1\DC1	5221	2	12/14/2001 10:27:19 ...
userAccountControl	5223	Contoso-Site1\DC1	5223	4	12/14/2001 10:27:19 ...

Figure 4-10. *Viewing replication meta-data using Replication Monitor.*

The high-watermark and up-to-dateness vector are used together to limit replication traffic. The high-watermark identifies the latest change that a domain controller received from another specific domain controller, so the sending domain controller does not need to resend changes. The up-to-dateness vector identifies the most recent changes that have been received from all other domain controllers that contain a replica of the partition, so that the sending domain controller does not have to send any directory updates that the receiving domain controller has received from another replication partner.

Change Stamps and Conflict Resolution

The last property that is used to manage the replication between domain controllers is a *change stamp*. Whenever an attribute is updated, this modification is marked with the change stamp. The change stamp is then sent with the update when it is replicated to other domain controllers. The change stamp is used to determine which change will be accepted in the case of a replication conflict. The change stamp consists of three components:

- **Version number** This is used to track the number of changes that have been made to an attribute on an object. When an object is created, the version number on all attributes is set to 1 even if the attribute is left blank. When a blank attribute is assigned a value, the version number remains at 1. However, when the attribute is updated after the initial change, the version number increments by one each time.

- **Last write time** This is used to track when the last write occurred to the attribute. The time value is recorded on the server where the attribute is updated and is replicated with the object to other domain controllers.

- **Originating server** This is the GUID for the server where the last originating update to the attribute was applied.

These three components form the change stamp for every modification to an attribute. When the attribute is replicated to another domain controller, this change stamp information is replicated with the attribute. If the same attribute is changed on two different domain controllers at the same time, this change stamp is used to determine which attribute is accepted as the final change. If a conflict arises, the decision as to which is the final change is made in the following order:

1. **Version number** The change with the highest version number is always accepted. This means that if the change on one domain controller is version 3, and the change on the other domain controller is version 4, the version 4 change will always be accepted.

2. **Last write time** The next value used to determine which value is accepted is the last write time. If the version numbers are identical, the change with the most recent time stamp will be accepted.

3. **Server GUID** If the version numbers are identical and the timestamps are identical, the server database GUID is used to determine which change is accepted. The change coming from the server with the higher GUID will be accepted. These GUIDs are assigned when the domain controllers are added to the domain and the assignment of the GUID is arbitrary.

Real World Replication Conflicts

Some network administrators seem to get very concerned about the possibility of replication conflicts and the potential for lost or overwritten data. In most companies, the chances of a replication conflict happening are slim. First, replication conflicts are dealt with at a per-attribute level. (If a user's telephone number is changed on one domain controller at the same time that the user's address is changed on another domain controller, no conflict is created.) Second, most companies have a centralized department where all changes to user accounts are made, so the chances of two people making different changes to the same attribute at the same time are remote. If the administration of user accounts is delegated to a department level, each department would make changes only to the user accounts for their department. So for most companies with a structured way of working with Active Directory objects, replication conflicts should occur rarely.

Active Directory, then, is able to resolve conflicts that are created when the same attribute on an object is modified on two domain controllers at the same time. However, there are at least two other types of conflicts that can arise:

- **Adding an object or modifying an object on one domain controller at the same time that the container object for the object is deleted on another domain controller** Take the example in which on one domain controller a new user is added to the Accounting organizational unit (OU). At the same time, on another domain controller, another administrator deletes the Accounting OU. In this case, the object that was added to the deleted container will be moved to the LostAndFound container in Active Directory.

- **Adding objects with the same relative distinguished name into the same container** An example of this conflict is when an administrator on one domain controller creates a user object with a relative distinguished name of BDiaz in the Accounting OU and at the same time, on another domain controller, a user with the same relative distinguished name is moved into the same OU or created in the same OU. In this case, the conflict resolution model will use the GUID assigned to the directory updated to determine which object is kept and which object is renamed. The object with the higher GUID is retained, and the object with the lower GUID is renamed to BDiaz#CNF:*userGUID,* where the number sign (#) is a reserved character. If the second user object is required, it can be renamed.

Replicating Object Deletions

The replication of object deletions is handled differently in Active Directory than other directory updates. When an object like a user account is deleted, the object is not immediately deleted. Rather, a tombstone object is created. The *tombstone object* is the original object with the *isDeleted* attribute on the object set to *true,* and most of the attributes for the object are removed from it. Only a few attributes that are required to identify the object such as the GUID, SID, USN, and distinguished name are retained.

This tombstone is then replicated to other domain controllers in the domain. As each domain controller receives the update, the modifications that were made on the originating domain controller are applied to each domain controller. The tombstone objects remain in the domain database for a specified period of time, called the *tombstone life-time*. At the end of the tombstone lifetime, set to 60 days by default, each domain controller removes the tombstone from its copy of the database. This process of removing the tombstones from the database is called *garbage collection*. By default, the garbage collection interval for the forest is set at every 12 hours. This means that every 12 hours, the garbage collection process runs and deletes any tombstones that have passed the tombstone lifetime value.

As described in Chapter 1, "Active Directory Concepts," Windows Server 2003 Active Directory provides improved support for lingering objects in Active Directory. A *lingering object* is an object that does not get deleted from a domain controller because it was offline or unable to replicate for an entire tombstone lifetime. To remove the lingering objects, you must use the Repadmin tool.

Tip The tombstone lifetime and the garbage collection interval can be modified using ADSI Edit or Ldp.exe. These properties are configured on the CN=Directory Service,CN=Windows NT,CN=Services,CN=Configuration, DC=*ForestRootDomain* object. The *garbageCollPeriod* and the *tombstoneLifetime* attributes define these settings. In most cases, these values do not need to be modified.

Configuring Intersite Replication

The most important reason for creating multiple sites in Active Directory is to control replication traffic between company locations, especially between locations that are separated by slow WAN connections. From the discussion so far in this chapter, one thing should be clear: The site configuration for your company will have a significant impact on the replication traffic across your network.

More Info Coming up with clear criteria for when to create an additional site is difficult because of the large numbers of variables that have to be included in this decision. Chapter 5 goes into detail about when you should consider creating additional sites. That chapter also covers many of the other design issues that you must consider when designing the site topology.

As described in Chapter 2, an Active Directory site is a network location in which all the domain controllers are connected to each other with fast network connections. One of the tasks of setting up an Active Directory network is determining where to draw the site boundaries and then connecting the sites together.

Creating Additional Sites

When Active Directory is installed, a single site called the Default-First-Site-Name (the site can be renamed) is created. If additional sites are not created, all subsequent domain controllers will be added to this site as they are installed. However, if your company has multiple locations with limited bandwidth between the locations, you will almost certainly want to create additional sites. Additional sites are created using the Active Directory Sites And Services administrative tool. To create a new site, right-click the Sites container, and then select New Site. From the Link Name list, you must choose which site link will be used to connect this site to other sites. Each site is associated with one or more IP subnets in Active Directory. Create additional subnets in the Subnets container in Active Directory Sites And Services and associate the subnets with the new site. Each site should have at least one domain controller and, ideally, a GC server. To move an existing domain controller into the site, you can right-click the domain controller object in its current Servers container and select Move. You are then given a choice about which site you want to move the domain controller into. If you install a new domain controller, it will automatically be located in the site where the IP subnet matches the domain controller's IP address. It is possible to create a site without any domain controllers in the site, but there is really no reason to do so.

Site Links

The Active Directory connectors that connect sites together are called *site links*. When Active Directory is installed, a single site link—called DEFAULTIPSITELINK—is created. If you do not create any additional site links before you create additional sites, each site is included in this default site link. If all of the WAN connections between your company locations are equal in terms of bandwidth and cost, you can just accept this default behavior. If all the sites are connected by one site link, the replication traffic between all sites will have exactly the same properties. If you make a change on this site link, the replication configuration for all sites will be modified. However, in many cases, you might not want to have the replication between all sites configured the same way. If you want to be able to manage replication differently between sites, you must create additional site links and assign the appropriate sites to the site links.

Creating a site link does not replace the work of ISTG; all it does is make it possible for ISTG to do its work. Once a site link is in place, ISTG will use the site link to create the required connection objects to replicate all the Active Directory partitions between each site.

The following are the configuration options on all site links.

- **Cost** The cost for a site link is an administrator-assigned value that defines the relative cost of the site link. The cost will usually reflect the speed of the network connection and the expenses associated with using the connection. This cost is important if there are redundant site links in the organization, that is, if there is more than one path for replication to travel from one site to another. In all cases, the lowest-cost route will be chosen as the replication path.

- **Replication schedule** The replication schedule defines what times during the day the site link is available for replication. The default replication schedule allows for replication to occur 24 hours a day. However, if the bandwidth to a site is very limited, you might want to have replication occur only during non-working hours.

- **Replication interval** The replication interval defines the intervals at which the bridgehead servers check with the bridgehead servers in the other sites to see if there are any directory updates. By default, the replication interval for site links is set at 180 minutes. The replication interval is only applied during the replication schedule. If the replication schedule is configured to allow replication from 10 P.M. to 5 A.M., by default, the bridgehead servers will check for updates every 3 hours during that time.

- **Replication transports** The site link can use either RPC over IP or SMTP as the replication transport. See "Replication Transport Protocols" later in this chapter for more details.

These options provide significant flexibility for configuring replication between sites. However, there are also some mistakes to avoid. To understand how these options work together, consider a company network like that shown in Figure 4-11.

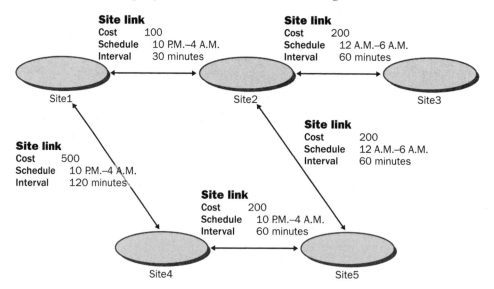

Figure 4-11. *A site link configuration.*

In Windows Server 2003 Active Directory, all site links are considered transitive by default. In Figure 4-11, Site1 has a site link to Site2 and to Site4, and Site2 has a site link to Site3 and Site5. Because of the transitive nature of the site links, this means that Site1 can also replicate directly with Site3 and Site5.

The site link costs define the path that replication traffic will take through the network. When KCC is creating the routing topology, it uses the accumulated costs for all site links to calculate the optimal routing. In the example shown in Figure 4-11, there are two possible routes between Site1 and Site5: The first route is through Site2; the second route is through Site4. The cost to route through Site2 is 300 (100+200) while the cost through Site4 is 700 (500+200). This means that all replication traffic will be replicated through Site2 unless the connection is not available.

When replication traffic crosses multiple site links, the site link schedules and replication intervals for each site link combine to determine the effective replication window and interval. For example, effective replication will occur between Site1 and Site3 only during the hours of 12 midnight to 4 A.M. (the overlapping time in the schedules) and the effective replication will happen every 60 minutes (the replication interval for the Site2–Site3 site link).

> **Note**   If the schedules for site links do not overlap, it is still possible for replication to occur between multiple sites. For example, if the Site1–Site2 site link is available from 2 A.M. to 6 A.M., and the Site2–Site3 site link is available from 10 P.M. to 1 A.M., changes to the directory will still flow from Site1 to Site3. The changes will be sent from Site1 to Site2, and then from Site2 to Site3. However, the replication latency would be almost a day in this case because changes replicated to Site2 at 2 A.M. would not be replicated to Site3 until 10 P.M.

Site Link Bridges

In some cases, you might want to turn off the transitive nature of site links and manually configure site link bridges. When you configure site link bridges, you define which site links should be seen as transitive and which site links should not. Turning off the transitive nature of site links can be useful when you do not have a fully routed network, that is, if not all segments of the network are available at all times (for example, if you have a dial-up or scheduled-demand dial connection to one network location). Site link bridges can also be used to configure replication in situations where a company has several sites connected to a fast backbone with several smaller sites connecting to each larger center using slow network connections. In such cases, site link bridges can be used to manage the flow of replication traffic more efficiently.

> **More Info**   Chapter 5 provides details about when and how to use site link bridges.

When you create a site link bridge, you must define which site links are part of the bridge. Any site links you add to the site link bridge are considered transitive with each other, but site links that are not included in the site link bridge are not transitive. In the example used earlier, a site link bridge could be created for the site links connecting Site1, Site2, Site4, and Site5. All of these site links would then be considered transitive, which means that a bridgehead server in Site1 could replicate directly with a bridgehead server in Site5. However, because the site link from Site2 to Site3 is not included in the site link bridge, it is not transitive. That means that all replication traffic from Site3 would flow to Site2, and from there it would flow to the other sites.

To turn off the transitive site links, clear the Bridge All Site Links option on the General tab of the IP Properties sheet. The IP object is located in the Inter-Site Transports container in the Active Directory Sites And Services administrative tool. Be careful when you do this, for you will now have to configure site link bridges for all sites if you want any transitive site connections.

Replication Transport Protocols

Windows Server 2003 Active Directory can use one of three different transportation techniques for replication:

- **RPC over IP within a site** All replication connections within a site must use an RPC-over-IP connection. This connection is synchronous, which means that the domain controller can replicate with only one replication partner at any one time. The RPC connection uses dynamic port mapping. The first RPC connection is made on the RPC endpoint mapper port (IP port 135). This connection is used to determine which port the destination domain controller is using for replication.

Tip If you are replicating the directory information through a firewall, or using routers with port filtering enabled, you can specify the port number that the domain controllers will use for replication. To do this, create the following registry key as a DWORD value and specify any valid port number: HKEY_LOCAL_MACHINE\SYSTEM\CurrentControlSet\Services\NTDS \Parameters\TCP/IP Port.

- **RPC over IP between sites** Replication connections between sites can also use RPC over IP. This RPC connection is the same as the intrasite connection with one important exception: by default all traffic sent between sites is compressed.

Note When you look at the two types of RPC-over-IP connections in the Active Directory Sites And Services administrative tool, you will notice that they are identified differently in the interface. The RPC over IP within a site is called *RPC*, and the RPC over IP between sites is called *IP*.

- **SMTP between sites** Replication connections between sites can also use SMTP to replicate information between sites. SMTP can be a good choice as a replication technique if you do not have a permanent and relatively fast connection between company locations. SMTP uses an asynchronous connection, which means that the domain controller can replicate with multiple servers at the same time. However, using SMTP also has some important constraints. First, SMTP can only be used to replicate information between domain controllers in different domains. Only the configuration directory partitions, schema directory partitions, and GC partitions can be replicated using SMTP. Second, replication through SMTP requires that the SMTP component in Internet Information Services (IIS) be installed on all domain controllers that will use SMTP for replication. The third constraint on SMTP replication is that you must install a Microsoft Certificate Authority (CA) in your organization. The certificates from this CA are used to digitally sign the SMTP messages sent between domain controllers.

Configuring Bridgehead Servers

As mentioned earlier, replication between sites is accomplished through bridgehead servers. By default, ISTG automatically identifies the bridgehead server as it calculates the intersite replication topology. To view which domain controllers are operating as bridgehead servers, you can use Replication Monitor. Just right-click any server name that is being monitored in Replication Monitor and select Show Bridgehead Servers. You have a choice about where you want to show the bridgehead servers: just for the server's site or for the entire enterprise. You can also view the bridgehead servers through Repadmin. To do this, open a command prompt and type *repadmin /bridgeheads*.

In some cases, you might want to control which domain controllers are going to operate as bridgehead servers. Operating as a bridgehead server can add a significant load to a domain controller if there are many changes to the directory information and replication is set to occur frequently. To configure which servers will be the bridgehead servers, access the computer objects in the Active Directory Sites And Services administrative tool, right-click the server name, and then select Properties. (Figure 4-12 shows the interface.) You are given the option of configuring the server as a preferred bridgehead server for either IP or SMTP transports.

The advantage of configuring preferred bridgehead servers is that you can ensure that the domain controllers you choose will be selected as the bridgehead servers. If you want complete control over which servers are used as bridgehead servers, you must configure a preferred bridgehead server for each partition that needs to be replicated into a site. For example, if a site contains replicas of the Contoso.com domain directory partition, the Fabrikam.com domain directory partition, the GC partition, and an application directory partition, you will need to configure at least one domain controller with a replica of each of these partitions. If you do not configure bridgehead servers for all of the partitions, ISTG will log an event in the event log and then choose a preferred bridgehead server for the partition. You can also configure multiple preferred bridgehead servers. If you do, ISTG will choose one of the identified servers as the bridgehead server.

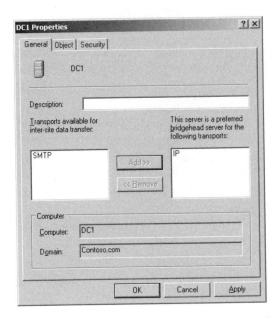

Figure 4-12. *Configuring a preferred bridgehead server.*

But you should configure this option with caution. Configuring preferred bridgehead servers limits ISTG's ability to choose the bridgehead server—it will always select a server that is configured as a preferred bridgehead server. If this server fails and no other servers have been designated as bridgehead servers for that directory partition, ISTG will not select another bridgehead server and replication will cease until the server is again available or until you have reconfigured the preferred bridgehead server options. If the preferred bridgehead server does fail, you can either remove the server as a preferred bridgehead server and allow ISTG to identify a bridgehead server, or you can choose another preferred bridgehead server.

Caution If the preferred bridgehead server does fail, and you choose to reconfigure the preferred bridgehead server, you will need to make any configuration changes in both sites. Because the bridgehead servers are not available, no information will be replicated between the sites until the configuration changes are made in both sites.

Monitoring and Troubleshooting Replication

One of the most useful tools for monitoring and troubleshooting replication is the Replication Monitor. This tool is installed as part of the Suptools.msi file from the Support\Tools directory on the Windows Server 2003 compact disc. To start Replication

Monitor, open a command prompt and type *replmon*. Replication Monitor opens with a blank management tool. To begin using Replication Monitor, click Edit on the menu bar to add one or more monitored servers to the monitored servers list. Once the servers have been added, you can monitor and manage almost all aspects of Active Directory replication using the tool. For example, you can monitor the current status of replication, the last successful replication, or any replication failures; force replication; and force KCC to recalculate the routing topology. Using this one monitoring tool, you can monitor replication on all of the domain controllers on your network.

A second useful tool for monitoring replication is Repadmin, also installed by Suptools.msi. To run this tool, open a command prompt and type *repadmin*. Repadmin provides much of the same functionality as Replication Monitor but through a command-line interface. Repadmin does provide the added functionality of being able to modify the replication topology by adding connection objects.

Note   For detailed information on how to use Replication Monitor and Repadmin, from the Start Menu, open Help And Support Center. Then, under Support Tasks, click Tools and then click Windows Support Tools. You are presented with an alphabetical list of all the support tools with excellent information about when you would use each tool as well as instructions on how to use the tools. You can also launch the tools from within the Help And Support Center.

Two standard server administrative tools are also useful for monitoring and troubleshooting replication. The first tool is the Event Viewer. One of the event logs added to all domain controllers is a Directory Service event log. Most of the directory replication-related events are logged in this event log, and this should be one of the first places you look when replication seems to be failing. The Performance administrative tool is useful for monitoring the amount of replication activity happening on the server. When a server is promoted to be a domain controller, the NTDS Performance Object is added to the list of performance counters. These performance counters can be used to monitor how much replication traffic there is as well as a wide variety of other Active Directory–related activities.

Tip   If you start noticing failures in Active Directory replication between domain controllers, the first thing you should check is DNS. Without a properly functioning DNS infrastructure, replication will not work.

Summary

One of the key aspects to managing Windows Server 2003 Active Directory is understanding how replication works. A stable replication environment is crucial in maintaining an up-to-date copy of all directory information on all the domain controllers in the forest, which is essential to ensure consistent user logon and directory search performance. This chapter provided a description of how directory replication works. The chapter first described how the replication topology is created between Active Directory domain controllers in the same site, and between domain controllers in different sites. The chapter then described the actual process of replication, including how replication is optimized to minimize the amount of network traffic that is created by Active Directory replication.

Part II
Implementing Windows Server 2003 Active Directory

The goal of the first part of this book was to help you understand the Microsoft Windows Server 2003 Active Directory directory service. Part II helps you implement Active Directory. The first step in implementing Active Directory is to create the architecture and design for your organization. The forest, domain, site, and organizational unit (OU) structures are unique in almost every company, and it takes knowledge and effort to create the right design for your particular environment. Chapter 5, "Designing the Active Directory Structure," provides you with an overview of this design process. Once you have created your Windows Server 2003 Active Directory design, you are ready to start installing Active Directory. Chapter 6, "Installing Active Directory," provides you with the concepts and procedures to complete the deployment of Active Directory. Many companies that are implementing Windows Server 2003 Active Directory are migrating from Microsoft Windows NT 4. Because Windows Server 2003 Active Directory is very different from the Windows NT directory service, this migration can be complex. Therefore, the migration from the Windows NT 4 version of a directory service to Windows 2003 Active Directory is the main topic in Chapter 7, "Migrating to Active Directory."

Chapter 5
Designing the Active Directory Structure

Deploying the Active Directory directory service in Microsoft Windows Server 2003 requires a great deal of planning and design. Active Directory can be deployed in any size organization, including large multinational corporations with hundreds of thousands of users and locations around the world. Creating an Active Directory design for a corporation of such a size requires a great deal of effort. However, even much smaller companies benefit greatly from time spent on the initial design.

This chapter provides an overview of the planning process that you must go through before you deploy Windows Server 2003 Active Directory. For the most part, this chapter assumes that you are working with a large corporation with multiple business units and locations. If you are working with a smaller company, many of the concepts discussed here will still apply.

This chapter begins by looking at the biggest question first: How many forests do you need in your network? From there the chapter moves on to discuss splitting the forests into domains and planning for the domain namespace. Once your domains are in place, you also need to create an organizational unit (OU) structure for each domain and then to configure sites.

> **Note** Designing a Windows Server 2003 Active Directory infrastructure is not significantly different from designing an Active Directory infrastructure in Microsoft Windows 2000. Windows Server 2003 includes some important improvements over Windows 2000, but the basic concepts of Active Directory have not changed. Because of this, this chapter assumes that you do not currently have Windows 2000 Active Directory deployed, but that you are migrating from Microsoft Windows NT 4 or from some other directory service.

Designing the Forest Structure

Probably the most important decision you need to make early in the design process is how many forests you will need. Deploying a single Active Directory forest means that it is easy to share and access information within the company. However, using a single forest for a large corporation also requires a significant degree of cooperation and trust between possibly diverse and disconnected business units. Ultimately, the number of forests you deploy depends on what is more important in your company: sharing information with ease across all the domains in the forest or being able to maintain fully autonomous and isolated control of a part of the directory structure.

Real World   Business Involvement in Active Directory Design

When you design Active Directory for a corporation, it is important to get the company's management involved in the design process. The business users are the primary consumers for the services provided by the Information Technology (TI) infrastructure, so it is essential that your design meet their requirements and have the support of their management.

The amount of involvement that business units require in the design process varies greatly among companies. In almost every organization, however, the involvement includes at least an approval of the high-level goals of the design project. These goals might revolve around issues such as accessibility of information, security, ease of management, and usability. Business managers are usually involved in high-level and highly visible decisions that cannot easily be changed after deployment. Among these decisions are how many forests and domains are needed in the network and the number of domain namespaces that are to be deployed.

Forests and Active Directory Design

An Active Directory forest is designed to be a self-contained unit. Inside the forest, it is easy to share information and collaborate with other users in the same unit. However, because the forest is a self-contained unit, the actions of one person can impact everyone else in the forest. As you design the highest level of the Active Directory infrastructure, you must decide whether you need to deploy one forest or multiple forests. Each forest is an integrated unit because it has the following characteristics:

- **Global catalog** The forest has one global catalog (GC). The GC makes it easy to locate objects in any domain in the forest and to log on to any domain in the forest regardless of which domain hosts your user account.

- **Configuration directory partition** All domain controllers share the same configuration directory partition. This configuration information is used to optimize replication of information throughout the forest, to store application information for Active Directory–enabled applications, and to share information through application directory partitions.

- **Trusts** All of the domains in the forest are connected by two-way transitive trusts. There is no option to change this.

Note   One of the best illustrations of the way a single forest is used to make collaboration easier is seen in how Microsoft Exchange 2000 Server uses forests. The forest boundary is also the boundary for the Exchange 2000 Server organization. Exchange 2000 Server stores most of its configuration information in the configuration directory partition, making it easy to manage message routing throughout a large organization. The global address list (GAL) is made up of all the e-mail recipients in the GC. Having a single Exchange 2000 Server organization is highly desirable for most companies. Within one organization, calendar information and public folders are accessible to everyone, and many types of collaborations are enabled by default. As soon as you deploy multiple organizations (and multiple forests), many of these benefits are lost or become much more difficult to configure.

While Active Directory makes the sharing of information easier, it also enforces a number of restrictions that require the different business units in a company to cooperate in several different ways. These restrictions include:

- **One schema** All the domains in the forest share a single schema. While this sounds simple enough, this might be the one reason for a corporation to deploy multiple forests. If one business unit decides to deploy an application that modifies the schema, all business units are affected. This might not seem like it would have much impact, but it can become overwhelming if twenty business units decide that they want to deploy applications that modify the schema. Every schema modification must be tested to ensure that it does not conflict with other schema changes. This testing takes a considerable amount of time and effort.

- **Centralized administration** Choosing to deploy a single forest means that some components of network administration must be centralized. For example, the only group with the right to change the schema would be the Schema Admins group. The only group with the right to add and remove domains from the forest would be the Enterprise Admins group. The Enterprise Admins group is automatically added to the domain local Administrators group on every domain controller in the forest. For some companies, this type of centralized administration is not acceptable. This is especially true for companies who are migrating from Windows NT 4 domains, which did not enforce centralized administration between multiple domains.

- **Change control policies** Because changes made to the forest can affect every domain, and because most significant changes should only be performed in a centralized manner, a well-defined change control policy must be in place.

- **Trusted administrators** Deploying a single forest requires a degree of trust from all administrators in all domains. Any administrator with the rights to administer a domain controller can make changes that will affect the entire forest. This means that all domain administrators must be highly trusted.

As you deal with the question of how many forests you need to deploy, you must assess each of these factors to determine your own needs.

Single or Multiple Forests

As mentioned earlier, the most significant question that you need to answer when creating your forest design is whether you will have a single forest or multiple forests. This decision must be made before deployment, because it is very difficult to change after deployment. There is no one-step process to merge forests; rather, you must move whatever objects you want in the new forest from the old forest. Also, there is no easy way to split a single forest into two. You must create a separate forest and then move objects from one to the other.

Almost all companies deploy a single forest. For most companies the benefits of a shared GC, built-in trusts, and a common configuration directory partition are more important than maintaining a complete separation of all administrative roles. As you work with designing Active Directory, your first choice should always be to deploy a single forest. Assume that you will be deploying a single forest, but be prepared to be convinced to do otherwise.

Having said this, there are clearly situations where multiple forests are the best option for a company. These situations include:

- Some companies do not have a strong requirement for intracompany collaboration. In some companies, business units operate quite independently of each other, with little need to exchange information other than e-mail. These companies are not giving anything up by deploying multiple forests.

- Some companies require a complete separation of network information. For security or legal reasons, a company might be required to ensure that some network information not be accessible to anyone outside a business unit. By default, the information in one forest is not visible in any other forest.

- Some companies require incompatible schema configurations. If two parts of the organization require a unique schema because they are deploying applications that make incompatible changes to the schema, you must create separate forests.

- Some companies cannot agree on centralized administrative procedures. If companies cannot agree on policies for forest or schema change control, or if they cannot agree on centralized administration, you will have to deploy separate forests.

Real World   Business Involvement and Forest Design

Few companies have technical reasons to deploy more than one forest. A forest can contain multiple domains, with each domain containing hundreds of thousands of objects. The domains can be deployed with multiple namespaces and with distinct administration for each domain.

However, as soon as you present to the decision makers in your organization the list of forest requirements such as centralized control, a common schema, or trusted administrators, you are sure to meet resistance. The biggest single reason why companies deploy multiple forests is company politics or the inability of different departments or business units to work out how to deal with the centralized components of managing a single forest. In some cases, the company cannot agree on a forest modification or schema modification process. In other cases, the fact that a domain administrator in one domain can affect all other domains in the forest means that a single forest is not acceptable. This is especially true in the common scenario where a number of formerly independent companies must now work together due to corporate takeovers or mergers.

Separate forests might be the answer for some of these companies, but you must also alert the decision makers to what they will lose if they do insist on multiple forests. Using multiple forests means that everyone gets complete autonomy, but also means that it is much more difficult to share information between business units.

- Some companies must limit the scope of trust relationships. Within a forest, all domains share a transitive trust, and there is no option to break these trusts. If your network environment requires a trust configuration where there cannot be a two-way transitive trust between all domains, you must use multiple forests.

For some companies, deploying multiple forests might be an appealing option. However, deploying multiple forests adds significant complexity to the network infrastructure. Some of these issues are:

- Increased administrative effort required to manage the network. At least one domain as well as the forest-level configuration must be managed in each forest.

- Decreased ability of users to collaborate. One example of this is searching for resources on the network. Users are no longer able to search the GC for resources in the other forest. Users must be trained in how to search for resources outside of the GC.

- Additional administrative effort required for users to access resources between forests. Administrators must configure the trusts rather than using the built-in trusts. If any information must be synchronized between the forests, this must also be configured.

Real World   Administrative Autonomy vs. Administrative Isolation

For some companies, the decision to deploy more than one forest will come down to whether the company requires administrative autonomy or administrative isolation between business units. In Active Directory, there are many types of administrative activity including both the configuration of the directory services (forest configuration, domain controller placement, Domain Name System [DNS] configuration) and management of the data in the directory service (managing user or group objects, group policies, and so forth).

Administrative autonomy means that you have complete administrative control over some component of the forest. You might have administrative autonomy at the forest level, domain level, or OU level. However, administrative autonomy does not mean that you have ultimate or exclusive control. For example, you might be able to completely administer your domain, but the Enterprise Admins group also has administrative permissions to your domain.

Administrative isolation, on the other hand, means that you have exclusive control over a component of the directory. If you have administrative isolation, no one else has any control over your part of the forest, and no one else can modify the directory service configuration or modify the data in your part.

Active Directory provides many ways to achieve administrative autonomy. Domain administrators can do anything they want in a domain. OU administrators can be given full rights to create and administer any types of objects in an OU. A single forest in Active Directory is designed for administrative delegation and autonomy.

However, if you require administrative isolation, the only way to achieve this is through the creation of separate forests. Part of the reason for this is because of the way Active Directory is designed. The Enterprise Admins group is automatically added to each domain's local Administrators group. The Domain Admins group has full administrative control over every object in the domain and is automatically added to the Administrators group on every computer in the domain. While the default configuration can be modified and the groups removed from the lower-level administrative groups, the higher-level administrators can always regain control of lower-level objects. This means that no part of the forest is isolated administratively.

Another reason a separate forest might be needed for administrative isolation is because of the possibility of malicious actions on the part of administrators in the domain. Anyone with administrative access to a domain controller can violate the administrative isolation of any other partition in the forest. An administrator might install software on the domain controller in one domain that modifies the directory information for every domain in the forest. The administrator might modify his or her own security identifier (SID) so that it appears that he or she is a member of the Enterprise Admins group and then use this access to make forestwide changes.

Likewise, if a user can shut down and restart the domain controller in Directory Services Restore mode, the user can modify information in Active Directory that will affect the entire forest.

All of the domain controllers and partitions in the forest are tightly integrated, and any change made on one domain controller will be replicated to all other domain controllers. There is no security check on the validity of replicated information; there is only a security check on making changes to the directory information. So, if a malicious administrator manages to make a change to the directory information, all other domain controllers will accept the replicated change without question. For these reasons, you must create separate forests if you require administrative isolation. In some cases, you might be required to guarantee complete isolation of a directory partition. If so, you must accept the added administrative effort and loss of collaboration that comes from deploying multiple forests.

Many companies, however, require administrative autonomy along with a reasonable assurance that administrators from other partitions in the forest will not act maliciously. This reasonable assurance can be addressed in most companies by doing the following:

- Putting only highly trusted administrators into groups that have administrative control over domain controllers. These groups include the Domain Admins group as well as the domain's local Administrators, Server Operators, and Backup Operators groups. Administrative tasks that do not require access to the domain controllers should be delegated to other groups.

- Physically securing the domain controllers with only highly trusted administrators given access to the servers.

- Auditing all actions performed by high-level administrators.

High-level administrators should log on using the administrative account only when necessary. These administrators should also have normal user accounts for day-to-day work.

Defining Forest Ownership

Regardless of how many forests you deploy, you will need to identify the forest owners for each forest. In technical terms, it is easy to define who the forest owners are. The Schema Admins group, the Enterprise Admins group, and the Domain Admins group in the root domain can be defined as the forest owners because they control what changes can be made to the forest. However, these roles are purely technical, and the people in these groups are almost never the final authority on whether modifications are actually made to the forest. For example, the Schema Admins group can change the schema, but a Schema Admins member will usually not have the authority to make the final decision on whether a request for a schema change will be approved.

Forest owners must possess a combination of technical expertise and business aware-ness. They should be people who understand the overall business requirements of an organization, but who also understand the technical implications of fulfilling all these requirements. Forest owners might decide that an application that modifies the schema will be deployed because it brings significant business value to the company. The schema administrator is then given the task of modifying the schema as required.

In a company with multiple business units, the forest ownership group should be made up of representatives from all the business units. While it is important that all business units be represented, this group must also be able to function efficiently. That is, a pro-cess must be in place so that the group can efficiently decide whether a forest-level change will be implemented. If implementing a global change takes an inordinate amount of time, individual business units might regret that they ever agreed to deploy a single forest.

Forest Change Control Policies

The first task for forest owners is to define a forest change control policy. The forest change control policy defines what changes can be made to the forest-level configuration and under what circumstances those changes can be made. Essentially there are two types of forest change: schema changes and configuration directory partition changes (for ex-ample, add or remove domains or application directory partitions or modify the site con-figuration).

The forest change control policy also defines the procedures for testing, approving, and implementing any forest change. This is especially significant for schema changes, be-cause schema changes are not easily reversed, and any schema change must be compat-ible with all other schema changes. The forest change control policy should define the testing procedure for schema changes, and the forest owners must maintain a test lab for testing these changes. The forest change control policy should require thorough testing of all forest-level changes, but should also ensure that the testing can be done expedi-tiously. If each change request takes a very long time to process, the frustration level for the users will keep increasing.

The forest change control policy should be in place before you deploy Active Directory. In companies with diverse and separate business units, coming up with this policy might be difficult and time consuming, but it will not be any easier after Active Directory has been deployed. If business units cannot agree on a forest change control policy before deployment, you might need to make the decision to deploy multiple forests.

Designing the Domain Structure

Once the question of how many forests you will deploy has been settled, the next step is to determine the domain structure within each of the forests. Your first task is to document the current directory services configuration and determine how much of the current infrastructure can be upgraded and what will need to be restructured or replaced. You will then determine how many domains you require as well as the domain hierarchy.

Domains and Active Directory Design

Domains are used to partition a large forest into smaller components, primarily for administration or replication purposes. The following domain characteristics are important in Active Directory design:

- **Replication boundary** Domain boundaries are replication boundaries for the domain directory partition and for the domain information stored in the Sysvol folder on all domain controllers. While other directory partitions like schema, configuration, and the GC are replicated throughout the forest, the domain directory partition is replicated only within one domain.

- **Resource access boundary** Domain boundaries are also boundaries for resource access. By default, users in one domain cannot access resources in another domain unless they are explicitly given the appropriate permissions.

- **Security policy boundaries** Some security policies can only be set at a domain level. These policies, such as password policies, account lockout policies, and Kerberos ticket policies, apply to all domain accounts.

Determining the Number of Domains

While most companies will deploy a single forest, many large companies will deploy multiple domains within that forest. Ideally, a single domain is the easiest to manage and provides the users with the least complex environment. However, there are also several reasons why companies choose to deploy multiple domains.

Choosing a Single Domain

For most companies, the ideal Windows Server 2003 Active Directory design will include many fewer domains than the company had in Windows NT. For some of these companies, multiple Windows NT domains might be combined into a single Active Directory domain. Many of the restrictions that resulted in companies deploying several domains

Real World **Current Directory Configuration and Active Directory Design**

An important requirement in Active Directory design is balancing the optimal design for a network with what is currently deployed. Whenever you get ready to create an Active Directory design, you must consider the current design and the implications of migrating from that infrastructure to Active Directory. If your current directory service consists of Windows NT 4 domains, you must collect the information about the current domains and consider the impact of upgrading those domains to Windows Server 2003 Active Directory. The current domain structure might not be ideal for upgrading to Active Directory design. However, upgrading the current domain structure is significantly easier (and less costly) than creating the ideal Active Directory structure and then migrating all of the domain objects to the new domains. You might be forced to work with a less-than-ideal Active Directory structure because you are required to upgrade the current domains. Of course, you might also find that the current structure is so far from the ideal structure that it is worth the extra work and cost of restructuring all the domains. Probably the most common scenario will be one where the current structure is almost acceptable, but you would like to make some changes. In this scenario, you might upgrade one or more domains and then merge other domains into the upgraded domains.

As you prepare your Active Directory design, you might want to create an ideal Active Directory design and then create another design based on the optimal upgrade scenario for the current environment. Chances are good that your final design will fall somewhere between these two designs.

This interaction between an ideal design and what is realistically possible illustrates another important aspect of Active Directory design: it is almost always an iterative process. You might start out with one design in mind, and as you gather additional information, you will likely need to modify that design. As you start testing the implementation or migration scenarios, you might again modify your Active Directory design.

It is important, however, that some parts of your design be finalized before you begin deployment. Implementation issues include deciding on the number of forests and domains as well as the domain namespace design. These issues are difficult to change after deployment has started. Other issues, such as final OU design and site design, are fairly easily changed after deployment.

in Windows NT have been removed in Windows Server 2003. The following factors make deploying a single domain a real possibility for many companies that had multiple Windows NT domains:

- The security database size restrictions have largely been alleviated in Active Directory, as the database can easily contain several hundred thousand objects. For all but the largest companies, the total number of objects in Active Directory will not exceed the possible number of objects in a domain.

- One of the reasons for creating additional domains in Windows NT was to limit or delegate administrative access. In Active Directory, the OU structure creates a hierarchy within a domain that makes it easy to delegate administration to specific parts of the directory and to limit administrative access.

- If your company frequently reorganizes, or if users move between business units, it is easy to move users between OUs in a domain. It is much more difficult to move users between domains.

- Single domains are easier to manage in that you need only be concerned with one set of domain-level administrators and one set of domain-level policies. Also, you need to administer only one set of domain controllers.

- The easiest scenario for managing group policies is in a single domain environment. Some group policy components are stored in the Sysvol folder on each domain controller in a domain. If you only have one domain, the group policies are automatically replicated to all domain controllers.

- A single domain provides the easiest environment to design authentication and resource access. With a single domain, you do not need to be concerned about trusts or about assigning access to resources to users in other domains.

Choosing Multiple Domains

While a single domain might be an ideal configuration for many companies, most large companies deploy multiple domains. There are many good reasons for doing so, including:

- Replication traffic must be limited. The domain directory partition, which is the largest and most frequently modified directory partition, is replicated to all domain controllers in a domain. In some cases, this might cause too much replication traffic between company locations (even if multiple sites are configured). This might be the case if there are slow network connections between company locations or if there are large numbers of users in multiple company locations. The only way to limit this replication traffic is to create additional domains.

- Any company locations that have only Simple Mail Transfer Protocol (SMTP) connectivity must be configured as separate domains. The domain information cannot be replicated through site links that use SMTP.

- The only way to have different password policies, account lockout policies, and Kerberos ticket policies is to deploy separate domains.

- If you need to be able to limit access to resources and restrict administrative permissions, you will want to deploy additional domains. For some companies, there might be legal reasons for creating separate administrative units.

- In some cases, you might create additional domains because the best migration path for the organization is to upgrade several of the current domains.

There are many good reasons for creating additional domains. However, each additional domain can add significant administrative and financial cost to an organization. Each additional domain requires additional hardware and additional administrators. Users will be accessing resources across trusts, which means greater complexity and potentially more points of failure. Users who travel between domains must authenticate to a domain controller in their home domain. Because of these additional costs, the total number of domains should be kept as low as possible.

Designing the Forest Root Domain

Another important decision you will need to make when designing an Active Directory solution for a large company is whether or not you should deploy a dedicated root domain (also called an empty root). A *dedicated root domain* is a domain that is dedicated to the role of operating as the forest root domain. That is, there are no user accounts or resources in that domain except for those needed to manage the forest. A forest with a dedicated root domain is shown in Figure 5-1.

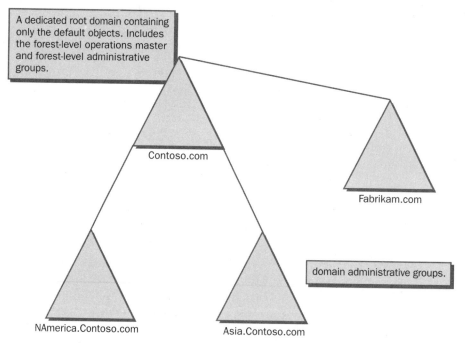

A dedicated root domain containing only the default objects. Includes the forest-level operations master and forest-level administrative groups.

Contoso.com

Fabrikam.com

domain administrative groups.

NAmerica.Contoso.com

Asia.Contoso.com

Figure 5-1. *A forest with a dedicated root domain.*

For most companies deploying multiple domains, a dedicated root domain is highly recommended. The root domain is a crucial domain in Active Directory structure. The root domain contains the forest-level administrative groups (the Enterprise Admins and Schema Admins groups) and the forest-level operations masters (the domain naming master and the schema master). Also, the root domain must always be available when users log on to domains other than their home domain or when users access resources in other domains. The root domain cannot be replaced; if the root domain is destroyed and it cannot not be recovered, you must rebuild the entire forest.

A dedicated root domain is easier to manage than a root domain that contains many objects. Because the directory database will be small, it is easy to back up and restore the root domain controllers. Further, there is almost no replication traffic between root domain controllers, so it is easy to locate domain controllers in several company locations to ensure redundancy. This also makes it easy to move the root domain to another location. Using a dedicated root domain makes it easier to limit the membership of the forest-level administrative groups. A dedicated root domain also never becomes obsolete, especially if the domain is given a generic name.

For these reasons, most companies that choose to deploy multiple domains should deploy a dedicated root domain. Even some companies that plan to deploy only one domain should consider the advantages of deploying a dedicated root domain.

The dedicated root domain requires some configuration that might not be applied to the other domains in the forest. First of all, because the root domain contains the forest operations master, the domain controllers for the root domain must be secured as much as possible. The forest domain also contains the groups that can modify the forest and schema. More than with any other domain, the members of the administrative groups in the root domain must be highly trusted. You probably will want to use the Restricted Group option in the Domain Security Policy to manage the membership of these groups. The DNS configuration of the root domain should also be as secure as possible. Because there are not likely to be any additional computers installed in the root domain, you should enable secure dynamic updates for the root domain DNS zone while the domain controllers are being installed, and then you should disable dynamic updates for this zone.

Designing Domain Hierarchies

Once the root domain design is in place, the next step is to determine how many additional domains you will need to deploy and how the rest of the domains will fit into the DNS namespace for the forest. Use the guidelines provided earlier to assist in determining how many domains you need to deploy. If the current directory service for the network is Windows NT, you will also need to examine the current domain design to determine how many domains you need to include in your Windows Server 2003 domain design.

Many large companies deployed Windows NT domains using a master domain or a multiple master domain model where one or more domains contained all of the user and global group accounts, and other domains contained the resources for the company. In some cases, companies had dozens of account domains and hundreds of resource domains. Often the account domains were organized around geographic regions or business units. Each account domain usually had one or more resource domains within the same geographic region or business unit. Figure 5-2 shows an example of what the domain configuration might have looked like.

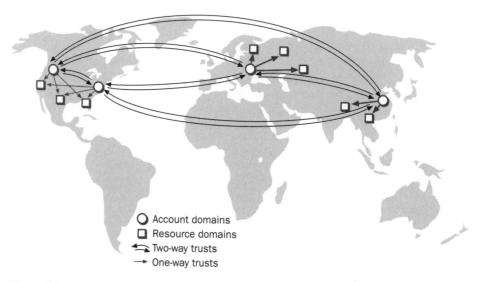

Account domains
Resource domains
Two-way trusts
One-way trusts

Figure 5-2. *A typical Windows NT model for multiple master account domains with resource domains.*

As these companies migrate to Active Directory, they can decrease the number of domains significantly. A common upgrade path for many of these companies is upgrading the account domains to Active Directory. Because Active Directory domains can contain so many more objects, in some cases the company might merge several multiple master account domains into one Active Directory domain. Once the account domains have been upgraded, the resource domains can then be restructured to become OUs in the Active Directory domain. In some cases, resource domains might be removed by attrition. For example, some companies might have deployed resource domains for the Exchange Server 5.5 infrastructure. As the Exchange organization is migrated to Exchange 2000 Server, the servers running Exchange 2000 Server could be deployed in the Active Directory domain. When the last server running Exchange Server 5.5 is removed from service, the Exchange domain can also be removed. Figure 5-3 shows a possible migration path for a company with multiple Windows NT 4 domains.

As you plan for additional domains in the forest, the domain boundaries will usually be determined by either the corporation's geographic locations or by the business units. In most cases, domains based on geography are preferable. The domain configuration is difficult to change after deployment, and the domains based on geography are not likely to require modification. Also, in most cases, the network topology matches the geographic configuration, so if you are creating additional domains to manage replication traffic, the geographically based domain is probably the best option. A domain design based on business units is usually the best option only if the business units are quite autonomous. If each business unit manages its own directory service, domains based on business units make sense.

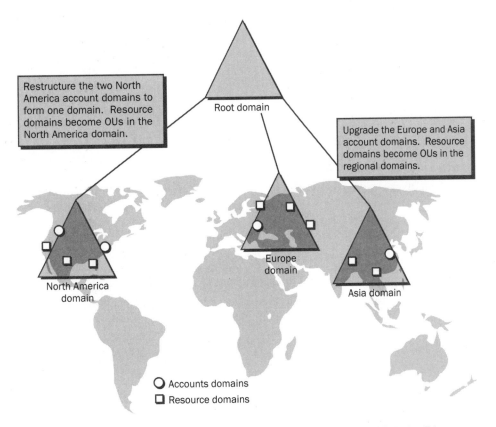

Figure 5-3. *Upgrading Windows NT 4 domains to Windows Server 2003 Active Directory.*

Domain Trees and Trusts

As you add more domains to the forest, you can add the domains in either a single-tree or multiple-tree configuration. If you add all of the domains in a single tree, all the domains will have a contiguous namespace (that is, they will fall under the root domain namespace). This is often the best design for a centralized corporation where all the business units are known by one name. However, if the corporation has several business units with distinct identities, there is likely to be considerable resistance to using another business unit's namespace. In this case you will add domains in separate trees, thus creating several namespaces.

From a functional point of view, there is almost no difference between deploying a single tree or multiple trees. In either case, all the domains will share a transitive trust with all other domains, and they will also share the GC and configuration container. The primary complicating factor with multiple trees is designing the DNS namespace and configuring the DNS servers. But with the addition of conditional forwarders and stub zones, even this design has become much simpler in Windows Server 2003.

If you deploy multiple domains, and if users frequently access resources in other domains or log on in domains other than their home domain, you might want to include shortcut trusts in your domain design. Shortcut trusts are used to improve performance for resource access or logon between domains. The default trust configuration between domains in Active Directory is either a parent-child trust or a tree root trust. Each parent and child pair share a two-way trust, and the roots of each tree share a two-way trust. Because the trusts are transitive, this means that all the domains in the forest trust each other. However, when a user logs on in a domain other than the home domain, the logon process might have to traverse the entire trust path. For example, a corporation might have a domain structure as illustrated in Figure 5-4. If a user with an account in the Asia.Fabrikam.com domain logs on in the Canada.NAmerica.Contoso.com domain, the initial logon request would go to a domain controller in the Canada domain. The logon request would be referred up the trust path to the NAmerica domain, then to the Contoso domain, then to the Fabrikam domain, and finally to the Asia domain. A shortcut trust can shorten the trust path. For example, if a shortcut trust is configured between the Canada domain and the Asia domain, the logon request could be forwarded directly to a domain controller in the Asia domain.

Tip Because shortcut trusts add more administrative overhead, they should be implemented only if necessary. They will be necessary only if the trust path includes more than four or five domains, and if users frequently log on or access resources in domains other than their own.

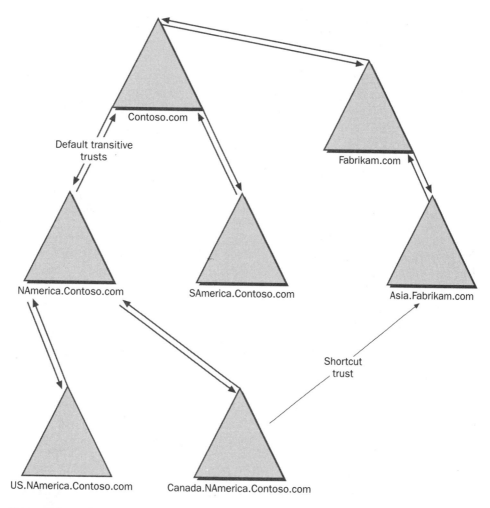

Figure 5-4. *A shortcut trust can be used to optimize resource access between domains.*

Changing the Domain Hierarchy

Your domain plan should be completed before you begin deployment because it is difficult to change the domain configuration after deployment. Windows Server 2003 does provide the option of renaming domains in a Windows Server 2003 forest that is running in Windows Server 2003 functional level. This includes the option of moving a domain from one tree to another within the forest, but not the option of replacing the forest root domain. Essentially, the domain rename option allows you to change the naming structure of the forest but not to make more fundamental changes. For example, if you decide to change the business units in each domain, you must move a large number of objects between domains. To do this, you must use a tool like Microsoft's Active Directory Migration Tool version 2 (ADMT) or a third-party migration tool. ADMT can be found in the /I386/ADMT folder on the Windows Server 2003 compact disc.

Defining Domain Ownership

For each of the domains included in the Active Directory design, you must assign a domain owner. In most cases domain owners are business unit administrators or the administrators in the geographical region where the domain has been defined.

> **Note** If you are deploying a dedicated root domain, the domain owners of the domain are also the forest owners. The only real functions performed in a dedicated root domain are forest functions, so it makes sense that the forest owners also own the root domain.

The role of the domain owner is to manage the individual domain. Tasks include:

- **Creating the domain-level security policies** These include the password policies, account lockout policies, and Kerberos ticket policies.

- **Designing the Group Policy configuration at the domain level** The domain owner might design the group policies for the entire domain and delegate the right for OU-level administrators to link group policies to OUs.

- **Creating the top-level OU structure in the domain** After the top-level OU structure has been created, the task of creating subordinate OUs can be assigned to OU-level administrators.

- **Delegating administrative rights within the domain** The domain owner should establish the administrative policies for the domain level (including policies on naming schemes, group design, etc.) and then delegate rights to OU-level administrators.

- **Managing the domain-level administrative groups** As mentioned earlier, the administrators in each domain must be highly trusted because their actions can have forestwide implications. The domain owner's role is to limit the membership of the domain-level administrative groups and delegate lower-level administrative rights whenever possible.

Designing the DNS Infrastructure

Once you have decided how many domains you will need to deploy and determined the domain hierarchy, the next step is to design the DNS infrastructure for your network. Active Directory in Windows Server 2003 requires DNS, as each domain name is now a part of the DNS namespace. A key design decision is to determine where to locate Active Directory domains within that namespace. In addition to designing the namespace, you must also design the DNS server configuration. If the company already has a DNS infrastructure in place, you might have to design your namespace to fit into the current namespace, as well as configure the Windows Server 2003 DNS servers to interoperate with the existing DNS servers.

Examining the Existing DNS Infrastructure

The first step in designing the DNS infrastructure is to examine the current DNS infrastructure. In most cases, DNS in Active Directory needs to interact with the current DNS infrastructure. This interaction might mean simply configuring a forwarder to an existing DNS server. Or you might decide to use the current DNS server as the primary DNS server for Active Directory and not even deploy DNS in Windows Server 2003. Active Directory requires DNS to operate; however, you have several options on how to deploy DNS.

As you examine the current DNS infrastructure, do the following:

- Document all of the DNS domain names currently in use within the company. This should include names that are used on the Internet as well as names that are only used internally.

- Document any additional names that the company has registered with the Internet naming authorities. Often a company might only be using the .com name on the Internet, but might also have registered the other top-level domain names like .net or .org. You might choose to use one of these domain names for your internal namespace.

- Document the current DNS server configuration. This documentation should include the types of DNS servers currently deployed on the network (such as Windows-based DNS servers, the Berkeley Internet Name Domain [BIND] [including version number], or Lucent VitalQIP). In addition, the DNS configuration should include information about forwarders, zone delegations, and primary and secondary server configurations.

Namespace Design

Once you have gathered the information on the current DNS infrastructure, you are ready to start designing your Active Directory namespace.

Internal and External DNS Namespaces

One of the first questions that you must answer before beginning the namespace design is whether you want to have the same internal and external DNS namespace. Essentially this has to do with whether or not you want to expose the internal namespace to the Internet.

Using the Same Namespace Internally and Externally

Some companies might choose to use the same DNS name internally and externally. In this case, a company would have registered only one DNS name on the Internet. For example, as shown in Figure 5-5, Contoso might decide to use Contoso.com both internally and externally.

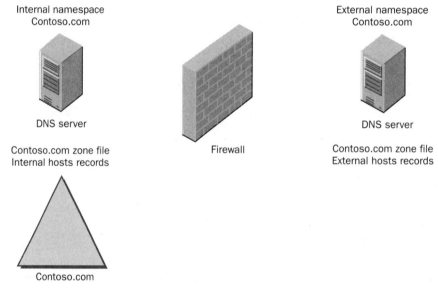

Figure 5-5. *Using a single DNS namespace.*

Caution Regardless of whether you use the same or different internal and external namespaces, your internal DNS server should never be accessible to external clients. The internal DNS server will host all domain controller records as well as possibly the records for all computers on your network (if you have dynamic DNS [DDNS] enabled). The only records that should be accessible from the Internet are the records for resources that need to be accessible from the Internet. For most companies, the list of externally available resources consists of the addresses for the SMTP servers, Web servers, and possibly a few other servers. Using the same namespace does not mean that you should use one DNS server or zone file internally and externally.

The primary advantage of using the same namespace internally and externally is that it provides a consistent experience for the end user. The user always uses the same domain name for any connection to the corporate network. The user's SMTP address and the user principal name (UPN) will use the same domain name as the public Web site. When the user needs to access Web-based resources, he or she can use the same name both internally and externally (although he or she might not access the same server). Another advantage of using the same namespace is that only one DNS name needs to be registered.

The primary disadvantages of using the same namespace have to do with security and administrative effort. Many companies are concerned about exposing the internal DNS name to the Internet and see this as a potential security risk. Using the same namespace internally and externally can complicate the DNS administration because the DNS administrators must now administer two different zones with the same domain name. Using the same name can also complicate some client configurations. For example, most proxy clients can be configured to interpret specified domain names as internal so that the client will connect them directly without going through the proxy server. Using the same name can complicate this configuration.

Using a Different Namespace Internally and Externally

Most companies use a different namespace internally and externally. For example, a company might decide to use Contoso.com as the external namespace and a name like Contoso.net or ADContoso.com for the internal namespace. (See Figure 5-6.)

Note Any difference in the domain names means that you are using a different namespace internally. For example, if you are using Contoso.com as the external namespace, Contoso.net, ADContoso.com, and AD.Contoso.com are all different namespaces. AD.Contoso.com will require a different DNS configuration than the other two, but all three are unique.

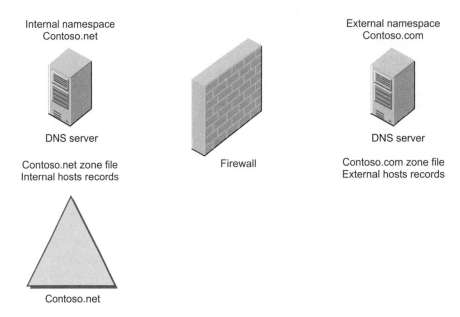

Figure 5-6. *Using separate namespaces internally and externally.*

Often the unique internal namespace is chosen for security reasons, that is, to prevent the internal namespace from being exposed to the Internet. Also, the DNS and proxy configurations are easier to manage with the unique namespace. The primary disadvantage to using a unique namespace is that the company might need to register additional DNS names with the Internet naming authorities. While registering the internal DNS name with the Internet naming authorities is not a requirement, it is recommended. If you do not register the name, and another company does register it, your users will not be able to locate Internet resources with the same domain name as the internal namespace.

Namespace Design Options

The actual names that you choose for your DNS namespace are flexible and will be determined largely by the current DNS infrastructure. If you do not have a DNS infrastructure in place (not an uncommon scenario in Windows NT networks), and if you have already registered the domain name that you want to use for Active Directory, your design might be fairly simple. However, if you already have an existing DNS infrastructure in place and must interoperate with that environment, your DNS design can be quite complex.

If you do not have an existing DNS infrastructure in place and you have one or more second-level domain names already registered for your company, your DNS namespace design will be quite simple. In this case, you can choose the registered second-level domain name as the root domain name and then delegate child domain names for additional domains in the same tree, or additional second-level domain names for additional trees in the forest. Figure 5-7 shows an example.

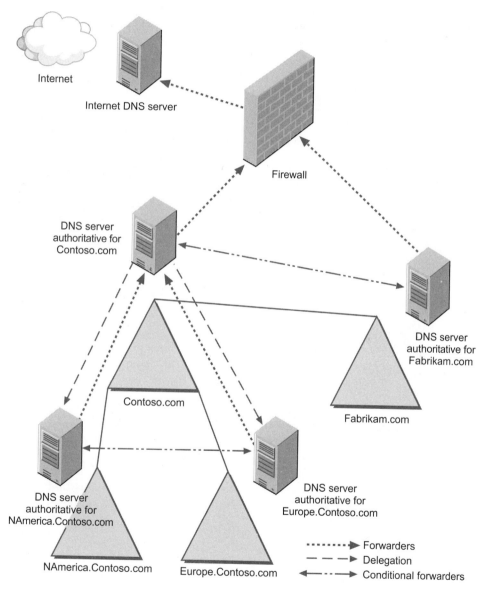

Figure 5-7. *DNS namespace design with no existing DNS infrastructure.*

Internal and External Namespaces

The issue of using an internal namespace that is different than the external, public namespace can lead to a significant amount of discussion within the company. In some cases the best technical answer may be to use different namespaces internally and externally, but business owners might have strong resistance to using anything other than the Internet namespace. Often, the reason for this is name branding: some companies have spent years and millions of dollars creating a name brand that customers instantly recognize. The corporate Web sites and SMTP addresses for all users reflect this namespace. Some companies might even have multiple public identities, with several business units within the company, each with its own name branding. Most of the time, business users are resistant to showing any name other than their recognizable corporate name to the external world.

The good news is that you can use different namespaces internally and externally and still maintain only one namespace externally. For example, Contoso might decide to use Contoso.net as the internal namespace and Contoso.com as the public namespace. The internal namespace can be almost completely hidden from everyone but network administrators. The SMTP addresses for all users can still be alias@contoso.com, and all the Web servers can still use the Contoso.com Web suffix. If required, the UPN for all users can even be configured as alias@contoso.com despite using a different internal namespace.

Figure 5-7 also illustrates how the DNS servers would be configured in this scenario. The Contoso.com DNS server is authoritative for its domain and contains delegation records to NAmerica.Contoso.com and Europe.Contoso.com as well as conditional forwarders or stub zones for the Fabrikam.com domain. The Fabrikam.com DNS server is authoritative for its zone and contains conditional forwarders or stub zones for Contoso.com. To resolve Internet addresses, the tree root servers could be configured with a forwarder pointing to a server on the Internet, or they could be configured with the Internet root hints.

The DNS design can be slightly more complicated if you have an existing internal DNS infrastructure. In this case, you have at least three options for integrating with the current infrastructure. The first option is to use only the current DNS infrastructure, including the domain name, for Active Directory. For example, Contoso might be using Contoso.net as its internal namespace and using BIND DNS servers to provide the DNS service. The company could decide to use Contoso.net as the Active Directory domain name and continue to use the current DNS servers (providing they support service locator [SRV] records).

Alternatively, the company could decide to use the same domain name but move the DNS service to a DNS server running Windows Server 2003. In either case, very little reconfiguration of the DNS servers is required. The DNS servers can continue to use the same forwarders or root hints for Internet name resolution.

Tip   When you configure the DNS servers for Internet name resolution, you have two options: you can use forwarders, or you can configure the DNS servers with root hints. The use of forwarders is generally more secure in that you can config-ure the internal DNS server to forward to one or two external DNS servers. This can simplify the configuration of the firewall. Using root hints might result in better redundancy because you remove the single point of failure. If one root hint server does not respond, the DNS server will simply contact another.

The second option with an existing DNS infrastructure is to choose a different DNS name for Active Directory domains. For example, Contoso might be using Contoso.net as the current internal DNS namespace and decide to deploy Active Directory domains using AD.Contoso.net as the domain name. (See Figure 5-8.)

In this case, a DNS server can be deployed as the primary name server for AD.Contoso.net with delegation records for NAmerica.AD.Contoso.net and Europe.AD.Contoso.net. This DNS server might be the same DNS server as the authoritative server for Contoso.net, or you might choose to deploy an additional DNS server. If you do deploy an additional DNS server for the Active Directory domain, you must configure the forwarders and root hints for this DNS server.

The third DNS design that you can use with an existing DNS infrastructure is one in which the Active Directory domain(s) are child domains to the existing internal namespace. For example, Contoso might decide to create a subdomain, AD.Contoso.net, as the Active Directory domain. (See Figure 5-9.)

In this case, the DNS server for the Contoso.net would be configured with a delegation record for the AD.Contoso.net domain. The AD.Contoso.net DNS server would then be configured with a forwarder record pointing to the Contoso.net DNS server.

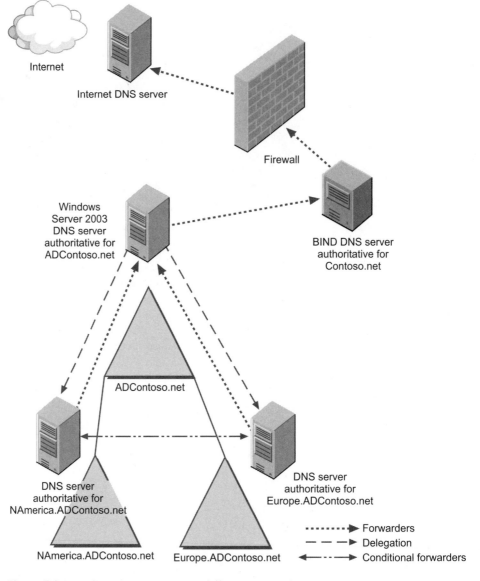

Figure 5-8. *Configuring DNS to use a different internal namespace.*

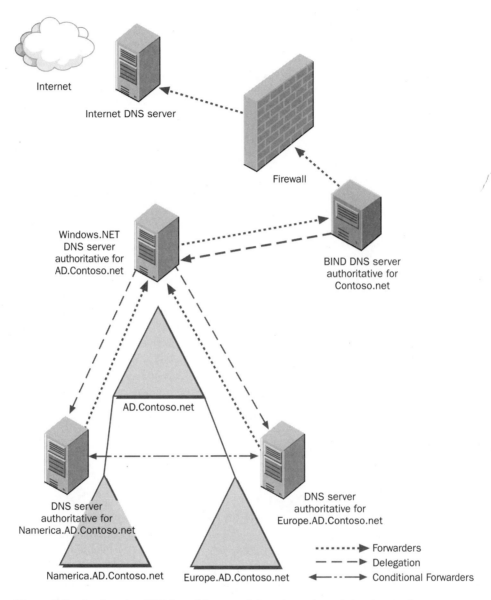

Figure 5-9. *Configuring DNS by adding a subdomain to the existing internal namespace.*

Probably the most complicated DNS design configuration you will ever face would be if a company decided to combine all of the ways for integrating DNS with the internal namespace. For example, as shown in Figure 5-10, a company might already be using Contoso.net and Fabrikam.net as internal namespaces. When the company decides to deploy Active Directory, it might choose to add child domains under the existing domains as well as to create a new domain tree called NWTraders.net. By configuring forwarders and root hints, the DNS servers could resolve any DNS names in the organization.

This DNS namespace does not determine Active Directory hierarchy, however. In the example shown in Figure 5-10, the AD.Contoso.net domain might be an Active Directory root domain, with NAmerica.AD.Contoso.net and Europe.AD.Contoso.net being child domains and AD.Fabrikam.net and NWTraders.net operating as root domains for additional trees in the Active Directory forest.

Integration with the Current DNS Infrastructure

Almost all large companies already have a DNS infrastructure in place. In many cases, the DNS is used primarily for name resolution to UNIX servers or to provide the DNS services users need for Internet access. In many cases, the DNS services are provided by BIND DNS servers running on UNIX servers. Because of Windows NT's dependence on NetBIOS names and Windows Internet Naming Service (WINS), as opposed to host names and DNS, many Windows administrators have had very little to do with DNS. This has changed with the release of Active Directory in Windows 2000 and Windows Server 2003. As described in Chapter 3, "Active Directory and Domain Name System," Windows Server 2003 requires DNS for clients to be able to locate domain controllers. Because of this total reliance on DNS, where the DNS service should be hosted has become a critical point of discussion in Active Directory design.

Most companies with an existing DNS infrastructure in place are not likely to just remove the current infrastructure and move everything to Windows Server 2003. This means that the DNS requirements for Active Directory will have to interoperate with the current DNS infrastructure.

There are two options for integration if the current BIND DNS infrastructure is to be maintained. The first option is to use non-Microsoft DNS servers and host the required DNS zone information for Active Directory on these servers. This is certainly a possibility. The only absolute requirement for DNS is that the server must support SRV records. In addition, you probably want to ensure that the DNS servers also support dynamic updates (especially if you are planning on registering all of the client IP addresses in DNS) and incremental zone transfers. If the current infrastructure uses BIND DNS servers, BIND 8.1.2 servers support SRV records and dynamic updates. In addition to the support provided by BIND 8.1.2, BIND 8.2.1 supports incremental zone transfers. As long as you are using one of these recent versions of BIND, you can continue using the BIND DNS servers. (If you are using Lucent VitalQIP DNS servers, Version 5.2 and later are BIND 8.2.2 compatible.)

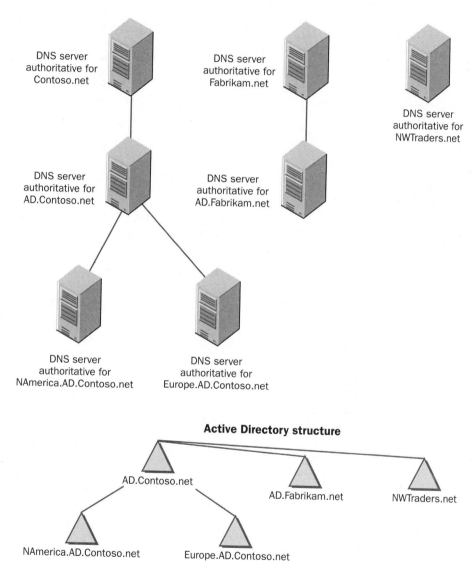

Figure 5-10. *Configuring DNS by adding child domains to the existing domains.*

Real World Choosing Which DNS Server to Use

The question of whether to use DNS servers running Windows Server 2003 or use non-Microsoft DNS servers can lead to heated discussions with no satisfactory resolution. Large companies have been running BIND DNS servers for many years, and the DNS administrators are often very knowledgeable, experienced, and reluctant to give up the DNS services to a Microsoft platform. Often these administrators express concerns about the stability, reliability, and security of DNS on Microsoft servers.

One approach to this discussion is to take the position that it really does not matter how the DNS service is provided. As long as the DNS servers support SRV records, Windows Server 2003 Active Directory can work with any DNS server. What is absolutely critical, however, is that the DNS service always be available. If the DNS service ever shuts down during working hours, no clients or servers will be able to find any Active Directory domain controllers. So the crucial question becomes which DNS server will provide the reliability that Active Directory needs.

Long discussions regarding the reliability of various servers seem to miss the mark. No single server can ever be completely reliable, so the question to ask is which DNS server provides the best options for eliminating a single point of failure and spreading the service availability across multiple servers. Windows Server 2003 provides excellent options for providing this reliability across multiple servers, especially if Active Directory integrated zones are used. With Active Directory integrated zones, every DNS server can have a writable copy of the DNS information. Active Directory integrated zones also address the security concerns by implementing secure updates.

Many companies have decided to stay with the BIND DNS servers, and these servers have provided the required functionality without any problems. Some companies have decided to move the primary DNS to Microsoft DNS servers and to retain the BIND DNS servers as secondary name servers. Almost any configuration will work, and as long as the DNS servers are always available, it really does not matter which option a company uses.

The second option for integrating the Windows Server 2003 DNS with BIND is to deploy both types of DNS. Many companies use the BIND DNS server as the primary name server for the internal namespace. For example, Contoso might be using BIND for name resolution for Contoso.com. If Contoso decides to deploy Active Directory and use DNS servers running Windows Server 2003, they have a number of options. If Contoso wants to use Contoso.com as the Active Directory DNS name, they can move the primary zone to the DNS server running Windows Server 2003 and maintain the BIND DNS server as a secondary name server. Or the DNS server running Windows Server 2003 could be the secondary name server to the BIND DNS server.

Note   You can use BIND DNS servers and Windows Server 2003 DNS servers for the same namespace. Both DNS servers can operate as either primary or secondary name servers for each other's zone information. However, if you are planning to use Active Directory integrated zones, the BIND DNS zone must be configured as a secondary zone. An Active Directory integrated zone cannot be a secondary zone.

Contoso might also decide to deploy Active Directory using a different domain name than that currently used on the BIND DNS servers. For example, the company might decide to use Contoso.net as the Active Directory DNS name. In this case, the DNS servers running Windows Server 2003 can be configured as the authoritative servers for Contoso.net and the BIND servers as authoritative for Contoso.com. The DNS server running Windows Server 2003 can then be configured with a conditional forwarder to the BIND DNS server for Contoso.com. Active Directory domain might also be deployed using AD.Contoso.com as the domain name. In this case the Contoso.com BIND DNS servers will be configured with a delegation record delegating any lookups for the AD.Contoso.com domain to the DNS servers running Windows Server 2003. The DNS servers running Windows Server 2003 could be configured with a forwarder pointing to the BIND DNS server.

Tip   The earlier section in this chapter on planning the DNS namespace illustrated a number of possible scenarios for DNS namespace deployment. The DNS servers discussed in the namespace planning section are essentially interchangeable: any of the DNS servers could be BIND servers, and any of the DNS servers could be DNS servers running Windows Server 2003. Theoretically, you could even use Windows Server 2003 DNS to host the external DNS name and use BIND DNS for Active Directory domains.

Designing the Organizational Unit Structure

Once the domain-level design is complete, the next step is to create an OU design for each domain. As described in Chapter 2, "Active Directory Components," OUs are used to create a hierarchical structure within a domain. This hierarchy can then be used to delegate administrative tasks or to apply a set of Group Policies to a collection of objects.

Organizational Units and Active Directory Design

Windows NT domains use a flat namespace, that is, all of the objects in the domain are at the same level. There is no way to assign administrative control of one object in the domain without giving the same level of administrative control over all other objects in the directory. OUs in Active Directory change this by creating a hierarchy of objects within a single domain. By using OUs, you can give someone administrative control over only one part of the domain, or even grant someone very limited administrative access over that part of the domain.

When you design the OU structure, you are grouping a collection of objects together for the purpose of administering the objects in the same way. For example, you might want to install a common set of applications for all the users in a particular department. By grouping all of the users into an OU, you can assign a Group Policy to that OU that automatically installs the required software. You might also want to group objects together for the purpose of assigning an administrator for that group of objects. For example, if you have a remote office with a local administrator, you can create an OU, put all the user and computer objects in the remote office into that OU, and then delegate the administration of that OU to the local administrator.

OUs have several characteristics:

- OU design does not have any implications for DNS namespace design. OUs are given directory names within a DNS namespace. For example, an OU might have the distinguished name of OU=ManagersOU,OU=AdministrationOU,DC=Contoso,DC=Com. In this case, the DNS name is Contoso.com, and the OU names are LDAP names inside the DNS namespace.

- OUs can be created inside of other OUs. By default, administrative rights and Group Policy settings set at upper-level OUs are inherited by child OUs. This default behavior can be modified.

- OUs are transparent to end users. When a user searches Active Directory for any object, the user's application will query the GC for the information. The user does not need to be aware of the OU structure to log on or to locate objects in Active Directory.

- Compared to the other Active Directory components, such as domains and forests, the OU structure is easy to modify after deployment. Also, moving objects between OUs is just a matter of right-clicking the object and selecting Move from the context menu.

Designing an OU Structure

In most companies, you have a considerable amount of flexibility when you create the OU design. However, as you create the OU design for each domain, there are a number of factors to consider.

Real World   Corporate Structures and OU Design

The first tendency when creating an OU structure might be to mimic the company's organization chart. This might work in some companies, but it could result in an ineffective OU structure in other companies. For example, the corporate organizational chart is usually based on business units with no regard for where users are actually located. Perhaps the members of the business units are scattered in multiple locations around the world. Grouping these users into a single OU could be quite inefficient.

However, examining the corporate structure and organizational model is often a good place to start with the OU design. For example, if the company is highly centralized and hierarchical, the OU structure will probably reflect that model. If the company structure gives a great deal of autonomy to business units or geographic locations, the OU design should reflect this approach. As you examine the corporate structure, also examine the information technology (IT) management structure. In some companies, separate business units are given a great deal of autonomy to manage the business as they want, but the IT management might still be strongly centralized. In this case, you will design the OU structure based on the IT management structure, not on the business management structure.

OU Design Based on Delegation of Administration

One of the reasons for creating an OU structure is to be able to delegate administrative tasks. Many companies that have merged Windows NT resource domains into a single Active Directory domain might still want to delegate the administrative tasks that the domain administrators in the resource domain used to do. Some companies have multiple locations with local network administrators in each location, and they might want to delegate administration for each of those locations. Other companies might want to be able to delegate a specific administrative task. For example, perhaps they want to give one or two people in each department the right to reset user passwords in the department as well as to modify the user information for all the users in the department.

All of these options, and many more, are possible by creating an OU structure in Active Directory and then delegating administrative access. You can grant almost any level of administrative access at an OU level. For example, if you create an OU for a remote office, you can grant the administrator in that remote office full control of all the objects in that office. This administrator can then perform any administrative task in that OU, including creating child OUs and delegating permissions to other administrators. If you create an OU for each department, you can grant very specific rights, such as the reset password right, to a few users in the department. You can even grant administrative rights based on the types of objects in an OU—the department administrators might be able to modify user accounts but not group objects or computer objects. Chapter 9, "Delegating the Administration of Active Directory," goes into detail about delegating administration. You should read that chapter before creating your OU design.

For most companies, the top-level OUs will be designed based on the requirement to delegate administration. The top-level OU will likely be based on geographic locations or business departments. Often these OU boundaries will also be administrative boundaries.

OU Design Based on Group Policy Design

The second reason for creating OUs is to manage the assignment of group policies. Group Policies are used for change and configuration management of desktops. With group policies, you can provide users with a standard desktop configuration, including the automatic installation of a set of applications. group policies can also be used to control what changes users can make to their computers and to configure many of the security settings. Almost all of the group policies in Active Directory will be assigned at an OU level, so the deployment of group policies will play an important part in the OU design.

As you plan the OU structure, you will group together objects that require the same group policy settings. For example, if all the users in one department require the same set of applications, these can be installed using a group policy. The users might also need a standard set of mapped drives. The logon scripts for the users can be assigned using a group policy. Perhaps you want to apply a security template to all of the file servers in your organization. To do this, group all of the file servers into an OU and assign the security template using a group policy.

In most companies, the lower levels of the OU design will be determined primarily by the need to apply group policies. By default, all group policies are inherited from parent OUs. This means that you can apply a group policy to many departments high in the OU structure, and then apply more specific group policies at a lower level. If you want to modify the default inheritance of group policies, you can do so by creating an OU and blocking any policy inheritance at that OU level. This strong dependency on group policies for the OU design means that you must understand the group policy functionality and requirements for your organization. Chapter 11, "Introduction to Group Policies," Chapter 12, "Using Group Policies to Manage Software," and Chapter 13, "Using Group Policies to Manage Computers," discuss in detail what you can do with group policies.

Creating an OU Design

As you begin the OU design, you should begin with the top-level OUs first. Top-level OUs are harder to modify after deployment because of all of the OUs under the top-level

OUs. This also means that the top-level OUs should be based on something static in the organization. Usually these OUs are based on geographic regions or business units.

A geographically based OU design is likely to be the most resistant to change. Some companies seem to reorganize frequently but rarely change the geographic configuration of the company. An OU structure based on geographic locations also works well if the corporation uses a decentralized administrative model, especially when the administration is geographically based. If each geographic location (either a single office or a central office with several branch offices connected to it) has its own set of network administrators, the geographic OUs can be used to delegate administrative tasks to these administrators. The primary drawback for a geographically based OU structure is if there are multiple business units in every geographic location. For example, if every department is represented in each office in the company, it might be more effective to use a business-unit–based OU structure at the top level.

The second most common top-level OU structure is one based on business units. In this model, a top-level OU is created for each business unit within the corporation. This type of configuration is most appropriate if a company has only one location or if many of the administrative tasks are delegated at a business-unit level. One of the problems with an OU structure based on business units is that the top-level OUs might need to be modified in the event of a corporate reorganization.

Most large corporations will actually use a combination of geographically based and business-unit–based OUs. One of the most common configurations is a top-level OU based on geographic regions, with the next level OUs within each region based on business units. Some companies might choose a top-level OU based on business units and then create a geographically based OU structure under these top-level OUs.

Figure 5-11 illustrates what an OU design might look like for a large company.

In this example, the top-level OUs include the Domain Controllers OU (all domain controllers are located in this OU) and an OU for the domain-level administrators. Top-level OUs might also include a Service Account OU for all of the service accounts used in the domain. Creating an OU at the top level for special user accounts like service accounts simplifies the administration of these accounts. The top-level OUs might also include a Servers OU if all of the servers are centrally managed. In addition to these administrative OUs, there can be top-level OUs based on the geographic locations for the corporation. The geographically based OUs might be used primarily to delegate administrative tasks.

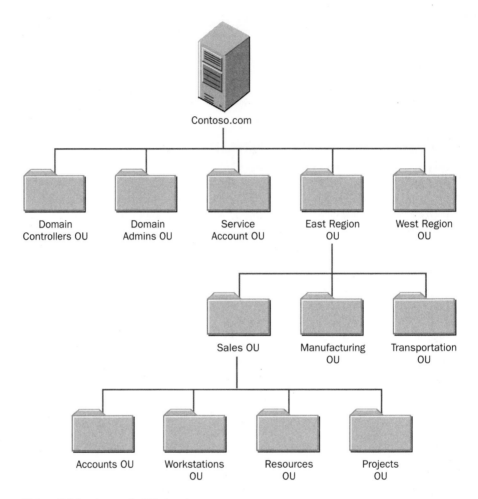

Contoso.com

Domain Controllers OU

Domain Admins OU

Service Account OU

East Region OU

West Region OU

Sales OU

Manufacturing OU

Transportation OU

Accounts OU

Workstations OU

Resources OU

Projects OU

Figure 5-11. *A sample OU structure.*

The second-level OUs in each geographic region are based on the business units in each region. The business-unit OUs might be used to delegate administration, but are also likely to be used to assign group policies. Under the business-unit OUs are OUs based on departments within the business units. At this level, the OUs will be used primarily to assign group policies or to assign specific administrative tasks such as the right to reset passwords. The department OUs might contain several other OUs:

- **Accounts OU** This OU contains the user and group accounts for the department. In some cases, the account OUs might be further split up into OUs containing groups, user accounts, or remote users.

- **Workstations OU** This OU contains all the user workstations and might include separate OUs for Windows NT workstations, Windows 2000 workstations, Microsoft Windows XP Professional workstations, and portable computers.

- **Resources OU** This OU contains the resources linked to the OU. This could include objects like domain local groups, servers, printers, and shared folders.

- **Application or project-based OUs** If a group of people and resources are working on a particular project or application that requires unique management, you can create an OU structure for those users and then group the users, resources, and computers needed for that project in this OU.

Tip   Theoretically, there is no limit to how many levels your OU structure can have. However, it is generally a best practice not to have more than ten layers. For most companies, an OU structure that is four or five levels deep is all you will ever need.

As you work on creating the OU design, ensure that you document the design carefully. This design will include a diagram of OU structure, a list of all the OUs, and the purpose for each OU. Also, if you are using the OU to delegate administrative tasks, document the rights delegated at each OU level. As you deploy group policies linked to each OU, document the group policy configuration.

Designing the Site Topology

All of the design topics discussed so far have dealt primarily with the logical aspects of Active Directory design, with little regard for the actual network topology in the organization. Before you can deploy Active Directory design, you must deal with the issue of site design, which will be directly impacted by the network topology.

Sites and Active Directory Design

In Active Directory, sites are specific organizational entities and are used to manage network traffic. This is done in three primary ways:

- Replication between sites is compressed so replication between sites uses less bandwidth than replication within a site. Further, replication can be scheduled to ensure it occurs when few other demands are being placed on the network.

- Client logon traffic will remain within the site if the local domain controller is available.

- Active Directory–aware applications like Distributed File System (DFS) can be added to the network to limit client access traffic to the local site.

Networking Infrastructure and Site Design

Because site design is so dependent on the networking infrastructure, the first step in creating a site design is to document that infrastructure. The documentation should include:

- A wide area network (WAN) and local area network (LAN) topology diagram detailing the corporate network. The diagram should include the total bandwidth and the available bandwidth between all company locations.

- A listing of all the company locations where the computers are connected with a fast network connection. The definition of a fast network connection will vary depending on factors such as the number of users in the location, the total number of objects in the domain, and the number of domains in the forest. As well, you will need to determine how much of the total bandwidth is available for replication. In most cases, the network connections within a site should have at least 512 kilobits per second (Kbps) of available bandwidth; in a large company, you might want to consider at least 10 megabits per second (Mbps) as the minimum network connection within a site.

- For each location, detail the number of users, the number of workstations and servers, and the local Internet Protocol (IP) subnets.

Creating a Site Design

Once you have collected the information about the corporate network, you are ready to design the sites. To begin, examine each location where the computers are connected with a fast network connection. How many users are there in the location? Are there enough users in the location to require a domain controller in the location? What are the network connections from this location to other locations in the company?

Every site should have a domain controller, and most sites should also have a GC server. This means that if you are trying to decide whether to create a site for a company location with a small number of users and a slow network connection to other company locations, the question is really whether you want to put a domain controller into that site. One way to answer this question is to determine which option will result in the least network traffic across the network link. Which will create more traffic: the clients logging on to a domain controller in another location or the replication traffic between domain controllers? In addition to determining which option results in heavier traffic, you also need to consider other factors. If you do not put a domain controller in the location, you need to consider the work disruption to the users if the network connection fails and the users cannot log on to the domain. You might also consider whether a server is required in the location for other reasons. If you are deploying a server running Windows Server 2003 in the location anyway, can it also serve as a domain controller for the site?

Tip As you create an Active Directory design for a company, the general rule of keeping things as simple as possible applies to everything but sites. When you are planning the forest, domain, or OU structure, simplicity should be one of your primary goals. However, creating additional sites for all of the company locations separated by slower network connections provides significant benefit without a significant increase in administration. So this might be the only time in the Active Directory design process that the simplest solution might not be the best solution.

Once you have determined how many Active Directory sites you will require, the next step is to create the design for each site. Each site in Active Directory is linked to one or more IP subnets, so as you create the design for each site, you should identify which subnets will be included in each site. If you decide not to deploy a domain controller into a company location, you must determine which site this location will belong to and add that IP subnet to the appropriate site. This ensures that the clients in the remote location will connect to the domain controllers that are closest to them.

Once you have created the sites, the next step is to create the replication topology for the sites. To do this, configure site links between company locations. For each site link, plan the schedule and replication interval as well as the site link cost. If you want to designate replication bridgehead servers for each site, identify all Active Directory partitions that will be located in the site and designate a bridgehead server for each partition.

Calculating the cost for each of the site links can be complicated, especially if there are multiple possible routes between company locations. If there are multiple routes, you need to assign the costs for the site links so that the optimal route is used for Active Directory replication. One way to determine what cost to assign to each site link is to create a table linking network bandwidth to site link cost. An example is shown in Table 5-1.

Table 5-1. Linking Network Bandwidth to Site Link Costs

Available bandwidth	Site link cost
Greater than or equal to 10 Mbps	10
10 Mbps to 1.544 Mbps	100
1.544 Mbps to 512 Kbps	200
512 Kbps to 128 Kbps	400
128 Kbps to 56 Kbps	800
Less than 56 Kbps	2000

Using the information outlined in this table, you can assign a cost to each site link. Then calculate which route the replication traffic will take through the network if all links are available. Also calculate the effects of a network link failure. If there are redundant paths within the network, ensure that the site link costs are configured so that the optimal backup path will be selected in the event of link failure.

Another option to manage Active Directory replication is to turn off site link bridging. In most cases, you should not turn off site link bridging because if site link bridging is enabled, all site links become transitive. That means that if Site A has a site link to Site B, and Site B has a site link with Site C, Site A can replicate directly with Site C. In most cases, this is the desired behavior. However, there are exceptions where you might want to turn off site link bridging. For example, a company might have several hub sites throughout the world, with several smaller offices connecting to the hub sites using slow or medium network connections. (See Figure 5-12.) If the hub sites are connected with fast network connections, the automatic site link bridging is acceptable. However, if the network connections between the hub sites are fairly slow, or if most of the bandwidth is used for other applications, you might not want to have transitive connections.

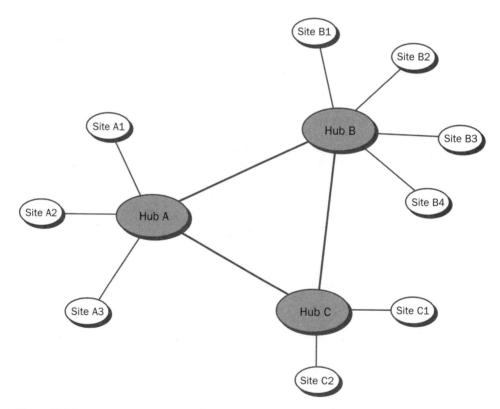

Figure 5-12. *Configuring site link bridging.*

In Figure 5-12, the network connection between Hub A and Hub B might have limited available bandwidth. If the default site link bridging is not modified, the bridgehead server in Hub A will replicate with the bridgehead server in Hub B, but also with the bridgehead servers in other sites connected to Hub B. This means that, potentially, the same replication traffic could cross the network connection five times. To modify this, you can turn off site link bridging and then create manual site link bridges. To turn off site link bridging, open the Active Directory Sites And Services administrative tool and access the IP object properties under the Inter-Site Transports container. On the General tab for the IP Properties sheet, clear the Bridge All Site Links option. You can then create site link bridges for all of the site links between the hub sites and the smaller sites connecting to the hub sites. Once this is configured, all replication from Hub A will flow to Hub B, and then it will be distributed to all the sites connected to Hub B.

Caution If you reset the Bridge All Site Links option, you turn off the transitive site connections, meaning that all site links in the organization are no longer transitive. If you then want to have any site link bridging, you must manually configure it. For this reason, use this option with caution.

Designing Server Locations

As part of the site design, you will also need to determine where to locate the servers running Windows Server 2003 needed to provide the required directory services. In most cases, once you have completed the site design, locating the servers is not complicated.

Locating DNS Servers

As you know, DNS is a critical service in Windows Server 2003 Active Directory. Without DNS, clients cannot locate Active Directory domain controllers, and domain controllers cannot locate each other to replicate. This means that DNS should be deployed in every location in your organization, with the possible exception of very small offices with only a few users.

The DNS service in Windows Server 2003 provides several deployment options. As a result, you can put a DNS server in an office where you do not put a domain controller. For example, you might not want to put a domain controller in a small office with a very slow network connection to a central office because of the amount of replication traffic to the domain controller. However, you might still put a DNS server in that office because DNS can be configured to produce little or no replication traffic. If you configure a DNS server as a caching-only server, it will still optimize client lookups but create no zone transfer traffic. Or you might configure the DNS server with stub zones for Active Directory domains. Because the stub zones contain only a few records, there will be very little replication traffic to the remote office.

Site Design for Branch Offices

One of the special cases for site design is when a company has several hundred small locations with domain controllers in each location. This scenario complicates Active Directory design and deployment in a number of ways. One example is the time that it takes for the Knowledge Consistency Checker (KCC) to calculate the replication topology. With every extra site, it takes longer to calculate the routing topology. While KCC is running on a domain controller, it can use 100 percent of the CPU time on the server. With a large number of sites, the domain controller running Inter-Site Topology Generator (ISTG) at the central office might run at 100 percent CPU utilization constantly and still never complete the calculation. Another complication has to do with the replication window. If the site connector is configured with a schedule to replicate for only 6 hours every night, you might find that you must deploy multiple bridgehead servers to complete the replication to all remote locations every night. Even setting up domain controllers for each site is complicated in this scenario. If the network connection is very slow and you simply install a domain controller in the site and then populate the directory by replication, the initial replication for a large directory may take hours.

Windows Server 2003 provides several significant enhancements that make the deployment of Active Directory in this scenario easier than it was in Windows 2000. Enhancements to the calculation algorithm used by the ISTG process greatly reduces the amount of time required to calculate the intersite replication topology. The option to build a domain controller and populate Active Directory from backup media means that building a domain controller in a remote office does not create as much replication traffic.

Despite these enhancements, designing and deploying Active Directory sites in a company with hundreds of sites is still a special case. If you are dealing with this type of environment, the best resource available is the Active Directory Branch Office Planning Guide, available on the Microsoft site at *http://www.microsoft.com/windows2000/techinfo /planning/activedirectory/branchoffice/default.asp*. Though this guide was prepared for the Windows 2000 Server environment, many of the concepts are still applicable to Windows Server 2003.

Locating Domain Controllers

As a general rule, a domain controller should be located in most company locations where there are a significant number of users. There are at least two reasons for locating a domain controller in a company location. First, if the network fails, the users can still log on to the network. Second, it ensures that the client logon traffic does not cross the WAN connection to a different location. Ideally, for the sake of redundancy, you should put two domain controllers in each location. If you do deploy a domain controller in a company location, then you should also create a site for that location so that all logon traffic stays within the site.

There are also two reasons why you might decide not to put a domain controller into a company location. If the replication traffic to the domain controller in the location is higher than the client logon traffic, you could simply configure the location so that the clients log on to an adjacent location. Also, if the location does not have any means of physically securing the servers, you might not want to put a domain controller at that location. If you do decide not to deploy a domain controller in a company location, you have two ways to manage which domain controllers the clients will log onto. First, you can configure a site for the office, and then configure a site link to one of the existing sites. Second, you can add the IP subnet for the office to an existing site.

Another issue that you need to plan for if you are deploying multiple domains is the forest root domain controller locations. These domain controllers are required whenever a user accesses a resource in another domain tree or when a user logs on to a domain in a domain tree other than their own. Because of this, you should locate forest root domain controllers in any offices where there are a large number of users or where a significant amount of traffic will be directed to the root domain controllers. If your company has a network topology that includes regional hub offices, you should deploy a root domain controller in each of the hub offices.

> **Caution**   Because of the importance of the root domain and the impact to the forest if the root domain is ever lost, the forest root domain controllers should be geographically distributed. Even if there is no good reason to put a root domain controller in offices outside of the head office, you want to do so just to provide geographic redundancy. Like all domain controllers, however, the root domain controllers should never be located in an office where they cannot be physically secured.

Locating Global Catalog Servers

GC servers are required for users to log on to domains that are running at a functional level of at least Windows 2000 native functional level, or when a user searches Active Directory for directory information. If the domain is running Windows 2000 native functional level, you should put a GC server in every site. However, this ideal must be balanced with the replication traffic created by putting a GC server in every site. If you have a very large enterprise, with several large domains, the GC replication traffic will be significant. As a general rule, put a GC server in every site, with multiple GC servers in large sites.

One of the enhancements to Windows Server 2003 Active Directory is the fact that it does support logons to a domain without access to a GC server by supporting *universal group membership caching*. When universal group membership caching is enabled, domain controllers can cache the universal group memberships for users in the domain. The first time the user logs on to the site, the user's universal group membership must be retrieved from a GC server. After the first logon, however, the domain controller will cache the user's universal group membership indefinitely. The universal group membership cache on the domain controlle`r is updated every 8 hours by contacting a designated GC server. To enable universal group membership caching, open the Active Directory Sites And Services administrative tool and expand the site object for the site where you want to enable this setting. Right-click the *NTDS Site Settings* object and select Properties. (See Figure 5-13.) On the Site Settings tab, select the Enable Universal Group Membership Caching option and, in the Refresh Cache From drop-down list, select the site where the closest GC server is located.

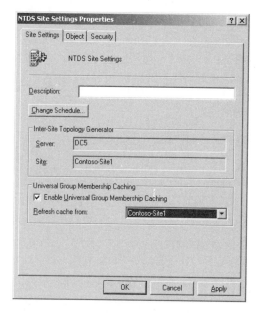

Figure 5-13. *Configuring universal group membership caching.*

Tip Deploying Exchange 2000 Server creates significantly more load on the GC servers. Exchange 2000 Server does not have its own directory service, so it depends on the GC. When a client views the GAL, the client is presented with all the e-mail recipients listed in the GC. When the Exchange server needs to locate a user's address to deliver e-mail, it will query the GC. If you are deploying Exchange 2000 Server, you must locate a GC in every location where you have deployed a server running Exchange 2000 Server, and you will need to increase the total number of GC servers.

Locating Operations Master Servers

The most important operations master for day-to-day operations is the primary domain controller (PDC) emulator. This server is especially important if the domain is running in Windows 2000 mixed functional level or Windows Server 2003 interim functional level because all of the Windows NT 4 backup domain controllers (BDCs) will rely on the PDC emulator for directory synchronization. Also, if your organization includes many down-level clients without the Directory Services Client installed, these clients must connect to the PDC emulator to change their passwords. Even in native mode, the PDC emulator still receives priority updates of user password changes. As a result, the placement of the PDC emulator is significant. The PDC emulator should be placed in a central location where the maximum number of clients can connect to the server.

The placement of the other operations masters is not as crucial. When deciding where to locate the operations masters, use the following guidelines:

- If possible, the schema master, domain naming master, and the relative identi- fier (RID) master should be located in a site with another domain controller as a direct replication partner. The reason for doing this is for disaster recovery purposes. If one of these servers fails, you might have to seize the operations master role to another domain controller. Ideally, you would like to seize the role to another domain controller that is fully replicated with the original op- erations master. This is more likely to be the case if the two domain controllers are in the same site and are configured as direct replication partners.

- The RID master must be accessible to all domain controllers through a remote procedure call (RPC) connection. When a domain controller requires more RIDs, it will use an RPC connection to request them from the RID master.

- The infrastructure master should not be located on a GC server if you have more than one domain. The infrastructure master's role is to update user display name references between domains. For example, if a user account is renamed and the user is a member of a universal group, the infrastructure master updates the username. If the infrastructure master is located on a GC server, it will not function because the GC is constantly updated with the most recent global infor- mation. As a result, the infrastructure master will never detect any out-of-date information and thus never update the cross-domain information.

- If an organization has a central location where most of the users are located, all the operations masters should be put in that site.

Summary

Active Directory design is a topic that could take up an entire book by itself. As described in this chapter, Active Directory design consists of designing the top-level components first and then moving to lower-level components. This means that the first step in Active Directory design is to create the forest design. This is followed by the domain design, DNS design, and finally the OU design. For companies with multiple locations, the site design is another component of Active Directory design.

Chapter 6
Installing Active Directory

The process of installing Active Directory directory service on a server running Microsoft Windows Server 2003 is straightforward. This is due to the well-designed Active Directory Installation Wizard; the user interface used to install the service. When Active Directory is installed on a server running Windows Server 2003, the computer becomes, *de facto*, a domain controller. If this is the first domain controller in a new domain and forest, a pristine directory database is created, ready and waiting for you to populate the directory service objects. If this is an additional domain controller in an existing domain, the replication process will soon propagate to this new domain controller all of the directory service objects of this domain. In the case of an upgraded Microsoft Windows NT 4 domain controller, the accounts database will automatically be upgraded to Active Directory after the Windows Server 2003 network operating system (NOS) is installed on that domain controller.

This chapter will present the information necessary for you to successfully navigate through the Active Directory Installation Wizard, as well as discuss two other methods of installing Active Directory: unattended installation and installing from restored backup files. Finally, it will present the process of removing Active Directory from a domain controller.

Prerequisites for Installing Active Directory

Any server running Windows Server 2003 that meets the prerequisites described in the following section can host Active Directory and become a domain controller. In fact, every new domain controller begins as a stand-alone server until the Active Directory installation process is complete. This process will accomplish two important goals. The first is to create or populate the directory database, and the second is to start Active Directory so that the server is responding to domain logon attempts and to Lightweight Directory Access Protocol (LDAP) requests.

The directory database, you will recall from Chapter 2, "Active Directory Components," is stored on the hard disk of the domain controller as the Ntds.dit file. During the installation of Windows Server 2003, the Ntds.dit file is stored in the %systemroot%\system32 folder on the local drive. Then, during installation of Active Directory, Ntds.dit is copied to a location identified during the installation process, or to the default folder

%systemroot%\NTDS if no other location is specified. By having the Ntds.dit file copied to the hard disk during the Windows Server 2003 installation, Active Directory can be installed at any time without having to access the installation media.

Note While Active Directory can be installed without access to the installation media, installing a Domain Name System (DNS) server and its associated management tools does require the installation files. Be sure to have the Windows Server 2003 compact disc close at hand during the installation process.

The next several sections examine the prerequisites for Windows Server 2003 to host Active Directory.

Hard Disk

Ultimately, the amount of hard disk space required to host Active Directory will depend on the number of objects in the domain and in a multiple domain environment, and whether the domain controller is also a global catalog (GC) server. To install Active Directory on a server running Windows Server 2003, the following minimum hard disk requirements should be met:

- 15 megabytes (MB) of available space required on the system install partition
- 250 MB of available space for the Active Directory database Ntds.dit
- 50 MB of available space for the extensible storage engine (ESENT) transaction log files. ESENT is a transacted database system that uses log files to support rollback semantics to ensure that transactions are committed to the database.

In addition to the above-listed hard disk requirements, at least one logical drive must be formatted with the NTFS v5 file system (the version of NTFS used in Microsoft Windows 2000 and Windows Server 2003) to support the installation of the Sysvol folder.

More Info Ultimately, the amount of hard disk space you require for your Active Directory installation will depend on the number of objects in your domain and forest. To learn more about planning disk space requirements for Active Directory, see the "Planning Domain Controller Capacity" article at *www.microsoft.com /technet/prodtechnol/windowsserver2003/evaluate/cpp/reskit/adsec/part1 /rkpdscap.asp*.

Network Connectivity

After installing Windows Server 2003, and prior to installing Active Directory, verify that the server is properly configured for network connectivity. To do this, attempt to connect to another computer on the network, by either typing the UNC path or the IP address of the target computer into the Address line of Windows Explorer, or by using the Ping utility (for example, from the command line, type *ping 192.168.1.1*). Take all necessary steps to optimize the network segment that the new domain controller will reside on. To do this, use a network monitoring tool, such as Network Monitor, to ensure that there is sufficient bandwidth to support the authentication and replication traffic that the domain controller will generate.

> **Note**   Network Monitor is not installed by default in Windows Server 2003, and it must be installed using the Windows Components Wizard in the Add/Remove Programs application in Control Panel. For more information on installing Network Monitor, and using it to analyze network traffic issues, search for "Network Monitor" (including the double quotation marks) in the Windows Server 2003 Help and Support Center.

Before installing Active Directory, you should also configure the Internet Protocol (TCP /IP) settings on the Local Area Connection Properties sheet. To access this dialog box, right-click the Local Area Connection object in the Network Connections folder in Control Panel and select Properties. On the Local Area Connection Properties sheet, select Internet Protocol (TCP/IP), then click the Properties button. On the Internet Protocol (TCP /IP) Properties sheet, do the following:

- On the General tab, configure the computer with a static IP address.
- On the General tab, if the domain controller you are installing is *not* going to serve as a DNS server, you should configure the DNS server address with the IP address of the DNS server that is authoritative for the domain. See the following section for more information on configuring DNS for Active Directory installation.
- On the Advanced TCP/IP Settings page (click Advanced on the General tab) click the WINS tab, and configure the server with the IP address of the Windows Internet Naming Service (WINS) server that the domain controller will use.

DNS

As mentioned in previous chapters, Active Directory requires DNS as its resource locator service. Client computers rely on DNS to locate the domain controllers so that they can authenticate themselves and the users who log on to the network as well as to query the directory to locate published resources. Furthermore, the DNS service must support service locator (SRV) resource records, and it is recommended that it also support dynamic updates. If DNS has not been previously installed on the network, the Active Directory Installation Wizard will install and configure DNS at the same time as Active Directory.

If DNS is already in place on the network, you should verify that it is configured to support Active Directory. The Dcdiag command (available as part of the tool set created when you install the \Support\Tools\Support.msi file on the Windows Server 2003 compact disc) can be used to verify this capability. To verify that the current DNS implementation will support Active Directory, use the following command:

*dcdiag /test:dcpromo /dnsdomain:**domainname** /newforest*

This command will verify that the DNS server is authoritative for the domain *domainname* and can accept dynamic updates for new domain controllers. For more information on using the dcdiag tool, type *dcdiag /?* at the command prompt.

If DNS is not available on the network, you will be prompted to install the DNS Server service during Active Directory installation. If the domain controller you are installing will also be a DNS server, be sure to carefully plan the DNS namespace that you will be using. See Chapter 5, "Designing the Active Directory Structure" for more information on designing the DNS namespace.

If you will be installing the DNS Server service at the same time as Active Directory, configure the DNS server setting on the computer to point to itself before installing Active Directory. To accomplish this, open the Internet Protocol (TCP/IP) Properties sheet and set the Preferred DNS Server address to the local computer IP address. See Figure 6-1 for an illustration of this setting.

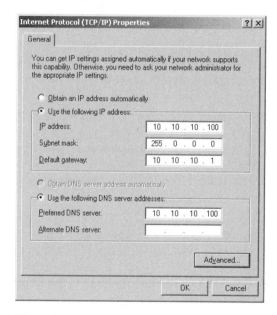

Figure 6-1. *Configuring the DNS Server settings.*

Administrative Permissions

To install or remove Active Directory, you must supply account credentials with administrative account permissions. But the type of account permissions you must have in order to install an Active Directory domain depends on the type of domain you are creating. The Active Directory Installation Wizard checks account permissions before installing the directory service. If you are not logged on with an account with administrative permissions, the wizard prompts you to provide the appropriate account credentials.

When you choose to create a new forest root domain, you must be logged on as a local administrator, but you are not required to provide network credentials. When you choose to create either a new tree-root domain or a new child domain in an existing tree, you must supply network credentials to install the domain. To create a new tree-root domain, you must provide account credentials from a member of the Enterprise Admins group. To install an additional domain controller in an existing domain, you must provide credentials that have permissions to join the computer to the domain and to create an *NTDS Setting* object in the configuration directory partition. The Domain Admins global group has this level of permissions.

Active Directory Installation Options

To start the installation of Active Directory, you can use one of several graphical interfaces, or start it from the command line. The graphical interfaces will install and configure the directory service as well as create and initialize the directory data store. Since Active Directory requires a DNS implementation to be authoritative for the planned domain, the installation process will install and configure the DNS Server service if an authoritative DNS server is not already in place.

There are several methods for starting the installation of Active Directory. These include:

- Configure Your Server Wizard
- Active Directory Installation Wizard (Dcpromo.exe)
- Unattended installation

Configure Your Server Wizard

Manage Your Server appears automatically after a new installation or upgrade to Windows Server 2003 is completed. This interface displays a list of all of the network services that are installed on the server, and it enables you to install additional services. Figure 6-2 shows the interface.

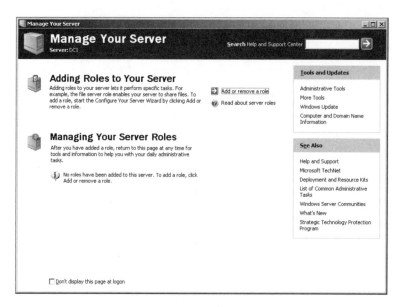

Figure 6-2. *The Manage Your Server interface.*

From Manage Your Server, you can choose to add the domain controller role to the server. You can either do this by selecting the pre-designed Typical Settings for a First Server selection, or by selecting the domain controller role. If you select the typical first server setting, the automated process will also add the DNS server service, and the DHCP service. This highly automated installation routine installs Active Directory using the default choices for many of the options that are presented using the full-featured installation interface—the Active Directory Installation Wizard. If you are planning to install Active Directory with all of the default installation options, the Configure Your Server Wizard provides a fool-proof interface for installing the service.

Active Directory Installation Wizard (Dcpromo.exe)

The Active Directory Installation Wizard can be started by typing *dcpromo.exe* in the Run dialog box or at the command prompt. There are two available command-line parameters for use with Dcpromo.exe:

- The */answer*[:***answerfile***] parameter is used to perform an unattended installation of Active Directory. Include in this parameter the filename of the unattended-answer file that contains all of the necessary information to complete the installation process.

- The */adv* parameter is used to start the Active Directory Installation Wizard when the domain controller will be created from restored backup files. When you add the */adv* parameter, you will be prompted for the path to the restored backup files during the installation process.

Detailed information on the key decision points is provided in the "Using Active Directory Installation Wizard" section of this chapter.

Unattended Installation

In addition to the graphical user interface for installing Active Directory, the installation process can be run in an unattended, or silent, mode by typing *dcpromo.exe /answer:**answerfile***, where *answerfile* represents the filename of the answer file that you have created. The unattended installation script file passes values for all of the user-input fields that you would ordinarily complete when using the Active Directory Installation Wizard. For any key that is not defined in the answer file, the default value will be used for that key, or the user interface will appear so that you can enter the required value. Creating the answer file for unattended installations will be covered later in this chapter.

Using the Configure Your Server Wizard

To install Active Directory using the Configure Your Server Wizard, you can select to add a new role from the Manage Your Server wizard, or you can select the Configure Your Server Wizard from the Administrative Tools folder.

➲ **To install Active Directory using the Configure Your Server Wizard, perform the following steps:**

1. In Manage Your Server, click Add Or Remove A Role, or select Configure Your Server Wizard from the Administrative Tools folder. This launches the Configure Your Server Wizard.

2. On the Preliminary Steps page, click Next. Wait a few moments while the Wizard detects your Local Area Connections settings.

3. On the Configuration Options page, to install Active Directory, as well as the DNS Server service, and the Dynamic Host Configuration Protocol (DHCP) service, select Typical Configuration For A First Server. To only install Active Directory, select Custom Configuration, and then click Next. Figure 6-3 shows the interface. The remainder of this procedure assumes you select the Custom Configuration option.

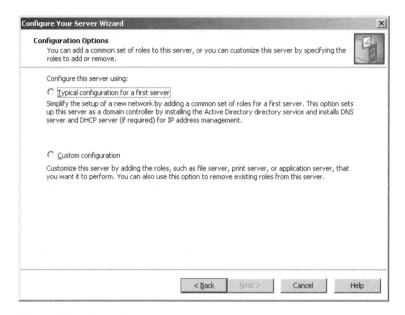

Figure 6-3. *The Configuration Options page.*

4. On the Server Role page, select Domain Controller (Active Directory) and then click Next. Figure 6-4 shows the interface.

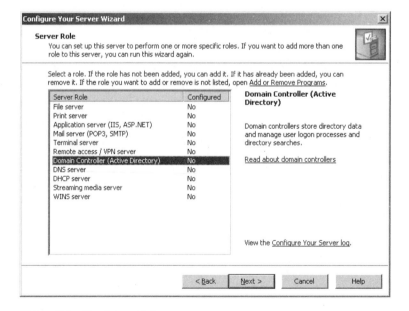

Figure 6-4. *The Server Role page.*

5. On the Summary Of Selections page, confirm your server role choice, and click Next. The Applying Selections page appears while the selected services are being configured.

6. To create the domain controller role, the Active Directory Installation Wizard's Welcome page appears. Figure 6-5 shows the interface. Once the Active Directory Installation Wizard's Welcome page appears, the process is the same as if you had launched the Active Directory Installation Wizard from the command line or run command. A detailed description of the Active Directory Installation Wizard decision points is provided in the next section. Complete the Active Directory Installation Wizard and then click Finish. After the Active Directory service is installed and configured, you are prompted to restart your server.

Figure 6-5. *The Active Directory Installation Wizard's Welcome page.*

Using the Active Directory Installation Wizard

The Active Directory Installation Wizard is as straightforward as a wizard comes. All of the options in the wizard are well explained and presented in a logical order. Rather than stepping you through this otherwise self-explanatory process, this section will discuss the key decision points one encounters when installing Active Directory.

To start the Active Directory Installation Wizard, type *dcpromo* in the Run dialog box or at the command prompt. The Active Directory Installation Wizard's Welcome page appears.

Operating System Compatibility

Domain controllers running Windows Server 2003 are more secure than those running previous versions of the Windows NOS, and the Active Directory Installation Wizard provides information on how this security affects client logon. The default security policy for domain controllers running Windows Server 2003 requires two new levels of domain controller communication security: Server Message Block (SMB) signing, and encryption and signing of secure channel network traffic.

These domain controller security features present a problem for down-level client computers when logging on. The following Windows client operating systems (OSs) do not natively support either SMB signing or secure channel encryption and signing:

- Microsoft Windows for Workgroups
- Microsoft Windows 95 and Windows 98
- Microsoft Windows NT 4 (Service Pack 3 [SP3], and earlier)

If your network supports the listed client OSs, then you must take the following remedial action to enable them to log on to a domain controller running Windows Server 2003:

Table 6-1. Enabling Client OSs to Log On to Active Directory

Client OS	Action needed
Windows for Workgroups	Upgrade the operating system.
Windows 95/Windows 98	Upgrade the operating system (recommended) or install the Directory Services Client.
Windows NT 4	Upgrade the operating system (recommended) or install Service Pack 4 (or later).

The Directory Services Client is a client-side component that enables down-level client OSs (Microsoft Windows 95, Windows 98, and Windows NT 4) to take advantage of many of the features of Active Directory supported by Windows 2000 Professional or Microsoft Windows XP Professional. These features include the Distributed File System (DFS) and Active Directory Search capability. See the Active Directory client extension page at *http://www.microsoft.com/windows2000/server/evaluation/news/bulletins /adextension.asp* for information on downloading and using the Directory Services Client on Windows NT 4 SP6a systems. Note that the previous name for the Directory Services Client was Active Directory Client Extension, a name you will still encounter in many Microsoft Web site articles.

Figure 6-6 shows the Operating System Compatibility interface.

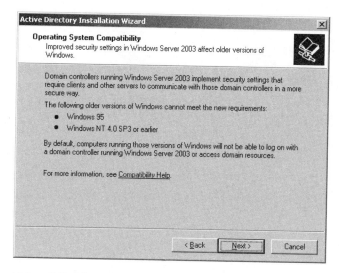

Figure 6-6. *The Operating System Compatibility page.*

Domain and Domain Controller Types

The first decision you must make in the installation process is what type of domain controller is to be created. You must select either to create the first domain controller in a new domain or to create an additional domain controller for an existing domain. Figure 6-7 shows this interface. The default option is to create a new domain and a new domain controller. If you choose to create an additional domain controller in an existing domain, be aware that all local accounts that exist on the server will be deleted, along with any cryptographic keys that are stored on the computer. You will also be prompted to decrypt any encrypted data, because it will be inaccessible after Active Directory is installed.

If you choose to create a new domain, you then must choose whether to create a root domain in a new forest, a child domain in an existing domain, or a new domain tree in an existing forest. Figure 6-8 shows the interface. Consult your Active Directory design documentation (see Chapter 5) to determine the nature of the domain you are creating. To create either a child domain in an existing domain or a new domain tree in an existing forest, you must supply the appropriate network credentials to continue with the installation process. No network credentials are required to create a new forest root domain.

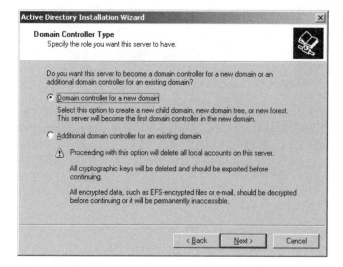

Figure 6-7. *The Domain Controller Type page.*

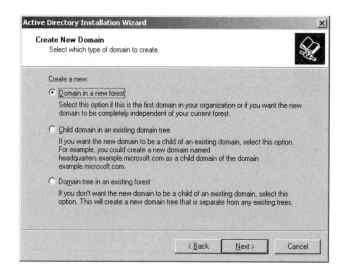

Figure 6-8. *The Create New Domain page.*

Naming the Domain

When creating a new domain controller for a new domain, you must provide both the full DNS name and the NetBIOS name. Figure 6-9 shows the first stage of this interface. There are specific rules you must follow when creating these names.

The full DNS name must contain a unique name for the new domain, and, if creating a child domain, the parent domain must be included in the DNS name and the parent domain must be available. For example, if you are creating the new domain NAmerica in the Contoso.com domain tree, the full DNS name that you must provide would be NAmerica.Contoso.com. When naming the domain, available characters include the case-insensitive letters A through Z, numerals 0 through 9, and the hyphen (-). Each component of the DNS domain name (the sections separated by the dot [.]) cannot be longer than 63 bytes.

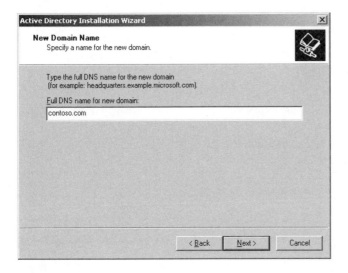

Figure 6-9. *The New Domain Name page.*

After you have entered a DNS name for the domain, you must select a NetBIOS name. Figure 6-10 shows this interface. The NetBIOS name is used by earlier versions of Windows to identify the domain's name. It is a best practice to accept the automatically generated NetBIOS name, which is derived from the previously entered DNS name. The only other restriction to the NetBIOS name is that it does not exceed fourteen characters. Additionally, the NetBIOS name must be unique on the network.

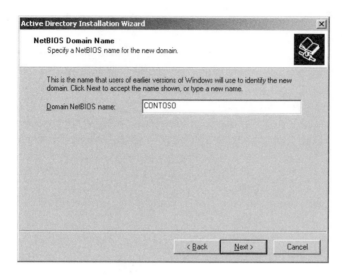

Figure 6-10. *The NetBIOS Domain Name page.*

File Locations

The Active Directory Installation Wizard prompts you to select a location to store the Active Directory database file (Ntds.dit), the Active Directory log files, and the Sysvol shared folder. You can either select the default locations or you can specify the locations for these folders. Figure 6-11 shows this interface.

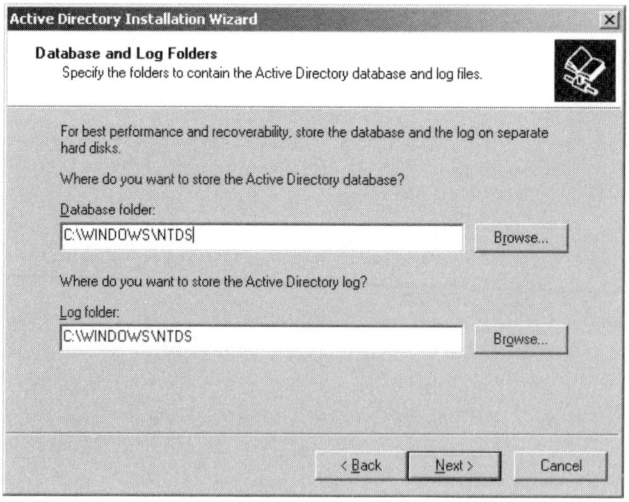

![Active Directory Installation Wizard — Database and Log Folders dialog. Title: "Database and Log Folders. Specify the folders to contain the Active Directory database and log files." Text reads "For best performance and recoverability, store the database and the log on separate hard disks." "Where do you want to store the Active Directory database?" Database folder: C:\WINDOWS\NTDS with Browse... button. "Where do you want to store the Active Directory log?" Log folder: C:\WINDOWS\NTDS with Browse... button. Buttons: Back, Next, Cancel.]

Figure 6-11. *The Database And Log Folders page.*

The default location for both the directory database and the log files is the %systemroot%\system32 folder. However, for best performance, you should configure Active Directory to store the database file and the log files on separate physical hard disks. The Sysvol shared folder default location is %systemdrive%\Windows. The only restriction on selecting the location for the shared Sysvol folder is that it be stored on an NTFS v5 volume. The Sysvol folder stores all of the files that must be accessible to all clients across an Active Directory domain. For example, logon scripts must be accessible to all clients upon logging on to the domain, and they are stored in the Sysvol folder. Figure 6-12 shows this interface.

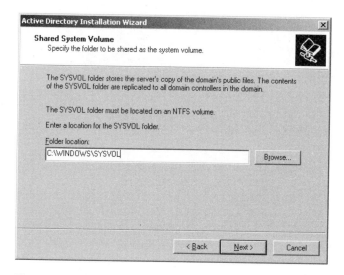

Figure 6-12. *The Shared System Volume page.*

Verify or Install a DNS Server

Active Directory requires DNS to be installed on the network so that client computers can locate domain controllers for authentication. The DNS implementation must also support SRV records to achieve this end. Microsoft recommends that the DNS implementation support dynamic updates. The DNS solution on the network can either be a non-Microsoft DNS solution or a DNS server running Windows NT 4 (SP4), Windows 2000 Server, or Windows Server 2003.

If the computer on which you are installing Active Directory is not a DNS server, or if the Active Directory Installation Wizard does not verify that a DNS server is properly configured for the new domain, the DNS Server service can be installed during the Active Directory installation. (If you are installing an additional domain controller in an existing domain, it is assumed that DNS is in place, and this verification step is skipped.) If a DNS implementation is located on the network but is not configured properly, the Active Directory Installation Wizard DNS Registration Diagnostics window provides a detailed report of the configuration error. At this point, you should make any necessary changes to the DNS configuration and retry the DNS diagnostic routine. As an advanced option, you can continue with the Active Directory installation and manually configure DNS later. Figure 6-13 displays the results of the DNS diagnostics performed while the Active Directory Installation Wizard is running. It also shows the three options for continuing past this point. Notice that the second option, to install and configure the DNS server on this computer, is the default choice in the situation where a DNS server is not found.

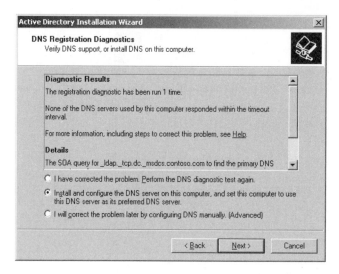

Figure 6-13. *Active Directory Installation Wizard's DNS Registration Diagnostics page.*

If you select the default option to install and configure the DNS server, the DNS server and the DNS Server service will be installed during the installation of Active Directory. The primary DNS zone will match the name of the new Active Directory domain, and it will be configured to accept dynamic updates. The preferred DNS server setting (on the TCP/IP properties sheet) will be updated to point to the local DNS server. (Remember, configuring the local computer IP address before Active Directory installation was recommended earlier in this chapter.)

More Info When the DNS Server service is installed by the Active Directory Installation Wizard, the DNS zone is created as an Active Directory integrated zone. For more information on configuring Active Directory integrated zones, see Chapter 3, "Active Directory and Domain Name System."

Selecting Default Permissions for User and Group Objects

Both Windows Server 2003 and Windows 2000 implement more strict security for user and group object attributes than was available in Windows NT 4. Specifically, access to user objects and group membership is no longer accessible to anonymous user logons by default in the later operating systems. To preserve backward compatibility with pre-Windows-2000-based applications and services (such as Microsoft SQL Server and Remote Access Service [RAS]), Active Directory must be configured to weaken the default security to allow anonymous access to these directory service objects. This is accomplished by adding the Everyone and the Anonymous Logon special groups to the Pre-Windows 2000 Compatible Access local group.

During the installation of Active Directory, you must select the default permissions for user and group objects. On the Permissions page you must select one of two options, as shown in Figure 6-14:

- Permissions Compatible With Pre-Windows 2000 Server Operating Systems
- Permissions Compatible Only With Windows 2000 Or Windows Server 2003 Operating Systems

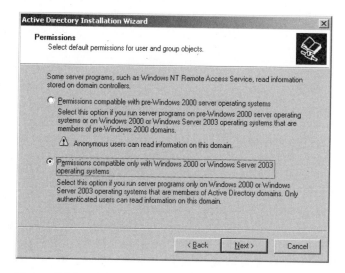

Figure 6-14. *The Permissions page.*

Which option should you choose? If your network environment will include Windows NT servers as well as services or applications that require Windows NT security for users and groups, you should accept the default selection of Permissions Compatible With

Pre-Windows 2000 Server Operating Systems. If your network environment includes only servers running Windows 2000 or Windows Server 2003, or if it will not be running any pre-Windows 2000 server programs, select Permissions Compatible Only With Windows 2000 Or Windows Server 2003 Operating Systems. Keep in mind that, with the default option, anonymous users will be able to access Active Directory data, thus representing compromised security.

After you have upgraded all servers and server programs in the domain to Windows 2000 or Windows Server 2003, you can (and should) reestablish the default Windows Server 2003 permissions for user and group objects. To do this, simply remove all members of the Pre-Windows 2000 Compatible Access local group. In a Windows Server 2003 domain, the members will be the Everyone SID and the Anonymous Logon SID.

To remove the members of this group using the Active Directory Users And Computers administrative tool, open the Builtin container and then double-click the Pre-Windows 2000 Compatible Access group (expand the Name column if necessary). On the Members tab of the group Properties sheet, select both SIDs and click Remove. To use the command line to remove the members of this group, type the following command:

```
net localgroup "Pre-Windows 2000 Compatible Access" Everyone "Anonymous
Logon" /delete
```

With either method, you must reboot every domain controller in the domain for the group membership change to take effect.

Completing the Installation

The final stages of the Active Directory Installation Wizard are straightforward. They involve setting the Directory Services Restore Mode password and reviewing the Summary page. The Directory Services Restore Mode password is used for authenticating to the registry-based security accounts management (SAM) database when the domain controller is started in this special recovery mode. Figure 6-15 shows this interface. The Summary page reports all of the options selected during the Active Directory Installation Wizard.

When you select Finish on the Completing Active Directory Installation window, Windows Server 2003 starts the process of installing and configuring Active Directory on the server. If this is the first domain controller in a new domain, this process is relatively quick, because only the default domain objects are created, and the directory partitions are quickly created. If you are installing an additional domain controller for an existing domain, after the domain controller is created, all of the directory partitions must be fully synchronized. To allow you to delay this full replication process until after the computer restarts, a Finish Replication Later button appears at the beginning of the initial replication process. Select this option to allow the normal replication process to synchronize the directory partitions on this domain controller at a later time.

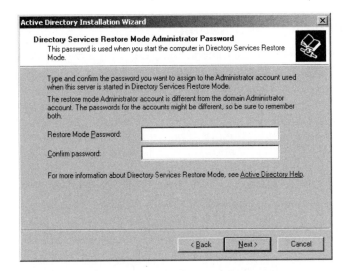

Figure 6-15. *The Directory Services Restore Mode Administrator Password page.*

Since the initial replication of the directory partition data can be time-consuming, especially across slow network links, Active Directory in Windows Server 2003 offers the new feature of installing an additional domain controller from restored backup files. This feature is discussed in detail later in this chapter.

Best Practices   After you install Active Directory, you should open the Active Directory Users And Computers administrative tool and verify that all of the Builtin security principals were created, such as the Administrator user account and the Domain Admins and Enterprise Admins security groups. You should also verify the creation of the "special identities" such as Authenticated Users and Interactive. Special identities are commonly known as groups, but you cannot view their membership. Instead, users will automatically be joined to these groups as they log on or access particular resources. These special identities, however, are not displayed in the Active Directory Users And Computers administrative tool by default. To view these objects, select View and then select Advanced Features. This will display additional components in the tool that are not visible by default. Now, open the Foreign Security Principals container. There you will find the objects S-1-5-11 and S-1-5-4, which are the Authenticated Users SID and the Interactive SID, respectively. Double-click these objects to view their properties and default permissions.

Performing an Unattended Installation

To install Active Directory without user interaction, you can use the /answer[:*filename*] parameter with the Dcpromo command. With this parameter you must include the filename for the answer file. The answer file contains all of the data that is normally required during the installation process. You can also install Active Directory while installing Windows Server 2003 in unattended mode. In this scenario, you will use the *E:\J386\winnt32 /unattend[:**unattend.txt**]* command, where *unattend.txt* is the name of the answer file used for the full Windows Server 2003 installation. (It is assumed that the CD-ROM drive is drive E and that you have the Windows Server 2003 installation disc in that drive.) Specifically, *Unattend.txt* must contain the [DCInstall] section to be able to install Active Directory.

To perform an unattended installation of Active Directory after the Windows Server 2003 operating system has been installed, you will create an answer file that just contains the [DCInstall] section of the answer file. To execute this limited unattended installation, at the command prompt or in the Run dialog box type *dcpromo /answer:***answerfile** (where *answerfile* is the name of the answer file). The answer file is an ASCII text file that contains all of the information required to complete the pages of the Active Directory Installation Wizard. To create a new domain in a new tree in a new forest, with the DNS Server service automatically configured, the contents of the answer file would look like this:

```
[DCInstall]

UserName=admin_username
Password=admin_password
UserDomain=admin_domain
DatabasePath=
LogPath=
SYSVOLPath=
SafeModeAdminPassword=password
ReplicaOrNewDomain=Domain
NewDomain=Forest
NewDomainDNSName=DNSdomainname
DNSOnNetwork
DomainNetbiosName=NetBIOSdomainname
AutoConfigDNS=yes
AllowAnonymousAccess=yes
CriticalReplicationOnly=yes
SiteName=
RebootOnSuccess=yes
```

For keys with no values set, or if a key is omitted, the default value will be used. The required keys for the answer file will change depending on the type of domain to be created (new or existing forest, new or existing tree). For more information regarding keys and appropriate values, see *http://support.microsoft.com/default.aspx?scid=kb%3ben-us%3b223757*. An additional key that can be used for promoting a domain controller using a restore from backup media is ReplicationSourcePath. To use this key, assign the value of the location of the restored backup files that will be used to populate the directory database for the first time. (This is the same as the path to the restored backup files that is selected when using this feature through the Active Directory Installation Wizard.) See the following section, "Installing Active Directory from Restored Backup Files," for more information on this feature.

> **Note**   For information on creating the unattended answer file for installing Active Directory, right-click the Deploy.cab file in the Support\Tools folder of the Windows Server 2003 compact disc, select Explore from the shortcut menu, right-click Ref.chm, select Extract, then double-click Ref.chm in the extract target location. The Deploy.cab file also includes Setupmgr.exe, the Setup Manager utility, a GUI that is used to create the *Unattend.txt* file for installing Windows Server 2003 including Active Directory (creates the [DCInstall] section). This cabinet file also includes the "Microsoft Windows Corporate Deployment Tools User's Guide" (Deploy.chm), which describes the unattended answer file section headings, keys, and values for each key in the [Unattended] and the [DCInstall] sections of the *Unattend.txt* file.

Installing Active Directory from Restored Backup Files

In Windows Server 2003 you have the ability to install an additional domain controller, using the Active Directory Installation Wizard, with the initial population of the three directory partitions being copied from the restore of a previously created backup set instead of across the network using the normal replication process. The benefit of this feature is that new domain controllers can be fully synchronized much faster. Otherwise, relying on the normal replication process to create the domain partitions may take hours or days. This method will most likely be used in environments with either low network bandwidth or very large directory partitions (or both). The process of installing from a restored backup is not designed for restoring failed existing domain controllers; System State restores are still the prescribed method for accomplishing that task.

After the domain controller is synchronized using the restored backup data, replication will occur to update the new domain controller with any changes that have occurred since the backup set was created. To minimize this replication time, always use a recent backup of the Active Directory data. Specifically, the backup set cannot be older than the tombstone lifetime of the domain, which has a default value of 60 days. The System State backup must be from a Windows Server 2003 domain controller within the same domain in which the new domain controller is being created—backups from a Windows 2000 domain controller are incompatible with this feature. The only other restriction is that the backup file be restored to a local drive and accessed from a logical drive letter (UNC paths and mapped drives are not allowed as part of the */adv* parameter). For more information on creating a backup of the Active Directory partitions, see Chapter 15, "Disaster Recovery."

➲ **To create an additional domain controller from restored backup files, perform the following steps:**

1. Create and verify a System State backup on a domain controller in the domain. Restore this backup to a local drive or network location where it can be accessed (by drive letter) by the server running Windows Server 2003 that is to be promoted.

2. On the server running Windows Server 2003 that is to be promoted, start the Active Directory Installation Wizard from the command line or the Run dialog box using the */adv* parameter. Type *dcpromo /adv*.

3. On the Domain Controller Type page, select Additional Domain Controller For An Existing Domain.

4. On the Copying Domain Files page, select the location of the restored backup files.

5. In the Copy Domain Information dialog box, select the location of the restored backup files for this domain.

6. Complete the rest of the Active Directory Installation Wizard as described in the previous sections.

Creating an additional domain controller from the restored backup files still requires network connectivity and an available domain controller, in the same domain, during the Active Directory installation process. The contents of the Sysvol share, for example, are replicated to the new domain controller outside of this process. Replication will still take place between an up-to-date and the newly-promoted domain controller for all objects created after the backup set was created.

More Info For organizations deploying Active Directory that have a number of small remote sites connected by slow links to either a regional hub or data center, see the "Active Directory Branch Office Guide" at *http://www.microsoft.com /windows2000/techinfo/planning/activedirectory/branchoffice/default.asp*. This series includes both a planning guide and a deployment guide to assist you in designing a deployment strategy for installing Active Directory in a branch office scenario, as well as the step-by-step procedures to implement the strategy.

Removing Active Directory

Active Directory is removed from a domain controller using the same command that is used to install it—Dcpromo.exe. When you run this command on a computer that is already a domain controller, the Active Directory Installation Wizard notifies you that it will uninstall Active Directory if you choose to proceed. What Wizard pages follow depend on whether the domain controller from which you are removing Active Directory is the last domain controller for the domain or not. This section will discuss the implications of removing Active Directory from both the last domain controller and an additional domain controller in a Windows Server 2003 domain.

What happens to the domain controller when you remove Active Directory? At a high level, the directory database is deleted, all of the services required for Active Directory are stopped and removed, the local SAM database is created, and the computer is demoted to a stand-alone or member server. More specifically, what happens will depend on whether the domain controller is an additional domain controller, or the last domain controller in the domain or forest.

To remove Active Directory from a domain controller, type *dcpromo* at the command prompt or in the Run dialog box. Your first decision is to determine whether the domain controller is an additional domain controller or the last domain controller in the domain. See Figure 6-16 for an illustration of the Wizard page that prompts you for that decision.

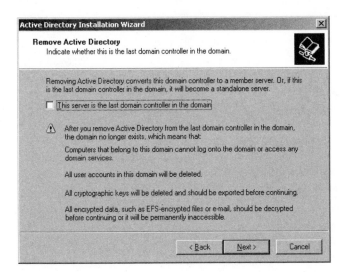

Figure 6-16. *The option to remove the last domain controller.*

Next, the Active Directory Installation Wizard displays a list of all of the application directory partitions found on the domain controller. If this is the last domain controller in the domain, then this is the last source for this application data. You may want to back up or otherwise protect this data before continuing to use Active Directory Installation Wizard, which will delete these directory partitions. If the domain controller from which you are removing Active Directory is also a DNS server, there will be at least two application directory partitions to store the zone data. See Figure 6-17 for an example of DNS application directory partitions found while uninstalling Active Directory.

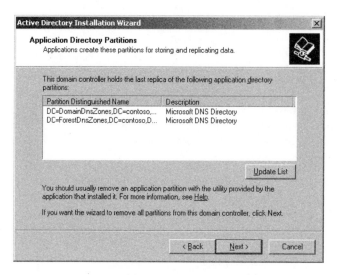

Figure 6-17. *Removing the DNS application directory partitions.*

After you confirm the removal of the application directory partitions, you are prompted to enter a new password for the local Administrator account. Finally, review the Summary page and complete the removal of Active Directory. You must restart the computer to complete the process. After the computer restarts, it will hold the role either of member server or stand-alone server.

Removing Additional Domain Controllers

Removing Active Directory from additional domain controllers is not as intricate as removing Active Directory from the last domain controller in a domain or forest. This is because with additional domain controllers, there are replicas of the directory partitions stored on the other domain controllers, so no data is actually lost. A number of interesting changes do occur on the domain controller as Active Directory is uninstalled. These include:

- All operations master roles are transferred to other domain controllers in the domain.
- The Sysvol folder and all of its contents are removed from the domain controller.
- The *NTDS Settings* object and cross-references are removed.
- DNS is updated to remove the domain controller SRV records.

- The local SAM database is created to handle local security policy.
- All Active Directory–related services that are started when Active Directory is installed (such as Net Logon) are stopped.

Finally, the computer account type is changed from domain controller to member server, and the computer account is moved from the Domain Controllers container to the Computers container. To remove Active Directory from an additional domain controller, you must be logged on as either a member of the Domain Admins or the Enterprise Admins group.

> **Note**   When removing Active Directory from an additional domain controller, make sure that there are other GCs available in the domain. GCs are required for user logon, and this role is not automatically transferred as the operations master roles are.

Removing the Last Domain Controller

In addition to all of the interesting things that occur when an additional domain controller is removed, there are specific events that occur when the last domain controller in a domain is removed. Most importantly, of course, the removal of the last domain controller in a domain serves to remove the domain itself. Likewise, if the domain controller is the last in a forest, the forest is also removed. The events associated with the removal of the last domain controller in a domain include:

- Active Directory Installation Wizard verifies that no child domains exist. Removal of Active Directory is blocked if child domains are found.
- If the domain to be removed is a child domain, a domain controller in the parent domain is contacted and changes are replicated.
- All objects related to this domain are removed from the forest.
- Any trust objects on the parent domain controller are removed.

Finally, after Active Directory is removed, the computer account type is changed from a domain controller to a stand-alone server. The server is then placed in a workgroup called Workgroup.

The administrative permissions required to remove the last domain controller in a child domain or in a tree-root domain are that you either be logged on as a member of the Enterprise Admins group or that you provide enterprise administrator credentials during the running of the Active Directory Installation Wizard. If you are removing Active Directory from the last domain controller in the forest, you must be logged on either as Administrator or as a member of the Domain Admins group.

Unattended Removal of Active Directory

Removal of Active Directory can be automated in a fashion similar to the unattended installation previously discussed. In fact, the same command line is used to remove Active Directory as is used to install it. The only difference is the content of the answer file.

To perform an unattended removal of Active Directory, at the command line or in the Run dialog box, type *dcpromo /answer:***answerfile** (where *answerfile* is the filename of the answer file that you create). The answer file contains the key values that represent the decisions discussed earlier for using the Active Directory Installation Wizard to uninstall Active Directory. A key value of note is *IsLastDCInDomain*, which can have the value of *Yes* or *No*. If you set the value of this key to *Yes*, then you have indicated that you are removing Active Directory from the last domain controller in the domain, and the domain itself will be removed. A sample answer file for removing an additional domain controller is reproduced below:

```
[DCInstall]
RebootOnSuccess=Yes
IsLastDCInDomain=No
AdministratorPassword=password
Password=password
UserName=Administrator
```

Summary

In this chapter you were introduced to the major decisions you must make during a Windows Server 2003 Active Directory installation. While the mechanics of installing Active Directory are straightforward, the decisions that you will make should be carefully planned and must fit into your Active Directory design plan. Similarly, removal of Active Directory is a simple procedure, but you must consider the impact on the rest of your directory services infrastructure caused by removing a domain controller. This chapter also introduced a new Active Directory installation feature, installing an additional, or replica, domain controller from restored backup files. This feature will greatly reduce the amount of time it takes to install an additional domain controller due to the time it takes to synchronize the directory partitions.

Chapter 7
Migrating to Active Directory

Chapter 6, "Installing Active Directory," covered the key decisions you will have to make when installing Active Directory directory service on a server-class computer. For ease of understanding, that chapter assumed a "green field" environment—one with no pre-existing directory service infrastructure to consider. Chapter 6 emphasized the importance of the Active Directory namespace and the Domain Name System (DNS) namespace. In reality, a green field environment will not often be encountered. More likely, the organization that is moving (or *migrating*) to Active Directory and Microsoft Windows Server 2003 will be coming from some pre-existing directory services environment. This chapter examines the migration to Windows Server 2003 Active Directory from an existing Microsoft directory services environment—specifically, from a Microsoft Windows NT 4 security accounts management (SAM) or the Microsoft Windows 2000 Active Directory platform. Migration scenarios from non-Microsoft directory services technologies, such as Novell Directory Services (NDS) or NetWare 3 Bindery, or UNIX-based directory services implementations, are outside the scope of this chapter.

More Info The Microsoft Web site hosts a great many pages of information on migrating to Windows servers from other platforms. For more information on migrating from a UNIX or Linux environment, see the "Migrating to Windows from UNIX and Linux" section of the Windows Web site at *http://www.microsoft.com /windows2000/migrate/unix/default.asp*. For more information on migrating from a Novell NetWare environment, see "NetWare to Windows 2000 Server Migration Planning Guide" at *http://www.microsoft.com/windows2000/techinfo/planning /incremental/netmigrate.asp*. For comprehensive information on migrating to Windows 2000 Server as well as Windows server technologies, see "Migrating to Windows" at *http://www.microsoft.com/windows2000/migrate/*.

This chapter begins with a discussion of the different migration path options you have when moving to Windows Server 2003 Active Directory. It then looks at the key points of each migration path and the procedures required for performing the migration.

Note The primary focus of this chapter is on the Windows NT 4 to Windows Server 2003 directory service migration process. This migration scenario represents the greatest change in technology and, as a result, is a complex process. Because Windows Server 2003 Active Directory is not substantially different from Windows 2000 Active Directory, the migration process is not very complex. Key points of the Windows 2000 migration scenarios are covered in the sections "Upgrading from Windows 2000 Server" and "Upgrading Then Restructuring," later in this chapter. Therefore, unless otherwise identified, the migration processes described in this chapter pertain to the Windows NT 4 to Windows Server 2003 directory services migration scenario.

Note that, unless otherwise specifically limited, references to Windows 2000 Server include Windows 2000 Server, Windows 2000 Advanced Server, and Windows 2000 Datacenter Server.

Migration Paths

If directory services migration can be described as getting from Point A to Point B, then Point A is your current directory services infrastructure; Point B is your desired Windows Server 2003 Active Directory structure. The first decision you need to make when planning to migrate to Windows Server 2003 Active Directory is how to get to "Point B." Not surprisingly, there are several ways to get from A to B on what are called *migration paths*. Your migration path will be the fundamental component in the overall plan that is your *migration strategy*. Your migration strategy includes how you intend to migrate, what directory services objects you will move, and in what order you will move them. A best practice for any directory services migration project is to document every detail of the migration strategy into an actionable document called the *migration plan*.

There are three migration paths from which to choose:

- Domain upgrade
- Domain restructure
- Upgrade then restructure

A domain upgrade migration path is achieved by upgrading the operating system on a down-level domain controller to Windows Server 2003. In the case of Windows NT 4, when a down-level domain controller is upgraded, the directory services are also upgraded from the Windows NT 4 SAM database to Windows Server 2003 Active Directory. Using the earlier example, Point A is upgraded from Windows NT 4 or Windows 2000 to Windows Server 2003 and becomes Point B. At the time of completion, Point A ceases to exist. The domain upgrade migration path is the least complex migration method. For this reason, you might consider it the default migration option.

The second option is the domain restructure migration path. During a domain restructure, directory services objects are copied from the existing directory services platform (Point A) to Windows Server 2003 Active Directory (Point B). This process is also referred to as *cloning*. In a domain restructure, Point A and Point B coexist. When all of the directory services objects are migrated from A to B, and all clients and computers have been configured to use the new directory service, Point A can simply be turned off. If your specific conditions indicate that a domain restructure is the appropriate migration path, there are several additional considerations to take into account as compared to a domain upgrade migration path. These factors are discussed in the sections that follow.

The third migration path, the upgrade-then-restructure migration path, is also known as the *two-phase migration*, or the *hybrid* migration. In short, the upgrade-then-restructure method is achieved by first upgrading the Windows NT 4 domain or domains and then migrating the accounts into new or existing Windows Server 2003 domains. This method combines the short-term benefits of the domain upgrade path and the long-term benefits of the domain restructure. You will see how this migration path offers these benefits as you read the migration path decision criteria later in this chapter.

The next few sections outline the advantages and disadvantages of each of these three paths.

The Domain Upgrade Migration Path

A domain upgrade, also known as an *in-place* upgrade, is the most straightforward of the three migration choices. It is the process of determining that a domain upgrade is the best path for your organization, however, that might prove a more difficult task. In a domain upgrade, the existing directory services platform is converted to Active Directory at the same time that the domain controller is upgraded to Windows Server 2003. One reason that a domain upgrade is a straightforward procedure is because you do not have the opportunity to modify the domain structure during the upgrade. For example, if you are the administrator for the NAmerica domain of Contoso.com, a Windows NT 4–based domain environment, then by definition you will be the administrator of the NAmerica domain in Windows Server 2003 after the upgrade. In a domain upgrade, you do not have the opportunity to change the domain structure, or even the domain name, of the source domain.

Note   In migration parlance, the *source domain* is the domain from which you are migrating, what was referred to earlier as "Point A." The domain structure that you are migrating to is known as the target domain—"Point B." In a domain upgrade scenario, the original domain is considered the source domain until such time as the Active Directory installation is complete, at which point the target domain is realized.

Windows NT 4 Upgrade

Perhaps the most common migration scenario is the Windows NT 4 directory services migration to Windows Server 2003 Active Directory. Despite its age, Windows NT Server 4 maintains a stronghold in the enterprise network operating system (NOS) marketplace. As of the date of publication, Microsoft has announced retirement plans for Windows NT Server 4 and will phase out the support channels for the product over the course of the next several months. With the release of Windows Server 2003, many organizations that chose not to upgrade to Windows 2000 Server will be upgrading to Windows Server 2003 Active Directory.

Windows 2000 Server Upgrade

An even more straightforward migration path is available for current Windows 2000 Server customers who are planning to upgrade to Windows Server 2003. Many of the directory service's architectural changes were most likely implemented either when customers created their Windows 2000 network environment or when they upgraded from Windows NT Server 4. The customer migrating to Windows Server 2003 Active Directory from Windows 2000 is most likely planning to capitalize on the new features available in the Windows Server 2003 version of Active Directory.

More Info For more information on the new features available in Windows Server 2003 Active Directory, see "What's New in Windows Server 2003 Active Directory" in Chapter 1, "Active Directory Concepts."

As with the Windows NT 4 to Windows Server 2003 upgrade scenario, the Active Directory migration is accomplished by upgrading the operating system on the domain controllers. Once the upgrade is complete, you can begin to take advantage of the desirable new features in Windows Server 2003 Active Directory. Might a Windows 2000 Server customer choose to perform a domain restructure instead of a domain upgrade? Yes, for the same reasons you will see a Windows NT Server 4 customer choose to restructure the domain--because the directory services infrastructure no longer meets the business needs of the organization. The Windows 2000 Server customer will most likely upgrade the NOS and then restructure, rather than perform a pure domain restructure.

There are two pre-migration steps you must perform when you upgrade from Windows 2000 Server to Windows Server 2003. You must first prepare the Active Directory forest and then prepare the Active Directory domain for Windows Server 2003. Fortunately, there are two tools provided in the \I386 folder on the Windows Server 2003 compact disc to help you complete these tasks: ForestPrep and DomainPrep. The procedures for preparing the forest and domain prior to upgrading are covered later in this chapter in the "Upgrading from Windows 2000 Server" section.

Renaming the Domain

Upgrading either a Windows NT 4 or a Windows 2000 domain to a Windows Server 2003 Active Directory domain does not change the name of the domain. One of the new features in Windows Server 2003 Active Directory is the set of Domain Rename tools. Once all the domains are running Windows Server 2003 and the forest functional level has been raised to Windows Server 2003, you can use the Domain Rename tools to change the name of the upgraded domain to meet the current needs of your organization. The tools provide the following functionality:

- Can rename the domain without repositioning any domain in the forest
- Can create a new domain tree structure by repositioning domains within a tree
- Can create new domain trees

The domain rename tools can be used to modify the name of the forest root domain, but you cannot modify which domain is the forest root domain. You cannot add or remove domains from the forest using these tools. To rename Windows Server 2003 domains, you must first install the Windows Server 2003 Domain Rename tools. These tools, Rendom.exe and Gpfixup.exe, are available on the Windows Server 2003 compact disc at \VALUEADD\MSFT\MGMT\DOMREN. The Windows Server 2003 Domain Rename tools are also available from the Microsoft Web site at *http://www.microsoft.com /windowsserver2003/downloads/domainrename.mspx*. Domain Rename is only available for Windows Server 2003 and is not supported by Windows 2000 domains.

For more information on using the Domain Rename tools, see the "Understanding How Domain Rename Works" article at *http://www.microsoft.com/windowsserver2003/docs /Domain-Rename-Intro.doc*. For detailed deployment procedures for the Domain Rename tools, see the "Step-by-Step Guide to Implementing Domain Rename" article at *http: //www.microsoft.com/windowsserver2003/docs/Domain-Rename-Procedure.doc*.

The Domain Restructure Migration Path

In performing a domain restructure, a new Windows Server 2003 directory services infrastructure is created, and the directory services objects are then migrated into this new environment. An obvious advantage of this migration path is that the original Windows NT 4 environment is unaffected during the creation of the target environment, also known as the *pristine forest*. While the image of a glistening, undisturbed woodland is certainly appealing, it will not take long to fill it up with directory services objects—namely your users, groups, and computers. The good news is that a domain restructure is a selective process. Unlike a domain upgrade, you get to choose what objects you want to migrate to the new platform. (A domain upgrade is an all-or-nothing proposition—every object in the Windows NT 4 domain is upgraded to Windows Server 2003 and Windows Server 2003 Active Directory.) A domain restructure project is a perfect time to dump all of those duplicate, nonactive, test, and otherwise defunct user and group accounts. They will disappear when you cut over to the new domain model and repurpose those old domain controllers.

Moving vs. Cloning

User, group, service, and computer accounts, also called *security principals*, are migrated from SAM, the Windows NT Server 4 directory service, to Active Directory. This migration can be performed in two ways; accounts can be either *moved* or *cloned*. Moving an object removes the original security principal in the source domain during the migration process. Moving is a destructive process, and it does not preserve the source domain objects for the purposes of rollback (disaster recovery). Cloning is the process of creating a new, identical security principal in the target domain based on the object in the source domain. The preferred method of transferring the security principals into the Windows Server 2003 pristine forest is cloning. Moving of security principals is more commonly performed when doing an interforest migration between two Windows Server 2003 forests, or between a Windows 2000 forest and a Windows Server 2003 forest.

The upgrade-then-restructure migration scenario is covered in the section "Upgrading then Restructuring," later in this chapter.

Understanding SID History

When you migrate user accounts from one domain to another, how do those user accounts maintain access to resources, such as printers and shared folders?

Consider the following example: During a domain restructure operation, you migrate a batch of user accounts from a Windows NT 4 domain to a Windows Server 2003 domain. Upon completion of the account migration, you instruct the users to log on to the new domain and reset their passwords. User X successfully logs on to the target domain and then attempts to access a pre-existing shared folder on a file server running Windows NT 4 Server—one that he has been accessing for months. Will User X be able to access the folder?

The answer is yes, thanks to the *SID-History* attribute.

SID-History is an attribute of Active Directory security principals (such as User accounts and Group accounts) that is used to store the former security identifiers (SIDs) of that object. So, for example, if User X in the example above had in the Windows NT 4 domain, the SID of S-1-5-21-2127521184-1604012920-1887927527-324294, that same value would now appear in the *SID-History* attribute field for the newly created Windows Server 2003 account object. As groups are migrated from the Windows NT 4 domain to the Active Directory domain, the SID from the Windows NT 4 domain is also retained in the *SID-History* attribute for the group. As users and groups are migrated, the migrated user accounts are automatically assigned to the migrated groups in the Windows Server 2003 domain. This means that the access assigned to the groups in the Windows NT 4 domain is retained during the migration process. During the migration process, the SID from the source domain is moved to the *SID-History* attribute. The new SID generated by the target domain controller is placed in the *SID* attribute of the migrated account.

How does this preserve access to resources following a migration? When User X attempts to access the shared folder on the Windows NT 4 file server, the security subsystem checks his access token to ensure that he has the necessary permissions to the folder. The access token not only contains User X's SID and the SIDs of all the groups that he or she belongs to, but all the *SID-History* entries for both the user and group accounts as well. When a match is found between the discretionary access control list (DACL) on the folder's security descriptor and the previous SID (now included in the access token by way of the *SID-History* attribute), permission is granted and the folder is accessed.

How much of this does the end user need to know? None. How much of this do you as an administrator need to know? All of it. Accessing resources is the most troublesome area of user account migration. By understanding how permissions are maintained following a migration, you as the administrator can effectively troubleshoot resource access issues. During the migration, you might need to take additional steps to ensure that the *SID-History* field is populated. You will learn more about this when examining the Windows Server 2003 migration utility: the Active Directory Migration Tool (ADMT).

How does SID-History work in a domain upgrade scenario? The answer is: not at all. During a domain upgrade, the SID is maintained with the user and group accounts. User X will be able to access resources as normal. How does SID-History work in an upgrade-then-restructure scenario? The answer is: the same as in the pure domain upgrade scenario—resource access is preserved by maintaining the original object's SID in the *SID-History* attribute. The only difference is that Active Directory requires that SIDs can only appear one time throughout the forest—including both the *SID* and *SID-History* fields. As a result, in an upgrade-then-restructure scenario, security principals must be moved rather than cloned.

The Upgrade-Then-Restructure Migration Path

As described earlier, the upgrade-then-restructure migration path is a combination of the two main migration paths. First the Windows NT 4 domain is upgraded to Windows Server 2003 and Windows Server 2003 Active Directory. Then, as your migration schedule allows, the accounts are restructured into new or existing Windows Server 2003 domains. This method provides the benefits of a domain upgrade (speed, low risk, high level of automation) with the long-term benefits of a domain restructure (creates a new domain model, is implemented in phases, clears out old and unnecessary account objects).

The advantage of the upgrade-then-restructure domain migration path is time, in several dimensions. First, upgrading the domains from Windows NT 4 to Windows Server 2003 is the most expedient migration path. Next, the process of restructuring the account objects can be performed over time, as your schedule, resources, and budget allow. Another benefit of this path is that it allows the network administrators the opportunity to get familiar with the new directory services environment before diving into a domain redesign or a somewhat risky migration project. This path also has the benefit to end users that their network services world does not change overnight—first they are upgraded to a new NOS, and then, over time, restructured into a different domain model.

Determining Your Migration Path

Keep in mind when deciding on a migration path that it is a per-domain decision and that it is completely legitimate to use different migration paths for different domains within your organization. A popular migration strategy is to upgrade the Windows NT 4 master accounts domain and then restructure the Windows NT 4 resource domains into the new Windows Server 2003 domain. Or, if your Windows NT 4 domain model is geographically oriented, you might upgrade one or two of the larger domains and then restructure the smaller domains into these larger ones, preserving their administrative autonomy through organizational units (OUs). Both of these scenarios are examples of *domain consolidation*.

Now that you have learned the basics of the three different migration paths, let's take a look at the decision criteria used to choose among these paths.

Migration Path Decision Criteria

The following questions are relevant in determining the most appropriate migration path for your organization:

1. Are you satisfied with your current domain model? Does the existing Windows NT 4 domain model meet your current organizational and business needs?

2. How much risk can you tolerate in migrating to a new domain model?

3. How much time do you have available to perform the migration?

4. What is the amount of system uptime required over the course of the migration project?

5. What resources are available to complete the migration?

6. What is the migration project budget?

7. How many server-based applications that will not run on Windows Server 2003 will need to be supported after the migration?

Imagine the possible answers to these questions on a spectrum from low to high, with domain upgrade aligning with the low end of the spectrum and domain restructure aligning with the high end. For the upgrade-then-restructure migration path, you will likely see a combination of business requirements on each side of the spectrum, or somewhere in the middle. See Figure 7-1 for an illustration of this conceptualization.

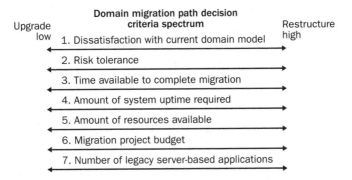

Figure 7-1. *The domain migration path decision criteria spectrum.*

Choosing the Domain Upgrade Path

Keeping in mind the questions asked above, let's look at the conditions that would indicate what domain upgrade migration path best suits your organization.

Satisfaction with Current Domain Model

If there are no major changes desired of the domain model as part of the upgrade to Windows Server 2003, the domain upgrade will provide the easiest migration path. The name of the domain will remain the same, as will the existence of all user and group accounts. A domain upgrade is an "all or nothing" proposition—you will simply be creating a Windows Server 2003 version of your current directory services implementation.

Risk Tolerance Is Low

In addition to offering the easiest migration path, a domain upgrade is also the lowest-risk method. The process is carried out automatically when you upgrade the operating system on Windows NT 4 Server–based domain controllers. Without user interaction, there are few opportunities for error. The disaster recovery methodology for a domain upgrade is relatively straightforward as well. If the upgrade fails, turn off the upgraded primary domain controller (PDC), promote any up-to-date backup domain controller (BDC) to the PDC, and start again.

Limited Time Available to Complete Migration

While the migration timeline is not often the most decisive factor in selecting a migration path, it can be a significant consideration for smaller organizations with limited resources to dedicate to the migration project. Because there are far fewer steps involved in a domain upgrade than in a domain restructure, it takes less time to complete overall. In comparison, a domain restructure requires sufficient time to both create and test the target domain infrastructure, and the time necessary to migrate all of the accounts from the source to the domain. Very large organizations might not be able to migrate all of the objects at one time, so it is not uncommon for a domain restructure to occur in several phases over a period of time. In contrast, a domain upgrade is a linear process and must be completed once begun.

Low System Uptime Required

Another timeline consideration is the amount of directory services uptime needed during the migration process. During a domain upgrade, the account objects (users, groups, computers) are themselves upgraded into Windows Server 2003 objects. As a result of this process, these resources are not available during the migration itself. A domain upgrade incurs network resource access downtime for the period of time necessary for the NOS upgrade to complete. Depending upon the size of your Windows NT 4 domain and the number of verification steps you put in place, this can certainly take the better part of a day (if all goes according to plan). So, an organization that will choose a domain upgrade migration path will need to accommodate some amount of directory services downtime.

Limited Resources Available

Because the domain upgrade is a less complex operation, or at least a highly automated one, it will require fewer resources to perform this migration path. Organizations that are not able to staff the more complex tasks of a domain restructure might choose this path.

Migration Project Budget Is Small

A domain upgrade is a less expensive proposition than a domain restructure for the simple fact that you can use the existing server hardware. That is not to say that you would want to do that—in fact, a NOS upgrade is likely a perfect time to upgrade the hardware for domain controllers and other mission-critical servers (e-mail, Web servers, etc.). However, if your current server hardware is functionally capable of running Windows Server 2003, you can spend less money performing a domain upgrade. For one thing, you will avoid having to purchase additional servers needed to create the pristine forest environment required of a domain restructure. Other contributing budgetary factors will be the lower resources required (including minimized contract spending and lost-opportunity costs for full-time resources) as well as the reduced test spending (as there are fewer migration tasks to test).

Server-Based Applications that Won't Run on Windows Server 2003

A domain upgrade is a good choice if the domain controllers you want to upgrade are not running a network service or line-of-business application that requires Windows NT Server 4 as the operating system. These applications can include a fax or communication application, an accounting application, or any other server-based application that does not get upgraded very often. If these services and applications exist in your organization, it is well worth your time to test all of your line-of-business applications on a

Windows Server 2003 computer and determine that the applications are functioning properly. If you determine that you have applications that will not run on Windows Server 2003, you have several choices: you can postpone the upgrade until a compatible version of the application is available or a suitable substitute is found; transfer the application off the domain controller onto a member server in the domain (if possible); or not upgrade that Windows NT Server 4–based member server until the new version becomes available. Keep in mind that a Windows NT 4–based member server can coexist indefinitely on your Windows Server 2003–based network.

Note To support Windows NT 4 BDCs on your Windows Server 2003 network, be sure not to raise the domain functional level from the default value of Windows 2000 mixed or, if there are no Windows 2000 Servers in the domain, above the Windows Server 2003 interim functional level.

Choosing the Domain Restructure Path

The following are the characteristics of an organization that is well suited to select the domain restructure migration path.

Not Satisfied with Current Domain Model

If the current Windows NT 4 domain model no longer meets the business or organizational needs of your organization; is out of date due to mergers, acquisitions, spin-offs, or other organizational changes; or otherwise reflects a less than optimal network services platform for your organization, your best choice is to select the domain restructure migration path. This will enable you to start fresh with an Active Directory design that meets both your business and organizational needs. Considering the time and effort it will take to deploy Active Directory throughout your enterprise, it only makes sense to start with a design that will make your life as easy as possible.

Risk Tolerance Is High

As previously stated, the domain restructure path is a more complex, higher-risk process than a domain upgrade. There are more tasks to perform and more things that can go wrong. And when things go wrong during a directory services migration, the result is unhappy users who cannot log on, access necessary resources, or get to their e-mail Inboxes. If you are equipped to manage this risk, do not avoid performing a domain restructure. How do you manage these risks? Planning, testing, training, and support.

Sufficient Time Available to Complete the Migration

Being more complex and involving more tasks, the domain restructure takes more time. However, if your migration project schedule is sufficient to permit the necessary planning, testing, and migration tasks, do not avoid the domain restructure path.

High System Uptime Required

If you work in an organization where system uptime is a critical metric, for example in an e-commerce business where every minute of downtime is computed by the accountants as lost revenue, a domain restructure is a good choice. Since the domain restructure migration path involves the creation of a separate pristine forest and leaves the source environment essentially unchanged, directory services uptime is preserved by having users continue to function in the existing environment. You can migrate either large or small batches of users during non-peak hours and leave those new accounts inactive until such time as you are ready to cut over (make the transition from the original directory service environment to Windows Server 2003 Active Directory).

Adequate Resources Available

Because there are more tasks involved with a domain restructure than with a domain upgrade, it will require more resources. Be sure you will be adequately staffed to handle the additional workload of a domain restructure when selecting this migration path. Do not forget to account for all of the routine responsibilities your staff will not be performing due to the time spent on the restructure. Chances are that you will not be able to suspend network backup procedures for several weeks because your technicians are setting up a test lab—so be sure to backfill existing roles if you are doing the migration with in-house staff. Alternatively, there are plenty of consulting groups that specialize in migration projects—you might want to outsource some or all of the project. This will save the time and money involved in training your in-house resources to perform all of the migration tasks.

Unconstrained Migration Project Budget

For a variety of reasons, a domain restructure will require a greater budget than a domain upgrade. Many of these additional expenses are related to the number and complexity of the required tasks in domain restructuring. There is also the budget consideration of the hardware requirements to build the pristine forest environment into which you will migrate your directory services objects. However, if you are now at the point of upgrading from Windows NT 4, these hardware expenses are likely to occur in any of the three migration scenarios.

Server-Based Applications Require Windows NT Server 4 as the NOS

If you maintain network services or line-of-business applications that will only run on Windows NT Server 4–based domain controllers, you obviously will not want to perform a domain upgrade for the domain that contains these computers. This fact might influence you to migrate the security principals through a domain restructure instead, and then to upgrade the domain controller after the application or service has either been moved to a member server or you are able to implement a Windows Server 2003–compatible version or alternative to this application.

Choosing the Upgrade-Then-Restructure Path

If you find that your company does not meet the conditions described above for favoring either the upgrade or restructure migration paths, or if perhaps you see your organization as fitting both, you might choose the third alternative—upgrade then restructure. You might consider the upgrade-then-restructure migration path if you want the quick benefits of going to Active Directory (including delegated administration, Group Policy, and application publishing, to name a few) as well as the long-term benefits of a domain restructure (such as fewer, but larger, domains and a domain design in line with your business and organizational goals).

A crucial question to ask when considering the upgrade-then-restructure path is "Will your current domain model function adequately in the Windows Server 2003 environment?" ("Adequately," of course, is highly subjective, and each network administrator will have to decide for him- or herself whether the company can continue to support this aggregation of prior operating systems through a migration, and if so, for how long.) If the answer is "yes," you can perhaps best achieve your migration goals through the upgrade-then-restructure path.

Real World   **Domain Consolidation through Restructuring**

One of your migration goals might be to consolidate the number of domains in your organization. Large organizations might have hundreds of domains meeting the directory services needs of their users. Why have the number of domains grown out of control? One reason is the rather low size limit of the SAM database (approximately 80 megabytes [MB] as a performance limit, given current hardware standards; 40 MB on older systems). As organizations grow, they must add more Windows NT 4 domains to meet the additional capacity requirements. Another reason for the "domain bloat" phenomenon is the master domain model itself. The master domain model utilizes account domains for user and group accounts, and it uses resource domains for shared resources (computers, printers, etc.) and the local groups that control the permissions to resources. As more shared resources are brought onto the network, the number of resource domains grows as well. The result is too many domains—and a lot of administrative headaches. An organization that fits this description is a good candidate for a domain restructure, with an Active Directory design goal of reducing the number of domains. Active Directory domains in Windows Server 2003 can support millions of objects, so you can consolidate the number of account domains necessary to meet the capacity demands of your business. And through the introduction of OUs, you can achieve the same level of administrative authority as was available in the Windows NT 4 resource domain model, without the security risk of having to make all resource administrators members of the Domain Admins group. An organization with hundreds of Windows NT 4 domains might migrate to an Active Directory design of a single domain.

Once you have determined the best migration path for your domains, it is time to get to work. The following sections detail the steps necessary to migrate your directory services infrastructure from Windows NT 4 to Windows Server 2003.

Preparing for Migration to Active Directory

Preparation for the migration from Windows NT 4 to Windows Server 2003 and Active Directory will occur in the following phases:

1. Planning the migration
2. Testing the migration plan
3. Conducting a pilot migration

Additionally, you should plan for a period of maintenance and support to follow the deployment. However, this is not unique to a directory service migration project, and it is not discussed in this section.

More Info   For more information on performing a Windows NT 4 to Windows Server 2003 directory services migration, see the article "Upgrading Windows NT 4.0 Domains to Windows Server 2003" at *http://www.microsoft.com/technet /prodtechnol/windowsserver2003/evaluate/cpp/reskit/adsec/part1 /rkpdswnt.asp.* There is also the "Domain Migration Cookbook" at *http: //www.microsoft.com/technet/prodtechnol/windows2000serv/deploy/cookbook /cookintr.asp.* Though focused on the Windows 2000 Server, this collection of white papers is a technical walkthrough of a Windows NT 4 migration project and includes procedures and best practices for upgrading and restructuring. These procedures and practices are essentially all still relevant in the Windows Server 2003 environment.

Planning the Migration

To ensure a successful migration to Windows Server 2003 and Active Directory, be sure to spend sufficient time planning the migration, whether it be an in-place upgrade of domain controllers or a complete restructure of the domain model. The end result of your planning process will be a migration plan: a thorough documentation of every task you need to perform to complete the migration. Once tested, this plan will serve as the script by which you complete the numerous and varied tasks of your domain migration.

Document the Current Environment

The first step in planning for your Active Directory migration is to understand and document your existing directory and network services platform. It will probably amaze you to learn how much you do not know about the servers, services, and applications running on your domain controllers. Use this audit as an opportunity to clean out the cobwebs, and perhaps to remove redundant or unused elements from your network. Not only will you make your network more efficient and easier to support, you might also reduce the amount of work you have to do during the directory services migration.

Once the current environment is documented, you can make intelligent choices about how and when to migrate to Active Directory.

Here are a few of the elements you will want to document in creating your migration plan:

- **Current Windows NT 4 domain structure** Before you begin the migration, you must have a clear picture of what you are migrating from. This information will be vital when you plan the rollout of the migration. It is a best practice to document the following information about your current directory and network services and the environment in which they run:
  - All domains in your organization (both account and resource domains)
  - All trust relationships between domains (including the type and direction of the trust)
  - All user, global, and local group accounts, as well as computer accounts
  - All service accounts and other hard-coded accounts that are necessary to start network services or applications
  - All system and security policies that are in place in your organization
- **Current Windows NT 4–based network services** Document all of the network services in use in your enterprise, including the server on which they are running. You will want to make sure that your migration plan accounts for the implementation of these services. You should document the following services:
  - DNS servers
  - Dynamic Host Configuration Protocol (DHCP) servers, as well as the scope settings
  - Windows Internet Naming Service (WINS) servers
  - Remote Access Service (RAS) servers (This one is critical; see the note below.)
  - File and print servers

Caution Windows NT 4–based RAS servers use NULL sessions to determine dial-in permissions and to determine if any other dial-in settings, such as call-back telephone numbers, are configured for remote users. By default, Active Directory does not accept object attribute queries by using NULL sessions. Without proper planning, the interoperability of remote access services in a mixed environment can cause legitimate dial-in users to be denied remote network access. To avoid RAS conflicts during a migration, you can upgrade the Windows NT 4 RAS servers as early as possible in the process. If you will be supporting a mixed environment during the migration, you must lower the default Active Directory security by selecting the Permissions Compatible With Pre-Windows 2000 Server Operating Systems option during the Active Directory Installation Wizard.

- **Current Windows NT 4–based server hardware and software configurations** This is especially important in an upgrade scenario where you might be planning on reusing the server hardware in the upgraded domain environment. You will want to ensure that any repurposed server will meet the hardware requirements of Windows Server 2003. It is also important to document the software configuration of each server and to ensure that all applications and services are accounted for in the new environment. For both domain controllers and member servers, this list should include:

  - Number of processors and processor speed
  - RAM
  - Storage systems
  - NOS running on each server (You might find that you have a collection of NOSs, which might have different upgrade paths.)
  - Operating system running on workstations (This will determine how you implement system policies and logon scripts.)
  - All line-of-business applications running on the Windows NT 4 domain controllers (You must document their Windows Server 2003 compatibility status and whether they need to be tested on the new platform.)

This list is a somewhat generic list. You should scrutinize your network for any additional characteristics that will present a challenge to your migration objectives. Now that you have a clear picture of where you are—Point A—it is time to plan your journey to point B.

Creating the Deployment Script

The migration deployment script is the step-by-step task list of what migration steps you will perform, and in what order. This document will be your instruction sheet when it is time to throw the switch. By the time you start, it will have been tested, revised, and reworked several times.

If you are performing a domain upgrade, your deployment script will be relatively simple; it will list all of the PDCs and BDCs you need to upgrade, the order in which they will be upgraded, the steps you will take to ensure continued network services throughout the upgrade process, and whatever validation steps you need to perform to ensure success. A domain restructure deployment plan, on the other hand, will be a much more detailed document. This document will list the user, group, computer, and service accounts you will be migrating; the source and target domain of each; the timing of the migrations; and the steps necessary to cut-over the users to the new environment. The restructure deployment plan will also detail all necessary validation steps.

Real World   A Domain Upgrade Example

Here is a brief example of a domain upgrade migration. Italics are used in this example to show the site-specific names and data, which will most likely be different in your environment. Notice the validation steps throughout the procedure list.

⊃   **To perform a domain upgrade migration, complete the following steps:**

1. Install the latest Windows NT Server 4 service pack on all *Contoso* domain controllers.

2. Synchronize all domain controllers in the *Contoso* domain.

3. Back up the BDC named *DC7* to tape. Perform test restore from image to verify dataset. Secure tape and label as pre-upgrade image.

4. Take *DC7* offline and secure. This is now the backup server for rollback.

5. Using Server Manager, send a network message to users connected to the PDC named *DC1* one hour prior to the NOS upgrade.

6. Start the NOS upgrade to *DC1* after all users are disconnected. (This process includes installing Active Directory and might take several hours.)

7. After *DC1* reboots following the upgrade process, perform the following validation steps:

    -   Check event log for no errors on start-up of all services (domain controller, DNS, WINS, RAS).

    -   Open the Active Directory Users And Computers snap-in. Verify that user accounts were upgraded properly.

    -   Log on as upgraded test user *Upgrade1*, password = *P@ssw0rd*. Document results of logon in test document in project folder. Escalate to the migration project manager if not successful.

    -   Access shared folder *ITStaff\Policies*\ and open the *PersonalSoftware.doc* file. Make a change and save this file. Did this folder open? Did this file open? Were there any errors?

And so on. Your procedure should be sufficiently detailed so that it can be easily followed without relying on memory. Relying on memory when the network access of all domain users is at stake is not a good idea.

Best Practices In the procedure described in this "Real World" sidebar, you are instructed to log on with the test user account *Upgrade1*. It is a best practice to create as many test accounts as you will need to test access to the network after an upgrade or a restructure. A test account can be configured exactly as you want, without relying on the correct permissions setup on a real account or relying on your own administrative account, which may not reveal issues with logon that an account without administrative permissions might encounter. You might want one test account for logon across the local area network (LAN), another for logon from a remote site, and another for testing remote access.

Now that you have detailed everything that you will do right, it is time to document what you will do when things go wrong—the disaster recovery plan.

Designing the Recovery Plan

Your disaster recovery plan—or simply recovery plan, to be optimistic—is the equivalent of the migration plan, but it is used when the validation tasks listed earlier are not successful. As you develop your migration plan, determine not only what you will do to validate the success of your migration steps, but also think about what you can do to restore the domain to its last known good state. By doing this, you will maintain access to resources for your users, and you can then troubleshoot your migration plan and try again. This section will cover some of the basics of disaster recovery planning for your migration to Active Directory.

Recovering from a Failed Domain Upgrade

To prepare for recovery from a failed domain upgrade, perform the following tasks:

1. Add a BDC to any Windows NT 4 domain that has only a single domain controller. This will ensure a recovery path if the single domain controller were to fail during the upgrade.

2. Synchronize all BDCs with the PDC. This will ensure that the SAM database is up-to-date.

3. Back up the PDC. Additionally, perform a test restore of the backup dataset to verify that the backup was successful.

4. Take a fully synchronized BDC offline and secure it away. By doing this, you preserve a copy of the SAM database that you can use to recover the domain if necessary, without having to reinstall the server and restore the backup.

5. Periodically put this secured BDC back on the network and restart it. This will keep the SAM database up to date. Be sure to do this while the domain is still at either the Windows 2000 mixed functional level (the default mode for upgraded domain controllers) or the Windows Server 2003 interim functional level (if no Windows 2000 Server domain controllers are present). After the functional level of the domain has been raised, you will no longer be able to replicate between Windows Server 2003 domain controllers and down-level BDCs.

⊃ **To recover from a failed domain upgrade on the PDC, perform the following steps:**

1. Shut down the upgraded domain controller. This domain controller is considered a PDC on a Windows NT 4 domain and will prevent the successful completion of the next step.

2. Put the offline BDC back on the network and promote it to a PDC. This will start the replication of the preserved SAM to all remaining Windows NT 4 BDCs on the network.

By performing this procedure, you will have restored your Windows NT 4–based network to working order. The remaining recovery tasks are to troubleshoot the failed upgrade, adjust your deployment plan accordingly, and start again.

Recovering from a Failed Domain Restructure

Since you are migrating accounts from a Windows NT 4 domain to Windows Server 2003 Active Directory, your disaster recovery plan will be relatively simple. The domain restructure process is a nondestructive process, and the Windows NT 4 environment remains fully functional throughout the migration. If the migration of accounts were to fail, it would certainly be inconvenient, but it would not affect users' ability to continue functioning on the Windows NT 4 network.

⊃ **To ensure that you can recover from a failed domain restructure, perform the following steps:**

1. Add a BDC to any Windows NT 4 domain that has only a single domain controller. This will ensure a recovery path if the single domain controller were to fail during the domain restructure process.

2. Synchronize all BDCs with the PDC. This will ensure that the SAM database is up to date.

3. Back up the PDC. Additionally, perform a test restore of the backup dataset to verify that the backup was successful.

If the domain restructure is not successful, the recovery plan is to continue working in the Windows NT 4 environment, troubleshoot the failure, retest the deployment plan, and try again. If the Windows NT 4 SAM is corrupted during the migration of accounts, use the backup to restore the accounts database. This corruption would be illustrated by objects not appearing in User Manager or by users not being able to log on.

Testing the Migration Plan

There are several good reasons to test your migration plan:

- It validates that the migration steps will achieve the desired results.
- It provides an opportunity to determine the time necessary to complete the full migration.
- It gives you an opportunity to become familiar with the tools and procedures you will use in your migration to Active Directory.

Be sure to test all elements of the migration. Review your migration plan, and build test cases for each different procedure you will have to perform. Do not forget to test your recovery plan as well—during a rollback to the Windows NT 4 domain would be a bad time to discover an error in your plan. As your testing reveals errors in the migration plan, update the plan as necessary, and retest the plan until it works as expected.

Best Practices When testing your migration plan, create a test environment that resembles your production environment as closely as possible. But when you do so, make sure that your test environment is completely isolated from your production environment.

Conducting a Pilot Migration

Before deploying the migration organization-wide, you should conduct a pilot rollout of the migration to a limited and controlled group of users. This will enable you to carefully observe the results of the migration in a controlled environment, before executing the full migration plan. The pilot rollout has several advantages:

- It tests your migration plan in the production environment.
- It provides an opportunity to discover unforeseen errors in the migration plan.
- It provides another opportunity for you to become familiar with the migration tools and processes.

As with your testing phase, the pilot migration will give you an opportunity to evaluate the results of your migration plan and make adjustments as necessary. Be sure to retest any modifications and redeploy the modifications to the pilot group before deploying the migration to the organization.

Note   You will not be able to "pilot" a domain upgrade; it is an all-or-nothing event. Given the opportunity, though, you should upgrade smaller domains first, and then tackle the larger ones. Domain restructures, on the other hand, can be rolled out in phases. Take advantage of this by deploying your restructure to a controlled group of users.

Once the pilot deployment is complete and all bugs have been worked out from the migration plan, you are ready to migrate to Windows Server 2003 Active Directory.

Upgrading the Domain

Upgrading the domain is the second stage of the process of upgrading to Windows Server 2003. (The first stage is the upgrade of the NOS.) When upgrading a domain controller running either Windows NT Server 4 or Windows 2000 Server, after the NOS upgrade is complete and the computer restarts, the Active Directory Installation Wizard begins automatically. You should complete the Active Directory Installation Wizard according to your Active Directory design document. Once the Active Directory Installation Wizard is complete, the directory service is updated to Active Directory for Windows Server 2003.

More Info   For more information on designing your Active Directory structure, see Chapter 5, "Designing the Active Directory Structure." For more information on using the Active Directory Installation Wizard, see Chapter 6, "Installing Active Directory."

There are several different steps you must perform during an upgrade, depending on what version of Windows you are upgrading from. The first part of this section describes the processes of upgrading the domain from Windows NT Server 4. It then examines an upgrade from Windows 2000 Server.

Note   If you have a version of Windows NT earlier than 4, you cannot upgrade directly to Windows Server 2003. You must first upgrade to Windows NT 4 and apply Service Pack 5 (SP5) or later before upgrading the operating system.

Upgrading from Windows NT Server 4

When upgrading to Active Directory and Windows Server 2003 from Windows NT Server 4, the first part of the process is to upgrade the operating system. After the NOS upgrade is complete and the computer restarts, you will complete the upgrade of the domain by finishing the Active Directory Installation Wizard. This section describes the steps necessary to prepare for and execute an upgrade to Active Directory from Windows NT Server 4.

More Info This section only discusses the processes necessary to prepare for and implement an upgrade to Active Directory in Windows Server 2003. Because this process begins with an upgrade of the Windows NT Server 4 operating system to Windows Server 2003, you should first familiarize yourself with all of the technical requirements necessary to upgrade the NOS. For more information on upgrading to Windows Server 2003 for small installations (one to five servers), see the "Installing and Upgrading the Operating System" page on the Microsoft Web site at *http://www.microsoft.com/technet/prodtechnol/windowsserver2003 /proddocs/entserver/installing_windows_2000_server.asp*. For larger installations, see the Microsoft Windows 2003 Server Deployment Kit at *http://www.microsoft.com/windowsserver2003/techinfo/reskit/deploykit.mspx*.

Before You Begin

Before you begin the upgrade process, there are several preparatory steps that you either must or should take, with each performed on the Windows NT 4 PDC that is to be upgraded. The following list describes these steps:

- Clean up the SAM database. Remember, with a domain upgrade, everything in the SAM database will be upgraded to Active Directory. It is a best practice to "clean up" the database before the upgrade. This will most likely reduce the volume of accounts that need to be migrated to Active Directory and will result in lower disk space usage on your Windows Server 2003 domain controllers. Keep in mind that the existing user accounts database can expand by as much as a factor of ten when upgrading to Active Directory. Cleaning up the SAM includes the following tasks, which can be completed using the Windows NT 4 User Manager For Domains administrative tool or the Net User command.
  - Remove duplicate user accounts.
  - Consolidate duplicate group accounts.
  - Remove unused user, group, and computer accounts.
  - Remove local group accounts for resources that no longer exist.
  - Install Windows NT 4 Service Pack 5 or later. You can download all of the supported Service Packs for Windows NT 4 on the Microsoft Web site at *http://www.microsoft.com/ntserver/nts/downloads/default.asp*.

Upgrading the PDC First

The first domain controller in your Windows NT 4 domain to upgrade is the PDC. This is a must. If you were to attempt to upgrade a BDC before the PDC, an error would occur. This is because Windows NT 4–based domains can only have one PDC in the domain at a time. Since all Windows Server 2003 domain controllers are in effect PDCs to a Windows NT 4 domain, you must upgrade the PDC first in order not to violate this rule.

Best Practices Rather than upgrade the existing PDC in your domain, it is a best practice to build a clean Windows NT 4 BDC, promote it to the PDC, and then upgrade that domain controller to Windows Server 2003. This extra step ensures that you can start with a domain controller that is hardware compatible with Windows Server 2003 and that the server does not have a history of modifications that might prevent a clean upgrade.

After this process is complete and you have validated that all network and directory service functionality is intact, you can then start adding more domain controllers by installing new domain controllers or upgrading the existing BDCs. As long as you remain in the default functional level of Windows 2000 mixed or, in the absence of any servers running Windows 2000 Server, as long as you raise the functional level to Windows Server 2003 interim, you will be able to support both Windows Server 2003 domain controllers and Windows NT 4 backup domain controllers. If, when, and how quickly you choose to upgrade the BDCs is up to you.

When all of the domain controllers are upgraded to Windows Server 2003, you can raise the domain and forest functional levels. For more information on functional levels, see "Understanding Functional Levels" later in this chapter.

➲ **To upgrade the PDC, complete the following steps:**

1. Insert the Windows Server 2003 compact disc in the CD-ROM drive. If Autorun is enabled on your CD-ROM drive, the Setup program will automatically start. If the Setup program does not automatically start, you can launch Setup.exe from the root folder of the compact disc.

2. When the Windows Server 2003 Setup program starts, select the Install Windows Server 2003 option.

3. After the Setup program collects information about your current operating system, select the Upgrading To Windows Server 2003 option.

4. Provide the information as necessary to complete the Setup program.

5. When the system upgrade to Windows Server 2003 is complete, the computer will restart. After the computer restarts, the Active Directory Installation Wizard starts automatically.

6. Complete the Active Directory Installation Wizard as necessary to meet your Active Directory design goals. After the Active Directory installation is complete, your computer will automatically restart.

When your computer restarts after you have completed step 6, the upgrade to Active Directory is complete.

Verifying the Upgrade to Active Directory

There are several steps that you should take to verify that Active Directory has been installed successfully on your upgraded domain controller. Some of these steps are diagnostic in nature, others are functional. Let's take a look at the functional tests first:

- Verify that all user, group, and computer accounts were migrated to Active Directory. To test this, open the Active Directory Users And Computers administrative tool and review the list of account objects. You might not want to verify each one, but be sure to select several Windows NT 4 accounts and verify that they exist on the upgraded domain controller.

- Verify trust relationships using the Active Directory Domains And Trusts administrative tool.

- Check the Event Viewer system log for any errors that occurred upon starting the Active Directory service.

- Verify that you can create new users on the Windows Server 2003 domain controller. On the upgraded domain controller, open the Active Directory Users And Computers administrative tool, and create a new test user account.

- Verify that users can log on to the domain. From a workstation in the domain, attempt to log on as a user in the upgraded account. You can either use a live user account or create a pre-upgrade test user account for this purpose.

- Verify replication to BDCs. After you create the new test user, above, open User Manager For Domains on a BDC running Windows NT Server 4, and verify that the user is replicated. Additionally, you can disconnect the Windows Server 2003 domain controller from the network and log on to the network as the test user, with a Windows NT 4 BDC processing the logon request.

Additionally, there are several Active Directory diagnostic tools available in the Support Tools package on the Windows Server 2003 compact disc. You can install these tools on your upgraded Windows Server 2003 domain controller by running the Suptools.msi file from the \SUPPORT\TOOLS folder on the Windows Server 2003 compact disc. The diagnostic verification steps you can perform are:

- To test for successful Active Directory connectivity and functionality, run the Domain Controller Diagnostic tool (from a command prompt, type *dcdiag*). A successful test returns a series of "passed" results.

More Info Dcdiag, a component of the Windows Server 2003 Support Tool collection, analyzes the state of domain controllers in a forest and provides detailed information about how to identify abnormal behavior in a system. Domain controllers are identified and tested according to directives entered by the user at the command line. For more information on the Dcdiag tool, type *dcdiag /?* at the command prompt.

- If this is not the first Active Directory domain in the forest, type *repadmin /showreps* at a command prompt to test for successful replication between Active Directory domain controllers. A successful test returns a message indicating a successful replication event with each inbound and outbound replication partner.
- To test for successful replication to BDCs, type *nltest /bdc_query:**domainname*** where *domainname* is the name of the replicated domain. A successful test returns "status = success" for each BDC in the domain.

After you have verified a successful upgrade of the PDC, you can begin to upgrade the BDCs.

Upgrading the BDCs

It may not be necessary to upgrade the Windows NT 4 BDCs. All of the domain information is upgraded to Windows Server 2003 Active Directory with the upgrade of the PDC. Your goal, after the PDC upgrade, is to bring additional Windows Server 2003 domain controllers online to support the directory service needs of the domain. You can do this either by installing new Windows Server 2003 domain controllers or by upgrading the existing BDCs. Installing new Windows Server 2003 domain controllers is the preferred choice because you eliminate the risk from upgrading a BDC with an unknown (or worse, troubled) history. The fresh installation of Windows Server 2003 on these additional domain controllers ensures that the computer is in a pristine state from the beginning.

Why might you choose to upgrade the BDC? Only, perhaps, if there were applications running on the BDC that would be inconvenient, or impossible, to reinstall on the new domain controller.

If you determine it is necessary, the process of upgrading the remaining BDCs is essentially the same as upgrading the PDC. Again, it is a two-step process, where you first upgrade the NOS, and, after the computer restarts, you use the Active Directory Installation Wizard to install Active Directory and promote the server to a domain controller. You do have the option of not running the Active Directory Installation Wizard. In this case, the computer will remain a member server in the Windows Server 2003 domain. Keep in mind that if you do this, the SAM database information on this server will be lost. Your Active Directory design documentation will dictate how many domain controllers you will need in your Windows Server 2003–based domain, and your migration plan will dictate which of the remaining BDCs should be promoted to domain controllers after the NOS upgrade and which should be left as member servers.

Preventing Domain Controller Overload

Domain controller overload, in the context of a domain upgrade scenario, can occur when you have Windows 2000 Professional and/or Windows XP Professional client computers on your Windows NT 4–based domain, and you then upgrade the PDC to Windows

Server 2003. This presents a potential domain controller overload condition on the single Windows Server 2003 domain controller because Windows 2000 Professional and Windows XP Professional computers that have joined an Active Directory domain will communicate only with a Windows 2000 Server or Windows Server 2003 domain controller for any action that requires these clients to contact a domain controller. If you have a large number of upgraded client computers—or new client computers—running the above-mentioned desktop operating systems, you should take the necessary steps to eliminate the risk of a single point of failure (the upgraded PDC). These steps are detailed below.

One means of preventing domain controller overload is to bring additional Windows Server 2003 domain controllers online as quickly as possible. If, however, your migration plan does not call for the immediate upgrade of all Windows NT Server 4–based BDCs or the addition of new Windows Server 2003 domain controllers, you can modify the registry on the upgraded PDC in such a way that the Windows Server 2003 domain controller emulates the behavior of a Windows NT 4 domain controller for all Windows 2000 Professional and Windows XP Professional clients. To enable Windows NT 4 emulation mode, perform the following steps on the upgraded Windows NT 4 PDC:

1. After the computer has been upgraded from Windows NT 4 to Windows Server 2003, but before you install Active Directory (before running the Active Directory Installation Wizard), open the Registry Editor (type *regedit* in the Run dialog box).

2. Create the *NT4Emulator* value in the following registry key: HKEY_LOCAL_MACHINE\SYSTEM\CurrentControlSet\Services\Netlogon\Parameters

3. Select Edit, then New, and then DWORD Value. Replace the New Value #1 name with *NT4Emulator*, and press Enter.

4. On the Edit menu, click Modify. In the Edit DWORD Value dialog box, type *1* in the Value Data text box, and then click OK.

5. Save the changes, and close the Registry Editor.

6. Start the Active Directory Installation Wizard by typing *dcpromo* from the Run dialog box.

Repeat this process on each newly installed Windows Server 2003 domain controller or each upgraded Windows NT 4 domain controller until sufficient Windows Server 2003 domain controllers exist so that the overload condition is not an issue.

Keep in mind that this is a temporary solution to a hopefully temporary problem. After all of your planned Windows NT 4 domain controllers have been upgraded to Windows Server 2003, you should either set the value of NT4Emulator to *0x0* or delete the key for each of the computers you modified.

Neutralizing NT 4 Emulation

For some computers, you will have to modify the registry so that they ignore the NT4Emulator setting. These are, specifically, computers running Windows Server 2003 or Windows 2000 Server that will be promoted to domain controllers, and computers running Windows 2000 Professional or Windows XP Professional that will be used to administer the domain using Active Directory administrative tools. For these computers, there is a neutralize facility that enables them to contact the Windows Server 2003 domain controllers as usual.

➲ **To neutralize the NT4Emulator setting, perform the following steps:**

1. Start Registry Editor (type *regedit* in the Run dialog box).

2. Create the *NeutralizeNT4Emulator* value in the following registry key: HKEY_LOCAL_MACHINE\SYSTEM\CurrentControlSet\Services\Netlogon\Parameters

3. Select Edit, then New, and then DWORD Value. Replace the New Value #1 name with *NeutralizeNT4Emulator*, and press Enter.

4. On the Edit menu, click Modify. In the Edit DWORD Value dialog box, type *1* in the Value Data text box, and then click OK.

After all of the Windows NT 4 BDCs have been installed or upgraded to Windows Server 2003, you have nearly completed the upgrade to Windows Server 2003 and Active Directory. The final step in the domain upgrade process is to raise the domain and forest functional level from Windows 2000 mixed (default) to Windows Server 2003.

Raising the Functional Level

After you have upgraded all of the domain controllers to Windows Server 2003, you must raise the domain and forest functional levels to optimize the benefits of upgrading the network operating system. This section describes the process of raising both the domain and forest functional levels. For information on the nature of functional levels, see "Understanding Functional Levels" later in this chapter.

To raise the domain functional level, perform the following steps on a domain controller in the upgraded domain:

1. Open the Active Directory Domains And Trusts administrative tool.

2. In the console tree, right-click the domain for which you want to raise functionality, and then click Raise Domain Functional Level.

3. In Select An Available Domain Functional Level, do one of the following:

   - To raise the domain functional level to Windows 2000 native, click Windows 2000 Native, and then click Raise.

   - To raise the domain functional level to Windows Server 2003, select Windows Server 2003, and then click Raise.

After you have raised the domain functional level (to at least Windows 2000 native), you can raise the forest functional level to Windows Server 2003. This will enable the full forest-wide Active Directory functionality available through Windows Server 2003. To raise the forest functional level, perform the following steps:

1. Open the Active Directory Domains And Trusts administrative tool.

2. In the console tree, right-click the Active Directory Domains And Trusts node, and then click Raise Forest Functional Level.

3. In Select An Available Forest Functional Level, select Windows Server 2003, and then click Raise.

Caution   The procedure to raise the domain or forest functional level cannot be reversed. To restore a lower functional level to a domain or forest, you must uninstall Active Directory (which deletes the domain when Active Directory is uninstalled from the last domain controller in the domain), and then reinstall the directory service.

Understanding Functional Levels

Functional levels are used in Windows Server 2003 to enable appropriate sets of Active Directory features for those domain controllers that can support them. The level of functionality you select for your enterprise is dictated by the version of the Windows operating system running on the domain controllers. Functional levels can be set for both the domain and the forest. When the forest is set to Windows Server 2003 functional level, all of the features of Active Directory are available.

The concept of functional levels is similar to the mixed mode and native mode settings introduced in Windows 2000 Server. This implementation has been expanded in Windows Server 2003 to accommodate the additional new features of Active Directory. Functional levels are used to provide backward compatibility for down-level domain controllers.

There are four different domain functional levels: Windows 2000 mixed (the default), Windows 2000 native, Windows Server 2003 interim, and Windows Server 2003. When you have upgraded all of your down-level domain controllers in a domain to Windows Server 2003, you should raise that domain's functional level to Windows Server 2003. Raising the domain functional level from Windows 2000 mixed to either Windows 2000 native or Windows Server 2003 will enable such features as SID History, Universal Groups, and group nesting.

There are three different forest functional levels: Windows 2000, Windows Server 2003 interim, and Windows Server 2003. To enable all features of Active Directory, as soon as all domains in the forest are operating at a functional level of Windows 2000 native or higher, you should raise the forest functional level to Windows Server 2003.

Caution   Do not raise the forest functional level to Windows Server 2003 if you have, or intend to have, any domain controllers running Windows NT Server 4 or Windows 2000 Server. Once the forest functional level has been raised to Windows Server 2003, it cannot be changed back to Windows 2000 mixed or Windows 2000 native, and you will no longer be able to support the down-level domain controllers in your forest.

Upgrading from Windows 2000 Server

The process of upgrading the domain from Windows 2000 Active Directory to Windows Server 2003 Active Directory is a straightforward one compared to the Windows NT 4 upgrade. Windows 2000 Server–based networks are already using Active Directory for directory services, so this is more of a pure upgrade scenario than a migration. There are a few unique steps to a Windows 2000 upgrade that you will need to be aware of before starting the upgrade.

Specifically, you will need to "prepare" the Windows 2000 Active Directory domain and forest for an upgrade to Windows Server 2003 Active Directory. These processes will update the existing domain and forest structures to be compatible with the new features of Windows Server 2003 Active Directory.

Best Practices   Before preparing the domain (and the forest in which it is located), you should apply Windows 2000 Server Service Pack 2 (SP2) or later to all domain controllers running Windows 2000 Server. You can download the latest and all supported service packs for Windows 2000 Server from the Microsoft Web site at *http://www.microsoft.com/windows2000/downloads/servicepacks/default.asp*.

Preparing the Forest

To prepare the Active Directory forest for an upgrade to Windows Server 2003 Active Directory, you will use an administrative tool, Adprep.exe, to make the necessary changes to the Active Directory schema. Remember, this process is completed *before* the upgrade to Windows Server 2003 is initiated.

To prepare the forest for an upgrade of the first Windows 2000 Server domain controller to Windows Server 2003, perform the following steps:

1. Locate the server that is the schema master. To do this, open the Active Directory Schema Microsoft Management Console (MMC) snap-in, right-click the Active Directory Schema node, and then click Operations Master. In the Change Schema Master dialog box, note the name of the current schema master.

2. Back up the schema master. You might need to restore this image if the forest preparation is not successful.

3. Disconnect the schema master from the network. Do not reestablish the connection until step 8 in this procedure.

4. On the schema master, insert the Windows Server 2003 compact disc into the CD-ROM drive.

5. Open a command prompt, change to the CD-ROM drive, and open the \I386 folder.

6. Type *adprep /forestprep*. To run *adprep /forestprep*, you must be a member of the Enterprise Admins group and the Schema Admins group in Active Directory, or you must have been delegated the appropriate authority.

7. To verify that the command has run without errors, open the Event Viewer and check the system log for errors or unexpected events. If you identify error messages related to the forest preparation process, address those errors before continuing with the next step. If you are unable to troubleshoot the errors, use the Active Directory Diagnostic tool (by typing *dcdiag* in the Run dialog box) to test the functionality of the domain controller. If you are unable to resolve these errors, restore the schema master from backup and investigate the corrective steps so that the forest preparation can be completed successfully.

8. If *adprep /forestprep* has run without errors, reconnect the schema master to the network.

This completes the forest preparation for a domain upgrade from Windows 2000 Server to Windows Server 2003. The next step is to prepare the domain.

Tip Before you begin your domain preparation, wait for the changes made to the schema master to replicate to the infrastructure master. Remember that if the servers are in different sites, you will need to wait longer for the replication to complete. If you try to perform the domain preparation process before the changes have replicated, an error message will notify you that more time is needed.

Preparing the Domain

Domain preparation is very similar to forest preparation. To complete this task you will identify and prepare the infrastructure master role holder instead of the schema master, as in the previous process.

➲ **To prepare each domain for an upgrade of the first Windows 2000 Server domain controller in a domain to Windows Server 2003, perform the following steps:**

1. Locate the server that is the infrastructure operations master. To do this, open the Active Directory Users And Computers administrative tool, right-click the domain node, and then click Operations Masters. On the Infrastructure tab of the Operations Masters sheet, note the name of the current infrastructure operations master.

2. On the server functioning as the infrastructure operations master, insert the Windows Server 2003 compact disc into the CD-ROM drive.

3. Open a command prompt, change to the CD-ROM drive, and open the \I386 folder.

4. Type *adprep /domainprep*. To run *adprep /domainprep*, you must be a member of the Domain Admins group or the Enterprise Admins group in Active Directory, or you must have been delegated the appropriate authority.

5. To verify that the *adprep /domainprep* command has run without errors, open the Event Viewer and check the system log for errors or unexpected events. If *adprep /domainprep* ran without errors, you have successfully prepared the domain for an upgrade from Windows 2000 Server to Windows Server 2003.

Once again, you should wait until the changes made to the infrastructure master replicate to the other domain controllers in the forest before upgrading any of the other domain controllers. If you begin to upgrade one of the domain controllers before the changes have replicated, an error message will notify you that more time is needed.

Now that the domain and forest are prepared for the upgrade to Windows Server 2003 and Active Directory, you can begin the upgrade process.

Upgrading the Domain Controllers

Unlike the domain controllers in Windows NT 4, all domain controllers in a Windows 2000 network are PDCs, in a sense. That is to say, each domain controller has the same ability to write to the Active Directory database, authenticate users, and respond to queries. With the exception of the Operation Master role-holders, all domain controllers are equal. That being said, it does not matter what domain controller you choose to upgrade first.

The upgrade process from Windows 2000 is the same as that described for the Windows NT 4 to Windows Server 2003 upgrade scenario. It is again a two-step process: You first upgrade the NOS to Windows Server 2003, and you then run the Active Directory Installation Wizard to install Active Directory.

Restructuring the Domain

The domain restructure migration path is most often chosen by organizations that want or need to change their Active Directory structure. To perform a domain restructure, you will first create the desired forest and domain structure and then migrate the existing Active Directory objects into this new structure. At the time of its creation, the new structure is also known as the pristine forest.

Note   The domain restructure migration path is also known as an interforest migration (migration from one Active Directory forest to another). The focus of this migration path walkthrough is on the Windows NT 4 to Windows Server 2003 domain migration, which is considered an interforest process. A Windows 2000 Active Directory to Windows Server 2003 Active Directory restructure, for the purposes of this chapter, is considered an intraforest migration and is discussed in the section "Upgrading then Restructuring."

The job of migrating the Active Directory objects (which includes user, group, and computer accounts, as well as trusts and service accounts) is made easier through the use of domain migration tools. There are a number of tools available for this task, both from Microsoft and from third-party software vendors. Here is a list of available, or soon-to-be available, domain migration tools and their manufacturers. Be sure to select the version of the tool that supports migrations to Active Directory domains in Windows Server 2003. Include in your domain migration planning process the task of researching the available migration tools and determining which product will best meet your needs.

- Active Directory Migration Tool (ADMT). This tool is available on the Windows Server 2003 compact disc in the \I386\ADMT folder. Double-click Admigration.msi to install the tool.

- An evaluation version of bv-Admin for Windows 2000 and Windows Server 2003 migration from BindView Corporation (*http://www.bindview.com/products /Admin/winmig.cfm*).can be requested from the product Web site.

- A trial version of Domain Migration Administrator (DMA) from NetIQ *(http: //www.netiq.com/products/dma/)* is available for download from the product Web site.

- A trial version of Domain Migration Wizard (DMW) from Aelita Software*(http: //www.aelita.com/products/DMW.htm)* is available for download from the product Web site.

The remainder of this section on restructuring the domain will focus on the conceptual aspects of the migration process, not the intricacies of a particular domain migration tool. Where necessary, the process will be described in the context of Active Directory Migration Tool (ADMT) from Microsoft.

Before going into detail about migrating Active Directory objects, a word about the organization of this section is in order. The domain restructuring tasks that follow are broken out by account domain and resource domain categories. This somewhat artificial organization is meant to reflect the prescribed domain structure of a Windows NT 4–based network, where an enterprise would consist of account domains (which contain the user and global group accounts); resource domains (which contain the computer and resource accounts such as printers; and the local groups) that are used to control access to these resources. Figure 7-2 illustrates the account domain and resource domain organizational model.

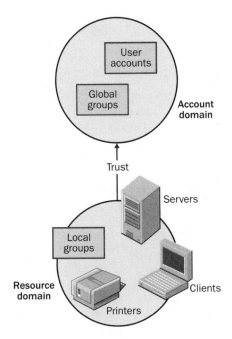

Figure 7-2. *The Windows NT 4 account domain and resource domain organizational model.*

What if you don't have account and resource domains in your Windows NT 4 enterprise environment? Then ignore the distinction. Just review the content relevant to the type of directory objects you need to migrate. This construct is only useful for discussing the order in which you should migrate objects and to provide context for the process of doing so.

Creating the Pristine Forest

The pristine forest includes the Widows Server 2003 target domain into which you will be migrating your existing Windows NT 4 accounts—your Point B on the journey from A to B. With a domain restructure migration path, you have the opportunity to create the optimal domain environment for your organization. Hopefully, this step comes at the end of a lengthy and thoughtful Active Directory design process, and all components of your Active Directory structure are clearly defined in your design document. For more information on the design process, see Chapter 5.

Tip   When installing Active Directory in the pristine forest, on the Permissions page of the Active Directory Installation Wizard, select the Permissions Compatible With Pre-Windows 2000 Server Operating Systems option. This setting allows anonymous user accounts to access domain information and is required to clone security principals. To obtain this option, you must have selected the Custom Configuration option on the Custom Options page of the Configure Your Server Wizard.

After you have implemented your target domain structure, there are several steps you must take to prepare for the migration of accounts.

Raising the Functional Level

The Windows Server 2003 target domain must be running in either Windows 2000 Native or Windows Server 2003 domain functional level to perform a domain restructure. The default domain functional level for a new Windows Server 2003 implementation is Windows 2000 mixed. If your target domain will include both Windows 2000 Server domain controllers as well as Windows Server 2003 domain controllers, you should raise the functional level to Windows 2000 native. If your new domain will include only Windows Server 2003 domain controllers, you should select Windows Server 2003 functional level. Keep in mind that the raising of the domain functional level is an irreversible process—once you raise the level, it cannot be lowered again.

Creating the Migration Account

The first user account you might choose to create in your pristine forest is the one necessary to perform the migration. By creating a specific user account for the migration, you can ensure that the account meets all of the security requirements necessary to perform the tasks involved with a domain restructure. Additionally, you exercise the security best practice of not logging in using the Administrator account. For example, you can create a new user account (such as Migrator) or several accounts (Migrator1, Migrator2, etc.) if you plan to have several trusted administrators performing the migration. This way, you can track the events performed by each account holder and avoid having a shared account with administrative privileges.

For migrating user, group, and service accounts, the account must be a member of the Domain Admins group in the target domain if you are using SID History to preserve access to resources. The account should also be a member of the Administrators group in the Windows NT 4 source domain.

Creating the Trusts

Because the migration process requires the granting of administrative permissions to accounts from a different domain, you will have to create several trusts to be able to migrate accounts from the source domain (or domains) to the target domain. In the Windows Server 2003 target domain and the Windows NT 4 source domains, create a one-way trust from each of the source domains (trusting) to the target domain (trusted).

After you create these trusts, validate them using the Active Directory Domains And Trusts administrative tool in Windows Server 2003 and the Server Manager administrative tool in Windows NT Server 4.

Modifying the Registry

To create a secure communication channel between the source and target domain controllers, there is a system registry modification that must be made on the Windows NT 4 source domain controller. If for some reason you choose not to make this modification before installing ADMT, the tool will make this change on first use. You will be prompted to restart the PDC after the change is made by ADMT.

Setting this value enables remote procedure calls (RPCs) over the Transmission Control Protocol (TCP) transport. Setting this value does not diminish the security of the Windows NT 4 system in any way.

On the source PDC, open the registry and create the following key:

> *HKEY_LOCAL_MACHINE\SYSTEM\CurrentContolSet\Control\Lsa*

Create the value *TcpipClientSupport*, using a DWORD setting of *1*.

Best Practices   If you plan to migrate user account passwords at the same time as the user accounts (as opposed to expiring the Windows NT 4 user passwords and having the user create a new password upon first logon to the Windows Server 2003 domain), there is a second registry edit you will need to make. On the source PDC, edit (or create, if it does not already exist) the following registry key to support password migration:

HKEY_LOCAL_MACHINE\SYSTEM\CurrentControlSet\Control\Lsa

For the value *AllowPasswordExport*, set the DWORD to *1*

For more information on password migration, see the ADMT Help facility.

Installing Active Directory Migration Tool

ADMT is an administrative tool available from Microsoft for the purpose of migrating directory service objects from one domain to another. ADMT can perform both *interforest* migrations (moving accounts from one forest to another) and *intraforest* migrations (moving accounts within a forest). Migrating from Windows NT 4 to Windows Server 2003 is an example of an *interforest* migration. ADMT provides both a graphical user interface (GUI) and a scripting interface, and it can be run on both Windows 2000 and Windows Server 2003 target domain controllers.

ADMT version 2.0, the version available on the Windows Server 2003 compact disc, supports the following tasks for completing your domain migration:

- User account migration
- Group account migration
- Computer account migration
- Service account migration
- Trust migration
- Exchange directory migration
- Security translation on migrated computer accounts
- Reporting to view the results of the migration events
- Functionality to undo last migration and retry last migration

One of the advantages of ADMT as compared to other domain migration tools is that it is included with the Windows Server 2003 product. The installation folder is located at \I386\ADMT on the Windows Server 2003 compact disc.

> **More Info**   In addition to the ADMT installation files, the ADMT folder on the Windows Server 2003 compact disc contains a Readme.doc document, which provides important information on the ADMT. Be sure to read this document before installing or using the tool. For the most up-to-date version of this document, see the Windows 2000 Active Directory Migration Tool site at: *http://www.microsoft.com/windows2000/downloads/tools/admt/default.asp*. On this site, you can also download the ADMT tool itself, but ensure that it is equal to or more recent than the version on the Windows Server 2003 compact disc.

To install ADMT on the target domain controller, perform the following steps:

1. On the Windows Server 2003 compact disc, open the \I386\ADMT folder.

2. Double-click Admigration.msi to install ADMT on your computer.

3. Accept the licensing agreement and accept the default settings on the wizard pages.

After the ADMT is installed, it can be started from the Administrative Tools folder on the Start menu. The ADMT starts as an MMC snap-in, with all of the Wizards available from the Action menu. See Figure 7-3 for an illustration of the available Wizards in the ADMT.

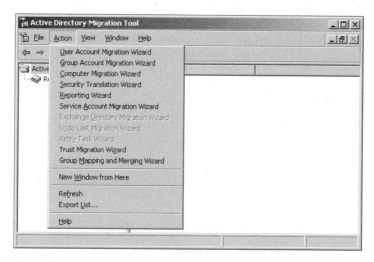

Figure 7-3. *The Wizards available in the ADMT.*

Enabling Auditing in the Target and Source Domains

The domain restructuring process requires that auditing must be enabled for the success or failure of account management operations in both the source and the target domains.

⮑ **To enable auditing on the Windows Server 2003 target domain, perform the following steps:**

1. Open the Active Directory Users And Computers administrative tool, right-click the Domain Controllers container, and select Properties.

2. On the Domain Controllers Properties sheet, select the Group Policy tab.

3. Select the Default Domain Controllers Policy, and click Edit.

4. Expand Default DomainControllers Policy\Computer Configuration\Windows Settings\Security Settings\Local Policies\Audit Policy, double-click Audit Account Management, and then select both the Success and the Failure options.

5. Force replication of this change to all domain controllers in the domain, or wait for the change to replicate automatically.

⮑ **To enable auditing on the Windows NT 4 source domain, perform the following steps:**

1. Open the User Manager For Domains administrative tool, select Policies, and then select Audit.

2. Verify that Audit These Events is selected and that, for User And Group Management, both Success and Failure are selected.

Additionally, you must create a new local group on the source domain controller for ADMT internal auditing purposes. The name of this new, empty group is *sourcedomainname*$$$ (for example Contoso$$$). ADMT will create this group automatically when run for the first time if you do not create it in advance.

Modifying Anonymous Access to the Target Domain

If you do not select the Permissions Compatible With Pre-Windows 2000 Server Operating Systems option when installing Active Directory, you can add the Everyone group to the Pre-Windows 2000 Compatible Access group by typing *net localgroup "Pre-Windows 2000 Compatible Access" everyone /add* at the command prompt and then pressing Enter.

After the group membership change is made, you must also ensure that the Everyone group permissions apply to anonymous users. To do this, open the Active Directory Users And Computers administrative tool, right-click the Domain Controllers container, and select Properties. On the Group Policy tab, edit the Default Domain Controllers Policy object.

In the Group Policy Object Editor, expand Default Domain Controllers Policy\Computer Configuration\Windows Settings\Security Settings\Local Policies\Security Options, and double-click Network Access: Let Everyone Permissions Apply To Anonymous Users. Check Define This Policy Setting, select Enabled, and then click OK.

Migrating Account Domains

A Windows NT 4 account domain contains primarily the user and group accounts that access network resources. In a domain restructure migration scenario, you will migrate the directory services objects in the account domains before migrating the resource domains. This order of operations is preferred because it preserves access to resources during the migration project.

To migrate an account domain, complete the following steps:

1. Establish trusts between the Windows Server 2003 target domain and the Windows NT 4 resource domains.
2. Migrate global group accounts.
3. Migrate user accounts (with or without passwords).

This section presents the best practices to keep in mind when completing an account domain migration.

Establishing Trusts

To preserve access to resources for migrated users, you must create one-way trusts from each Windows NT 4 domain that contains resources that the migrated users need to access, to the Windows Server 2003 target domain. Creating a trust is a two-step process.

The first step is performed on the Windows Server 2003 domain controller for the target domain. Add each Windows NT 4 resource domain to the Domains That Trust This Domain list on the target domain's Properties sheet by using the Active Directory Domains And Trusts administrative tool. You will create a password to secure this trust, and you will need it when creating the second half of the trust.

The second step is on the Windows NT 4 resource domain PDC. Using User Manager For Domains, add the Windows Server 2003 target domain to the Trusted Domains section. To complete this task, you will need to provide the password created in the first step described earlier. You should receive a status message if the trusts have been successfully created.

Migrating Global Group Accounts

The order of operations for migrating accounts is global groups first, then users. This preserves group membership when user accounts are later migrated to the target domain, and it preserves access to resources. When you migrate global groups from Windows NT 4 to Windows Server 2003, a new SID is created for the new global group. The SID from the source domain is added to the *SID-History* attribute for each new group object. You will recall that by preserving the SID from the source domain in the *SID-History* field, users can continue to access resources on the not-yet-migrated Windows NT 4 resource domains.

By cloning the global group accounts (using a domain migration tool such as ADMT), you will create in the target domain the skeletal group structure as defined in your Active Directory design. As user accounts are later migrated, they will automatically join the groups of which they were members in the source domain.

The process of migrating global groups from Windows NT 4 to Windows Server 2003, in this case using the ADMT Group Account Migration Wizard, is a straightforward one:

➲ **To migrate global groups from Windows NT 4 to Windows Server 2003 using the ADMT Group Account Migration Wizard, perform the following steps:**

1. Identify the source and target domains. If the domain names do not appear in the drop-down list, you can type them in.

2. Select the Windows NT 4 global groups that you want to migrate to Windows Server 2003.

3. Select the OU to which you want to add the global groups in the target domain.

Note   ADMT only enables you to select a single OU as the destination container of the migrated global group accounts. Keep this in mind as you plan the migration of your global groups. Rather than select *all* of the source global groups, you might want to select all of the groups that will be migrated to a specific OU. Then, you can rerun the Group Account Migration Wizard to migrate the groups which are to be stored in another OU.

---

4. Select the desired group options. This includes whether or not to copy the group members (that is, the user accounts) at the same time as copying the groups. The default is not to copy group members. Copying group members at the time you migrate the group might be an expeditious choice if yours is a smaller organization and migrating by groups is an acceptable staged approach. In larger organizations, however, the top-level global groups (such as Employees) is too large a body of users to migrate at one time.

Once the global groups are migrated over to Windows Server 2003, it is time to start migrating the user accounts.

Migrating User Accounts

The migration of user accounts does not have to be done all at once. In fact, it is a good idea to plan carefully the order and timing of migrating the users. Because you will be preserving access to Windows NT 4–based resources during the migration, this process can be stretched out over days, weeks, or months. Things to keep in mind when migrating user accounts are:

- How many new users can your IT group support at one time?
- What set of users should be moved together?
- What set of users are not able to accommodate the inconveniences of a domain restructure at a certain time?

These business drivers will determine the order and timing of the user account migration process. So the first step in migrating user accounts is to determine the sets of users to migrate and when to perform the migration.

The actual migration of user accounts is procedurally very similar to the migration of global group accounts.

➲ **To migrate user accounts from Windows NT 4 to Windows Server 2003 and Active Directory using the ADMT User Account Migration Wizard, perform the following steps:**

1. Select the source and target domains.
2. Select the Windows NT 4 user accounts you want to migrate.
3. Select the destination OU in the target domain.
4. Select whether or not you want to migrate user account passwords. Using ADMT, you have the choice to do one of the following:

   - **Create new, complex passwords** In this case, a text document (comma-separated value [.csv] format) is created that maps user names to the new passwords. You then have the task of communicating the password to the migrated users.
   - **Set password same as user name** In this case, the password is set to the *username* value. Since both this option and the one above pose a security risk, the *User Must Change Password At Next Logon* attribute is set for the migrated user in the target domain.
   - **Migrate passwords** This option migrates the user passwords from the source domain to the target domain. Selecting this option requires you to identify the password migration source domain controller.

More Info   The *password migration source domain controller* is a domain controller in the source domain that is configured as the Password Export Server (PES) by installing the password migration DLL. Password migration is a separate component of ADMT and can be installed on any domain controller (BDC recommended) in the source domain from the Windows Server 2003 compact disc. To install the password migration DLL on a Windows NT 4 domain controller, open the \I386\ADMT\PWDMIG folder and double-click the Pwdmig.msi file. The PES maintains a database of the source domain user passwords and creates a secure communication channel to the target domain for the purpose of migrating these passwords. For more information on installing and using the password migration feature to migrate user account passwords, see the Readme.doc document in the \I386\ADMT folder on the Windows Server 2003 compact disc, or on the Windows 2000 Active Directory Migration Tool site at: *http: //www.microsoft.com/windows2000/downloads/tools/admt/default.asp.*

5.   Manage the account state with account transition options. With the help of ADMT, you can manage the transition from the source account to the target account on the Account Transition Options page. This enables you to control the state of the target domain account (enabled, disabled, or same as source) and the source domain account (disabled, or enabled for a configurable number of days).

Best Practices   A common scenario is to migrate batches of user accounts but not activate (enable) the accounts until you complete the migration. At that time you can programmatically activate all of the user accounts and cut over to the target domain. For security reasons, it is a good idea not to have an account active in both the source and the target domains. If your plan is to have users log on to the Windows Server 2003 domain immediately after their accounts are migrated, use ADMT to disable the source domain account during the migration. Alternatively, if you want to allow users to have the Windows NT 4 domain to fall back on during the migration, use ADMT to disable the source domain account some number of days after ADMT runs.

Decommissioning the Account Domain

The final step in migrating the account domain to Windows Server 2003 is to decommission the source domain. A Windows NT 4 account domain is decommissioned after you have verified that all necessary user and group accounts have been migrated to Windows Server 2003 and that all network services are otherwise provided in the (formerly) pristine forest. To decommission the account domain, simply turn off the domain controllers. After a period of time (during which you monitor for any indications of interrupted network or resource access), the domain controllers can either be upgraded to Windows Server 2003 or reinstalled with the Windows Server 2003 operating system and then promoted to domain controllers or left as member servers.

Best Practices It is recommended that you do not decommission the Windows NT 4 account domain before migrating the resource domains. The reason for this is that shared local groups and local groups in the resource domains will not resolve member names from the account domain (instead, the group membership for the local group will display "account unknown"). While there is no effect on user access to resources, it is important not to delete the "account unknown" entries because this will break the access to resources preserved by using SID History. After all of the resource domains have been restructured, you can decommission all Windows NT 4 source domains.

Now that you have migrated the global groups and user accounts, you have completed the process of migrating the account domain. At this point, your users are logging on to the Windows Server 2003 domain, and they are seamlessly accessing their shared network resources from the Windows NT 4 resource domains. Thanks to SID History and your migration skills, end users are unaware of the mixed environment in which they are working—it's business as usual. To complete your domain restructure project, as your project timeline allows, you will now want to migrate the resource domains to Windows Server 2003.

Migrating Resource Domains

The next phase of the domain restructure scenario is to migrate the Windows NT 4 resource domains.

To migrate the resource domains:

1. Satisfy the additional security requirements.
2. Identify the service accounts running on member servers.
3. Migrate computer accounts (member servers and workstations).
4. Migrate shared local groups.
5. Migrate service accounts.
6. Decommission all of the source domains.

Additional Security Requirements

There are two additional security-related steps you must take to enable the migration of Windows NT 4 resources to Windows Server 2003:

1. Make sure that the target domain's Domain Admins group is a member of the local administrators group on the Windows NT 4 resource domain. This will provide the necessary administrative rights on every member server and workstation in the resource domain so that you can migrate the resources in the domain.

2. Create a second trust from the target domain to the resource domain. In the "Creating the Pristine Forest" section earlier in this chapter, you were instructed to create a trust from all of the resource domains to the target domain. By establishing this second trust, you will have created two one-way trusts between the resource and target domains. Use the Active Directory Domains And Trusts snap-in to verify that this trust has been established.

Identifying Service Accounts

Service accounts are special user accounts that are used to operate services on computers running Windows NT 4 and Windows Server 2003. Most services operate under the Local System Authority (LSA) account. When you migrate the resource domain, you must first identify all of the services that are configured not to run under the LSA.

Migrating service accounts is a two-stage process. First, you must identify the service accounts. Then, after the computers running Windows NT 4 are migrated to the Windows Server 2003 target domain, the identified service accounts can be migrated.

➲ **To identify the service accounts operating in the Windows NT 4 source domain using ADMT, perform the following steps:**

1. Open the Service Account Migration Wizard.
2. Select the source and target domains.
3. In the source domain, select all of the computers on which you want to search for service accounts. To complete this task, you will need to consult your pre-migration documentation of the existing domain environment.
4. Finish the Service Account Migration Wizard.

At this point, the Wizard has identified all the service accounts running on the computers you identified. This information is stored in the ADMT database until it is needed later for the actual migration of these accounts. Migration of the service accounts occurs after the migration of the computer accounts themselves.

Migrating Computer Accounts

The computer accounts that reside in a Windows NT 4 resource domain include all of the Windows NT Server 4 member servers, as well as all of the computers running Windows NT Workstation 4, Windows 2000 Professional, and Windows XP Professional. Migrating computer accounts will clone all of the computer accounts from the source domain to an OU in the target domain.

Note You cannot migrate domain controller computer accounts because you cannot change the domain to which a Windows NT 4 domain controller belongs without reinstalling the operating system. Domain controllers must be moved to the Windows Server 2003 domain rather than migrated. Windows NT 4 domain controllers are moved to the Windows Server 2003 Active Directory domain by upgrading the operating system to Windows Server 2003 and then making the computer a domain controller in the target domain. Alternatively, after upgrading the operating system, you can choose to not install Active Directory and leave the upgraded server as a member server in the target domain.

⊃ **To migrate computer accounts using ADMT, complete the following steps:**

1. Open the Computer Migration Wizard.

2. Select the source and target domains.

3. From the source domain, select the computer accounts you want to migrate.

4. Select the OU in the target domain into which you want to migrate the computer accounts.

5. Select any computer objects for which you want to translate security for accounts previously migrated from the account domain to the target domain. This process updates the discretionary access control lists (DACLs) for the resources on the migrated computers with the new target domain SIDs of the migrated group and user accounts. The available objects include:

   • Files and folders

   • Local groups

   • Printers

   • Registry

   • Shares

   • User profiles

   • User rights

Tip If you choose not to translate security for the above-listed objects during the running of the Computer Migration Wizard, you can do it later using the Security Translation Wizard in ADMT. The integral component of the Security Translation Wizard is the same as the Translate Objects page in Computer Migration Wizard. The first page in the Security Translation Wizard queries whether you want to translate security for previously migrated objects. If running the Security Translation Wizard after you have migrated computer accounts, select the Previously Migrated Objects option.

6. Configure the restart of the migrated computer. To move a computer account from one domain to another, ADMT dispatches an agent to make the change on the computer itself. To complete the computer account migration process, the computer being migrated must be restarted. ADMT enables you to configure the amount of time after the Wizard completes before the computer restarts.

7. Complete the Computer Migration Wizard. When the Wizard is finished, click on View Dispatch Log to verify the success of the *dispatch agent*. This is the component that updates the domain membership of the computer and then restarts the computer. The dispatch log is very useful for troubleshooting failed computer account migrations.

Migrating Shared Local Groups

Shared local groups are simply local groups on a Windows NT 4 domain controller. Shared local groups are often used to organize access rights. If this is the case in your enterprise, you must migrate these shared local groups to the target domain to preserve access to resources for migrated users. The process for migrating shared local groups is not much different from the process for migrating global groups that was described in the section "Migrating Account Domains" earlier in this chapter.

Note   It is not necessary to migrate local groups on member servers or workstations. These local groups are (also) used to grant access to the resources on the computer, and they reside in the SAM on the member server or workstation. Because the SAM always moves with the computer, it is not necessary to move these accounts. You do need to translate security for these local groups to update the SID references for the new domain accounts. Review the Computer Migration Wizard description provided earlier in this chapter for more information on translating security during a computer migration.

➲ **To migrate shared local groups using ADMT, complete the following steps:**

1. Open the Group Account Migration Wizard.

2. Select the source and target domains.

3. Select the shared local group that you want to migrate.

4. Select the OU into which you want to migrate the group account.

5. Ensure that you select the Migrate Group SIDs To Target Domain option.

6. Allow the Group Account Migration Wizard to run to completion in order to finish migrating the shared local groups to the target domains.

Migrating Service Accounts

Now that the computer accounts are migrated to the target domain, you can complete the second phase of the service account migration process. You will recall that at the beginning of the resource domain migration process, you identified the service accounts that were used to operate services on member services. At this point in the process, you will migrate those service accounts from the Windows NT 4 resource domain to the Windows Server 2003 target domain. This procedure will ensure that all of the services not running under the LSA will continue to start the required services after the member server is migrated to the target domain.

➲ **To migrate the service account using ADMT, complete the following steps:**

1. Open the User Account Migration Wizard.
2. Select the source and target domains.
3. Select the service accounts that you want to migrate.

Tip If you do not recall the account name of the previously identified service accounts, you can review the contents of the dispatch agent log file, Dctlog.txt, which is located in the %userprofile%\Temp folder. For example, if you are logged on to the Windows Server 2003 computer as Migrator1, you will find this file in C:\Documents and Settings\Migrator1\Temp.

4. Select the OU in the target domain into which you want to migrate the service accounts.
5. Complex password generation will be used for service account migration. Regardless which password migration option you choose on the Password Options page, ADMT will always use the complex password option. ADMT recognizes that the user account you are migrating is a service account, and it will grant the account the right to log on as a service.

Note If the service accounts that you are migrating have local rights inherited only from membership in a local group (such as "log on as a service" as a member of the local administrators group), you must fix these rights by running the Security Translation Wizard. If this is the case, on the Translate Objects page of the Security Translation Wizard, select the *Local Groups* and the *User Rights* objects for the migrated member server that contained the local group through which the rights were inherited. This is the computer on which the security translation will take place.

Decommissioning the Source Domains

Now that all the account domains and resource domains have been migrated to Windows Server 2003 and Active Directory, you can decommission the Windows NT 4 source domains. At this point, the only computers left in the source domains are the domain controllers. If your migration plan calls for moving these domain controllers to the Windows Server 2003 target domain, you can move these computers to the target domain. There is a fairly complex process of taking the domain controllers offline, upgrading, promoting, demoting, and promoting again to make these Windows NT 4 computers domain controllers in the new domain. A more straightforward approach, however, is to ensure that all necessary data has been moved off of these servers, and to then perform a New Installation of the Windows Server 2003 operating system.

The final task is to remove all of the trusts that were created to perform the migration. Using the Active Directory Domains And Trusts administration tool, select each of the trusts to the now-defunct Windows NT 4 domains, and click Remove.

Upgrading then Restructuring

The third migration path to examine is the upgrade-then-restructure path, or the intraforest migration. Recall from earlier in this chapter that the upgrade-then-restructure approach first involves an upgrade of the down-level domain controllers to Windows Server 2003 (which preserves the original domain hierarchy), followed by a domain restructuring where directory services objects are migrated from the upgraded source domains to the target domain (or domains). Having read the sections of this chapter on domain upgrades and domain restructuring, you already are familiar with the tasks necessary to complete an upgrade-then-restructure migration to Active Directory. Due to Windows Server 2003 security requirements, however, you will see that account migration works differently in an intraforest scenario than in an interforest scenario.

The process of restructuring the domain after an upgrade to Windows Server 2003 does not necessarily have to occur right away. Domain restructuring can also be considered an Active Directory management skill, so that your Active Directory structure can change as your business changes.

This section will focus on how an upgrade-then-restructure migration is different from what you have already learned about the domain restructure migration path. This section does not discuss a specific tool, as these technical differences will apply to any domain migration tool that you choose.

An intraforest migration differs from an interforest migration in the following ways:

- In an intraforest migration, to preserve access to resources using SID History, accounts must be moved instead of cloned. However, moving account objects in the intraforest scenario is a destructive process and in that process, the user, group, and computer accounts from the source domain are deleted as the new accounts are created in the target domain. As a result, you will not be able to maintain the "parallel environment" that offered a convenient fall-back environment in the interforest restructure scenario.

- In an intraforest migration, to maintain group membership rules, you must move user accounts and the groups to which they belong at the same time. This is called a *closed set*. This is different from a migration from a Windows NT 4 source domain to a Windows target domain, where user accounts and group accounts can be migrated either together or separately. ADMT does not calculate a complete closed set, however, so you must be very careful when migrating users who are members of global groups. If you migrate a group whose membership includes a user account that is a member of another global group, and if that global group is not recursively a member of any groups being migrated at this time, it will break the membership between that user account and the global group that is not included. Other group types (such as universal groups) do not have this issue because they can contain members outside of their domains.

Configuring Interforest Trusts

As an alternative to performing the interforest migration process described in the preceding section, you can use interforest trusts, or *forest trusts*, from one Windows Server 2003 forest in order to access resources in another disjoined Windows Server 2003 forest.

One of the significant enhancements in Windows Server 2003 Active Directory over Windows 2000 Active Directory is the option to create trusts between Active Directory forests. In Windows 2000 Active Directory, you can only create a trust between a single domain in one forest and a single domain in another forest. In Windows Server 2003 Active Directory, you can configure a trust between the forest root domains. This trust can be a one-way or a two-way trust. After the trust is created, you can use global groups or universal groups from one forest to grant permissions to resources in another forest.

Note   Creating a trust between the two forests only enables the sharing of re-sources between the forests. All of the other forest-level distinctions still apply after the trust is created. For example, creating the trust does not mean that the forests will share a global catalog (GC) or a common schema.

When you create a forest trust in Active Directory, the trust automatically enables name suffix routing between the two forests. With name suffix routing, users can use their user principal names (UPNs) when logging on to any domain in either forest. For example, if you create a forest trust between the NWTraders.com forest and the Contoso.com forest, users from the Contoso.com forest can log on to a workstation in the NWTraders.com forest using their *alias*@contoso.com UPN. Name suffix routing is applied by default to all first-level domain names available in the forest. This includes both the default UPN suffixes and any alternative suffixes configured in the forest. The only time the name suffix routing does not work between forests is if the same UPN suffix is configured in both forests. If the Contoso.com UPN suffix is configured in the NWTraders.com forest, users from the Contoso.com forest will not be able to log on to the NWTraders.com forest using their UPN.

When you first enable the forest trust, all of the first-level domain suffixes are automati-cally routed in the UPN trust. All child domain suffixes are routed implicitly through the parent domain suffix. If you add another UPN suffix to a forest after the trust is created, you must enable name suffix routing for the new suffix. You can do this by verifying the trust between the domain or by manually adding the new suffix to the Name Suffix Routing tab on the trust's Properties sheet.

To create a forest trust, the forest must be running at Windows Server 2003 functional level. Only members of the Enterprise Admins group in a forest have permission to cre-ate forest trusts.

⊃ **To create a forest trust, use the following procedure:**

1. Start the Active Directory Domains And Trusts administrative tool. Right-click the name of the forest root domain and select Properties. Select the Trusts tab.

2. Click New Trust. The New Trust Wizard starts. Type in the domain name of the forest root domain in the other forest.

3. You are then given a choice of what type of trust you want to configure. Fig-ure 7-4 shows the interface. You can create an external trust or a forest trust. An external trust is a nontransitive trust, while a forest trust is always transitive. Select Forest Trust.

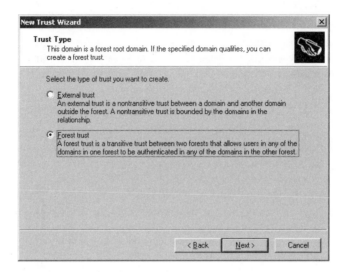

Figure 7-4. *Configuring the trust type for a forest trust.*

4. You are then given a choice about the direction the trust will flow. Figure 7-5 shows the options available.

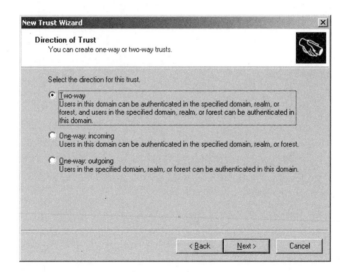

Figure 7-5. *Configuring the forest trust direction.*

5. You are then given a choice of whether to create the trust only for this domain or for the other domain as well. (These two domains are the forest root domains in each forest.) The forest trust can only be configured between the forest root domains. Figure 7-6 shows these choices. If you chose to configure both sides of the trust at one time, you have to type in the name and password for the Enterprise Admins account that exists in the other forest. If you chose to set up the trust for this domain only, you are asked to type in a password that will be used to configure the initial trust. You must then use this password to configure the trust in the forest root domain from the other forest.

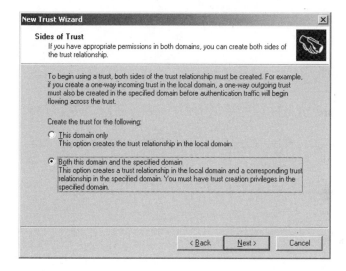

Figure 7-6. *Choosing to configure one side or both sides of a trust.*

6. You are then given the choice of the level of authentication to be granted for both the outgoing trust and the incoming trust. Figure 7-7 shows the interface for the outgoing trust authentication level. This option allows you to carefully control access to resources between the forests. If you choose to apply forest-wide authentication, the users from one forest will have access to all servers and resources in the other forest. This is the same configuration as the trusts between the domains within a forest. Users from one domain in a forest can access resources in any other domain in either forest, provided they have been given permission to access the resource. You can also apply selective authentication for the forest trust. In this case, you must explicitly give the users or groups from one forest permission to access servers in another forest. You can do this by granting the users or groups the Allowed To Authenticate right in Active Directory.

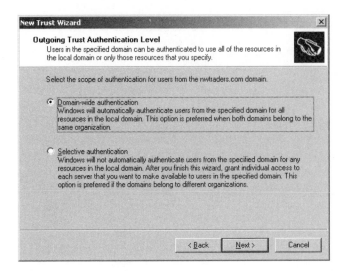

Figure 7-7. *Configuring the level of authentication for a forest trust.*

7. After configuring the trust, you are given the option to automatically verify the trust.

Summary

This chapter explored the different migration paths to go from either a Windows NT 4 directory service or Windows 2000 Active Directory to Windows Server 2003 Active Directory. The three primary migration paths—upgrade, restructure, and upgrade-then-restructure—were described. There are several criteria you can use to determine which migration path is right for your organization. For organizations that are satisfied with their current domain structure, the upgrade migration path is the least complicated, least risky means to upgrade the directory service from Windows NT Server 4 or Windows 2000 Server to Windows Server 2003. If your domain structure is not in line with your current business or organizational model, you will need to restructure your domain. Regardless of the chosen path, careful planning, testing, and piloting of your migration plan is critical to the success of your migration project.

This chapter also examined the key decision points for performing a Windows NT Server 4 upgrade and a Windows 2000 Server upgrade. Next, the process of restructuring Windows NT 4 account domains and resource domains, using ADMT, was discussed. Then the upgrade-then-restructure migration path, also known as an intraforest migration, was distinguished from a domain restructure. A discussion of the interforest trust feature of Windows Server 2003 completed this chapter.

Part III
Administering Windows Server 2003 Active Directory

The first two parts of this book explained the concepts and components of the Microsoft Windows Server 2003 Active Directory directory service and provided you with information about how to design, implement, and deploy Active Directory. After you deploy Active Directory, you must also administer Active Directory to provide the maximum benefit for your company. Part III details many of the administrative processes that you will use to do this. One of the primary reasons for deploying a directory service is to provide security, so Chapter 8, "Active Directory Security," begins by describing the concepts behind Windows Server 2003 Active Directory security. Chapter 9, "Delegating the Administration of Active Directory," expands on this discussion by describing ways that you can delegate administrative permissions within your domain. Chapter 10, "Managing Active Directory Objects," introduces you to the management of Active Directory objects. One of the most powerful features in Active Directory is Group Policy, which can be used to manage thousands of computers using Active Directory. Chapter 11, "Introduction to Group Policies," Chapter 12, "Using Group Policies to Manage Software," and Chapter 13, "Using Group Policies to Manage Computers," all focus on group policies and explain how to use these tools to implement software distribution and manage client computers.

Chapter 8
Active Directory Security

One of the primary reasons for deploying a directory service like Active Directory is to provide security on the corporate network. Every company stores business-critical information on file servers on the network. Managing secure access to the information is critical to ensure that only properly authorized users have access to the data. Almost all companies deploy e-mail servers such as Microsoft Exchange 2000 Server and want to provide users with secure access to their mailboxes. Microsoft Windows Server 2003 Active Directory provides this level of security.

This chapter begins by introducing the basics of Active Directory security. Active Directory directory service uses several basic building blocks and concepts to provide security on a Windows Server 2003 network. After an introduction to the security basics, this chapter will focus on one essential component of that security. This component consists of the authentication and authorization functions and is used by Active Directory to ensure that users are who they say they are (authentication) and to provide access to the resources the user should have access to (authorization). Windows Server 2003, like Microsoft Windows 2000, uses Kerberos as the primary security protocol, so much of this chapter will focus on understanding the role of Kerberos in authentication and authorization.

Active Directory Security Basics

There are some basic concepts needed to understand how Active Directory security works on a Windows Server 2003 network. Essentially, Active Directory security consists of two types of objects and the interaction between the two objects. The first object is a *security principal,* or an object that represents a user, group, service, or computer that needs access to some resource on the network. The second object is the resource itself, which is the object that the security principal needs access to. To provide the proper level of security, Active Directory must have some way of determining the identity of the security principal and then giving the right level of access to the resources.

Security Principals

Security principals are the only objects in Active Directory that can log on to Active Directory and be granted permission to access resources on the network. A security principal is an object in Active Directory that represents a user, group, service, or computer. Every security principal is assigned a security identifier (SID) when the object is created. The SID is made up of two parts. The first part is a domain identifier, and all security principals in a domain have the same domain identifier. The second part of the SID is the relative identifier (RID), which is unique for each security principal in an Active Directory domain.

The SID is an essential component when configuring security for resources on a Windows Server 2003 network. When you grant permission to a resource, you use the security principal's display name, but Windows Server 2003 actually uses the SID to manage access to the resource. When a user tries to access a resource on a server in the domain, the operating system grants permission to the user's SID, rather than the person's name. This means that if a user's display name is changed, the permissions granted to the user do not change. However, if a user object is deleted and then re-created with the same name, the user will not be able to access the same resources because the SID will be different.

Access Control Lists

The other component that is included in Active Directory security is the entity that a security principal needs to access. This entity may be another object in Active Directory such as an organizational unit (OU), a printer object, or even a security principal. The entity may also be a resource such as a file on a server running Windows Server 2003 or a mailbox on a server running Microsoft Exchange 2000 Server.

The permissions that have been granted to these objects are located in an access control list (ACL), also called a *security descriptor*. Every object in Active Directory or on an NTFS file system partition has a security descriptor. The security descriptor includes the SID of the security principal that owns the object as well as the SID for the object's primary group. In addition, every object has two separate ACLs: a discretionary access control list (DACL) and a system access control list (SACL). The DACL lists the security principals that have been assigned permission to the object as well as the level of permissions that have been assigned to each security principal. The DACL is made up of a series of access control entries (ACEs). Each ACE lists one SID and then identifies the level of access that the SID has to the object. The ACE includes entries for all types of security principals. For example, a user account might have Read permissions to a file and a security group might have Full Control. The DACL for the file will have (at least) two ACEs, one granting the user Read permission and another granting the group Full Control.

The SACL lists the security principals whose access to the resource needs to be audited. The list of ACEs in the SACL indicates whose access is to be audited and the level of auditing required.

> **Note**   The DACL can contain ACEs that grant access to a resource as well as ACEs that deny access. The ACEs that deny access are always listed first in the ACL, so they are evaluated first by the security subsystem. If an ACE denies access to the resource, the security subsystem does not evaluate any other ACEs. This means that an ACE that denies permission to a resource always overrides any ACE that grants access to a specific SID.

Access Tokens

The connecting point between the security principal's SID and the ACL is the *access token*. When a user is authenticated through Active Directory, the user is assigned an access token during the logon process. This token includes the user's primary SID, the SIDs for any groups to which the user belongs, and the user's privileges and rights.

The access token is used by the security subsystem whenever a user tries to access a resource. When the user tries to access a resource, the token is presented by the client workstation to any thread or application that requests security information before allowing access to a resource. For example, when a user tries to access a mailbox on a server running Exchange 2000 Server, the access token is presented to the server. In this case, the security subsystem on the server running Exchange 2000 Server will compare the SIDs in the access token to the permissions granted in the ACL. If the permissions granted to the SID allow it, the user will be able to open the mailbox.

Authentication

In order for the security processes, including their use of SIDs and ACLs, to work properly, there must be some way for a user to gain access to the network. Essentially, users must be able to prove that they are who they say they are so that they can retrieve their access token from the domain controller. This process is called *authentication*.

Authentication occurs during the initial client logon process. When the user sits down at a Windows 2000 or Microsoft Windows XP Professional computer and enters Ctrl+Alt+Del, the Winlogon service on the local computer switches to the logon screen and loads the Graphic Identification and Authentication (GINA) dynamic-link library (DLL). By default, this is the Msgina.dll. However, third parties can build alternative GINAs (for example, the NetWare client uses the Nwgina.dll). After the user has typed in the username and password and has selected a domain, GINA passes the entered credentials back to the Winlogon process. The Winlogon service passes the information to the Local Security Authority (LSA). The LSA immediately applies a one-way hash to the user's password and deletes the clear text password that the user typed in. The LSA then calls the appropriate Security Support Provider (SSP) through the Security Support Provider Interface (SSPI). Windows Server 2003 provides two primary SSPs for network authentication, the Kerberos SSP and the NT LAN Manager (NTLM) SSP. If Windows 2000, or later, clients are logging on to a Windows 2000 or Windows Server 2003 network, the Kerberos SSP is selected and the information is passed to the SSP. The SSP then communicates with the domain controller to authenticate the user. The Kerberos authentication process will be covered in detail later in this chapter.

If the logon procedure succeeds, the user is authenticated and granted access to the network. If the user has logged on to a domain, and if all the resources that the user needs to access are in the same forest, this is the only time that the user will be authenticated. Until the user logs off, all the permissions the user gets on the network are based on the initial authentication.

Authorization

Authorization is the second step in the process of gaining access to network resources, and it takes place after authentication. During authentication, you are proving your identity by typing in the correct username and password. During authorization, you are given access to resources on the network. Another way to think about this is to say that during authentication the access token is created for you. During authorization, you present the access token to a server or service and request access to a resource. If the SIDs in your access token match the SIDs in the ACL that grant access, you are given access to the resource.

Kerberos Security

So far this chapter has covered the basics of Active Directory security without discussing the actual mechanism that implements the security. The primary mechanism for delivering authentication in Active Directory is the Kerberos protocol. The Kerberos protocol was first developed by engineers at the Massachusetts Institute of Technology (MIT) in the late 1980s. The current version of Kerberos is version 5 (Kerberos v5), which is described in RFC 1510. The Windows Server 2003 implementation of Kerberos is fully RFC-1510 compliant, with some extensions for public key authentication.

Kerberos is the default authentication protocol for Windows 2000 Active Directory and for Windows Server 2003 Active Directory. Whenever a Windows 2000 or later client authenticates to Active Directory, the client will always try to use Kerberos. The other protocol that can be used to authenticate to Active Directory is NTLM, which is supported primarily for backward compatibility for older clients. Kerberos has a number of advantages over NTLM:

- **Mutual authentication** With NTLM, authentication is only one way, that is, the server authenticates the client. With Kerberos, the client can also authenticate the server, ensuring that the server that is responding to the client request is the correct server.

- **More efficient access to resources** When a user tries to access a network resource on an NTLM-based network (such as Microsoft Windows NT 4), the server where the resource is located has to contact a domain controller to check the user's access permissions. On a Kerberos-based network, the client connects to the domain controller and acquires a session ticket to connect to the resource server. This means that the resource server does not need to connect to the domain controller.

- **Improved trust management** NTLM trusts are always one-way, nontransitive, and manually configured. Kerberos trusts are automatically configured and maintained between all the domains in a forest and are transitive and two-way. In addition, Kerberos trusts can be configured between forests and between Windows Server 2003 Kerberos domains and other Kerberos implementations.

- **Delegated authentication** When a client connects to a server using NTLM authentication, the server can use the client credentials to access resources only on the local server. With Kerberos authentication, the server can use the client credentials to access resources on another server.

Note   Windows Server 2003 also supports authentication through Secure Sockets Layer/Transport Layer Security (SSL/TLS), Digest authentication, and Passport authentication. Since these authentication services are primarily used in an Internet environment for authentication to Microsoft Internet Information Services (IIS) 6.0, these authentication options will not be discussed.

Introduction to Kerberos

There are three components in a Kerberos-based system. First of all, there is the client who needs to gain access to network resources. Second, there is the server that manages the network resources and ensures that only properly authenticated and authorized users can gain access to the resource. The third component is a Key Distribution Center (KDC), which serves as a central location to store user information and as a central service to authenticate users.

The Kerberos protocol defines how these three components interact. This interaction is based on two key principles. First of all, Kerberos operates based on the assumption that authentication traffic between a workstation and server crosses an insecure network. This means that no confidential authentication traffic is ever sent across the network in clear text. A practical example of this is that the user password is never sent across the network, not even in an encrypted form. The second principle is that Kerberos operates based on a shared secret authentication model. In a shared secret authentication model, the client and the authenticating server share a secret that is not known by anyone else. In most cases, this shared secret is the user password. When the user logs on to a network secured by Kerberos, the user password is used to encrypt a packet of information. When the Kerberos server receives the packet, it decrypts the information using the copy of the password stored on the server. If the decryption is successful, then the authenticating server knows that the user knows the shared secret and access is granted.

> **Note** When the user logs on, he or she will usually type in their password. The domain controller checks to see if that password is accurate. However, because Kerberos operates with the assumption that the network is insecure, this checking is done without sending the password across the network.

One of the problems with a shared secret authentication model is that the user and the server managing the network resource must have some way of sharing the secret. If one user is trying to access a resource on one server, a user account can be created on the server with a password that only the user knows. When the user tries to access the resources on the server, that user can present the shared secret (password) and gain access to the resource. However, in a corporate environment, there may be thousands of users and hundreds of servers. Managing distinct shared secrets for all of these users would be impractical. Kerberos deals with this issue by using a Key Distribution Center (KDC). The KDC runs as a service on a server on the network and manages the shared secrets for all users on the network. The KDC has one central database of all user accounts on the network, and it stores the shared secret for each user (in the form of a one-way hash of the user's password). When a user needs access to the network and resources on the network, the KDC confirms that the user knows the shared secret and then authenticates the user.

> **Note** In Kerberos terminology, this central server that manages user accounts is a KDC, as discussed previously. In the Windows Server 2003 implementation of Kerberos, this server is called a domain controller. Every Active Directory domain controller is a KDC. In Kerberos, the boundary defined by the user database on one KDC is called a realm. In Windows Server 2003 terminology, this boundary is called a domain.

Each KDC (which runs as the Kerberos Key Distribution Center service in Windows Server 2003) is made up of two separate services: the Authentication Service (AS) and the Ticket-Granting Service (TGS). The AS is responsible for the initial client logon and issues a Ticket-Granting Ticket (TGT) to the client. The TGS is responsible for all session tickets that are used to access resources on the Windows Server 2003 network.

The KDC stores the account database used for Kerberos authentication. In the Windows Server 2003 implementation of Kerberos, the database is managed by the directory system agent (DSA), which runs within the LSA process on each domain controller. Clients and applications are never given direct access to the account database; all requests must go through the DSA using one of the Active Directory interfaces. Every object within the account database (in fact, every attribute on every object) is protected with an ACL. The DSA ensures that any attempts to access the account database are properly authorized.

Tip   When Active Directory is installed on the first domain controller in the domain, a special account named krbtgt is created in the domain. The account cannot be deleted or renamed and should never be enabled. The account is assigned a password when it is created and the password is automatically changed on a regular basis. This password is used to create a secret key that is used to encrypt and decrypt the TGTs issued by all the domain controllers in the domain.

Kerberos Authentication

Kerberos authentication begins when the Kerberos security provider is called by the LSA on a Microsoft Windows 2000 Professional or Windows XP Professional workstation or a server running Windows 2000 Server or Windows Server 2003. When a user logs on by typing a username and password, the client computer applies a one-way hash to the user's password to create a secret key, which is cached in secure memory on the workstation. A one-way hash means that the password cannot be derived from the hash.

To perform a client logon process, the client and server systems follow these steps:

1. The Kerberos SSP on the workstation sends an authentication message to the KDC. (See Figure 8-1.) The message includes:

    - The username

    - The user realm (domain name)

    - A request for a TGT

    - Preauthentication data, which includes a time stamp, plus possibly other data

    The preauthentication data is encrypted using the secret key derived from the user password.

2. When the message arrives at the server, the server examines the username and then checks the directory database for its copy of the secret key associated with the user's account. The server decrypts the encrypted data in the message with the secret key and checks the time stamp. If the decryption is successful and the time stamp is recorded as being within 5 minutes of the current time on the server, the server prepares to authenticate the user. If the decryption fails, the user must have entered the wrong password, and the authentication fails. If the time stamp is more than 5 minutes off the current time on the server, the authentication will also fail. The reason for the small time difference is to prevent someone from capturing the authentication packets and then replaying them at a later time. The default maximum allowable time difference of 5 minutes can be configured on the domain security policies.

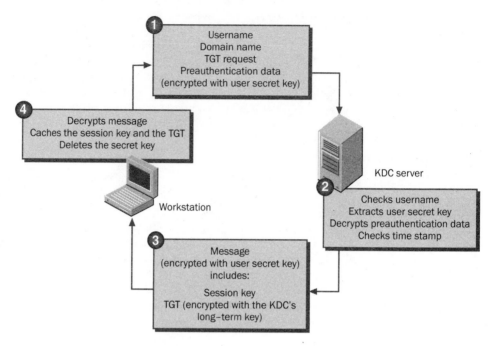

Figure 8-1. *Getting a Kerberos TGT.*

3. After the user is authenticated, the server sends the client a message that includes a *session key* and a *TGT*. (See Figure 8-1.) The session key is an encryption key that the client will use to interact with the KDC instead of using the client's secret key. The TGT is a session ticket that grants the user access to the domain controller. For the lifetime of the TGT, the client will present the TGT to the domain controller whenever the client needs access to resources on the network. The entire message from the server is encrypted using the user's secret key. In addition, the TGT is encrypted using the server's long-term secret key.

4. When the packet arrives at the client computer, the user's secret key is used to decrypt the packet. If the decryption is successful and the time stamp is valid, the user's computer assumes that the KDC is authentic because it knew the user's secret key. The session key is then cached on the local computer until it expires or until the user logs off the workstation. This session key will be used to encrypt all future connections to the KDC. This means that the client no longer needs to remember the secret key, and it is deleted from the workstation cache. The TGT is stored in an encrypted form in the workstation cache.

Note The Kerberos protocol includes the Authentication Service (AS) Exchange, which is the subprotocol used to perform the initial authentication for the user. The process just described uses the AS Exchange subprotocol. The initial message sent by the client to the KDC is called a KRB_AS_REQ message. The server response to the client is called a KRB_AS_REP message.

5. At this point, the user has been authenticated, but the user still does not have any access to resources on the network. The TGT is a session ticket that grants access to the KDC, but to gain access to any other resources on the network, the user must acquire another session ticket from the KDC. (See Figure 8-2.) The client workstation sends a session ticket request to the KDC. The request includes the user's name, the TGT granted during authentication, the name of the network service that the user wants access to, and a time stamp that is encrypted using the session key that was acquired during the AS Exchange process.

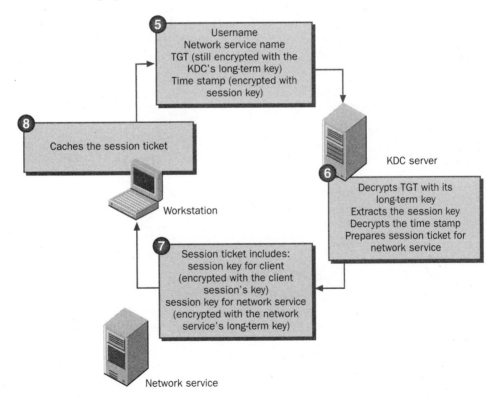

Figure 8-2. *Acquiring a Kerberos session ticket for a network resource.*

6. The KDC decrypts the TGT using its long-term key. It then extracts the session key from the TGT and decrypts the time stamp to ensure that the client is using the correct session key and to ensure that the time stamp is valid. If the session key and time stamp are acceptable, the KDC prepares a session ticket for the network service.

7. The session ticket includes two copies of a session key that the client will use to connect to the required resource. The first copy of the session key is encrypted using the session key the client obtained during the initial logon. The second copy of the session key is intended for the network service and includes the user's access information. This part of the session ticket is encrypted using the network service's secret key, which is unknown to the client workstation but known to both the KDC and the network service because the server where the resource is located is a member of the KDC realm.

8. The client workstation caches both parts of the session ticket in memory.

Note The process described in steps 5 through 8 uses the Ticket-Granting Service (TGS) Exchange subprotocol. The session ticket request sent by the client is called a KRB_TGS_REQ message; the server response is a KRB_TGS_REP message.

9. The client now presents the session ticket to the network service to gain access. (See Figure 8-3.)

10. The network service decrypts the session key in the session ticket using the long-term key that it shares with the KDC. If this decryption is successful, the network service knows that the ticket comes from a trusted KDC. The network service then decrypts the user's access token using the session key and checks the user access level. The client request also includes a time stamp, which is encrypted with the session key and checked by the server.

Note The process described in steps 9 and 10 uses the Client/Server (CS) Exchange subprotocol. The client request is called a KRB_AP_REQ message.

Assuming the authentication and authorization are successful, the client is given access to the server resources. If the client needs subsequent use of the resource or service, the session ticket is pulled from the client's ticket cache and reissued to the target resource server. If the session ticket has expired, the client has to return to the KDC to obtain a new ticket.

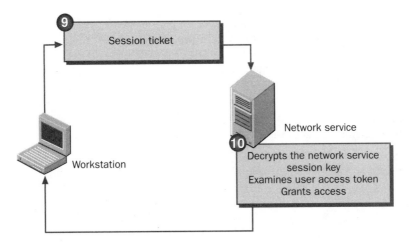

Figure 8-3. *Accessing the network service.*

More Info You can view the contents of the client cache by using two tools available for download from the Microsoft Web site. KList.exe provides a command-line interface to view and delete the Kerberos tickets. The Kerberos Tray tool (Kerbtray.exe) provides a graphical user interface (GUI) for viewing the tickets. Figure 8-4 shows an example of the information provided by the Kerberos Tray tool. The Kerberos Tray tool is available at *http://www.microsoft.com/windows2000 /techinfo/reskit/tools/existing/kerbtray-o.asp* and the KList tool is available at *http://www.microsoft.com/windows2000/techinfo/reskit/tools/existing/klist-o.asp.*

Figure 8-4. *Viewing Kerberos tickets using the Kerberos Tray tool.*

This process of gaining access to a resource on the network means that the KDC is only involved during the initial client logon and the first time the client tries to access a resource on a specific server. When the user first logs on, that user is given a TGT that gives the client access to the KDC during the lifetime of the ticket. When the client tries to connect to a network resource, the client contacts the KDC again and gets a session ticket to access that resource. This session ticket includes the user's access token. When this token is presented to the server where the resource is located, the server can determine the level of resource-access the user should have.

Authenticating Across Domain Boundaries

The same authentication process applies when a user authenticates across domain boundaries. For example, a company may have a three-domain forest as shown in Figure 8-5.

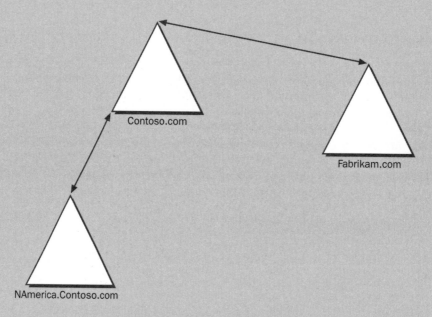

Figure 8-5. *Authentication across domain boundaries.*

If a user with an account in Fabrikam.com travels to the NAmerica.Contoso.com domain location and tries to log on to the network, the client workstation must be able to connect to a domain controller in the Fabrikam.com domain. In this case, the client computer sends the initial logon request to the NAmerica.Contoso.com domain controller. The domain controller determines that the user account is located in the Fabrikam.com domain, so it needs to refer the client workstation to that domain. If all of the domains were configured with shortcut trusts with each other, the domain controller could directly refer the client computer to a domain controller in the Fabrikam.com domain. However, if no shortcut trusts have been created, there is no direct trust between NAmerica.Contoso.com and Fabrikam.com. In this case, the NAmerica domain controller will refer the client computer to a domain controller in the Contoso.com domain. The referral includes a session key granting access to the domain controller in the Contoso.com domain. The session key was created when the NAmerica domain was added to the Contoso.com forest and the initial trust was created between the two domains. The session key guarantees that the logon request is coming from a trusted domain. The client computer then sends an authentication request to the Contoso.com domain. Now the client is referred to a domain controller in the Fabrikam.com domain. Again this referral includes a session key to access the domain controller. The client computer then sends a TGT request to the home domain controller in Fabrikam.com.

A similar process is followed when a client tries to gain access to a resource on a domain other than the user's home domain. In this case, the client needs to acquire a session ticket from a domain controller in the domain where the resource is located, so the client will be referred through the same process until it can connect to the right domain controller.

This authentication process has implications for forest design, especially if users frequently log on to domains other than their home domain or access resources in domains other than the home domain. If you are designing a forest with multiple domains, the client may have to traverse the entire trust path between the domains. If this happens often, you may want to put domain controllers for the root domains in locations close to the users. You can also use shortcut trusts so that the domain controller referrals can be sent directly to the appropriate domains.

Delegation of Authentication

One of the issues that can complicate accessing network services is that the network service may be distributed across multiple servers. For example, the client might connect to a front-end server that must connect to a back-end database server to collect some information. In this environment, the user's credentials (rather than the front-end server's credentials) should be used to access the back-end server so that the user will only get access to authorized information. In Windows 2000, Kerberos provides this functionality in two ways: using proxy tickets and using forwarded tickets. If proxy tickets are enabled, the client will send a session ticket request to the KDC requesting access to the back-end server. The KDC grants the session ticket and sets the PROXIABLE flag on the ticket. The client then presents the session ticket to the front-end server, which uses the ticket to access information on the back-end server. The main problem with proxy tickets is that the client must know the identity of the back-end server. The other option is to use forwarded tickets. If these tickets are enabled, the client will send an AS Exchange request to the KDC requesting a TGT that the front-end server will be able to use to access back-end servers. The KDC creates a TGT and sends it to the client. The client sends the TGT to the front-end server, which then uses the TGT to acquire a session ticket to access the back-end server on behalf of the client.

There are two significant concerns with the way delegation of authentication is implemented in Windows 2000. The first concern is that delegation of authentication can only be used if the client is authenticated using Kerberos. This means that all of the Windows NT, Microsoft Windows 95, and Windows 98 clients cannot use delegation of authentication. In Windows Server 2003, the client can use any authentication protocol. The second Windows 2000–related concern is related to the security of the delegation. In Windows 2000, once the front-end server obtains the forwarded ticket from the KDC, it can use the ticket to access any network service on behalf of the client. Windows Server 2003 provides the option for constrained delegation, which means you can configure the account so it is delegated for only specific services on the network (based on service principal names). Constrained delegation is available only when the domain is set to Windows Server 2003 functional level.

In order for the delegation of authentication to be successful, you must ensure that both the user account and the service or computer account are configured to support delegation of authentication. To configure this on a user account, access the user's Properties sheet through the Active Directory Users And Computers administrative tool, select the Account tab, then scroll through the Account Options list and make sure that the Account Is Sensitive And Cannot Be Delegated option is not selected. (This is not selected by default.) To configure the service account for delegation, you must first determine whether the logon account used by the service is a normal user account or whether it is the LocalSystem account. If the service runs under a normal user account, access the user's Account tab, make sure the Account Is Sensitive And Cannot Be Delegated option is not selected. (This is not selected by default.) If the service runs under a LocalSystem account, the delegation must be configured on the computer account's Properties sheet. (Figure 8-6 shows the interface.) To implement the Windows 2000 level of authentication, select the Trust This Computer For Delegation To Any Service (Kerberos Only) option. To implement the Windows Server 2003 enhancements, select the Trust This Computer For Delegation To Specified Services Only option. You can then select whether the client must authenticate using Kerberos only or can use any protocol and then select the services (based on service principal names registered in Active Directory) to which the computer can present delegated credentials.

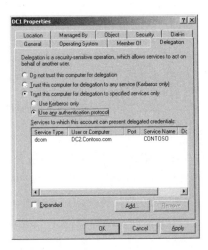

Figure 8-6. *Configuring constrained delegation on a computer account.*

Configuring Kerberos in Windows Server 2003

As mentioned earlier, Kerberos is the default authentication protocol for Windows 2000, or later, clients logging on to Active Directory. You can configure several Kerberos properties through the domain security policy. To access the Kerberos policy settings, open the Domain Security Policy from Administrative Tools and expand the Account Policies folder. (The interface is shown in Figure 8-7.)

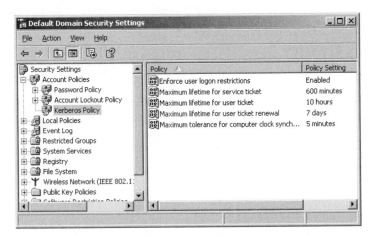

Figure 8-7. *Configuring the Kerberos settings through Domain Security Policy.*

- **Enforce User Logon Restrictions** This policy sets the option for the KDC to validate every request for a session ticket against the user rights setting on the target computer. If this policy is enabled, the user requesting the session ticket must have either the Allow Log On Locally right, if they are logging on interactively, or the Access This Computer From The Network right on the target computer. The Allow Log On Locally right and the Access This Computer From The Network right are assigned under Local Policies\User Rights Assignment in the Domain Security Policy. By default, this policy is enabled.

- **Maximum Lifetime For Service Ticket** This policy sets the maximum amount of time (in minutes) that a session ticket can be used to access a specific service. If the setting is zero minutes, the ticket will never expire. If the setting is not zero, the setting must be greater than 10 minutes and less than, or equal to, the setting for Maximum Lifetime For User Ticket. By default, the setting is 600 minutes (10 hours).

- **Maximum Lifetime For User Ticket** This policy sets the maximum amount of time (in hours) that a user's TGT can be used. After the TGT expires, a new one must be requested from the KDC or the existing ticket must be renewed. By default, the setting is 10 hours.

- **Maximum Lifetime For User Ticket Renewal** This policy sets the amount of time (in days) that a TGT can be renewed (as opposed to getting a new TGT). By default, the setting is 7 days.

- **Maximum Tolerance For Computer Clock Synchronization** This policy sets the maximum time difference (in minutes) that Kerberos will tolerate between the time on a client computer and the time on the domain controller that provides Kerberos authentication. If the time difference between the two computers is greater than this tolerance level, all Kerberos tickets will be refused. By default, the setting is 5 minutes. Be aware that if this setting is changed, it will revert to the default when the computer is restarted.

In most cases the default Kerberos settings are appropriate. In high security environments, you can decrease the settings for ticket lifetimes. However, as these settings are decreased, the clients will need to connect to the KDC more often, creating additional network traffic and additional load on the domain controllers.

Integration with Public Key Infrastructure

As mentioned earlier, Kerberos is based on a shared-secret authentication model. This provides excellent security but imposes one important limitation on providing access to a Windows Server 2003 network. This limitation is that every user that accesses the network must have a user account in the KDC account database. If a user does not exist in the database, he or she cannot be granted any access to the network.

This works well for a company where all the users who log on to the network are known and a user account can be created for each user. However, many companies are expanding the list of users who require access to network resources to include users who are not employees. A company may enter into a short-term partnership with another company and be required to provide access to network resources to employees from the other company. Or a company may want to provide specified customers with access to resources on the company network. In these scenarios, the list of people requiring access to the network might be very long, so creating a user account for each of the users would be impractical.

Public Key Infrastructure (PKI) has become the primary means for solving this problem of granting access to users who do not have a user account. PKI moves away from a shared-secret authentication model and replaces it with a certificate-based authentication model. In PKI, users are not authenticated based on the fact that they know the correct password, but they are authenticated based on the fact that they hold the right certificate. PKI is based on three essential concepts: public and private keys, digital certificates, and certificate authorities (CAs).

PKI begins with the concept that every user or computer involved in the information exchange has two keys: a private key and a public key. The private key is known only to one user. It can be stored on the computer's hard drive, as part of a roaming profile, or on a different device, such as a smart card. The public key, on the other hand, is made available to anyone who asks for it. The private and public keys are related, but there is no way to derive a private key from a public key. These public and private keys are used in a variety of ways.

One of the ways that the public and private keys are used is to encrypt information as it is sent across the network. A user's public key is used to encrypt the message. Because the public key is made available to anyone who requests it, anyone can send a message encrypted with a user's public key. However, the only key that can decrypt the message is the user's private key. That means that the only person who can decrypt a message that is encrypted using a public key is the person holding the private key. Anyone else capturing this packet on the network does not have the correct private key and therefore cannot read the message.

Another way that public and private keys are used is to digitally sign and seal messages sent between two users. A digital signature is used to ensure the identity of the sender of the message and also to ensure the integrity of the message. To create a digital signature, the entire message is sent through a mathematical hash. This hash creates a message digest, which is encrypted using the message sender's private key. The encrypted hash is sent with the message as a digital signature. When the message recipient gets the message, the same hash is applied to the message, creating a second message digest. Then the sender's public key is used to decrypt the digital signature. If the recipient's message digest is identical to the result of the decrypted signature, the integrity and authenticity of the message are confirmed.

The second component of PKI is the digital certificate. The purpose of a certificate is to identify the certificate holder. When a person or company applies for a certificate from a certificate authority (CA), the CA confirms the identity of the person or company requesting the certificate. When the certificate is granted to the user, the user is also given the associated public key as well as the private key for the certificate. The certificate is also digitally signed by the certificate authority, thus adding the certificate authority's stamp of authenticity to the certificate. The current standard for these certificates is X.509 v3. The certificate includes information about the person, computer, or service to which the certificate has been issued, information about the certificate itself, such as the expiration date, and information about the CA that issued the certificate.

The certificates required for PKI are issued by CAs,,which are network servers that manage the granting and revoking of certificates. Because of the importance of PKI for the Internet, a wide variety of CAs is currently available, including popular commercial CAs such as Verisign and Thawte. Most Internet clients like Microsoft Internet Explorer are automatically configured to trust certificates issued by these commercial CAs. You can also set up your own CA using Windows Server 2003. The Certificate Services included with Windows Server 2003 are a full-featured CA that can be used to issue certificates to people within your company or to people in partner organizations.

More Info   Planning and deploying a PKI requires a significant amount of effort. Windows Server 2003 provides the option to create a PKI using an enterprise CA that is tightly integrated with Active Directory. By deploying an enterprise CA, you can configure policies for automating most of the administrative effort involved in issuing and renewing certificates. The Microsoft Web site and Help And Support Center in Windows Server 2003 provide detailed information for setting up a PKI.

One of the main reasons for using certificates is to allow users who may not have an account in Active Directory to gain access to resources on the Windows Server 2003 network. For example, you may want to set up a secure Web site so that partner organizations or customers can get access to some confidential information on your network. However, in Windows Server 2003, permission to access network resources can only be granted to security principals. There is no option to assign permissions based solely on certificates. However, you can provide access to resources for users who have certificates, but not Active Directory user accounts, by mapping a certificate to a user account and then using the account to assign permissions.

Windows Server 2003 provides two different ways that a certificate can be mapped to a user account:

- **One-to-one mapping** In this case, a single certificate is mapped to a single Windows Server 2003 user account. With a one-to-one mapping, you must assign a certificate as well as create a user account for each user. This may be a good solution if you want remote employees of the company to access secure resources through a secure Web site. However, it does not simplify your administration. Nonetheless, with one-to-one name mapping you can control the level of access for each user.

- **Many-to-one mapping** In this case, many certificates are mapped to one Active Directory account name. For example, if you are creating a partner relationship with another company and the employees of the company need access to a secure Web site, you can create one user account. Then you can link as many certificates as you want to that one user account. For example, if that company has its own CA, you can create a rule that maps all certificates issued by that CA to one user account in your domain. Then you can assign permissions to network resources using that one account.

Tip   You can map certificates to user accounts through the Active Directory Users And Computers administrative tool or through the Microsoft Internet Information Server (IIS) Manager. In the Active Directory Users And Computers administrative tool, use the Name Mappings option that is available when you right-click a user account.

Integration with Smart Cards

Smart cards provide another option for integrating PKI with Kerberos authentication. When Kerberos is used without PKI, the shared secret between the client and the KDC is used to encrypt the initial logon exchange with the authentication service. This key is derived from the user's password and the same key is used to encrypt and decrypt the information. Smart cards use a PKI model in which both a public key and a private key are used to encrypt and decrypt the logon information.

A smart card contains the user's public and private keys plus an X.509 v3 certificate. All of these components are used when the user uses the smart card to authenticate to Active Directory. The logon process begins when the user inserts a smart card into the smart card reader and enters his or her personal identification number (PIN). The insertion of the smart card into the reader is interpreted as a Ctrl+Alt+Del sequence by the LSA on the computer, and the logon process begins.

The PIN is used to read the user's certificate and public and private keys from the smart card. The client then sends a regular TGT request to the KDC. However, rather than sending the preauthorization data (time stamp) encrypted with the user's secret key derived from the password, the client sends the public key and the certificate to the KDC. The TGT request still includes the preauthorization data, but it is digitally signed with the user's private key.

When the message arrives at the KDC, it checks the client certificate to ensure that it is valid and that the CA that issued the certificate is trusted. The KDC also checks the digital signature of the preauthorization data to ensure the authenticity of the message sender and the integrity of the message. If both of these checks come back positive, the KDC uses the user principal name (UPN) included on the client certificate to look up the account name in Active Directory. If the user account is valid, the KDC authenticates the user and sends a TGT including a session key back to the client. The session key is encrypted using the client's public key, and the client uses its private key to decrypt the information. This session key is then used for all connections to the KDC.

Tip   It takes a considerable amount of work to set up smart card logon for your network. First of all, you will have to deploy a CA to issue the certificates. Then you will have to set up smart card enrollment stations where users can get their smart cards, and the correct certificates and keys can be assigned to the cards. After the initial deployment, you will have to handle the administrative tasks of dealing with lost or forgotten cards. Smart cards provide excellent additional security on your network, but this additional security comes with considerable administrative effort.

Interoperability with Other Kerberos Systems

Because Kerberos is based on an open standard, it provides excellent opportunities for interoperability with other Kerberos-based systems. Any of the components that are part of the Windows Server 2003 Kerberos implementation can be replaced by a non-Windows equivalent. These three components are:

- The Kerberos client
- The Kerberos Key Distribution Center
- The network resource that is using Kerberos for authorization

There are four possible scenarios for interoperability:

- A Windows 2000 or Windows XP Professional client may be logging on to a domain controller running Windows Server 2003 and accessing resources on either a server running Windows Server 2003 or on another Kerberos-based service.
- A Windows 2000 or Windows XP Professional client may be logging on to a non-Windows KDC and accessing resources on either a server running Windows Server 2003 or on another Kerberos-based service.
- A non-Windows Kerberos client may be logging on to a Windows Server 2003 KDC and accessing resources on a server running Windows Server 2003 or on another Kerberos-based service.

- A non-Windows Kerberos client may be logging on to a non-Windows Kerberos implementation and accessing resources on a server running Windows Server 2003 or on another Kerberos-based service.

Windows Server 2003 can be configured to participate in any of these configurations. The easiest option is a homogenous solution in which either the entire environment is based on Windows Server 2003 Kerberos or on a non-Windows-based Kerberos implementation.

However, the Windows Server 2003 implementation of Kerberos also makes it fairly easy to interoperate with other Kerberos implementations. The easiest way to implement this is to create cross-realm trusts between the Windows Server 2003 domain and the non-Windows Kerberos realm. These realm trusts can be configured as transitive or nontransitive and as one-way or two-way. To configure a trust with another realm, open the Active Directory Domains And Trusts administrative tool and access the Properties sheet for the domain where you want to create a trust. On the Trusts tab, click New Trust, and the New Trust Wizard will start. Using this wizard you can create the Windows Server 2003 side of the trust with another Kerberos realm. Figure 8-8 shows the realm trust Properties sheet after it has been created.

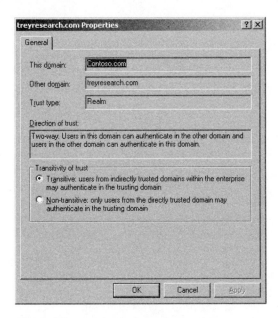

Figure 8-8. *Configuring a cross-realm trust.*

More Info   Microsoft provides a step-by-step guide to configuring Kerberos cross-realm trusts. This guide, entitled "Step-by-Step Guide to Kerberos 5 (krb5 1.0) Interoperability," is available on the Microsoft Web site at *http://www.microsoft.com/technet/prodtechnol/windows2000serv/howto/kerbstep.asp.*

NTLM Security

The second option for authenticating to a Windows Server 2003 domain controller is to use NTLM authentication. NTLM authentication is supported primarily for backward compatibility with client computers running Windows NT 4, Windows 95, and Windows 98. This protocol is used in the following situations:

- When a computer running Windows 95, Windows 98, or Windows NT authenticates to a Windows Server 2003 domain controller. The Directory Services Client must be installed on computers running Windows 95 and Windows 98 or these operating systems can only authenticate using the LAN Manager protocol.

- When a computer running Windows XP Professional or Windows Server 2003 authenticates to a server running Windows NT 4.

- When any client accesses a stand-alone server running Windows Server 2003.

- When a client running Windows XP Professional or Windows 2000 tries to log on to a Windows Server 2003 domain controller but is unable to authenticate by using the Kerberos protocol. In this instance, NTLM authentication can be used as an alternative protocol.

The NTLM protocol is significantly less secure than Kerberos. With Windows NT 4 Service Pack 4, Microsoft introduced a new version of the NTLM protocol called NTLMv2. This new version includes additional security, such as creating a unique session key each time a new connection is established as well as an advanced key-exchange process to protect the session keys.

Summary

This chapter provided a brief overview of the basic concepts of Windows Server 2003 Active Directory security, including the security principals, access control lists, authentication, and authorization. Most of this chapter focused on the primary means of providing authentication and authorization in Active Directory through the Kerberos protocol. Kerberos provides a secure mechanism for users to authenticate to Active Directory and to gain access to network resources. This chapter also discussed the integration of Kerberos with PKI, smart cards, and other implementations of Kerberos.

Chapter 9
Delegating the Administration of Active Directory

As explained in previous chapters, Microsoft Windows Server 2003 Active Directory no longer maintains the single flat namespace that was used in Microsoft Windows NT domains. Instead, Active Directory directory service provides a hierarchical view of the directory, first through the Domain Name System (DNS) hierarchy of multiple domains and then through the organizational unit (OU) structure within domains. This hierarchy creates an important administrative possibility: the option to delegate administrative permissions. In Windows NT domains, there had been no option to delegate administrative permissions within a domain. The permissions you were given in one part of the domain were the permissions you had throughout the domain. This has completely changed. Windows Server 2003 Active Directory provides powerful options for managing permissions and delegating administrative tasks within a domain.

This chapter builds on the discussion of Active Directory security started in Chapter 8, "Active Directory Security." This chapter begins by revisiting Active Directory security, detailing exactly what the access control lists (ACLs) on Active Directory objects look like. After explaining how control of each object is managed, this chapter discusses the delegation of those rights. To delegate these permissions, you can directly access the ACL of individual objects. Windows Server 2003 Active Directory also provides the Delegation Of Control Wizard to assign the permissions.

Active Directory Object Permissions

As described in Chapter 8, when a user logs on to a Windows Server 2003 network, he or she is granted an access token. That access token includes the security identifiers (SIDs) for the user account as well as the SIDs for all groups to which the user belongs. Once the user is logged on, the user tries to access a network resource, which could include an Active Directory object. Each network resource or Active Directory object has an ACL stored in its *NTSecurityDescriptor* attribute, which is made up of one or more access control entries (ACEs) that define what rights each SID has to an object. This security descriptor lists the object owner as well as a discretionary ACL (DACL) and a system ACL

(SACL). The DACL defines the permissions that all security principals have to the object. The SACL defines the audit settings on the object.

> **Note**   Every object in Active Directory has an ACL, which means that you can modify the permissions on that object. This includes objects visible through the Active Directory Users And Computers administrative tool as well as objects visible through the Active Directory Sites And Services administrative tool, ADSI Edit, or Ldp.exe. The primary focus of this chapter will be on objects visible through the Active Directory Users And Computers administrative tool, because almost all security administration will be done using this tool. However, many of the concepts and procedures discussed in this chapter can be applied to other Active Directory administrative tools. For example, you can use the fact that every object has an ACL to modify permissions for site objects in the Active Directory Sites And Services administrative tool. You can even use the Delegation Of Control Wizard that is discussed later in this chapter.

There are a number of different tools that can be used to view the security descriptor of any object in Active Directory. The most common tool is the Active Directory Users And Computers administrative tool. Even this tool can present several different views of the ACL. This is because the access permissions on an Active Directory object are broken into two categories: *standard permissions* and *special permissions*. Also, viewing the security information through the Active Directory Users And Computers administrative tool can be complicated by the fact that you can grant permissions to an object, to objects inside a container object, or to the attributes on an object.

Standard Permissions

To view the standard permissions for any Active Directory object in the domain directory partition, access the Security tab for that object's Properties sheet in the Active Directory Users And Computers administrative tool. (If the Security tab is not visible, select Advanced Features on the View menu, then reselect the object and open its Properties sheet.) The Security tab shows the standard permissions that are available for each object. Figure 9-1 illustrates the standard permissions for a user object.

Each object class in Active Directory has a different set of standard permissions. For example, an organizational unit (OU) is a container object that can contain child objects, so it will have a set of permissions that apply to child objects that would not be appropriate for a user object. However, some standard permissions such as Full Control, Read, Write, Create All Child Objects, and Delete All Child Objects apply to all objects.

Some Active Directory objects also have standard permissions that are applied to grouped sets of properties. For example, every user object has several property sets such as Public Information, Personal Information, or Web Information. Each of these property sets refers to a set of attributes, so granting access to this one property set provides access to a set of attributes. For example, the Personal Information property set includes attributes such as *homePhone*, *homePostalAddress*, *streetAddress*, and so on. Using the property sets to assign access to groups of attributes streamlines the process of assigning permissions.

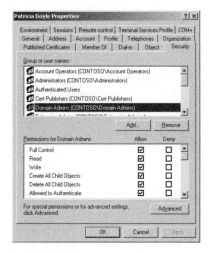

Figure 9-1. *Viewing the standard permissions on a user object.*

More Info   For a complete listing of the attributes included in each property set, search for "property sets" (including the opening and closing quotation marks) in Help And Support Center. The Active Directory schema defines which attributes are part of each property set by using the *rightsGuid* value for the property category (in the Configuration directory partition) and the *attributeSecurityGUID* for the schema object. For example, the *rightsGuid* value for cn=Personal-Information, cn=Extended-Rights, cn=configuration, dc=*forestname* is equivalent to the *attributeSecurityGUID* for cn=Telephone-Number, cn=Schema, cn=Configuration, dc=*forestname*. This means that the telephone number is included in the Personal Information property set.

In addition to the standard permissions, the Security tab also shows some extended rights. These rights include Receive As, Send As, Send To (all Microsoft Exchange 2000 Server-related rights), Change Password, and Reset Password. The list of permissions may also include Validated Write permissions. For example, Group objects require the Validated Write permissions to add/remove oneself as a member. The difference between a validated write and a normal write is that the validated write ensures that the value being written is valid. In this case, a user with permission to add/remove oneself as a member of a group will have permission to add only himself or herself to the group.

Special Permissions

One of the entries in the standard permissions list on the Security tab is Special Permissions. In addition to being able to grant standard permissions, you can also grant special permissions to Active Directory objects. These special permissions are much more granular and specific than standard permissions. To get access to the special permissions, click Advanced on the Security tab. Figure 9-2 shows the interface. Table 9-1 explains the columns on the interface.

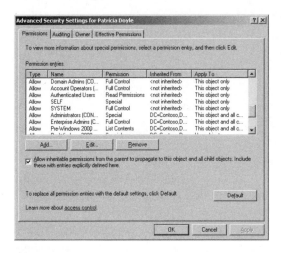

Figure 9-2. *Viewing the Advanced Security Settings for a user object.*

Table 9-1. Special Permissions Configuration Columns

Column	Explanation
Type	This value is set to either Allow or Deny. Normally, the interface sorts the permissions so that all Deny permissions are listed first, but the sort order can be changed by clicking any column header. Regardless of the order of appearance in this column, the Deny permissions are always evaluated first.
Name	This is the name of the security principal that this ACE applies to.
Permission	This column lists the level of permission granted for the security principal. Levels of permission can be standard rights, such as Full Control; special permissions such as Create/Delete User Objects; or just Special. The types of permissions available depend on the type of object.
Inherited From	This column lists the location where this permission is set.
Apply To	This column specifies the depth to which this permission applies. It has a variety of settings, including This Object Only, This Object And All Child Objects, or Only Child Objects.

Note The Default button on the Advanced tab resets the permissions on the object to the default permissions.

This interface lists all of the ACEs for the object. In many cases, the same security principals may be listed in multiple ACEs. For example, the Authenticated Users group is given permission to Read Permissions, Read General Information, Read Personal Information, Read Web Information, and Read Public Information in separate ACEs.

You can add and remove security principals, or you can edit the current permissions granted to a security principal, using this Advanced Security Settings interface. If you add or edit the permissions granted to a security principal, you are given two different options for assigning permissions. Figure 9-3 shows the first option, which is assigning permissions to the object.

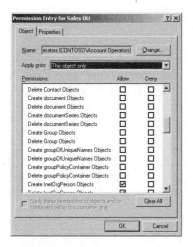

Figure 9-3. *Assigning special permissions to Active Directory objects.*

The Object tab is used to assign permissions that apply only to the object, to all child objects, or to specific child objects. For example, if you are assigning permissions at the OU level, you can grant permissions that apply to the object (the OU), to the object and all child objects, to all child objects, or to specific child objects (like user, group, and computer accounts). The permissions list varies depending on the type of object you are working with.

The second option for assigning permissions is to control the settings for the object properties. Figure 9-4 shows the interface.

The Properties tab is used to assign permissions to the individual properties for the object selected in the Name field of the Advanced Security Settings window. For example, if you are applying permissions to user objects, you are given the option of assigning Read and Write permissions to each attribute available on the object class.

Figure 9-4. *Configuring an object's property permissions.*

Note If this is the first time you have seen these options, you will probably have one of two reactions. One reaction is that this is great; you can finally assign the permissions the way you have always wanted to. The other reaction is one of aversion; you do not ever want to assign permissions at this level. Both reactions are appropriate. That is because, for the most part, you do not ever want to assign permissions at this level, but it certainly is useful when you have a very specific requirement.

Viewing the ACE using Ldp.exe

The graphical user interface (GUI) is the tool to use for managing this enormous collection of ACEs, but to enable you to truly appreciate the value of the GUI, spend a minute and look at the details of an ACE, using a tool like Ldp.exe. To view the ACL using Ldp.exe, open the Run dialog box and type *ldp*. (If Ldp.exe has not been installed on the computer, open the \SUPPORT\TOOLS folder on the Windows Server 2003 compact disc, and double-click Suptools.msi to install the Active Directory support tools.) Select the Connection drop-down menu and then select Connect. If you leave the server box empty, the server will connect to the local computer. You can also type in the server name. Once you are connected to the server, select the Connection drop-down menu and select Bind. If you are not logged in with a user account that has administrative rights, type in alternate credentials. Otherwise, leave the logon information blank. After binding to the domain, click the View drop-down menu and then select Tree. To view the entire domain, click OK. The domain OU structure will be listed in the left pane. (See Figure 9-5.)

To view the ACL for any object, locate the object in the tree view in the left pane. Then right-click the object and select Advanced, and then Security Descriptor. The ACL is stored in the *NTSecurityDescriptor* value on each Active Directory object. Ldp.exe then writes every ACE to the right pane, first in a cryptic format that looks like this:

```
(A;;CCDCLCSWRPWPDTLOCRSDRCWDWO;;;DA)
```

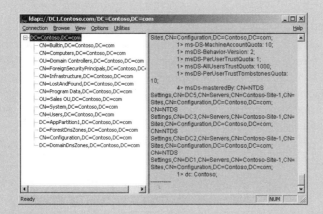

Figure 9-5. *Using Ldp.exe to view the domain properties.*

Each pair of letters in the first listing of the ACE corresponds to a specific permission. For example, CC means the user has the right to create all child objects. The last two letters in the ACE refer to the group or user that has the permissions (DA refers to the Domain Admins group). If the permissions are assigned to a user or group that does not have a well-known SID, the last part of each ACE lists the user or group SID. (To see a complete listing of all the possible permissions that can be assigned in an ACE, review the help information for the DsAcls command included with the Active Directory support tools. The DsAcls command-line tool can be used to assign or remove permissions to any object in Active Directory).

After many lines of this type of information, the Ldp.exe tool provides a more readable explanation for each ACE. For example, for the line above, the explanation looks something like this:

```
Ace[0]
        Ace Type:   0x0 - ACCESS_ALLOWED_ACE_TYPE
        Ace Size:   36 bytes
        Ace Flags: 0x0
        Ace Mask:   0x000f01ff
            DELETE
            READ CONTROL
            WRITE DAC
            WRITE_OWNER
            ACTRL_DS_CREATE_CHILD
            ACTRL_DS_DELETE_CHILD
            ACTRL_DS_LIST
            ACTRL_DS_SELF
            ACTRL_DS_READ_PROP
            ACTRL_DS_WRITE_PROP
            ACTRL_DS_DELETE_TREE
            ACTRL_DS_LIST_OBJECT
            ACTRL_DS_CONTROL_ACCESS
        Ace Sid:    Contoso\Domain Admins S-1-5-21-602162358-688789844-
            1957994488-512
```

Permissions Inheritance

Windows Server 2003 Active Directory uses a static permissions inheritance model. That is, when permissions are changed on a container object in the Active Directory structure, that permission is calculated and applied to the security descriptor for all objects in that container. This means that if permissions are changed high in the Active Directory structure and these permissions are applied to all child objects, calculating the new ACL for each object can be a processor-intensive process. However, this initial effort means that the permissions do not need to be recalculated when a user or process tries to access the object.

By default, all permissions are inherited in Active Directory. Most permissions set at the container level are inherited by all objects within that container, including other container objects. For example, if a user has permission to create user accounts in an OU, that user will also have permission to create user accounts in any child OU within that OU. In most cases, you are likely to accept the default permissions inheritance. If you have designed your OU structure with the goal of delegated administration, you will have created an OU structure where top-level administrators that require permissions to all Active Directory objects are granted permissions high in the hierarchy. As you move further down the hierarchy, you may be assigning permissions to other administrators who should have control over a smaller part of the domain.

In some cases, however, you may want to block higher-level administrators from having any administrative permissions to a specific child OU. For example, you may have created a child OU for a branch office in your company, and you may assign a local administrative group full control of the OU. You may, however, not want those local administrators to have access to any executive user accounts in the OU. To accomplish this, you can create an Executives OU within the branch office OU and then block permissions inheritance at the Executives OU level.

To block the inheritance of permissions on an Active Directory object, access the Advanced Security Settings window for the object (shown in Figure 9-2). Then clear the option to Allow Inheritable Permissions From The Parent To Propagate To This Object And All Child Objects. When you clear this option, you are presented with the option to copy the existing permissions or remove all permissions before explicitly assigning new permissions. (This interface is shown in Figure 9-6.)

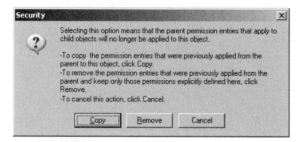

Figure 9-6. *Selecting the option to copy or remove permissions when blocking permissions inheritance.*

After you have blocked inheritance, you can configure the permissions on the objects. Blocking inheritance has a couple of implications:

- The permissions are blocked for the object and any child objects. This means that you cannot block the permissions inheritance at a container level and then reapply the inheritance from a higher container at a lower level.

- Even if you decide to copy the permissions before modification, permissions inheritance begins where you block the permissions. If you modify the permissions at a higher level, the permissions will not be inherited past the blocked permissions.

- You cannot be selective about what permissions are blocked. When you block permissions, all inherited permissions are blocked. Permissions that have been explicitly assigned to the object or child objects are not blocked.

Note   One of the possible concerns with blocking inherited permissions is that you might create an orphaned object where no one has any permissions. For example, you can create an OU, block all permissions inheritance to that OU, and assign the permissions to only one administrative group. You can even remove the Domain Admins group from the ACL of the OU so that the Domain Admins does not have any permissions under normal circumstances. If that administrative group gets deleted, the OU would have no group with administrative control. In this case, the Domain Admins group can always take ownership of the object and reassign permissions.

Effective Permissions

As discussed so far in this chapter, a user can get permissions to a specific object in Active Directory in several ways. These include:

- The user account may be granted explicit permissions to an object.
- One or more groups that the user belongs to may be granted explicit permissions to an object.
- The user account or one or more groups that the user belongs to may be given permissions at a container-object level and permissions inherited by lower-level objects.

All of these permissions are cumulative, that is, the user is granted the highest level of permissions from any of these configurations. For example, if a user is explicitly given Read permission to an object, the user belongs to a group that is explicitly given Modify permissions, and the user belongs to a group that is given Full Control at the container level, the user will have Full Control. When a user attempts to access an object, the security subsystem examines all of the ACEs that are attached to the object. All of the ACEs that apply to the security principal (based on user account or group SIDs) are evaluated and the highest level of permission is set. However, in addition to ACEs that grant permissions, Active Directory also supports Deny permissions. Deny permissions can be applied at two levels.

- The user object or one or more of the groups that the user belongs to may be explicitly denied permission to an object.
- The user object or one or more groups that the user belongs to may be denied permissions at a container level, and this denial of permission may be inherited to lower-level objects.

Deny permissions almost always override Allow permissions. For example, if a user is a member of a group that is given Modify permissions to an Active Directory object, and the user is explicitly denied Modify permissions to the object, the user will not be able to modify the object. This is because the ACEs that deny permissions are evaluated before the ACEs that allow permissions. If one of the ACEs denies permission to the security principal, no other ACEs are evaluated for the object.

The one situation where Allow permissions do override Deny permissions is when the Deny permissions are inherited and the Allow permissions are explicitly assigned. For example, you can deny a user the permission to modify any user accounts in a container. But, if you explicitly allow Modify permissions to an object within the container, the user account will have Modify permissions on that object.

Deny Permissions: Use Carefully

Using the Deny option to deny permissions can make your Active Directory security design very difficult to manage. There are a number of different scenarios where you may think about using the Deny permission. One is that you may want to use the Deny option to remove some permissions that are being inherited. For example, you may grant Modify permissions at a container level, but may want to change that to Read-Only further down the hierarchy. In this case you could deny the Write permission on any objects or properties further down the hierarchy.

Another scenario where you may think of using the Deny option is when you want to create a container that requires higher security. For example, you may have a container for all of the executives, and you may want to make sure that a normal user cannot read the executive account properties. You may choose to deny Read permissions on the container using the Domain Users group. Unfortunately, this denies everyone the right to read the directory objects, including all administrators. Because of the complications that can result from using the Deny option, you should use it with care.

In most cases, rather than denying permissions you can just ensure that a user or group has not been given permissions. If a user has not been granted any permissions and is not a member of any group that has been granted permissions, the user will not have any access. You do not need to use the Deny permission to prevent users from accessing objects in Active Directory.

One of the few scenarios in which it can be beneficial to use the Deny option is if you have a case where a group should be given permissions but one or more users in the same group should have a lower level of permissions. For example, you may have a group called Account Admins that is responsible for managing all user accounts in the domain. Some members of this group may be temporary employees who need to be able to manage all user accounts in the domain, but should not be able to modify any properties on executive accounts. In this case, you could assign the Account Admins group permission to manage all user accounts in the domain. Next, create an OU for the executive accounts, and create a group for the temporary members of the Account Admins group. Then deny the temporary users the right to modify any user accounts in the Executive OU.

As you can see, configuring security on Active Directory objects can involve managing a large number of interrelated variables. Many companies may start out with a fairly simple security design where a small group of administrators is given all the permissions in Active Directory. Most of the time, the initial Active Directory security configuration is clearly documented. However, as time goes by, this simple initial configuration often becomes much messier. Sometimes another group of administrators is given a set of permissions for a specific task and for a specific period of time. Granting the permissions is easy to do, but often the permissions are never removed. Often these security modifications made after the initial deployment are also not clearly documented.

For any Active Directory structure that has been deployed for some time, the current security configuration is likely more complex than was initially designed. Sometimes this results in users having more permissions than they should have. Fortunately, Windows Server 2003 provides a tool that can be used to easily determine the effective permissions a security principal has to any object in Active Directory.

To determine the effective permissions that a security principal has on an Active Directory object, access that object's properties through the appropriate Active Directory administrative tool. Select the Security tab, click Advanced, and then select the Effective Permissions tab. Figure 9-7 shows the interface for the Active Directory Users And Computers administrative tool. To determine the effective permissions for a specific user or group account, click Select and then search for the user or group name. After you have selected the name, click OK. The Effective Permissions page displays all of the permissions the security principal has to the Active Directory object.

Note   This tool has some limitations that may affect the effective permissions displayed. The tool determines the effective permissions based on inherited and explicitly defined permissions for the user account and the user's groups. However, the user may also get some permissions based on how the user logs on and connects to the object. For example, in Windows Server 2003, you can assign permissions to the Interactive group (that is, anyone logged on to the computer) or the Network Login group (that is, anyone accessing the information across the network). This Active Directory administrative tool cannot determine the permissions granted to a user based on these types of groups. Also, the tool can only determine permissions by using the permissions of the person running the tool. For example, if the user running the tool does not have permission to read the membership of some of the groups that the user belongs to, the tool will not be able to determine the permissions accurately.

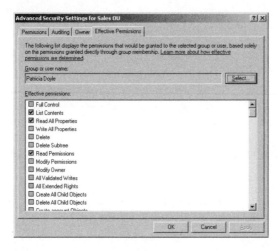

Figure 9-7. *Displaying the effective permissions for an Active Directory object.*

Ownership of Active Directory Objects

Every object in Active Directory must have an owner. By default, the user that created an object is the owner. The owner of an object has the right to modify permissions on the object, which means that, even if the owner does not have full control of an object, the owner can always modify the permissions on the object. In most cases, the owner of an object is a specific user account rather than a group account. One exception to this is when an object is created by a member of the Domain Admins group; the ownership of the object is then assigned to the Domain Admins group. If the owner of the object is a member of the local Administrators group but not a part of the Domain Admins group, the ownership of the object is assigned to the Administrators group.

To determine who the owner of an Active Directory object is, access that object's properties using the appropriate Active Directory administrative tool. Select the Security tab, click Advanced, and then select the Owner tab. Figure 9-8 shows the interface for the Active Directory Users And Computers administrative tool.

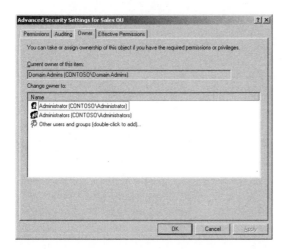

Figure 9-8. *Viewing the ownership of an Active Directory object.*

If you have the Modify Owner permission to the object, you can use this interface to modify the owner of the object. You can chose either to take ownership for your own account or to assign the ownership to another user or group. This last option is unique in Windows Server 2003 Active Directory. In Microsoft Windows 2000 Active Directory, you could only take ownership of an object; you could not assign the ownership to another security principal.

Administrative Privileges

The administrative permissions discussed so far have to do with specific permissions on Active Directory objects and define what actions the administrator can perform on those objects. In addition to these permissions, a user may also be able to perform some tasks in Active Directory because of the privileges assigned to him or her. The permissions discussed so far are based on the ACLs that are attached to each Active Directory object. User privileges are different because user privileges are applied to user accounts. User privileges are something that the user has because of who he or she is, not because he or she has permission to modify a particular Active Directory object. For example, there are two ways that you can give a user or group the right to add workstations to the domain. One option is to give the user or group permission to Create Computer Objects either at an OU level or at the Computers container level. This allows the user to add as many workstations as needed to the domain in the specified container.

Another way to allow a user to add workstations to the domain is to give him or her the privilege to add a computer to a specific domain. This privilege is a part of the Default Domain Controllers Policy. Any user who has this privilege can add up to ten workstations to the domain. By default the Domain Users group is granted this permission.

Auditing the Use of Administrative Permissions

An important aspect of ensuring that your Active Directory is as secure as possible is to create a carefully planned security configuration for the entire domain. This plan will clearly identify exactly what permissions each administrative group should have. Another essential component to domain security is the auditing of the use of those permissions. Auditing serves at least two purposes. First of all, it provides evidence for changes that have been made to the directory. If a change has been made to the directory, you may need to track down who has made the change. This is especially important if an incorrect or malicious change has been made to the domain information. A second purpose for auditing is to provide an additional check on the administrative rights being exercised throughout the domain. By examining audit logs occasionally, you can determine whether someone who should not have administrative rights is in fact exercising such rights.

There are two steps involved in enabling auditing of changes made to Active Directory objects. The first step is to enable auditing at the Domain Controllers OU level. This is done by accessing the Domain Controller Security Policy administrative tool: from the Microsoft Management Console (MMC), select File>Add/Remove Snap-in, click Add, and then add the Group Policy Object Editor. In the Group Policy Wizard, click Browse, then triple-click Domain Controllers.*domainname*.com (where *domainname* is the domain name where you are enabling auditing). Figure 9-9 shows the default auditing configuration in Windows Server 2003 Active Directory.

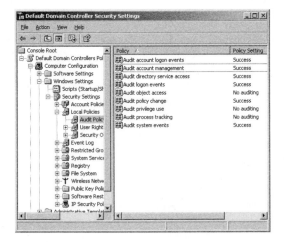

Figure 9-9. *Configuring auditing on the Default Domain Controllers OU.*

If you want to audit changes to Active Directory objects, you should ensure that Audit Account Management is enabled (configured). When this policy is enabled (configured), all modifications made to Active Directory objects can be audited. You can audit both successful changes to Active Directory and failed attempts at modifying Active Directory. By default, Windows Server 2003 Active Directory is configured to audit the success of all account management activities.

Enabling auditing at the domain controller OU level is the first step in enabling auditing. This makes it possible to configure auditing on the actual objects within that domain. To enable auditing on an object in Active Directory, access the object's Properties sheet through the appropriate Active Directory administrative tool. Then select the Security tab, click Advanced, and select the Auditing tab. Figure 9-10 shows the interface for the Active Directory Users And Computers administrative tool and the default audit setting for an OU in Active Directory.

To add more auditing entries, click Add and select which users or groups and what actions you want to audit. In most cases, you should select the Everyone group so that modifications made by anyone can be audited. Then you can select which activities you want to audit. You can audit all modifications made to any object in the container, to specific types of objects, or to specific properties. You can enable the auditing of all successful modifications, of all failed attempts to make modifications, or both. If you audit all successful modifications, you will have an audit trail for all changes made to the directory. If you enable failed attempts, you will be able to monitor any illicit attempts to modify directory information. Once auditing is enabled, all of the audit events are recorded in the Security log accessible through the Event Viewer.

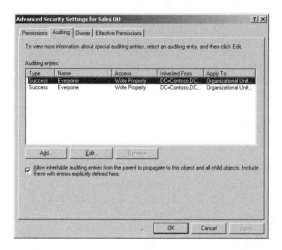

Figure 9-10. *Configuring auditing on Active Directory objects.*

Enabling auditing is easy. Managing auditing is much more difficult. If you enable the auditing of all directory modifications at the domain controller OU level, the Security log will grow very rapidly. Almost all of the events will be legitimate changes and thus of no interest to you except as an audit trail. However, interspersed among the legitimate changes may be a very small number of changes that you need to be aware of. The problem is finding the few interesting audit events among the large number of routine events. In some companies, one administrator may be given the task of reviewing the event logs every day. A better way to deal with this is to create some automated way of analyzing the event logs. Another way is to use a tool such as Microsoft Operations Manager (a separately priced product) to filter the events and raise alerts only on the interesting events.

More Info If you want to find out more about Microsoft Operations Manager, (MOM) you can go to the following web site: *http://www.microsoft.com/mom*. MOM provides a great deal of functionality that goes far beyond just monitoring security logs.

Delegating Administrative Tasks

This chapter has dealt with how to ensure the security of Active Directory objects. The discussion thus far has been in preparation for this section, which deals with using these security options to delegate administrative tasks. Because every object—indeed every property on every object—in Active Directory has an ACL, you can control administrative access down to any property on any object. This means that you can grant other Active Directory administrators very precise permissions so that they can perform only the tasks they need to do.

While you can get extremely specific about delegating administrative rights, you should maintain a balance between keeping things as simple as possible and still meeting your security requirements. In most cases, delegating administrative permissions in Active Directory falls under one of the following scenarios:

- **Assigning full control of one OU** This is a fairly common scenario when a company has multiple offices with local administrators in each office who need to manage all objects in the local office. This option may also be used for companies that have merged Windows NT resource domains into OUs in a single Active Directory domain. The former resource domain administrators can be given full control of all objects in their specific OU. Using this option means that you can almost completely decentralize the administration of your organization while still maintaining a single domain.

- **Assigning full control of specific objects in an OU** This is a variation on the first scenario. In some cases, a company may have multiple offices, but local administrators should have permission to manage only specific objects in the office OU. For example, you may want to allow a local administrator to manage all user and group objects, but not computer objects. In a situation where resource domains have become OUs, you may want OU administrators to manage all computer accounts and domain-local groups in their OU, but not to manage any user objects.

- **Assigning full control of specific objects in the entire domain** Some companies have highly centralized user and group administration, where only one group has permission to add and delete user and group accounts. In this scenario, this group can be given full control of user and group objects regardless of where the objects are located within the domain. This is also a fairly common scenario for a company with a centralized workstation and server administration group. The workstation team may be given full control of all computer objects in the domain.

- **Assigning rights to modify only some properties for objects** In some cases, you may want to give an administrative group permission to manage a subset of properties on an object. For example, you may want to give an administrative group permission to reset passwords on all user accounts, but not to have any other administrative permissions. Or, the Human Resources department may be given permission to modify the personal and public information on all user accounts in the domain, but not permission to create or delete user accounts.

It is possible to use all of these options, and any combination of these options, with Windows Server 2003 Active Directory. One way to configure delegated permissions is by directly accessing the ACL for an object and configuring the permissions. The problem with this option is that it can get quite complex because of the number of options available and the real possibility of making a mistake.

To make this task easier, Windows Server 2003 Active Directory includes the Delegation Of Control Wizard.

➲ **To use the Delegation Of Control Wizard, follow these steps:**

1. Open the Active Directory Users And Computers administrative tool and identify the parent object where you want to delegate control. In most cases, you will be delegating control at an OU level, but you can also delegate control at the domain or container level (for example, the Computers or Users container). Right-click on the parent object and select Delegate Control. Click Next.

2. On the Users Or Groups page, select the users or groups to which you want to delegate control. Click Add to search Active Directory for the appropriate users or groups.

3. Then, select the tasks that you want to delegate. The interface (shown in Figure 9-11) enables you to select from a list of common tasks or to create a custom task to delegate.

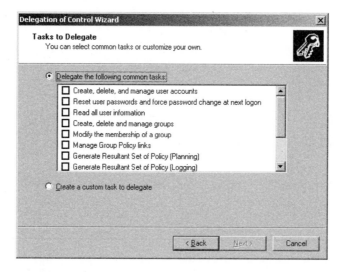

Figure 9-11. *Using the Delegation Of Control Wizard to select a common task or create a custom task to delegate.*

4. If you choose to create a custom task, you can choose the type or types of objects to which you want to delegate administrative permissions. (Figure 9-12 shows the interface.)

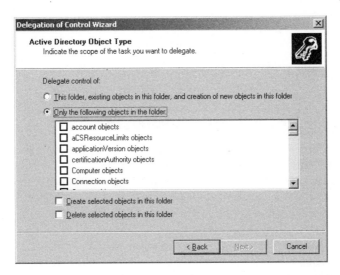

Figure 9-12. *Selecting the type of object or objects to which permissions will be delegated.*

5. After you have selected the type of object to which to delegate permissions, you can choose what levels of permissions you want to apply to the object. You can choose full control over the object, or you can delegate permissions to specific properties. (The interface is shown in Figure 9-13.)

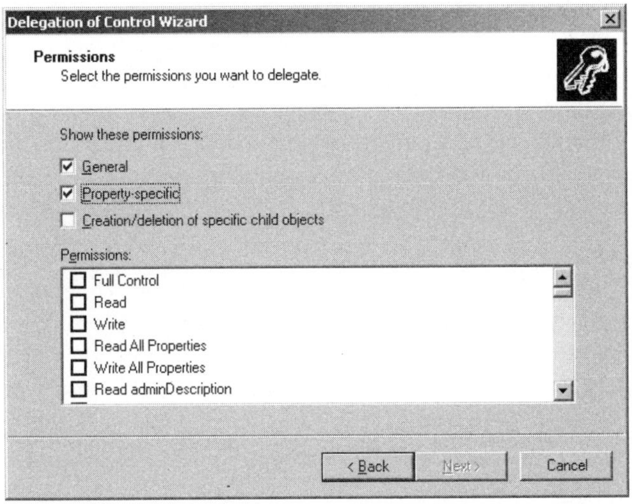

Figure 9-13. *Selecting the specific permissions to delegate.*

The Delegation Of Control Wizard makes it much easier to delegate control in a consistent manner than when configuring permissions through the ACL. However, the effect of either method is the same; that is, the ACL on the objects is modified to provide the appropriate level of access.

Customized Tools for Delegated Administration

Active Directory in Windows Server 2003 provides powerful options for delegating administrative tasks and assigning only the precise permissions that users need to have to perform specific tasks. To complement this delegation, Windows Server 2003 Active Directory also makes it easy to develop administrative tools that fit the user's task. For example, if you delegate the right to reset passwords for a single OU, you can also provide a very simple administrative tool that can only be used to reset passwords in the specified OU. Windows Server 2003 provides two options for creating these customized tools: You can either create a customized view of the regular MMC administrative tools, or you can create a taskpad that is a completely customized tool for administration.

Customizing the Microsoft Management Console

The first option for developing an administrative tool is to create a customized Microsoft Management Console (MMC) using one of the default snap-ins and then modify what the user can see in the MMC.

> **Caution** Simply creating the customized MMC does not grant or limit the user's rights to perform administrative tasks. Before creating the customized administrative interface, you must first delegate the correct level of permissions. For example, if you give a user the right to create user accounts at a domain level, and then you create an MMC that only allows the user to view one OU, the user can still create user accounts in any OU in the domain. If the user loads the regular Active Directory Users And Computers administrative tool or sits down at another desk with a different MMC, the user will be able to create the account anywhere.

To create the customized MMC, open the Run dialog box and type *mmc*. This opens an empty MMC. From the File menu, add the appropriate Active Directory administrative tool snap-in. If you create a custom MMC using the Active Directory Users And Computers snap-in, you would then expand the domain and locate the container object where you have delegated permissions. In the left pane, right-click on the container object and select New Window From Here.

This opens a new window with just the container object and all child objects visible. You can then switch back to the window that displays the entire domain and close the window. Then save the administrative tool and provide it to the users, who will administer only the part of the domain that is visible in the MMC. The MMC can be provided to the user in a number of ways. For example, you may install the MMC on his or her desktop, or you may create a shortcut to the administrative tool on a network share.

To make sure that the container administrators do not modify the MMC after you have given it to them, you can modify the MMC options by selecting Options from the File menu. You can configure the MMC to be saved in User Mode and modify the permissions on the MMC so that the end user cannot save any changes to the MMC. Figure 9-14 shows the interface. For full details on how to create customized MMCs, see the Help And Support Center.

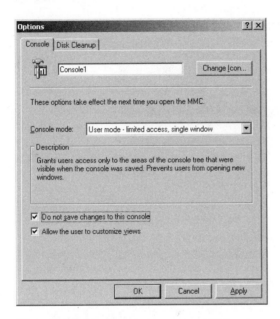

Figure 9-14. *Configuring a custom MMC to prevent changes to the MMC.*

Creating a Taskpad for Administration

A custom MMC is useful when a user requires full administrative control of a particular OU. However, if a user only has permission to perform limited tasks in a container, the taskpad provides an even simpler management tool.

Creating a taskpad consists of two steps. The first is creating a Taskpad view, and the second is assigning the tasks that the user can perform on the objects. To create a taskpad, create a customized MMC that contains the administrative snap-in that you want to use. Then locate the container where you have delegated the administrative permissions, and then right-click and select New Taskpad View. This starts the New Taskpad View Wizard. The Wizard presents you with options for what types of objects will be displayed in the taskpad and how the information will be displayed on the screen. After you have created the view, you can add tasks using the New Task Wizard. This Wizard allows you to define what types of tasks can be performed by the users of the taskpad. The list of available tasks depends on the types of objects that are visible in the taskpad. For example, if you select to view an OU that contains user accounts, you have the option of assigning tasks that can be performed on user accounts. As you finish creating the taskpad, you can also configure the taskpad setting so that the taskpad contains a very simple interface.

Figure 9-15 shows a completed taskpad that can be used by an administrator to reset passwords in a specific OU. To use the tool, the administrator simply selects a user account and then clicks Reset Password.

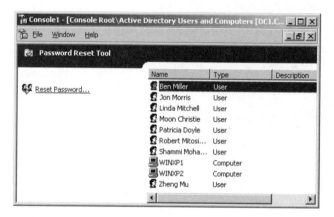

Figure 9-15. *A taskpad for resetting user passwords.*

Planning for the Delegation of Administration

As shown in this chapter, Windows Server 2003 Active Directory provides the tools you need to delegate administrative permissions in your domain. However, with all of the positive things you can do in delegating permissions, you also take the risk of assigning incorrect permissions. Incorrect permissions might mean giving people too many permissions, so that they can do things in Active Directory that they should not be able to do. Incorrect permissions can also mean assigning too few permissions, so that users cannot do the work they need to do. Creating a delegation structure that will provide users with the precise permissions they need requires a significant amount of planning. The following are some suggestions to help get this right:

- Carefully document the administrative requirements for all potential administrators. In most companies, you will find that there are various groups that need some administrative permissions in the domain. If the company has used Windows NT, many of these users could be members of the Domain Admins group. As you document the administrative tasks that these users need to perform, you will usually find that they really need a much lower level of access. Often the only way to document the level of administrative permissions each group needs is to document all of the administrative work they do every day. By documenting the activities they have to perform, you can design the precise permissions they need to have.

- Before making any changes to the production environment, test all security modifications in a test environment. Making a wrong security configuration can have serious implications for your network. Use the test lab to ensure that the modifications meet the permission requirements, but do not give any additional permissions that are not needed.

- Use the Effective Permissions page in the Advanced Security Settings window to monitor and test the permissions users have. The Effective Permissions page is a great new tool in Windows Server 2003 Active Directory that can be used to determine the precise permissions a user or group has in Active Directory. Use the tool in the test environment to ensure that your configuration is accurate, and use it again in the production environment to make sure that your implementation followed the plan.

- Document all the permissions that you assign. Of all the tasks assigned to network administrators, documenting changes made to the network seems to be the most disliked because it can be very tedious and not seen as important. As a result, documentation is often incomplete or out-of-date. The only way to effectively manage the security configuration on your network is to document the initial configuration and then to make a commitment to keep the documentation updated whenever one of the original settings is modified.

Summary

The option to delegate administrative permissions in Windows Server 2003 Active Directory provides a great deal of flexibility in how your domain can be administered. The delegation of administrative rights is based on the Active Directory security model, where every object and every attribute on every object has an ACL that controls what permissions security principals have to the object. According to the security model, all permissions are, by default, inherited from container objects to objects within the container. These two basic features of the security model mean that you can assign almost any level of permission to any Active Directory object. This flexibility can also mean a great deal of complexity if the security for Active Directory is not kept as simple as possible. This chapter provided an overview of security permissions, delegation of administrative rights in Active Directory, and some of the tools that can be used to manage this feature.

Chapter 10
Managing Active Directory Objects

The most common tasks that you will perform using Microsoft Windows Server 2003 Active Directory directory service will involve the management of Active Directory objects such as *users* and *groups*. Most companies will create an Active Directory design and implement it once. After the deployment, few changes will be made to most Active Directory objects. However, working with *user* objects and *group* objects is a significant exception to this rule. As employees join or leave the company, the administrator will need to spend time managing users and groups. Active Directory also contains other objects such as *printer* objects, *computer* objects, and *shared folder* objects that may require frequent administration.

This chapter discusses the concepts and procedures that you will use to manage Active Directory objects. It discusses the types of objects that can be stored in Active Directory and explains how to manage those objects. This chapter also discusses the primary interface that you will use for working with these objects, the Active Directory Users And Computers administrative tool, and some of the enhancements that have been made to this tool in Windows Server 2003.

Managing Users

Windows Server 2003 Active Directory makes available three different objects that are used to represent individual users in the directory. Two of these, the *user* object and the *inetOrgPerson* object, are security principals that can be used to assign access to resources on your network. The third object, the *contact* object, is not a security principal and is used primarily for e-mail.

User Objects

One of the most common objects in any Active Directory database is a *user* object. A *user* object, like any other Active Directory class object, is a collection of attributes. In fact, a *user* object can have over 250 attributes. In this way, Windows Server 2003 Active Directory is very different from the Microsoft Windows NT directory services, where *user* objects have very few attributes. Because it can provide all these additional attributes,

Active Directory is useful as a directory service in addition to simply being a database for storing authentication information. For example, Active Directory can become the primary location for most user information in your company. The directory can become the place where all user information such as telephone numbers, addresses, and organizational information is stored. Once users learn how to search Active Directory, they will be able to find almost any information about other users.

When you create a *user* object, you must populate some of its attributes. As shown in Figure 10-1, only six attributes are required when you create a user account. Of these six, the *cn* and the *sAMAccountName* attributes are configured based directly on the data you provide when you create the account. All of the other mandatory attributes, including the *security identifier* (SID), are automatically populated by the security system.

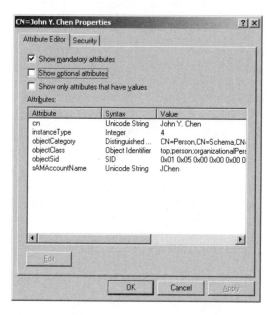

Figure 10-1. *Mandatory attributes for a user account viewed in Adsiedit.msc.*

When you create a user account, you can assign a value to many of the other *user*-object attributes. Some of these attributes are not visible through any user interface (UI). For example, each *user* object has an attribute called *Assistant* that is not visible through a UI. You can still populate this hidden attribute by using a script or a tool like Adsiedit.msc that directly accesses the attribute. You can also populate hidden attributes during a bulk import of directory information using either the Csvde or the Ldifde command-line utility. (See the Help And Support Center for details on these utilities.) One of the reasons you need to populate attributes that are not visible in a UI is so that you can still use that attribute for locating and modifying *user* objects. In some cases, the hidden attribute is available through the Find dialog box. For example, in the Active Directory Users And Computers administrative tool, to search for all users that have the same *Assistant* attribute, use the Advanced tab on the Find dialog box to create a query based on the *Assistant* attribute. Figure 10-2 shows the interface. In this interface, click Field, select User, and then select the attribute you wish to search for. Many of the hidden attributes can be found from this interface.

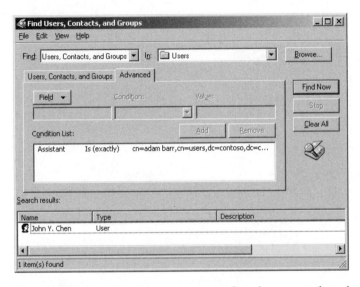

Figure 10-2. *Searching for a user account based on an attribute that is not visible in the UI.*

More Info   You can view and modify any attribute on a *user* object using a tool like Adsiedit.msc or Ldp.exe. A more efficient way to modify these attributes is to use scripts. You can greatly benefit from the use of scripts with Active Directory, which is written to allow and encourage the use of scripts. For information about using scripts to automate Active Directory management tasks, see the TechNet Script Center at *http://www.microsoft.com/technet/scriptcenter /default.asp*. The TechNet Script Center contains both scripting resources and sample scripts you can use to extend the administrative tasks you would otherwise perform through the Active Directory management consoles. Also see the Microsoft Press Online Web site at *http://www.microsoft.com/mspress/* for a bonus chapter on scripting, "Introduction to ADSI Scripting Using VBScript," written by Mike Mulcare.

You can manage most regular user administration tasks using the Active Directory Users And Computers administrative tool. To create a *user* object in the Active Directory Users And Computers administrative tool, locate the container where you want to create the object, right-click, and select New>User. When you create the user, you must provide at least the user's Full Name and User Logon Name. The Full Name data is used to populate the *cn* attribute for the user, while the User Logon Name data becomes the *sAMAccountName* value. Once you have created the user, you can access the object properties to fill in additional attributes for the user. Most of the attributes for the *user* object are easy to understand. The most important tab for administering a user account is the Account tab (shown in Figure 10-3). The user settings available on the Account tab are described in Table 10-1.

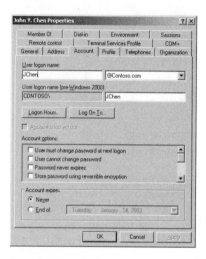

Figure 10-3. *The Account tab for a* user *object.*

Table 10-1. Account Properties for a *User* Object

Account setting	Explanation
User Logon Name	Identifies the user principal name (UPN) for this user
User Logon Name (pre-Windows 2000)	Identifies the pre-Microsoft Windows 2000 logon name using the *domain\username* format
Logon Hours	Establishes the hours when a user can log on to the domain
Log On To	Lists the computers (using NetBIOS computer names) where the user is allowed to log on
Account Is Locked Out	Identifies that the account has been locked out due to too many failed logon attempts
Account Options	Provides several options for settings, such as password policies and authentication requirements
Account Expires	Specifies when the account will expire

Naming *User* Objects in Active Directory

While it is true that every object in Active Directory must have a unique name, when discussing an object like a *user* object, this simple statement can become quite complicated, because a *user* object actually has a number of possible names. Table 10-2 lists all of the names that can be associated with a *username* and the scope within which that name must be unique.

Table 10-2. Username Uniqueness Requirements

Username	Uniqueness requirement
First name, initials, last name	No uniqueness requirement
Display name	No uniqueness requirement
Full name–The full name is used to populate the *cn* attribute on the user account. By default, the full name is created using the First Name, Initials, and Last Name fields from the New Object-User dialog box. This can be modified using Adsiedit.msc.	Must be unique within the organizational unit (OU)
User principal name–The UPN is made up of the logon name and the domain DNS name or an alternative UPN if additional UPN suffixes have been configured for the forest.	Must be unique within the forest
User Logon Name (pre-Windows 2000)	Must be unique within the domain

The UPN can be a very useful name for a user. A user can go to any domain in the forest and log on using his or her UPN rather than selecting his or her home domain when logging on. By default, the UPN suffix is also the Domain Name System (DNS) name for the domain. However, you can modify the UPN suffix. For example, you may be using a different DNS name internally than the one that is visible to the external Internet. In most cases, the Simple Mail Transfer Protocol (SMTP) e-mail address for all users would match the external DNS name. Your users may want to be able to log on to the domain using their SMTP addresses. You can enable this option by adding an alternative UPN suffix to the forest and then assigning this suffix to all user accounts. To create an additional UPN suffix, open the Active Directory Domains And Trusts administrative tool, right-click the Active Directory Domains And Trusts entry at the top of the left pane, and select Properties. Figure 10-4 shows the interface. Type in any alternative UPN suffixes that you wish to use.

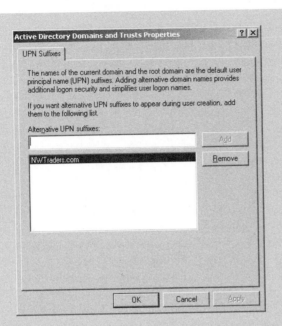

Figure 10-4. *Adding alternative UPN suffixes to your forest.*

inetOrgPerson Objects

One of the new objects that is available in Windows Server 2003 Active Directory is the *inetOrgPerson* object. The primary reason for including this object in Active Directory is because it is the primary user account used by other Lightweight Directory Access Protocol (LDAP) and X.500 directories that are Request for Comments (RFC) 2798-compliant. By enabling the *inetOrgPerson* object, Microsoft has made it easier to integrate Active Directory with other directories. Also, this will simplify the migration from other directories to Active Directory.

> **Note** If you are upgrading a Windows 2000 forest to Windows Server 2003, the *inetOrgPerson* object is created in the schema when you run the Adprep.exe command with the /forestprep switch. Adprep.exe can be found in the \I386 folder on the Windows Server 2003 compact disc.

The *inetOrgPerson* object can be created using the Active Directory Users And Computers administrative tool. To create an *inetOrgPerson* object in the Active Directory Users And Computers administrative tool, locate the container where you want to create the object, right-click, and select New>InetOrgPerson. You must provide at least the user logon name and the full name when creating the *inetOrgPerson* object. The *inetOrgPerson* is a subclass of the *user* object, which means that it has all of the characteristics of the user class, including that it acts as a security principal. The *inetOrgPerson* objects can be managed and used in all of the same ways that you would use any *user* object.

Contact Accounts

The third type of object that can be used to represent users in Active Directory is the *contact* object. *Contact* objects are different from *user* objects and *inetOrgPerson* objects in that *contact* objects cannot be security principals. Usually, *contact* objects are used for informational purposes only. To create a *contact* object in the Active Directory Users And Computers administrative tool, locate the container where you want to create the object, right-click, and select New>Contact. You must provide at least the full name when creating the *contact* object. In addition, when you create a *contact* object, you can populate a number of attributes for the object, including telephone numbers and addresses.

Contacts are useful in several scenarios. One way you can use contacts is if you have a user who cannot be a security principal in your domain, but whose contact information needs to be accessible. For example, you may have consultants working in your office who cannot log on to the network but whose contact information must be stored where it is easily located by anyone in the company. You can also use contacts to share information between forests. Your company may have merged with another company that has already deployed Active Directory. You can create cross-forest trusts between the two forests so that you can share network resources, but the global catalog (GC) in each forest will still only contain accounts for that single forest. You may want all or some of the accounts from both forests to be visible to the users. To enable this, you can use a tool like Microsoft Metadirectory Services (MMS) to create a *contact* object for every user account from the other forest and populate the *contact* object with the appropriate contact information.

> **More Info**   MMS is available through Microsoft Consulting Services or through an existing MMS partner. For more information, see *http://www.microsoft.com /windows2000/technologies/directory/mms/default.asp.*

Another way that *contact* objects are used is if you implement Microsoft Exchange 2000 Server. Unlike earlier versions of Exchange, Exchange 2000 Server does not have its own directory service. Instead, Exchange 2000 Server requires Active Directory, and it stores all of its directory information in Active Directory. In Exchange Server 5.5 and earlier, you can create a custom recipient. The custom recipient includes an e-mail address so you can send mail to the person, but the custom recipient does not have a mailbox on your Exchange servers. If you are using Exchange 2000 Server, a mail-enabled *contact* object replaces the custom recipient. When you mail-enable a *contact* object, you assign an e-mail address to the account. This mail-enabled contact will then be visible using an e-mail client. When you send mail to the contact, the mail is delivered to the correct e-mail address.

Managing Groups

One of the primary functions of a directory service like Active Directory is to provide authorization for access to network resources. Ultimately, all access to network resources is based on the individual user accounts. However, in most cases, you do not want to administer access to resources by using individual user accounts. In a large company, this would result in a great deal of administrative effort. Also, the access control lists (ACLs) on network resources would soon be unmanageable if you assigned permissions using individual user accounts. Because managing access to network resources using individual user accounts is unmanageable, you will create *group* objects to manage large collections of users at one time.

Group Types

Windows Server 2003 provides two different types of groups, called *distribution groups* and *security groups*. When you create a new *group* object, you are given the choice of which type of group you want to create. Figure 10-5 shows the interface.

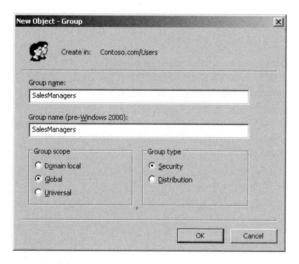

Figure 10-5. *Creating a new group in the Active Directory Users And Computers administrative tool.*

The most common type of group in Active Directory is the security group. A security group is a security principal and can be used to assign permissions to network resources. A distribution group cannot be a security principal. Because it cannot be used to assign access to resources, the distribution group has a very limited usefulness. The most common use for a distribution group is if you have installed Exchange 2000 Server and you need to group together users so that you can send e-mail to the entire group. If you have installed Exchange 2000 Server, you can mail-enable a distribution group and then add mail-enabled users and contacts to the group. You can then send mail to the whole group of users at one time.

Note   A distribution group is very similar to a distribution list in Exchange Server 5.5, but it is not the exact Exchange 2000 Server equivalent. In Exchange Server 5.5, you can use a distribution list to collect a group of users for e-mail purposes, but you can also use the distribution list to assign permissions to public folders on the Exchange server. In Exchange 2000 Server, you must use a mail-enabled security group if you want to assign permissions to a public folder.

You can convert distribution groups to security groups and back as long as your domain is running at least Windows 2000 native functional level. (For more information on functional levels, see Tables 2-1 and 2-2 in Chapter 2, "Active Directory Components.") If the group contains user accounts or contacts, the *user* or *contact* objects are not changed when the group type is changed.

Note   Because distribution groups have such a limited use in Active Directory, the focus of the rest of this chapter will be on security groups.

Group Scope

In Windows Server 2003 Active Directory, you can create groups with three different scopes: domain local, global, and universal. Table 10-3 lists the characteristics of each group scope.

Note   Universal groups are available only if the domain is set to at least Windows 2000 native functional level. *Nested groups* are groups that are members of other groups. The options for nesting groups depend on the domain functional level. For example, you can nest a global group in a domain local group at any functional level, but you can nest a global group inside another global group only if the domain functional level is Windows 2000 native or higher.

Domain local groups are fully functional only when the domain has been elevated to at least the Windows 2000 native functional level. If the domain is running in a Windows 2000 mixed functional level, domain local groups operate just like local groups on domain controllers in Windows NT 4. The group can be used to assign permissions to resources on the domain controllers but not on any other computers in the domain. If the domain has been switched to Windows 2000 native functional level, domain local groups can be used to grant permissions to resources on any server running Windows 2000 or Windows Server 2003.

Table 10-3. Active Directory Group Scopes

Group scope	Group membership can include:	Group scope includes:
Domain local	User accounts from any domain in the forest.	Can be used to assign access to resources only in the local domain.
	Global groups or universal groups from any domain in the forest.	Can be used on all servers running Windows 2000 or Windows Server 2003.
	User accounts or global or universal groups from any domain in a trusted forest.	
	Nested domain local groups from the local domain.	
Global	User accounts from the domain where the group is created.	Can be used to assign access to resources in all domains in the forest, or between trusted forests.
	Nested global groups from the same domain.	Can be used on any member server running Windows.
Universal	User accounts from any domain in the forest.	Can be used to assign access to resources in all domains in the forest or between trusted forests.
	Global groups from any domain in the forest or from a trusted forest.	Can be used only on servers running Windows 2000 or Windows Server 2003.
	Nested universal groups from any domain in the forest or from a trusted forest.	

Planning   How you use groups will vary depending on what servers you have deployed in your environment. If your domain contains only servers running Windows 2000 and Windows Server 2003, you can use domain local groups to assign permissions to all resources on these servers. However, you can also still use local groups on the member servers. Note that you will still have to use local groups on servers running Windows NT. In either case, the local groups can contain global groups from any domain in the forest. If you create the local groups on a server running Windows 2000 or Windows Server 2003, the groups can also contain universal groups from any domain in the forest or trusted forest.

Global group functionality has remained consistent in Windows Server 2003 Active Directory and Windows 2000 Active Directory. If the domain has been switched to at least Windows 2000 native functional level, you can nest global groups from the same domain inside other global groups. If your domain is running in Windows 2000 mixed or native functional level, you can use this option to deal with the limitation of 5000 users per group. If you have a very large group, you can create multiple subgroups and nest them in a single group. The nesting of groups can also be useful in other circumstances. For example, your company may have several unique business units, each of which has a group of managers and executives. You may decide to create a Managers global group for each business unit and then nest these global groups in a company-wide Managers group.

Universal groups are the most flexible groups in Active Directory, but this flexibility comes with a cost. Universal groups can contain members from any domain in the forest and can be used to assign permissions to resources in any domain in the forest. To make this possible, the membership list for all universal groups must be stored in the GC. The membership list is stored as a single attribute in the GC. This means that if your domain is running at the Windows 2000 native functional level, every time a member is added to the universal group, the entire membership list must be replicated to all other domain controllers. If the universal group contains thousands of members, this can result in a great deal of replication. This problem is not relevant if the domain has been switched to Windows Server 2003 functional level. When the domain has been promoted to this functional level, the domain controllers running Windows Server 2003 will replicate only the change to the membership list.

Using universal groups can also create other complications. Because the universal group can be used anywhere in the forest, and a member in the group can come from anywhere in the forest, a GC server must be available whenever a user tries to log on to the domain. If the GC is not available to determine universal group membership, the user will not be able to log on to the domain. This issue has been addressed in Windows Server 2003 Active Directory. If the domain has been switched to Windows Server 2003 functional level, you can configure all the domain controllers in a site to cache universal group membership. If you do this, the user's group membership is cached on the local domain controller when the user logs on. Then if the GC server is not available during logon, the local domain controller can use the cached universal group membership to authenticate the user. If the user has never logged on to the local domain controller before, this cached information will not be available, and the user will not be able to log on.

Caution   If a user does log on by using the cached universal group information, but the universal group permissions have been modified, those new permissions will not be applied to the local user until the universal group information is updated from a GC server.

Windows Server 2003 Active Directory contains a large number of built-in group accounts, both in the Users container and in the Builtin container. These groups have a wide variety of purposes and default permissions within the domain. The only groups that contain any members when you install a domain are the Administrators domain local group and the Domain Admins global group. The Administrator account that created the domain is added to both of these groups, and the Domain Admins group is added to the Administrators group. If the domain is the first domain in the forest, the Administrator account is also added to the Enterprise Admins global group and the Schema Admins global group.

Creating a Security Group Design

One of the detailed design components for Active Directory implementation is the security group design. Creating a security group design can be very detailed and painstaking work, especially in a large organization. This section will provide general principles for creating the security group design for your organization.

The first step in creating the security group design is to determine which of the group scopes to use. In many companies, there is a great deal of discussion about how to use the various groups. The use of groups in Active Directory is very flexible. For example, in a single domain, users can be added to a group of any scope in the domain, and the groups can be used to assign permissions to any resource in the domain. In a multidomain environment, there are several options for using universal groups, global groups, and domain local groups.

For most companies, the best way to use the various group scopes is to implement the following steps:

1. Add users to global or universal groups.
2. Add the global or universal groups to domain local groups.
3. Assign access to resources using the domain local groups.

In some companies there is significant resistance to creating both a domain local group and a global or universal group when one group will do, but there are also important reasons why using two groups is the best approach.

If the approach of using global or universal groups and domain local groups is followed, global or universal groups can be created based on the need to collect users who have something in common. In most cases, global or universal groups are based on a business department or on a functional purpose. For example, all members of the Sales department usually have more in common with each other than they do with members of other departments. Users may all require access to the same resources, or they may all need the same software installed. Group membership is also frequently organized on a functional basis. All managers may need to be grouped together, regardless of which business unit they are part of. All members of a project team will likely need access to the same project resources.

Domain local groups are usually used to assign permissions to resources. In many cases, the permissions may be closely linked to business departments or functions. For example, all members of the Sales department may require access to the same sales shared folder. All project team members usually require access to the same project information. In other cases, access to resources may cross the regular business or functional boundaries. For example, the company may use a shared folder to which everyone in the company has Read Only access. Or several departments and project teams may require access to the same shared folder. By creating a domain local group that is specific to a particular resource, you can easily manage access to the resource. You can then add the appropriate global or universal groups to the domain local group.

Often, users require different levels of access to shared folders. For example, a company might have a Human Resource shared folder where all employee policy information is stored. All users may need to be able to read the information in the folders, but only members of the Human Resources department should be able to modify the information in the folder. In this case, you would create two domain local groups for the shared folder. One group can be given Read Only permission, while the other group is given Full Control or Modify permissions. The Human Resources global group can then be added to the domain local group that has been assigned Full Control, and all other global groups that only need Read Only access can be added to the Read Only domain local group.

Using global groups and domain local groups in this way means that you can split the ownership of the global groups and domain local groups. An important security concern in any large corporation is ensuring that only the right users have access to any shared information. One step to ensuring this is to make sure that every group has an *owner*, also known as an authorizer. Only the owner can authorize any modification to the group configuration. The owner of the global group is usually a department administrator. The owner of a project-based global group is probably the project manager. These owners are the only people who can authorize any change to the membership list.

The owner of a domain local group is usually the data, or resource, owner. If every resource in your company has an owner who is the only person who can authorize any modifications to permissions to the shared resource, that person also becomes the owner of the domain local group that is associated with the resource. Before any global or universal group can be added to the domain local group, this owner must approve the modification.

Using the two levels of groups is particularly important in scenarios where you have multiple domains and users from each domain need access to a shared resource in one domain. As illustrated in Figure 10-6, you can create a global group in each domain and then add that global group to a domain local group in the domain where the resource is located.

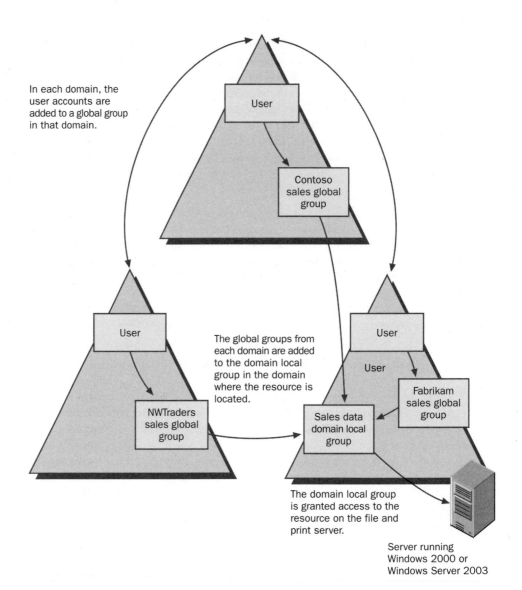

In each domain, the user accounts are added to a global group in that domain.

User

Contoso sales global group

User

The global groups from each domain are added to the domain local group in the domain where the resource is located.

User

User

NWTraders sales global group

Sales data domain local group

Fabrikam sales global group

The domain local group is granted access to the resource on the file and print server.

Server running Windows 2000 or Windows Server 2003

Figure 10-6. *Configuring resource access using global groups and domain local groups with multiple domains.*

Note Windows NT uses global groups and local groups, but does not have the option of using domain local groups. If you have Windows NT member servers in your domain, you will still need to use local groups on each server. If you have servers running Windows 2000 or Windows Server 2003 and your domain is running in at least Windows 2000 native functional level, you should use domain local groups whenever possible. If you do, you can use the domain local groups across multiple servers. As well, if you use domain local groups rather than local groups, you can move a resource between servers and use the same domain local group to assign permissions.

One of the questions that must be asked when creating the security group design is when to use global groups and when to use universal groups. In some cases, you do not have any option. For example, in Exchange 2000 Server, mail-enabled groups replace the distribution lists used in Exchange Server 5.5 to group e-mail recipients together and to assign access to public folders on the Exchange server. If you are using mail-enabled groups for Exchange 2000 Server, you should use a universal group. As you migrate from Exchange Server 5.5 to Exchange 2000 Server, you should replace each of the Exchange Server 5.5 distribution lists with a mail-enabled universal group. If you have more than one domain, you must use universal groups for these mail-enabled groups.

In most cases, the best practice when creating the universal group design in Windows 2000 Active Directory was to minimize the use of universal groups, especially if you had any sites that were separated by slow network connections. The reason for this recommendation was because of the replication issues with the GC. This recommendation is still valid if your forest is running in Windows 2000 functional level. However, if your Windows Server 2003 forest has been switched to the Windows Server 2003 or Windows Server 2003 interim functional level, this replication issue is no longer relevant. Also, the option to enable GC caching reduces the need to deploy a GC server in every site. Because of these enhancements, the decision of when to use universal groups or global groups is not so critical in Windows Server 2003 Active Directory. In most cases, you will be able to use global groups and universal groups almost interchangeably.

Managing Computers

Another type of object in Active Directory is the *computer* object. There are only two types of *computer* objects in Active Directory. The first is the *domain controller* object. A *domain controller* object is created when you promote a server to become a domain controller.

Domain controller objects are located by default in the Domain Controllers OU. While you can move domain controllers out of this OU, you should do so with caution. Many of the domain controller security settings are configured on the Domain Controllers OU, and moving a domain controller out of this container will effectively modify the security settings for any moved domain controllers.

The second type of *computer* objects are the objects for all other computers that are members of the domain. All other computer accounts are created in the default Computers container in Active Directory. In most cases, you will move the *computer* objects from this container into specific OUs. The reason for doing this is so that you can manage the computers differently. For example, you will probably want to manage the servers in your company differently from the workstations, so you will need to create two separate OUs. Often, workstations can be split up into smaller groupings. All the workstations in the Sales department will require different applications than the workstations in the Engineering department. By creating two OUs and moving the workstations into the appropriate OUs, you can manage the two types of workstations differently. Computer accounts are created in the domain when you join a computer to the domain. You can also pre-create computer accounts.

Note All computers running Windows NT, Windows 2000, Microsoft Windows XP Professional, and Windows Server 2003 must have a computer account in the domain. Computers running Microsoft Windows 95 or Microsoft Windows 98 cannot have accounts in the domain.

You will rarely manage the *computer* objects in Active Directory directly. If you right-click a computer account in Active Directory, you will see that there are very few management options. One option available is to reset the computer account. Use this option with caution, because when you reset a computer account, you break that computer's connection to the domain, and the computer must be rejoined to the domain.

An option that is very useful from an administrative point of view is the option to access the Computer Management application for any computer from Active Directory. Locate a computer in the Active Directory Users And Computers administrative tool, right-click the icon for the workstation or server you want, and choose Manage. The Computer Management Microsoft Management Console (MMC) opens focused on the workstation or server that you selected.

Note The fact that you will not likely perform a great deal of administration on the *computer* objects in Active Directory certainly does not mean that you will not be using Active Directory to manage computers. Chapter 11, "Introduction to Group Policies," Chapter 12, "Using Group Policies to Manage Software," and Chapter 13, "Using Group Policies to Manage Computers," deal with group policies, which provide powerful tools for managing computers.

Managing *Printer* Objects

A third group of objects in Active Directory consists of *printer* objects. You can create a *printer* object by publishing the printer in Active Directory. When you publish a printer in Active Directory, a *printer* object is created that stores printer attributes such as printer location, but also printer features such as printing speed, color printing capabilities, and other printer-specific functionality. The primary reason for publishing *printer* objects in Active Directory is to make it easier for users to locate and connect to network printers.

Publishing Printers in Active Directory

By default, any printer that is installed and shared on a server running Windows 2000 or Windows Server 2003 in an Active Directory domain is automatically published in Active Directory. If you do not want a printer on one of these servers to be automatically published in Active Directory, you can clear the option List In The Directory on the printer's Properties sheet. However, if the printer is located on a server running Windows NT or another operating system, you must manually publish the printer in Active Directory. To do so, locate the *container* object where you want to publish the *printer* object, and then right-click and select New>Printer. Then type in the Universal Naming Convention (UNC) path to the shared computer.

Tip If you are using Windows NT print servers, and you do not want to upgrade the print server to Windows 2000 or Windows Server 2003, you must manually publish all the printers on the Windows NT print servers in Active Directory. Microsoft has provided a script called Pubprn.vbs to automate this process. This script is located in the %systemroot%\system32 folder.

Publishing a printer in Active Directory is most useful when users need to search Active Directory for *printer* objects. When a printer is published in Active Directory, information about the printer is automatically populated on the printer's Properties sheet, accessed from the Active Directory Users And Computers administrative tool. This can be very useful information for a user who is looking for a specific printer. For example, the user may be looking for a color printer that also prints at least six pages per minute. If this information is stored in Active Directory, the client can use the A Printer On The Network option of the Search operation selected from the Start Menu to locate any printers that meet these requirements. Figure 10-7 shows the interface on a Windows XP Professional workstation. Once the network printer has been located, the user can right-click on the printer and select Connect to install the printer on the client machine.

If the *printer* objects are published in Active Directory, you can use the Group Policy Object Editor to manage the *printer* objects. Figure 10-8 shows the options for managing printer settings.

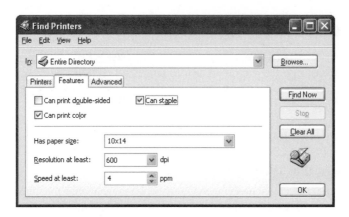

Figure 10-7. *Searching for printers in Active Directory.*

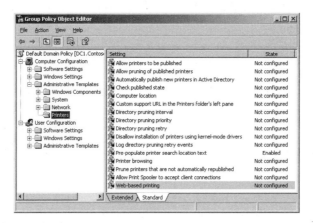

Figure 10-8. *Configuring printer settings using the Group Policy Object Editor.*

A couple of the options that you can configure using group policies manage printer pruning. These options refer to the fact that Active Directory will automatically delete the *printer* objects from Active Directory if the *printer* object becomes obsolete. For example, if a printer is removed from a print server, or if the printer is no longer shared on the server, printer pruning will remove the *printer* object. By default, one of the Active Directory domain controllers tries to contact each print server every 8 hours to confirm the validity of the printer information. If the print server does not respond, the *printer* object is deleted from Active Directory. Each time a print server running Windows 2000 or later restarts, it automatically reregisters the shared printers on the server in Active Directory. You can configure the printer pruning parameters using the Group Policy Object Editor.

One of the most interesting options in Active Directory for managing *printer* objects is the option to automatically pre-populate the printer location setting for users when they browse for a printer. Many companies with multiple locations have employees who travel between company locations. Most companies have meeting rooms that are in different parts of the building. Whenever users move from one part of the company to another, they usually need to be able to print, regardless of their location. If the user is unfamiliar with where the printers are in their current location, it can often take some time to find the closest printer.

You can simplify this search for printers by assigning each printer a location in Active Directory and then using the user's location to present a list of printers that are close to the user. This functionality is based on the site configuration in your network.

To enable printer location tracking, perform the following steps:

1. Open the Active Directory Sites And Services administrative tool, and locate the *subnet* object where you will enable printer tracking. Right-click on the *subnet* object and select Properties. Click the Location tab and enter the *location* value for this subnet. The location entry should be in the *location/sublocation* format (e.g., HeadOffice/3rdFloor).

2. Use the Group Policy Object Editor to enable the Pre-Populate Printer Search Location Text policy for a selected container. In most cases, you will do this at the domain level.

3. On your print server, access the Properties sheet for each printer. On the General tab, you can fill in the printer location. If you have completed the first two steps of this procedure, you can click Browse to locate the printer location. You can add more details to the printer location so that the printer location is more specific (e.g., HeadOffice/3rdFloor/Outside Meeting Room 5).

4. After you have enabled printer location tracking, users can easily locate the printer closest to them. When the user starts the Add Printer Wizard and searches for a printer in the Directory, the *Location* attribute is filled in based on the user's current site. Figure 10-9 shows the interface on a Windows XP Professional client. The user can then click Browse for a more specific printer location.

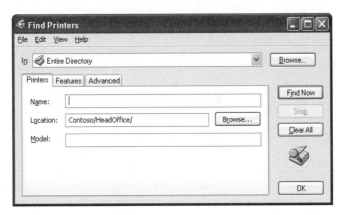

Figure 10-9. *Searching for* printer *objects in Active Directory using the* Location *attribute.*

Managing Published Shared Folders

Another object that you can publish to Active Directory is a *shared folder* object. To publish a shared folder on Active Directory, locate the Active Directory container where you want to publish the shared folder. Right-click the container and select New>Shared Folder. Then type in a name for the Active Directory object as well as the UNC for the shared folder. After you create the *shared folder* object in Active Directory, users can browse for the shared folder or search Active Directory for the object. After the users locate the object in Active Directory, they can right-click on the object and map a drive to the shared folder.

The primary advantage of publishing a shared folder to Active Directory is so that users can search for shares in Active Directory based on a variety of properties. When you create a *shared folder* object, you can provide a description for the shared folder. Figure 10-10 shows the interface. After creating the shared folder, you can open its Properties sheet to provide keywords associated with the shared folder. When clients need to locate the shared folder, they can search Active Directory using an argument based on the object name, keywords, or description.

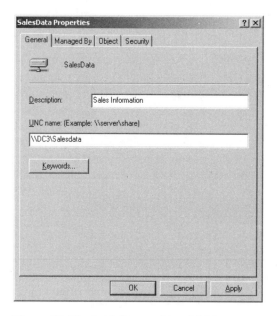

Figure 10-10. *Publishing a shared folder in Active Directory.*

The most significant limitation with publishing shared folders in Active Directory is that if you ever move the shared folder to another server, any client with a drive mapped to that shared folder will find that the mapping no longer works. This is because when you map a drive to a shared folder in Active Directory, the drive mapping on the client is still based on the UNC path to the share. For example, you may create and publish a shared folder called SalesInfo that points to \\Server1\SalesInfo. When a user browses to that shared folder in Active Directory and maps a drive, the drive mapping uses the \\Server1\SalesInfo syntax. If you ever move the folder to another server, the drive mapping will fail even if you change the Active Directory object to point to the new location.

Windows Server 2003 Active Directory Administration Enhancements

Windows 2000 marked the first release of Active Directory, and many of the administrative tools that came with Windows 2000 were limited in some important ways. The Windows Server 2003 administrative tools provide some enhanced functionality.

- **Drag and drop functionality** One of the most requested new features in Windows Server 2003 Active Directory was the option to drag and drop objects within Active Directory administrative tools. For example, you can now move a user from one OU to another by dragging and dropping the icon for the user account to the new OU. You can add an existing user to a group by dragging and dropping the icon for the user account to the group account.

- **Multiple item editing** Another useful new option is the ability to edit multiple objects at one time. In Windows 2000 Active Directory, you can modify only one object at time. With the Windows Server 2003 Active Directory Users And Computers administrative tool, you can make some changes to large numbers of objects at the same time. For example, suppose that all the users in the Marketing department are moved to another office building and you need to change the address for all user accounts. You can use the search tool to locate all of the user accounts with a *Department* attribute set to Marketing. Then select all of the accounts in the search results pane, right-click, and select Properties. You can now modify the common attributes for all accounts at the same time. Your domain must be in Windows Server 2003 functional level to allow multiple item editing.

- **Saved queries** In large organizations with thousands of users, administrators will almost always locate Active Directory objects by searching rather than browsing. The option to save queries means that you can create a search query once, and then retain it for reuse later. For example, you may want to perform a monthly check to see which user accounts have not been used to log on to the domain in the last 30 days. Right-click the Saved Query container and select New>Query to create a query that locates this information, and then once a month just click on the query to see the latest list.

- **Command-line tools** Windows Server 2003 Active Directory includes a number of new command-line tools to administer Active Directory objects. These command-line tools include Dsadd and Dsmod (used to add or modify Active Directory objects, respectively), Dsrm (to remove Active Directory objects), Dsmove (to move objects from one container to another), Dsquery (to find a list of objects), and Dsget (to display attributes of an object). (See the Help And Support Center for detailed information on how to use these command-line tools.)

Summary

This chapter provided an overview of the most common Windows Server 2003 Active Directory objects and procedures for administering Active Directory objects. A great deal of your administrative effort will be spent administering these objects. In particular, you will be administering group and user accounts as employees join and leave your company or as you create new groups to secure network resources. One of the complications that you may have to work with is that you can have three different objects that represent individual users: *user* objects, *inetOrgPerson* objects, and *contact* objects. As well, you have two different types of groups and three different scopes that you may need to work with. You will also spend your time administering objects such as *computer* objects, *printer* objects, or *shared folder* objects.

Chapter 11
Introduction to Group Policies

One of the most common topics of conversation among people paying for the setup of a corporate information technology (IT) infrastructure is the total cost of owning computers. Companies have calculated that the initial purchase or lease price of a computer is only a small part of the cost of managing and maintaining that computer over the years it will be used. The primary cost is the cost of the people managing those computers. If all client computers must be manually administered, the cost of owning those computers can very quickly grow to an unacceptable level. For many companies, the answer to this problem is to use some form of automation to manage computers. As much as possible, companies want to configure computer settings in one central location and have the settings apply to all client computers. Some of these settings can be used to lock down computers so that users cannot change their desktop configurations. Other policies can be used to install software on a select group of computers.

Group policies in Microsoft Windows Server 2003 Active Directory provide many of the tools needed to lower the cost of managing client computers. When you use group policies, you can configure policies in Active Directory directory service and then have those policies applied to some or all of the computers in your organization. This chapter introduces group policies and how to configure them in Windows Server 2003 Active Directory. Chapter 12, "Using Group Policies to Manage Software," and Chapter 13, "Using Group Policies to Manage Computers," deal with how to use group policies to perform certain tasks, such as managing user desktops and installing software.

Note Group policies are effective only for computers running Microsoft Windows 2000 or later. You can use group policies to manage servers running Windows 2000 and Windows Server 2003 and to manage client computers running Windows 2000 and Microsoft Windows XP Professional, but you cannot use group policies to manage client computers running Microsoft Windows NT, Windows 95, or Windows 98. If you are familiar with group policies in Windows 2000 Active Directory, you will see that most of the concepts are the same in both versions of Active Directory. You will also notice that there are significantly more options available in Windows Server 2003 Active Directory. Many of the new settings are specific to Windows XP Professional and ignored by Windows 2000 clients.

Group Policy Overview

Group policies in Windows Server 2003 Active Directory provide powerful tools to manage user desktops. As shown in Table 11-1, there are a number of things you can do with group policies.

Table 11-1. Group Policy Options

Configuration option	Explanation
Software installation and management	You can install software on computers and then maintain it by installing patches or upgrades. You can also uninstall the software packages. Software can be assigned to both users and computers.
Scripts	You can run startup and shutdown scripts as well as logon and logoff scripts. The scripts can be MS-DOS .bat files or Windows Script Host files.
Folder redirection	You can redirect some parts of the user's work environment, such as My Documents, the Start menu, or Desktop, to a network share where it can be backed up. This redirection is transparent to the user.
Security configuration	You can configure security settings using group policies. Some of these settings, such as password and account policies, must be configured at the domain level. Other security settings can be configured at any container level.
Administrative templates	You can use administrative templates to set registry values that limit what modifications users can perform on their computers.

There are two types of group policies. The first is the local group policy on every computer running Windows 2000, Windows XP, and Windows Server 2003. There can only be one local group policy, and it is the only group policy available on any computer that is not a member of a domain. The local group policy is also applied to all computers that are part of a domain. Many of the local policies can be the same as the domain group policies. However, because the local group policy is the first policy applied, the Active Directory group policies will often override the local group policy settings.

Note The local Group Policy Object (GPO) is stored on the local computer in the %systemroot%\System32\GroupPolicy directory.

The second type of group policy is the Active Directory group policy. Objects from this group policy are stored in Active Directory and can be applied in many different ways so that each policy can manage many different computers. When a Windows Server 2003 Active Directory domain is first created, two Active Directory group policies are created: the Default Domain Policy and the Default Domain Controllers Policy. The Default Domain Policy sets the account and password policies and can also be used to configure any other domain-wide settings. The Default Domain Controllers Policy is applied at the Domain Controllers organizational unit (OU) and is used to increase some of the security settings for domain controllers. In addition to these policies, you can create as many group policies as you want and link them to different locations in your Active Directory structure. Group policies can be linked to the site container, the domain container, or any OU container in your organization.

Both the local group policy and the Active Directory group policies have two groups of settings. One group of settings applies to computers, and the other group of settings applies to user accounts. Group policies can apply only to computers and users. Active Directory groups can be used to determine whether a particular group policy will be applied to a particular user. However, group policies are always applied to either user or computer objects.

The Active Directory–based Group Policy Objects (GPOs) are actually made up of two different objects. One of the objects is a Group Policy container (GPC) object that is accessed in the Active Directory Users And Computers administrative tool under the System\Policies container. (If you do not see the System container, select Advanced Features from the View menu.) Figure 11-1 shows several containers. The GPC contains the following information:

- **Version information** Maintained by both the GPC and Group Policy template (GPT) and used to make sure that the two objects are synchronized
- **List of components** Used to specify which group policy settings (computer, user, or both) are configured in this GPO
- **Status information** Used to specify whether the GPO is enabled or disabled

These details of the GPC object can be seen by viewing the object properties using a tool like ADSI Edit, but should only be modified through the Group Policy Editor.

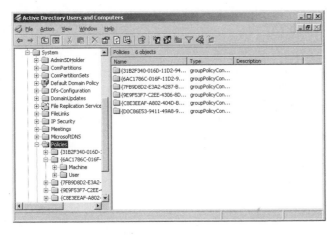

Figure 11-1. *Locating GPCs in Active Directory.*

Tip As you can see from Figure 11-1, the globally unique identifiers (GUIDs) that are used to identify the GPCs in Active Directory are not exactly easy to use. To determine the display name for each of the GPCs, you can use ADSIedit.msc. Locate the GPC in Active Directory using ADSI Edit, and then view the *displayName* attribute.

The second object that makes up the group policy is the GPT, which contains most of the actual settings for the group policy and is stored in the Sysvol folder on each domain controller. Each GPT includes the folders and contents listed in Table 11-2.

Table 11-2. The Contents of the Group Policy Template

Folder location	Contents
Adm	Contains the .adm files used to configure the administrative templates.
Scripts	Contains the scripts assigned by group polices.
User	Contains all the registry settings applied to the user by the policy. The settings are stored in a Registry.pol file.
User\Applications	Contains the application advertisement scripts for all applications deployed to users.
Machine	Contains all the registry settings applied to the computer by the policy. The settings are stored in a Registry.pol file.
Machine\Applications	Contains the application advertisement scripts for all applications deployed to computers.
{GUID}	Contains the file Gpt.ini, which provides the GPO's version number.

Both of these GPO components are replicated to all other domain controllers in the domain. The directory object (GPC) is replicated as part of the regular Active Directory replication. The Sysvol object (GPT) is replicated by the File Replication service (FRS).

Note If you have just created a new GPO or modified an existing object, the policies must replicate to all other domain controllers in the domain. You can use Replication Monitor to check the status of the replication. (Replication Monitor is one of the Active Directory tools installed when you double-click Suptools.msi in the \Support\Tools folder on the Windows Server 2003 compact disc.) To do so, open Replication Monitor and add the domain controllers to the Monitored Servers list. Then right-click the domain controller name, and select Show Group Policy Object Status. Figure 11-2 shows what the replication information looks like.

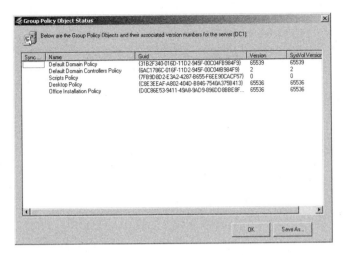

Figure 11-2. *Viewing Group Policy Object status using Replication Monitor.*

Implementing Group Policies

When you create a new GPO or modify an existing GPO, the changes are made on the primary domain controller (PDC) emulator by default. In most cases, you should accept this default to reduce the possibility of multiple administrators making incompatible changes to the group policy settings. However, if the PDC emulator is not available when you want to make the changes, you are given a choice of which domain controller to connect to. Figure 11-3 shows the choices. (You can also modify which domain controller will be changed by accessing the same interface through the View>DC Options menu in Group Policy Object Editor.) If you choose to connect to the domain controller with the Operations Master token for the PDC emulator, you are connecting to the PDC emulator. You can also choose to make the changes on the domain controller that you are currently connected to or on any domain controller.

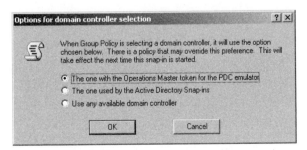

Figure 11-3. *Selecting the domain controller on which the GPO changes will be made.*

Creating GPOs

There are two ways to create new GPOs. The first option is to use an Active Directory administrative tool to access the container where you want to create a new GPO. Then right-click the container object and select Properties. Select the Group Policy tab. Figure 11-4 shows the Group Policy tab. To create a new GPO that will be linked to this container, click New.

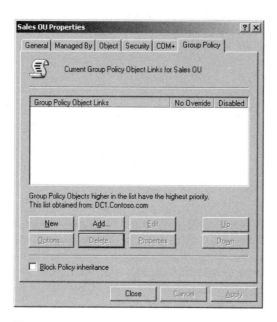

Figure 11-4. *Creating a new GPO linked to an OU.*

The second way to create a new GPO is to create a custom Microsoft Management Console (MMC) and add the Group Policy Object Editor snap-in into the MMC. When you select this snap-in, you are given the choice of which GPO you want to modify. By default, the snap-in will load the Local Computer Policy. However, you can click Browse to load any GPO from your domain or site. You can also use this tool to modify the local GPO for any computer where you have administrative rights. Figure 11-5 shows the options.

To create a new GPO while in the Welcome To The Group Policy Wizard, browse to the location in your domain where you want to create the new GPO and then click the Create New Group Policy Object button.

Regardless of which tool you use to create the new GPO, a new group policy is created and linked to the object where you create the GPO. Figure 11-6 shows a newly created GPO. You can then modify the GPO to meet your requirements.

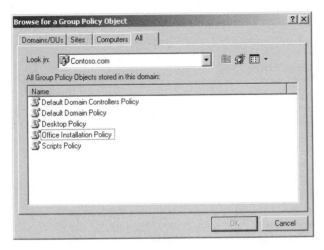

Figure 11-5. *Selecting the GPO to modify policies, while adding the Group Policy Object Editor MMC snap-in.*

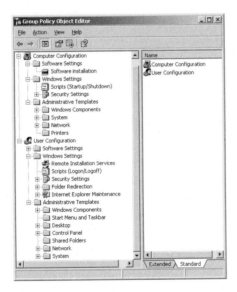

Figure 11-6. *Creating a new GPO loads the default group policy settings.*

Administering Group Policy Objects

Once you have created the GPOs, you can modify the configuration of the GPO. Most of these modifications will be configured from the Group Policy tab on the container object's Properties sheet where the GPO is linked. The interface is shown in Figure 11-4. Table 11-3 explains the configuration options available from this interface.

Table 11-3. Configuring GPO Settings

Interface option	Explanation
Add	Used to link previously created GPOs to this container object. When you click Add, you are presented with an interface similar to that shown in Figure 11-5. You can locate any GPO in your organization and link it to this container.
Edit	Used to modify the configuration options for the GPO, changing the actual contents of the GPO. When you click Edit, the interface shown in Figure 11-6 is presented.
Options	Used to configure the No Override option and to disable the GPO. These configuration options will be discussed in more detail in the section "Group Policy Inheritance and Application" later in this chapter.
Delete	Used to delete the GPO. When selecting this option, you are given the option of completely deleting the GPO from Active Directory or just deleting the link to this container object.
Properties	Used to configure whether the GPO applies to computers, users, or both. Also used to configure the security options for the GPO. These configuration options will be discussed in more detail in the section "Filtering Group Policy Application" later in this chapter.

Group Policy Inheritance and Application

GPOs can be linked to site objects, domain objects, and OU objects in Active Directory. Group policies can be linked to only these containers and cannot be connected to Active Directory container objects such as the Users container or the Computers container.

By default, group policy settings are inherited from top-level containers to lower-level containers. Therefore, all the group policies assigned to a user or a computer are applied every time the computer starts or the user logs on. The group policies are applied in the following order:

1. **Local group policy** The first group policy to be applied is always the local group policy.

2. **Site-level group policies** These group policies are linked to the site object in Active Directory.

3. **Domain-level group policies** These group policies are linked to the domain object in Active Directory.

4. **OU-level group policies** If the domain contains multiple levels of OUs, the group policies for the higher-level OUs are applied first and the group policies linked to lower-level OUs are applied next.

In some cases, more than one group policy might be applied at any of the Active Directory levels. If this is the case, the order that the GPOs are listed in the administrative interface, from bottom to top, determines the order in which they are applied. For example, Figure 11-7 shows three group policies applied to an OU. In this case, the Scripts Policy would be applied first, followed by the Desktop Policy, and then the Office Installation Policy.

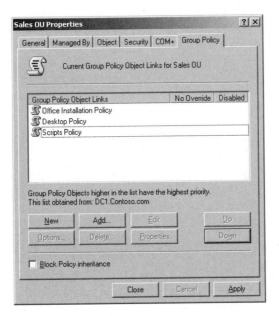

Figure 11-7. *Multiple group policies linked to the same container are applied from the bottom of the list to the top.*

The order in which group policies are applied is important if multiple group policies are modifying the same settings. For example, if a domain-level GPO removes the Run command from all computers and a lower-level OU GPO adds the Run command, the Run command will be available on all computers in the OU. This conflict arises only if the two policies modify the same setting. Similarly, a higher-level GPO might be configured to remove the Run command, and a lower-level GPO might be configured to remove a configuration icon from the Control Panel. Because there is no conflict between the settings, both will apply.

Most of the GPO settings include three configuration options: Enabled, Disabled, and Not Configured. If the setting is Enabled, whatever policy is configured by the option will be enforced. If the setting is Disabled, whatever policy is configured will be disabled. If the setting is enabled in a GPO that was applied earlier, the setting will be modified to be Disabled. For example, you might enable the setting to remove the Run command in a

GPO linked to a top-level OU. Then you could disable the setting to remove the Run command at a lower-level OU. When you disable this setting, the Run command will be available for all users in the lower-level OU. If the setting is set to Not Configured, the policy setting will not be modified and the setting that was inherited from a higher level will be maintained.

Modifying the Default Application of Group Policies

By default, all the group policies that apply to the computer and user accounts are applied in the Local/Site/Domain/Organizational Unit (LSDOU) order. So, within a container, every user and computer will be affected by the group policies. However, there are cases where you do not want this to happen; you might want to configure exceptions to the default application of group policies.

Group Policies and OU Design

As discussed in Chapter 5, "Designing the Active Directory Structure," one of the factors in creating the OU design is the application of group policies. Such consideration for group policies is especially important at the lower-level OUs, where the group policy requirements are probably the most important factor influencing the design. In most cases, this design should take advantage of the default inheritance of the group policy settings. This section, "Modifying the Default Application of Group Policies," details some of the ways to modify the default application of group policies, but one of your design goals should be to minimize the use of these options.

Even if it is one of your design goals, most large enterprises are simply too complex to always use the default inheritance. For example, you might create an OU design based on business units or departments because most users in the same business unit are likely to require the same desktop settings and the same set of applications. However, some of the users in each business unit are also likely to be part of a team that crosses department lines, either permanently or for specific projects. The other departments might have different software requirements, so the user might need to have access to both applications. Because these types of complex configurations are common in most enterprises, Windows Server 2003 Active Directory provides several options for modifying the default application of group policies.

Modifying the Inheritance of Group Policies

There are two ways to modify the default group policy inheritance. The first option is to block the policy inheritance at a container level. To block the policy inheritance, right-click the container where you want to modify inheritance and select Properties. Click the Group Policy tab, and select the check box for Block Policy Inheritance. Figure 11-8 shows the interface. Selecting this option means that group policy settings inherited from higher-level containers are blocked. The option to block policy inheritance can be useful when you have a policy that should be applied to a large group of users and computers in multiple OUs but where you do not want the policy applied to a specific group of users. A common example is a scenario where all users in the organization require that some parts of their desktop, such as the Run command or the Registry Editor, be locked down but network administrators still require full access to all tools. In this scenario, you can configure a group policy at the domain level that locks down all computers, create a separate OU for the network administrator accounts, and then block group policy inheritance at that level.

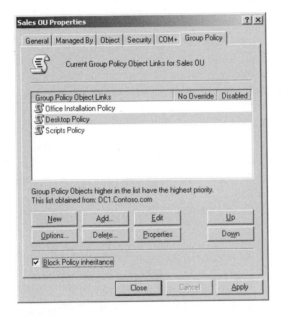

Figure 11-8. *Blocking group policy inheritance at an OU level.*

Caution   One of the limitations of blocking the inheritance of group policies is that when you select the option to block group policy inheritance, all group policy inheritance will be blocked. There is no way to selectively block inheritance by only specific group policies.

The second way to modify the default inheritance of group policies is to use the No Override option. This option is used to enforce a group policy even in containers where the option to block group policy inheritance is set. To configure a group policy for no override, locate the container object where the group policy is linked and then select the container's Properties sheet. Select the Group Policy tab, select the group policy, click Options, and select the No Override option. Figure 11-9 shows the interface.

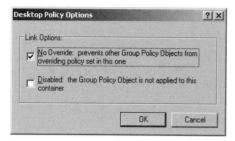

Figure 11-9. *Configuring the No Override option on a group policy.*

The No Override option can be useful when you have a group policy that applies to all users regardless of where they are located. For example, you might want to use group policies to manage the antivirus software on all client computers in your organization. In this case, you should select the top-level container that contains all the computers in your domain and apply the policy at that level. Then configure the group policy for No Override so that the settings are applied to all client computers.

No Override is set at the location where the GPO is linked to the container, not at the GPO itself. Therefore, if you link the GPO to more than one location in your domain and configure one of the links for No Override, the other links are not automatically configured for No Override. No Override is also set on a per-GPO basis—that is, setting the No Override option on one GPO linked to an OU does not affect the No Override option for other GPOs linked to the OU.

Note The No Override option forces group policy settings even if the inheritance is blocked. In addition to these group policy settings, the domain-level settings such as account policies and password policies also apply to all computers and users in the domain. Blocking policy inheritance has no effect on these policies.

Filtering Group Policy Application

The third way to modify the inheritance of group policies is to filter the application of group policies by using Active Directory groups. By default, when you create a group policy, the group policy is applied to all users and computers in the container. To understand why this is the case, view the Security tab for a newly created group policy. As shown in Figure 11-10, the Security tab for all GPOs is configured so that Authenticated Users have both Read permission and Apply Group Policy permission. Therefore, all authenticated users, including both computers and users, will be affected by the policy.

You can modify which users or computers will be affected by the group policy by modifying which accounts have the Apply Group Policy permission set for them. To configure this setting, first remove the Authenticated Users group from the Security tab or clear the Apply Group Policy check box. Then add the appropriate accounts to the access control list (ACL) and grant the accounts Read permission and Apply Group Policy permission.

Although you can modify permission by adding any security principal, it is a best practice to always use Active Directory groups rather than individual user or computer accounts.

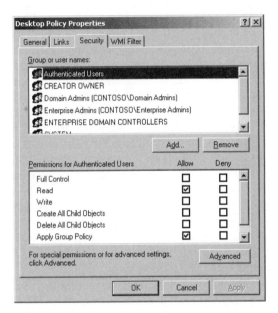

Figure 11-10. *Configuring the Security tab on a GPO's Properties sheet to modify GPO application.*

Tip   Although you can use groups to filter the application of group policies, you cannot apply group policies to groups. For example, if you link a group policy to a container that contains a global group but does not contain user accounts that are members of the global group, the group policies will not be effective. The user and computer accounts must be in the container object for the group policy to apply.

The option to apply group policies to a selective group is useful in a number of different scenarios. One example is where you need to install a particular software package for a group of users, but the user accounts are scattered in a variety of OUs throughout the domain. To install this application using group policies, you can link the GPO to a container object that contains all the user accounts and then modify the security of the GPO so that the policy applies only to the specified group. Another scenario where you might choose to filter the application of group policies is if you have a GPO that is assigned to a particular OU but you do not want the GPO to apply to all users in that OU. In this case, you have two options. First, you can create a group that contains all the user accounts that require the group policy and configure the Apply Group Policy permission for that group only. Second, you can create a group that contains all the user accounts that do not require the group policy and use the Deny setting on the Apply Group Policy permission to ensure that the policy does not apply to these users.

Tip If you remove the Apply Group Policy permission for a group, you should also remove Read Access. If you don't, the group policy is read every time the computer starts and every time members of the group log on, even if the policy is not applied, which can have a detrimental effect on startup and logon performance.

Tip Windows Server 2003 Active Directory also provides the option to filter the application of group policies based on Windows Management Instrumentation (WMI) filters. The WMI filters, which are written in the WMI query language, can be used to more precisely specify group policies that apply to a computer. For example, you can use this option to specify that a software package should only be installed on a computer with more than 200 MB of available disk space or on a computer with more than 64 MB of RAM. For more details on WMI filters, see the Help And Support Center and the WMI Software Development Kit on the Microsoft Web site at *http://msdn.microsoft.com/library/default.asp?url=/library/en-us/wmidsk/wmi /wmi_start_page.asp*.

Applying Group Policies to Users or Computers

Another way to modify the application of group policies is to configure the group policy to apply to only computers or only users, but not both. To do so, access the GPO's Properties sheet. An example is shown in Figure 11-11. You can choose to disable either the computer configuration settings or the user configuration settings.

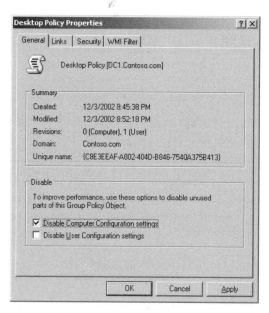

Figure 11-11. *Disabling the computer configuration settings for a GPO.*

> **Tip**   Most of the options for modifying the default application of group policies discussed in this section should be avoided because they can result in a group policy configuration that is complex and difficult to manage. However, using the option to apply the group policies to only users or computers should be used more frequently. In most cases, a group policy is configured to apply to either users or computers, but not both. Choosing the option to disable the computer or user configuration settings can significantly increase the group policy performance.

Disabling Group Policies

Another option that can be used to modify the application of group policies is to disable a group policy. To do so, access the GPO's Properties sheet and select Options. (The interface is shown in Figure 11-9.) By disabling the group policy, you can prevent the application of the group policy without changing any other settings. For example, you might have a group policy that needs to be run only occasionally or a group policy that is still in a pilot phase. You can create the group policy, link it to the appropriate container, and then disable the policy. You can then enable it as needed.

Group Policy Processing

Now that you know how to create GPOs and link them to containers within Windows Server 2003 Active Directory, the next step is to understand how the group policies are actually applied to the computers. When a computer starts and the user logs on, the group policies are applied in the following manner:

1. When the client computer starts, it reads the registry to determine the site where the computer is located. The computer sends a query to the Domain Name System (DNS) server requesting the Internet Protocol (IP) addresses of the domain controllers in the same site.

2. When the DNS server responds, the client computer connects to a domain controller in its site. As part of the authentication process with the domain controller, the client computer requests the list of all GPOs that apply to the computer.

3. The domain controller responds to the client with a list of all the GPOs that apply to the computer as well as the order in which the policies should be applied. The computer then retrieves the GPOs from the domain controller and applies the policies. The order in which the group policies are applied is based on the LSDOU configuration.

4. When the user logs on, the client computer again queries the domain controller, now requesting all GPOs that apply to the user. Again, the GPOs are applied in the appropriate order.

Tip Group policies are applied asynchronously on Windows XP clients. In Windows 2000, group policies are applied synchronously, which means that all computer policies must be completely applied before the user logon screen appears, and all user policies must be applied before the user desktop appears. Applying the policies asynchronously means that Windows XP should boot and the users should be able to log on more quickly.

You can use group policies to modify how other group policies are applied. These configuration options are set in the User Configuration\Administrative Templates\System\Group Policy or Computer Configuration\Administrative Templates\System\Group Policy folders. Figure 11-12 shows the options available in the Computer Configuration branch of the folder tree.

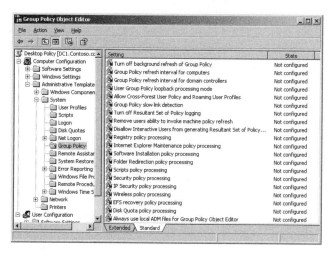

Figure 11-12. *Group Policy configuration options.*

The group policies are applied when the computer starts and when the user logs on. Once the user has logged on, the group policies are refreshed periodically. By default, the policies are refreshed every 90 minutes with up to a 30-minute variation to avoid overloading the domain controllers if many clients request the refresh at the same time. Group policies on domain controllers are refreshed every 5 minutes. You can use the configuration settings in the Group Policy folder to disable all background refreshing of group policies or to modify the refresh time for group policy.

There are two factors that can modify the default processing of group policies to a computer and user. The first factor is if the client computer detects a slow network connection during startup. If the computer detects a slow network connection during startup, only selective parts of the group policy are applied. By default, only the security settings and the administrative templates are applied across a slow network connection.

To determine whether the computer is using a slow network connection, the computer sends a zero-byte ping packet to the domain controller. If the response time is less than 10 milliseconds (ms), the network is considered fast and all group policies are applied. If the response time is more than 10 ms, the computer pings the domain controller three times with a 2-kilobyte (KB) packet. The computer averages the response times and uses this average to determine the network link speed. By default, if the network connection is greater than 500 kilobits per second (Kbps), all group policies are applied. If the computer detects a network connection that is less than 500 Kbps, the security settings and administrative template policies are applied but the other policies are not.

You can modify this default slow link configuration. One option is to modify the default definition of a slow link. This definition can be configured for computers in the Computer Configuration\Administrative Templates\System\Group Policy folder. Right-click Group Policy Slow Link Detection and select Properties. (Figure 11-13 shows the interface.) To modify the default slow link speed of 500 Kbps, select Enabled and then enter the value that you want to use.

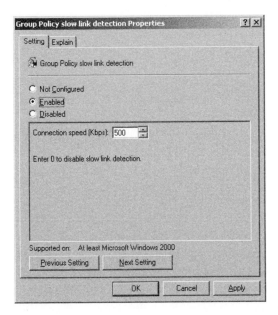

Figure 11-13. *Configuring the slow link detection value.*

By default, only the security and administrative template components are processed if the computer detects a slow network connection. There is no way to turn off these settings. However, you can configure some of the other settings so that they are processed across even a slow network connection. The Computer Configuration\Administrative Templates\System\Group Policy folder also contains the other options. For example, you might want to apply Internet Explorer Maintenance Policy Processing across the slow network connection. To enable this option, right-click this setting in the Group Policy folder and select Properties. Then click Enabled, and select how you want the policies to be applied. Figure 11-14 shows the options.

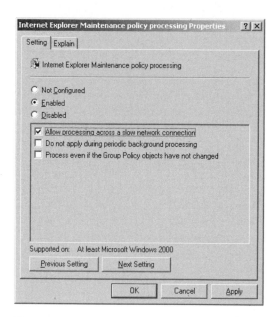

Figure 11-14. *Configuring slow link processing for Internet Explorer Maintenance Policy Processing.*

To enable this policy regardless of the network bandwidth, select Allow Processing Across A Slow Network Connection. The other two settings control whether the setting will be processed each time the policy is refreshed and whether the policy is applied even if it has not been changed.

The second option that can be used to modify the application of GPOs to the computer is to use the loopback option. The loopback option is used to modify the default application of group policies where the computer policies are set first and then the user policies are set. Because the user policy is set after the computer policy, the user policy will overwrite the computer policy for any conflicting settings. You can use the loopback policy to modify this configuration. By setting the loopback policy, you can ensure that the computer policies are applied last, thus overwriting any policies applied to the user. Group policy loopback is set using the User Group Policy Loopback Processing Mode option in the Computer Configuration\Administrative Templates\System\Group Policy container. Figure 11-15 shows the configuration options.

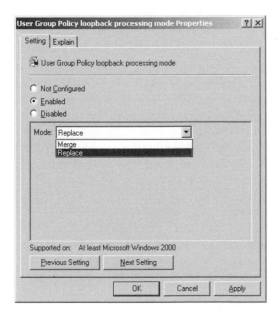

Figure 11-15. *Configuring the loopback processing of group policies.*

When you enable loopback processing, you have two additional configuration options. First, the Merge option means that the computer group policies are applied first, then the user policy is applied, and then the computer policy is applied again. Some of the user settings might not be modified by the computer policies. Only conflicting settings will be overwritten. Second, the Replace option means that only the computer policies are processed; the user policies are not processed.

The loopback option is useful in a variety of scenarios. One of the most common is when you need to lock down a computer that is located in a public place. For example, you might have a computer in a public office and allow employees to log on to the computer. Because the computer is publicly accessible, you might want to ensure that the computer is always locked down, regardless of who logs on to the computer. You can enable lockdown by putting the public computers into an OU and configuring a restrictive group policy for that OU. Then configure loopback processing for that OU. Now when a user logs on to the computer, the user will get a restrictive desktop. The user might get a much less restrictive desktop when he or she logs on to his or her regular workstation, but the loopback policy protects the public computer.

Delegating Administration of GPOs

As discussed in Chapter 9, "Delegating the Administration of Active Directory," one of the biggest advantages of Active Directory is the option to delegate many of the administrative tasks within the organization. The management of group policies is no exception; you can also delegate the management of this important administrative tool.

There are three options for delegating the administration of group policies. First, you can delegate the permissions to create, delete, and modify the GPOs. By default, only the Domain Admins group and the Group Policy Creator Owners groups have this right. The Group Policy Creator Owners group has an additional restriction in that the members of this group have permission to modify the settings only on group policies that they actually created. If you create a special group of administrators in your organization that will manage group policies, you can add those administrators to one of these groups. You can grant the right to create and delete group policies to any other group, but granting permission to create or delete GPOs is more complicated than most delegation of permission scenarios. Not only must you give the user permission in Active Directory to create GPOs, but also you must give the user permission to write data to the %systemroot%\Sysvol*domainname*\Policies folder, which is where the GPTs are stored. You can also give users or groups permission to modify specific GPOs by granting them Read and Write permission to the GPO in Active Directory.

The second option for delegating the administration of group policies is to delegate the right to manage group policy links. This option does not give the administrators permission to modify any GPO, but it does give them the right to add or remove GPO links at a container object. The easiest way to grant this level of permissions is to use the Delegation Of Control Wizard. In the Active Directory Users And Computers administrative tool, right-click the object that you want another user or group to control and then click Delegate Control to start the Wizard. When you start the Wizard at an OU level, one of the standard tasks that can be delegated is the permission to Manage Group Policy Links. Figure 11-16 shows the interface.

The third way to delegate the administration of group policies is to give users the right to generate the Resultant Set of Policy (RSoP) information. Again, you can use the Delegation Of Control Wizard to grant the right to generate the RSoP tool in either logging or planning mode. Figure 11-16 also shows this delegation option. You can also assign these permissions by editing the ACL on a container object by granting the user Write permissions to the *gPLink* attribute. Granting the user Write permissions to the *gPOptions* attribute gives the user permission to configure the blocking of group policies at that container level.

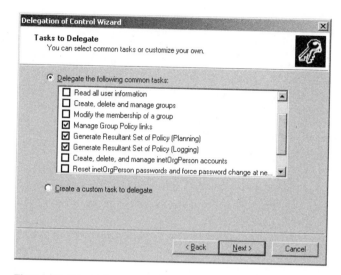

Figure 11-16. *Delegating the permission to Manage Group Policy Links.*

Implementing Group Policies Between Domains and Forests

You can use Windows Server 2003 group policies to enforce policies between domains and even between trusted forests. In both cases, there are some significant limitations and issues that you need to deal with before implementing such group policies.

After creating a GPO in a Windows Server 2003 Active Directory, you can link that GPO to any site, domain, or OU in the forest. The primary limitation with linking group policies between domains is that the GPOs are stored only on the domain controllers in the domain where the GPO is created. If you choose to link the GPO to a container in a different domain, you might need to deal with significant network bandwidth and security issues. For example, if a group policy is linked to an OU that is in a different domain than where the GPO was created, all the computers in the OU must be able to connect to a domain controller in the GPO source domain to download the group policy. If one of these domain controllers is in the same site as the client computers, network bandwidth will not be significantly impacted. However, if all domain controllers that have a copy of the GPO are in a different site across a slow wide area network (WAN) connection, the application of the group policy can be very slow and can seriously impact the available bandwidth. In addition, if the users from one domain must apply a group policy from another domain, the users and computers from the destination domain must have Read access to both the GPC in Active Directory and the GPT in the Sysvol folder. In most cases, it is better practice to create GPOs for each domain rather than share one GPO across multiple domains.

These issues also apply when using group policies between forests. Windows Server 2003 Active Directory provides the option to share group policies between trusted forests. This option can be useful when users travel between company locations that are in separate forests. In this scenario, a user logging on to a computer in another forest can still have his or her group policy from their home domain applied to him or her. Other functionality that is available between forests includes the following:

- The shares used for software distribution can be in a separate forest.
- Logon scripts can be located and read from a domain controller in another forest.
- Redirected folders and roaming user profile files can be located on a computer in another forest.

In each case, the network bandwidth and security issues might mean that you would rather implement separate GPOs in each forest than between forests.

Group Policy Management Tools

Group policies provide a great deal of functionality and flexibility for managing your client computers and servers. So far in this chapter, you have seen one of the tools that can be used to manage group policies: the Group Policy Object Editor. This section introduces several other tools that can be used to manage group policies.

RSoP Tool

Because so many options are available, configuring group policies can be complicated. For example, it can be difficult to determine exactly which policies apply to a particular user or group. If you have created multiple GPOs and linked them to various containers in your domain, it can be difficult to determine what the effective group policy setting is and which GPO any specific setting is coming from. One of the tools that you can use to make this task easier is the RSoP tool, which can be used to determine exactly what the effective policies are for any user or computer.

The RSoP tool can be used in two modes: logging mode and planning mode. In logging mode, the tool is used to locate and list all the group policies that apply to a computer or user account. In planning mode, it is used to determine the effect that changing a group policy configuration will have on a user or a computer. This modification can include moving a user from one container to another or adding the user or computer to a different security group.

To use the RSoP tool, create a custom MMC and add the Resultant Set of Policy snap-in. Then right-click Resultant Set Of Policy and select Generate RSoP Data. The Resultant Set Of Policy Wizard gives you a choice of running the tool in logging mode or in planning mode. If you choose logging mode, you can choose the computer and user. The tool then calculates all the group policy settings that are applied to the user and computer. As part of each setting, the tool also specifies which GPO is supplying the effective information for that setting.

If you run the RSoP in planning mode, you can choose a user, a computer, or both; or a container object for the user or computer account, or both. Figure 11-17 shows the interface. After selecting the user or the computer or both, you can test different scenarios for modifying the user or computer objects. For example, you can determine which group policies will be effective if the user connects to the domain across a slow link or what the effect of using the loopback setting will be for the user. You can also determine what the effect would be of moving the user or computer to another container in Active Directory or of adding the user or computer to another security group. After making your choices, the tool will calculate the effective group policies for the user and computer in the new configuration.

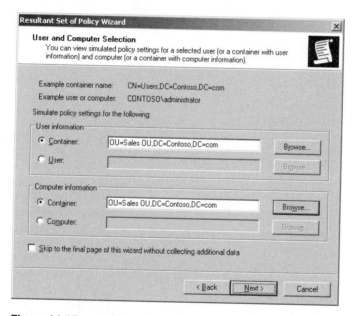

Figure 11-17. *Specifying the user and computer objects in RSoP planning mode.*

GPResult

GPResult is a command-line tool that provides some of the functionality that is provided by the RSoP tool. If you run the Gpresult command without any parameters, it returns the group policy information for the computer on which you run the command and for the logged-on user. The information includes the group policies that are applied to the computer and user, and the groups that each object belongs to. The command can also be run in verbose mode, in which the results will include all the effective group policy settings as well as all effective privileges that the user has. The tool can also be run from one computer to analyze the effective group policies for another user and computer. GPResult is installed on all computers running Windows XP Professional and Windows Server 2003. For complete information on using GPResult, see the Help And Support Center.

GPUpdate

The GPUpdate command-line tool replaces the Secedit /refreshpolicy command that is available in Windows 2000 Active Directory. It is used to force a refresh of the group policies for a computer or a user. If you type *gpupdate* at a command prompt, both the computer policy and the user policy are refreshed on the local computer. The tool can also be used to refresh group policies on other computers. One of the advantages the Gpupdate command has over the Secedit command is that the command can be used to log off users or even restart computers after the group policy is refreshed, which is useful when refreshing group policies that are only applied when the user logs on or when the computer restarts. For example, software distribution policies and folder redirection policies are only applied at startup or logon. By using the */logoff* or */boot* parameters, you can forcibly apply these policies at any time.

Group Policy Management Console

Using the built-in tools for group policy management is appropriate for a small organization where there are few group policies and a flat OU hierarchy where group policies are applied at only one or two levels. However, in large enterprises where there might be dozens of group policies and as many places where the policies are linked to containers, managing group policies can be much more complicated. To address this situation, Microsoft has designed a new tool, the Group Policy Management Console (GPMC). Figure 11-18 shows the interface for this tool.

Note At the time of this writing, Microsoft has indicated that the GPMC will be available as a free download shortly after Windows Server 2003 ships. This section is based on the Beta 2 version of the GPMC. Some of the functionality and interfaces in the final release might be different than shown here.

The GPMC provides a single tool that you can use to administer all group policy configurations for the entire organization. Table 11-4 summarizes the functionality that is available in the GPMC.

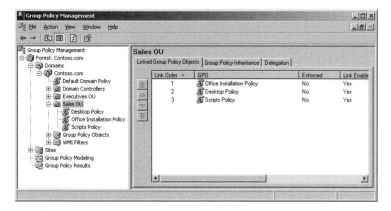

Figure 11-18. *The GPMC provides a single management tool to manage all group policies.*

Table 11-4. GPMC Configuration Options

Functionality	Configuration options
GPO Settings	Used to configure all the settings of the GPO.
GPO Links	Used to view and modify all places where a GPO is linked to container objects.
GPO Delegation	Used to view and modify the delegation of GPO creation and deletion, modification of GPO links, and the permission to generate RSoP data.
Security Filtering	Used to view and modify all filtering based on security groups.
RSoP Planning	Named "Group Policy Modeling" but uses the same wizard as the RSoP tool in planning mode.
RSoP Logging	Named "Group Policy Results" but uses the same wizard as the RSoP tool in logging mode.
Modify Inheritance	Used to set the No Override and the Block Inheritance settings.
Search	Used to search for any type of group policy–related object. For example, you can search for all GPOs that have enabled Folder Redirection.
Backup And Restore GPOs	Used to back up and restore individual GPOs or all the GPOs in a domain. Without this tool, the only way to back up and restore GPOs is to back up the System State data on a domain controller.
Scripting Interface	The GPMC exposes several Component Object Model (COM) objects that can be used to script the management of group policies. For more information, see the information on GPMC on the Microsoft Web site at *http://www.microsoft.com /windowsserver2003/gpmc/default.mspx*.

As you can see, the GPMC is a very powerful tool for managing group policies in an enterprise environment.

Group Policy Design

Group policies are powerful tools for managing computer configurations on your network. Implementing group policies can also be very complicated, and if implemented incorrectly, group policies can greatly impact the work environment for all users in your organization. This section describes a few best practices for designing the group policy implementation on your network.

More Info   Chapters 12 and 13 describe additional best practices for using group policies for software distribution and desktop management.

One of the important issues you will run into when designing the group policy configuration is how many group policies you will implement. Because all group policy settings are available in every GPO, you could theoretically configure all the required settings in a single GPO. Or you could deploy a separate GPO for every setting that you want to configure. In almost every case, the optimum number of GPOs will fall between these two extremes, and no one solution is right for all situations. When the client computer starts and the user logs on, all the applicable GPOs must be downloaded and applied to the local computer. Therefore, having fewer group policies usually enhances the startup and logon performance for the client. However, having only a few group policies that do many things can become much more difficult to document and manage. Also, if you have group policies that have only a few settings, it is much easier to reuse group policies across multiple OUs. In general, it is a good practice to use GPOs to configure only one group of settings. For example, you might use one GPO to set the security configuration, another to set the administrative templates, and another to install a software package.

Another design issue has to do with where you want to deploy the group policies. Usually you have a choice of deploying group policies high in the OU structure and then possibly using group filtering and group policy blocking to make sure that the group policies are applied to the appropriate computers or users. Or you might choose to apply most of the group policies lower in the hierarchy so that you can apply each policy at the right point in the hierarchy and avoid any complicated inheritance configuration. In most cases, a combination is probably the right answer. If you have some policies that need to be applied to all users in your domain, set those policies as high as possible. As you go down the hierarchy, the group policies will be much more specific.

Summary

This chapter has provided the framework for the next two chapters by explaining the configuration options for group policies in Windows Server 2003 Active Directory. This chapter discussed how to create and manage group policies using the tools available with Windows Server 2003. This chapter also discussed how group policies are inherited and applied to client computers. You can use the default inheritance model to set a group policy high in the OU hierarchy and have the GPO settings apply to many objects in the domain. You can also modify this default inheritance of group policy settings by blocking or filtering the inheritance. Chapters 12 and 13 focus on what you can actually do with group policies. Chapter 12 deals with how you can use group policies to distribute software to client computers, and Chapter 13 discusses how you can use group policies to manage a wide variety of desktop configuration options.

Chapter 12
Using Group Policies to Manage Software

Chapter 11, "Introduction to Group Policies," provided an overview of the basic features of, and how to deploy and manage, group policies in Microsoft Windows Server 2003 Active Directory. This chapter and the next chapter detail what you can actually do with group policies. This chapter discusses using group policies to manage software on client computers. Chapter 13, "Using Group Policies to Manage Computers," discusses several other ways that you can manage user desktops using group policies.

Managing software on client computers is one of the most important tasks that you will perform when managing a corporate network. The software installed on client computers includes the tools that users must have to get their work done. In many companies, a desktop computer will have a regular office suite of applications, such as Microsoft Office, as well as a wide variety of business-specific applications. In most companies, the standard client computer also requires a file compression application, antivirus software, and other applications.

Managing the software on user desktops can be a very labor-intensive task if an administrator must visit each desktop every time a new software package needs to be installed or upgraded. In a large company, just dealing with application errors can require several full-time administrators. In some cases, software updates must happen on a nightly or weekly basis. Many companies update their antivirus software at least weekly.

Using group policies to manage software can significantly reduce the effort required to manage user desktops. In fact, one of the biggest cost savings to be gained from deploying Active Directory directory service and group policies is in the area of software management.

Managing software in a corporate environment consists of much more than simply deploying the software. Many companies have a clearly defined software life-cycle management process that includes purchasing or building and testing the application, piloting the application to a small group of users, wide-scale deployment of the application, maintenance of the application after deployment, and finally, the removal of the application. Group policies in Active Directory can make most of these tasks more efficient.

Windows Installer Technology

In most cases, software management through group policies relies on the Microsoft Windows Installer technology. Windows Installer technology is used to install, manage, and remove software on Windows workstations. Windows Installer technology consists of two components:

- **A software installation package file (.msi file)** The .msi package file contains a database of information that contains all the instructions required to install and remove applications.
- **The Windows Installer service (Msiexec. exe)** This service manages the actual installation of software on the workstation. The service uses a dynamic link library (DLL) named Msi.dll to read the .msi package files. Based on the content of the software installation package file, the service then copies application files to the local hard disk, creates shortcuts, modifies registry entries, and performs all the tasks listed in the .msi file.

Using the Windows Installer technology has a number of benefits. One of the most important benefits is that any application can be largely self healing. Because the .msi file contains all the information needed to install the application, the same file can be used to repair an application that has failed. For example, if an application fails because a critical file has been deleted, the application will fail to start the next time the user selects the application. If the application has been installed using Windows Installer, the same .msi file that was used to install the application will be used to repair the application by reinstalling the missing file. The .msi file also enables cleaner uninstalls of applications.

Note Windows Installer technology is not specific to Windows Server 2003, Microsoft Windows XP Professional, or Microsoft Windows 2000, although the Windows Installer service is installed by default on these operating systems. Applications can be installed using the Windows Installer technology on other computers. You can install the Windows Installer service on computers running Microsoft Windows NT, Windows 95, and Windows 98. However, you can use group policies to distribute software only to computers running Windows Server 2003, Windows XP Professional, and Windows 2000.

Most software manufacturers now provide a .msi software installation package file with all new software. This is known as a *native Windows Installer file*. If the software includes a .msi file, you can use that file to install the software.

Creating a .msi file

In some cases, you might not have a native Windows Installer file. You might have an older application that does not have a native installer package. If you want to use

Windows Installer technology to deploy the application, you can create a .msi file to distribute the software.

➲ **To create an .msi file, perform the following steps.**

1. Create a clean installation of the operating system where you are going to create the installation software package file. No additional software should be installed on the operating system. The operating system that you use for this computer should be the operating system that will be running on the computer where you will be installing the application. If you want to install the application on both Windows 2000 and Windows XP Professional, usually you must create two separate .msi files.

2. Use a software packaging tool to take a snapshot of the operating system before you install the software. There are several software packaging tools available from vendors such as Wise.

3. Install the application on the workstation. Normally, you will use the native software installation process.

4. After you have installed the application, customize the application as you want. For example, you might want to create or remove shortcuts, add templates to a custom location, or customize the toolbar on the application. In some cases, you must open the application at least once to fully install all the components.

5. Use the software packaging tool to create a second snapshot of the workstation. This process creates the .msi software installation packaging file.

Once you have created the .msi file, you can use the Group Policy Software Installation process to distribute the software to the workstations.

Deploying Software Using Group Policies

After you obtain or create the Windows Installer file, you can deploy the application using group policies in Windows Server 2003 Active Directory. Group policies provide a means to advertise or make the application available for installation to workstations or users. After you configure the appropriate group policy, the next time the computer boots up, or the next time the user logs on, the fact that the new software package is available is advertised to the computer. The application is then ready to be installed on that computer.

Before you can advertise an application to users on the network, you must copy the software installation files, including the .msi file, to a network share that is accessible to all users. When you create the network share, you must ensure that all users or computers have appropriate access to the share. If you are assigning applications to computers, the computer accounts must have Read access. If you are assigning or publishing applications to users, the users must have Read access. (See the next section for details about assigning applications versus publishing applications.)

Deploying Applications

After creating the network share and copying the installation files to the share, you are ready to implement the Group Policy Objects (GPOs) that will advertise the application to the clients. You can create a new GPO or modify an existing GPO. The first choice that you have to make when configuring the GPO is whether you want to advertise the application to computers or to users. If you decide to advertise the application to computers, you will use the Computer Configuration\Software Settings container in the Group Policy Object Editor, and the application will be installed on the workstation the next time the workstation is rebooted. If you decide to advertise the application to users, you will use the User Configuration\Software Settings container in the Group Policy Object Editor, and the application will be available to the user the next time the user logs on.

Note   Chapter 11, "Introduction to Group Policies," introduced the Microsoft Group Policy Management Console (GPMC), a powerful tool you can use to administer all group policy configurations for the entire organization. Because it is designed as a single tool for group policy management, its user interface is quite different from the user interface found in the other Active Directory administrative tools. However, since GPMC is an optional add-on, the information provided in Chapters 11, 12, and 13 are presented using only the administrative tools and snap-ins provided as part of the Windows Server 2003 installation compact disc.

When you use a group policy to install applications, you have two choices for how the application will be advertised to the client. The first option is to *assign* the application, which can target either a computer or a user. The second option is to *publish*, which makes an application available, but only to user accounts.

When you assign an application to a computer, the application is completely installed the next time the computer is rebooted, which means that the application is installed for all users of a computer the next time they log on to that computer.

When you assign an application to a user, the application is advertised the next time the user logs on to the network. You can configure how the application is advertised, but most of the time, the application is added to the Start menu. The application is also added to the published applications list in the Add Or Remove Programs control panel. By default, the application is not installed when the user logs on but will be installed when the user activates the application from the Start menu or chooses to install the application through Add Or Remove Programs. You can also configure the install logic so that an application can be installed when the user tries to open a file with a file extension that is associated with the application. For example, if Microsoft Word is not currently installed on the user's computer, when the user double-clicks a file with a .doc extension, Word will automatically be installed. This process is often referred to as *extension activation*.

One of the new features in Windows Server 2003 Active Directory that is not available in Windows 2000 Active Directory is the option to completely install the software application when the user logs on rather than after user activation. Choosing this option means that the logon process will take longer to allow the application to be installed, but the application is then available to the client for use. This option is available only when the application is assigned to a user. Published applications cannot be completely installed until they are installed through Add Or Remove Programs or through extension activation. This option is also not applicable when the application is assigned to computers because the application is completely installed the next time the computer is rebooted.

When you publish an application to a user, the application is advertised the next time the user logs on to the network. In this case, however, the application is only advertised in the Add Or Remove Programs control panel. To install the application, the user must choose that option in Add Or Remove Programs. By default, published applications are also installed through extension activation.

In most cases, publishing an application is the best option if only some of the users require the application. For example, you might have a graphics application such as Microsoft Visio that only the network architects require all the time. However, some other users might need Visio. By publishing the application to the users, you are not installing the application on their desktops or adding it to their shortcuts, but you are making the application available for those who need it.

➲ **To advertise an application using a group policy, use the following procedure:**

1. Copy the software installation files to a network share. Configure the permissions on the share to ensure that all required users and computers have Read access to the installation files.

2. Locate the container—a site, a domain, or an organizational unit (OU)—where you want to advertise the application and access the container properties. Click the Group Policy tab. Create a new GPO, or click Edit to modify the properties of an existing GPO.

3. If you are advertising the application to user accounts, expand the User Configuration\Software Settings container in the Group Policy Object Editor, right-click Software Installation, select New, and then select Package. If you are advertising the application to computer accounts, expand the Computer Configuration\Software Settings container in the GPO, right-click Software Installation, select New, and then select Package.

4. Browse to the network location, or type in the network path where the installation files are located. You must use a network location and not a local drive letter on the server because the network location is advertised to the client computers. Select the appropriate .msi file.

Note If you do select the wrong network location or if you choose to modify the network location after deployment, you must re-create the software package. There is no means to modify the installation path for the software package.

---

5. When you select the .msi file, you are given a choice of how you want to advertise the software package. Figure 12-1 shows the options if you are advertising the application to user accounts. If you are advertising the application to computers, you can only assign the application.

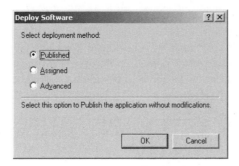

Figure 12-1. *Options for advertising the software package.*

6. If you chose to assign or publish the application, click OK. If you choose the Advanced option, you are presented with the Properties sheet for the package. This Properties sheet is discussed in the section "Configuring Software Package Properties" later in this chapter.

Once the GPO is configured, the application will be advertised to all clients in the container object. By default, the software installation component of a group policy is applied only when the user logs on (if the policy is applied to user accounts) or when the computer reboots (if the policy is applied to computer accounts). The GPUpdate command-line tool, which is included on all computers running Windows XP Professional and Windows Server 2003, can force a logoff or a reboot as part of the group policy update on the workstation. To force a logoff or a reboot, use the command *gpupdate /logoff* or *gpupdate /reboot*.

Software Distribution and Network Bandwidth

One of the most difficult aspects of managing software distribution using group policies is network utilization management. If you assign a large multi-megabyte application to a large group of users and all of those users install the application at the same time, the installation might take hours because of the significant increase in the volume of network traffic. There are a number of options for managing the network bandwidth. One option is to assign applications to computers and ask users to reboot the computers at the end of the day. You can also force a reboot of the workstation by using the GPUpdate command. If you apply this command to only a few workstations at a time, the impact on the network can be minimized. Another option is to assign applications to small groups of users at one time. In most cases, you might also want to avoid assigning applications that will be completely installed when the user logs on. If you advertise an application but allow the user to initiate the installation, you will be able to at least spread out the software installation over some time. Although none of these options is ideal, you can use them to at least manage the bandwidth to some extent.

Another way to manage network utilization if you have multiple sites is to use the Distributed File System (DFS). With DFS, you can create a logical directory structure that is independent of where the files are actually stored on the network. For example, you might create a DFS root named \\server1\softinst and then create subdirectories for all applications underneath that share point. With DFS, you can locate the subdirectories on multiple servers and configure multiple physical links to the same logical directories. If you use Active Directory–integrated DFS, you can even configure automatic replication of the folder contents between copies of the same directory. DFS is a site-aware application, which means that if you have multiple sites, the client computers will always connect to a copy of a DFS folder in their own site rather than cross a wide area network (WAN) link to access the folder on another site.

It is difficult to predict exactly what the effect of a network installation will be. One of the advantages of using group policies to install software is that you can easily perform a test to see what the effect is likely to be. For example, you can configure a GPO that includes the software package but make sure that GPO is not linked to any OU. You can then create a temporary OU, add a few user or computer accounts to the OU, and link the GPO to the OU. This configuration can be used to test how long it takes to install the applications to a small group of users. You can also pilot the software distribution by linking the GPO to a production OU but using group filtering to limit which users or computers will apply the GPO.

Regardless of the efforts you take to minimize the effect on the network, deploying a large application to a large number of users will always have some impact on the network. Since this is this case, you will probably have to plan on completing the installation over several days.

Using Group Policies to Distribute Non–Windows Installer Applications

In some cases, you might not want to go through the effort of creating a .msi file to install an application, but you might still want to use group policies to distribute an application. For example, you might have a simple application that must be installed on several workstations but that does not require any customization and is not likely to be upgraded. You can create and use a software installation settings (.zap) file to install this application.

A *.zap file* is a text file that contains the setup instructions for installing an application. In most cases, the .zap file will contain only the following lines:

```
[Application]
FriendlyName = "applicationname"
SetupCommand = ""\\servername\sharename\installapplication.exe""
```

The *FriendlyName* value is the name that will be displayed in the Add Or Remove Programs control panel on the client computer. The *SetupCommand* value is the path to the installation file for the application. You can use a Universal Naming Convention (UNC) path or a mapped drive for the *SetupCommand* value. If the application provides a means to customize the installation by using setup parameters, you can include the parameters in the *SetupCommand* value, following the setup path's closing double quotation marks. For example, the value might be

```
SetupCommand = "\\servername\sharename\setup.exe" /parameter
```

Note that if the command line includes a parameter, the setup path uses a single set of double quotation marks instead of the two sets of double quotation marks required in the earlier example.

After you have created the .zap file and copied the application installation files to a network share, you can publish the application to users. The application is added to the list of available applications in the Add Or Remove Programs control panel. Users can then select the application to install. Applications that are distributed through .zap files cannot be assigned to either computers or users, and they will not install using extension activation.

Using a .zap file has several important limitations compared to using Windows Installer files. First, the installation of the application using the .zap file runs the normal installation program for the application, which means that you cannot customize the installation unless the application provides setup parameters to customize the installation. Further, the installation using .zap files cannot run with elevated permissions during the installation, which means that a user might need to be a local Administrator to install the application. Applications installed using .zap files are also not self-healing. If the application fails because a file has been previously corrupted or deleted, the user might have to run the original installation procedure again manually to reinstall the application. An application that has been installed using a .zap file also cannot be easily upgraded or patched. Because of these drawbacks, this software installation technology has limited usefulness and should be used only when you are installing a simple application that is not likely to be upgraded.

Configuring Software Package Properties

After you create the software package, you can modify the package properties. To access the package properties, right-click the package and select Properties. Figure 12-2 shows the Deployment tab. Table 12-1 describes the options available on this Properties sheet.

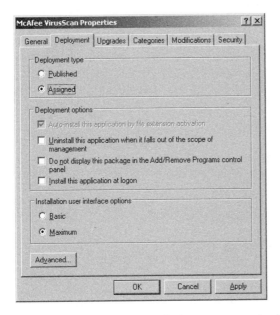

Figure 12-2. *Modifying the deployment properties for a software package.*

Table 12-1. Deployment Options for a Software Package

Setting	Explanation
Deployment Type	Use this option to specify how the application will be advertised to clients.
Auto-Install This Application By File Extension Activation	Use this option to enable or disable the option to install software when the user opens a file of a selected extension. This option is not available if you assign an application.
Uninstall This Application When It Falls Out Of The Scope Of Management	Use this option to control what occurs when the Group Policy no longer applies to the user or computer. For example, if the Group Policy is linked to user accounts in an OU, choosing this option means that the application will be uninstalled if the user account is moved out of the OU.

(continued)

Table 12-1. *(continued)*

Setting	Explanation
Do Not Display This Package In The Add/Remove Programs Control Panel	Use this option to control whether the application will be displayed in the Add Or Remove Programs control panel.
Install This Application At Logon	Use this option to completely install an application when the user logs on rather than wait for the user to initiate the installation. This option is not available when the application is published.
Installation User Interface Options	Use this option to control what is displayed for the user when the software is being installed. Selecting Basic means that only error messages and completion messages will be displayed. Selecting Maximum means that all software setup screens will be displayed.
Advanced	Use this option to configure additional settings for the software package. Options include installing 32-bit applications on 64-bit operating systems, installing the application even if it uses a different language than the destination operating system, and including Component Object Model (COM) components with the package so that the client can install the components from Active Directory. Figure 12-3 shows the interface.

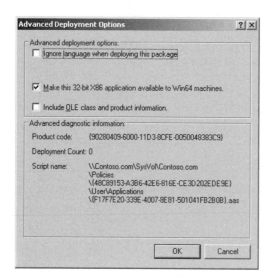

Figure 12-3. *Using the Advanced Deployment Options page to configure group policy software installation.*

Setting the Default Software Installation Properties

When you prepare to install software using group policies, you can configure the default settings for all software packages that are deployed using a specific GPO. You can access this interface by right-clicking the Software Installation container and selecting Properties. Figure 12-4 shows the interface.

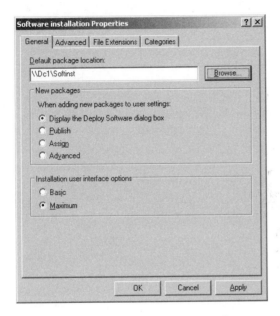

Figure 12-4. *Configuring the default software installation settings.*

You can use this procedure to set the options that will be displayed when you create a new software package in this GPO. You can also set the default location for the software installation files and configure the installation's user-interface (UI) settings.

Installing Customized Software Packages

Sometimes a company might want to customize the installation of a software package even if it comes with a native Windows Installer package. For example, you might need to create a custom installation of your word processing application to include custom dictionaries or templates. Or you might need to customize the installation of Microsoft Office to install only Microsoft Word and Microsoft Excel on every desktop while deploying the full Office suite to only selected users. If you work for an international company, you might need to deploy the same application in multiple languages.

You can customize the installation of a software package by creating a transform (.mst) file. The transform file contains instructions, in addition to the .msi file, that customize the installation. The easiest way to create a .mst file is if the software manufacturer has provided a tool to do so. For example, Microsoft includes a Custom Installation Wizard with the *Microsoft Office 2000 Resource Kit* and the *Microsoft Office XP Resource Kit*. When you start this Wizard, you have to select a .msi file, a name, and a location for the .mst file. Then the Wizard presents all the options for customizing the default installation of the software. You can customize almost every aspect of the installation, including removing previous versions of Office, customizing which components will be installed, and deciding where those components will be installed. You can migrate user settings if the installation is an upgrade of existing software, or you can custom-configure personal settings and security settings. You can add additional files to the installation (such as custom templates), add or remove registry keys, add or remove shortcuts to Office applications, and configure e-mail client settings.

After creating the transform file, you must create a new software package to deploy the custom installation. When you create the new software package, select the Advanced option when choosing the deployment method so that you can add the transform file before the package is completed. From the software package's Properties sheet, select the Modifications tab and then add the transform files. Figure 12-5 shows the Modifications tab.

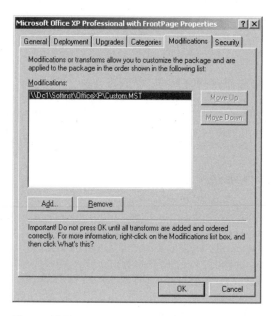

Figure 12-5. *Adding transform files to a software package.*

When you apply the transform file to the software package, all clients within the scope of the GPO that install the application will install the customized version. You can include more than one transform file with the software package. If you do, the transform files are applied starting from the top of the list, which means that transform files that are applied later in the installation process might overwrite earlier modifications.

Updating an Existing Software Package

Another very useful feature that is available when you use group policies to install software is the option to update existing software packages. There are basically two ways to update existing software packages: patching or installing a service pack on an existing application, and upgrading an application to a new version. If you are running Microsoft Office 2000, installing Service Release 1 for Office 2000 is an example of the first type of update, but installing Office XP is an example of the second type of update.

The two different methods for updating software require different procedures. If you are applying patches or a service pack to an existing application, you must first obtain a .msi file or a patch (.msp) file for the updated application. (Ideally, this file will come from the software manufacturer, but you can also create your own.) Copy the new .msi file and the other new software installation files into the same folder as the original .msi file, overwriting any duplicate files. Then redeploy the application. To do so, right-click the software package in the Group Policy Object Editor, select All Tasks, and then select Redeploy Application. The software package will be redeployed to all users and computers under that group policy.

If you are upgrading an existing application to a new version of the software, you will take a different approach. In this case, you must create a new software package to deploy the application. Then you can access the software package properties for the new application and select the Upgrades tab. Using the settings on this tab, you can create a link between the new software distribution package and an existing package. When you click Add from the Upgrades tab, you can choose which software package will be upgraded by this package. You can also configure whether the old application must first be uninstalled before the new application is installed. Figure 12-6 shows an example of upgrading Office 2000.

When you create the upgrade link, the Upgrades tab shows the new information. Figure 12-7 shows the interface. You can also use the Upgrades tab to make this a required upgrade. If you choose to make it a required upgrade, all software distributed by the previous GPO will be upgraded the next time the computer reboots or the user logs on. If you do not make it a required upgrade, the user can choose when to install the new application, either by activating the application from the Start menu or through the Add Or Remove Programs control panel. If you are using the same GPO for the upgrade software package as you used for the initial application, the original software package will show that the new package is upgrading it.

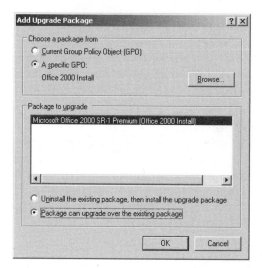

Figure 12-6. *Upgrading an existing software package.*

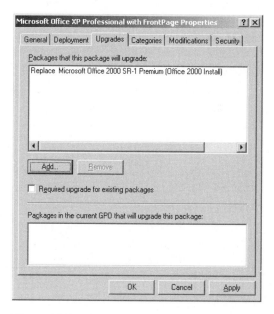

Figure 12-7. *The Upgrades tab on a software package's Properties sheet.*

Planning   The fact that it is so easy to upgrade an application through group policies does not mean that it should be taken lightly. Before deploying the upgrade, you should test the upgrade to ensure that it will not create problems with existing applications. You should also test the upgrade process to make sure that it will work smoothly in your organization. Once you have ensured that the upgrade will work, you still have to manage the deployment. If the application that you are upgrading has been deployed to several thousand users and you decide to make the upgrade a required upgrade, the users might have to wait a long time for the installation to be completed. You must still manage the deployment of the upgrade to minimize the impact on the network bandwidth.

Managing Software Categories

In a large organization, you might deploy dozens of applications using group policies. If you chose to publish most of these applications high in the domain hierarchy where the GPO applies to most users, users will see a long list of available applications when they open the Add Or Remove Programs control panel, which can lead to confusion. One way to minimize this confusion is to use software categories to present the users with a simpler view of the applications that they can install.

When you use software categories, you can present the user with grouped lists of applications. For example, as Figure 12-8 illustrates, you can create a category for each group of business applications. If a user is in the Administration business unit, he or she can select the Administration category and from there choose which application to install.

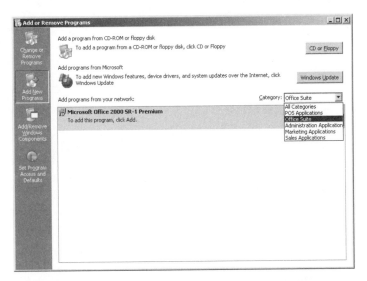

Figure 12-8. *Displaying software categories in Add Or Remove Programs.*

Windows Server 2003 Active Directory does not come with any predefined software categories, so you can create any categories you want. To create categories, open any existing GPO, right-click Software Installation under either Computer Configuration or User Configuration, select Properties, and then select the Categories tab. Figure 12-9 shows the interface. Software categories do not apply to individual GPOs but do apply to all GPOs in the domain. After creating the software categories, you can associate each of the software deployment packages with a category.

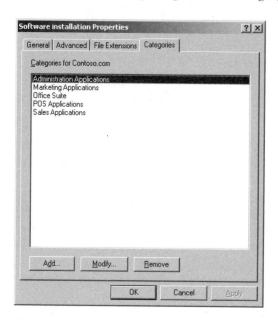

Figure 12-9. *Configuring software categories on a GPO.*

Configuring File Extension Activation

One of the means by which a user can initiate the installation of an application is through file extension activation. In most cases, you will have only one application that is linked to any specific file extension. However, in some cases, you might have more than one. For example, you might be upgrading Word 2000 to Word XP, and for several months you might have both versions of the software available for installation. In this case, you can configure which of the application versions will be installed when a user initiates the install through file extension activation.

To configure this option, in the Group Policy Object Editor, access the Software Installation Properties sheet under Computer Configuration or User Configuration. Select the File Extensions tab. Figure 12-10 shows the interface. The application that is listed first will be installed when the file extension is activated.

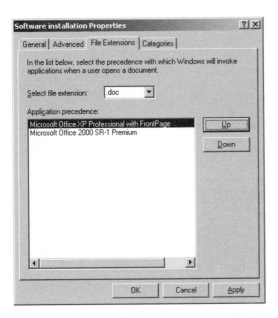

Figure 12-10. *Configuring file extension activation.*

Removing Software Using Group Policies

A group policy can be used to install applications, and it can also be used to remove previously installed applications. There are three options for using a group policy to remove software:

- Removing software as a preliminary step to installing a newer version of the software
- Removing software when the user or computer is moved outside the scope of management
- Removing software when you remove the software package

The first two options have been discussed earlier in the chapter. The last option requires some explanation. When you remove a software package from a GPO, you have a choice of how to manage the software that was installed by the GPO. Right-click the software package in the Software Installation listing, select All Tasks, and then select Remove. Figure 12-11 shows the dialog box that appears when you choose to remove a software installation package. If you choose Immediately Uninstall The Software From Users And Computers, the software will be uninstalled the next time the computer reboots or the user logs on. If you choose Allow Users To Continue To Use The Software,But Prevent New Installations, the application will not be removed from the workstations but users will no longer be able to install the application using this GPO.

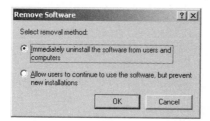

Figure 12-11. *Configuring the removal of software when removing a software package.*

Using Group Policies to Configure Windows Installer

Because most of the applications that you will install using group policies use the Windows Installer technology, you might also need to configure how Windows Installer applications are installed. Windows Server 2003 Active Directory provides several options for configuring how Windows Installer applications will be installed. Most of these settings can be configured by opening a GPO in Group Policy Object Editor and expanding Computer Configuration, then Administrative Templates, then Windows Components, and then Windows Installer. Figure 12-12 shows the interface. A few of the settings can be configured under User Configuration\Administrative Templates\Windows Components\Windows Installer. Table 12-2 explains the options that can be configured in both locations.

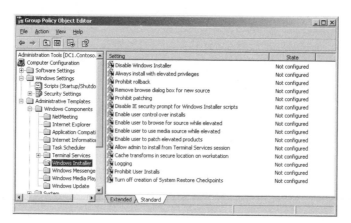

Figure 12-12. *Configuring the Windows Installer settings for computer objects.*

Table 12-2. Group Policy Setting Options for Windows Installer

Setting	Explanation
Disable Windows Installer (Computer Configuration only)	Use this option to enable or disable the installation of software using Windows Installer. If you enable the policy, you can then disable Windows Installer completely, enable Windows Installer for all applications, or disable Windows Installer for those applications that are not distributed through group policies.
Always Install With Elevated Privileges (Computer and User Configuration)	Use this option to allow users to install applications that require access to directories or registry keys that the user would normally not be able to access. Enabling this option means that Windows Installer will use the system permissions to install software.
Prohibit Rollback (Computer and User Configuration)	Use this option to disable the default Windows Installer behavior of creating files that can be used to roll back an incomplete installation.
Remove Browse Dialog Box For New Source (Computer Configuration only)	Use this option to disable the Browse button when the user wants to install a new feature using Windows Installer. Enabling this option disables the Browse button, which means that the user can install features only from administrator-configured sources.
Prohibit Patching (Computer Configuration only)	Use this option to prohibit the user from installing patches to programs using Windows Installer. Enabling this option provides enhanced security because it prevents the user from installing patches that might modify system files.
Disable IE Security Prompt For Windows Installer Scripts (Computer Configuration only)	Use this option to turn off the warning that the client receives when installing software through a browser interface, such as Microsoft Internet Explorer. You might want to use this option if most of your software is distributed through a Web site.
Enable User Control Over Installs (Computer Configuration only)	Use this option to give the user more control over the application installation. If you enable this option, the installation process will stop at each installation screen so that the user can modify the settings.
Enable User To Browse For Source While Elevated (Computer Configuration only)	Use this option to browse for alternate installation sources if the application is being installed with elevated permissions.
Enable User To Use Media Source While Elevated (Computer Configuration only)	Use this option to allow the user to use removable media as the installation source if the application is being installed with elevated permissions.
Enable User To Patch Elevated Products (Computer Configuration only)	Use this option to allow the user to install patches when the installation is running with elevated permissions.

(continued)

Table 12-2. *(continued)*

Setting	Explanation
Allow Admin To Install From Terminal Services Session (Computer Configuration only)	Use this option to allow Terminal Services administrators to install and configure software using a Terminal Services session.
Cache Transforms In Secure Location On Workstation (Computer Configuration only)	Use this option to cache the transform files used to install a customized application on the local workstation. This transform file is required to repair or repeat the software installation.
Logging (Computer Configuration only)	Use this option to configure Windows Installer to increase the default level of logging for the software installation.
Prohibit User Installs (Computer Configuration only)	Use this option to manage whether the applications assigned to a user will be installed. If you enable this option, you can configure the setting so that only computer-assigned applications will be installed. This setting can be useful if the computer is a kiosk or a shared computer. This option only applies to clients with Windows Installer v2.0 (or later) installed.
Turn Off Creation Of System Restore Checkpoints (Computer Configuration only)	Use this option to modify the default behavior on computers running Windows XP Professional where a System Restore checkpoint is automatically created before any application is installed.
Search Order (User Configuration only)	Use this option to modify the default search order in which Windows Installer searches for installation files. By default, Windows Installer will search the network first, then removable media, and then an Internet URL.
Prevent Removable Media Source For Any Install (User Configuration only)	Use this option to prevent users from using Windows Installer to install any application from removable media.

Planning for Software Distribution Using Group Policies

Using group policies to manage software can greatly decrease the amount of effort required to distribute and maintain software on client computers. However, taking advantage of this tool can be complicated, especially in a large company with many different software configurations for user desktops. Deploying group policies to manage software most effectively requires careful planning. This section outlines some of the things you should consider when doing this planning.

One of the factors that you must consider when deploying applications is whether to advertise the application to users or computers. In general, if most computers are shared computers, and every user requires a particular software package, you should assign the policy to computers. By assigning the policy to computers, the software is completely installed on the workstation the next time the workstation reboots and the software becomes available to all users. Assigning the software package to computers can also provide more options for managing network bandwidth. By using this option, you can configure a group policy during the day and then ask users (or use a remote tool) to reboot the workstations after regular working hours.

If only a few users require a software package, it is usually more efficient to assign or publish the application to user accounts. In some cases, a software package must be distributed to users in multiple OUs. The best way to distribute the software in such cases is to assign a group policy high in the Active Directory hierarchy and then filter the application of the GPO by security groups.

Another important decision to make when planning for software distribution is how many GPOs to use. At one extreme, you could use one GPO to distribute all software for a particular container, which will improve the client logon performance but could result in large and complicated GPO configurations. At the other extreme, you might choose to use many GPOs, with each GPO distributing a single application. In this case, the client logon performance might be affected because the computer has to read many GPOs. Companies use a variety of approaches to deal with this problem. One fairly standard approach is to create one GPO to install a standard set of applications that everyone needs and that is rarely modified. Additional GPOs are created for applications that are frequently updated (such as antivirus software) and for applications that are used by small groups of users.

You might also need to plan for software distribution across slow network links. Many companies have remote offices or remote users who connect to Active Directory using slow network connections. By default, the software distribution component of group policies is not applied when the client connects across a network connection that is less than 500 Kbps (kilobits per second). If the workstations on your network normally connect on a local area network (LAN) and only occasionally connect across a slow network connection, this default is probably acceptable. However, if you have network clients that almost always connect to the network across a slow network connection, you will need to prepare for these clients through some additional configuration.

One option is to leave the default software distribution as is but force a complete installation of the software when the user does connect to the LAN. You can use this option if the clients occasionally do connect to your LAN. If you have clients that never connect to the LAN, you might need to use means outside of Active Directory to distribute software. For example, you might choose to distribute software using removable media or through a secure Web site if the clients have a fast Internet connection and normally connect to Active Directory through a slow virtual private network (VPN) connection.

Most large companies have some form of automated process for building workstations. Companies can use disk cloning technology or Remote Installation Services (RIS) to rapidly build a standard desktop for a user. You can use this technology in combination with group policies to greatly optimize the distribution of software. For example, if you are using a disk cloning tool to build client workstations, you can build the client computer and then use a Group Policy to install a standard set of applications on the workstation. When this image is deployed to workstations, these applications can be managed using group policies. If you use RIS to install client machines, you can include the managed application in the RIS image for each department.

Perhaps the most important step in preparing to use a group policy to deploy software is to thoroughly test every software distribution before you deploy it. Most companies that use a group policy to distribute software maintain a distribution test lab that contains workstations that are representative of the workstations in the production environment. You can easily create a test OU in Active Directory and move these computer accounts and some test user accounts into this OU. Then use this test environment to test every software distribution.

Software Update Services—An Alternative for Updating Computers

One of the critical tasks for a network administrator is maintaining the operating system patch level for all computers on the network. Because of the effort involved, some companies do not update desktop computers at all or apply only the most critical updates. These companies usually update all the servers but rely on the Internet firewall and antivirus software to protect the workstations. Some companies have taken another approach and configure all their client computers to use the Windows Update site to download patches. These companies might even allow the business users to manage patches on their own. Choosing this option can lead to an administrative nightmare because of the inconsistent application of patches.

Using group policies can make the management of patches easier, but it does not solve the problem. Microsoft provides .msi files only for significant updates such as service packs, so it is a great deal of work to manage the patches. In response to this demand, Microsoft has provided the Software Update Service (SUS) as an alternative means to deploy updates to workstations.

SUS consists of a server component and a client component. To enable SUS, you must install the server component on a computer running Windows 2000 or Windows Server 2003. Then configure the service on the server to download all critical updates from the Windows Update site. This download can be automated or manual. Once the updates are downloaded and tested, you can configure the service to distribute the updates to all clients. The SUS client can be installed on computers running Windows 2000 Professional and Server (with Service Pack 2 or later), Windows XP Professional, or Windows

Server 2003. Windows 2000 Service Pack 3 and Windows XP Professional Service Pack 1 include the SUS client component. The client computer uses the SUS client component to connect to a SUS server to download and install patches.

The SUS service can be managed using group policies. In the Group Policy Object Editor, using the settings under Computer Configuration, select Administrative Templates, select Windows Components, and then select Windows Update to configure how automatic updates will be managed on the workstation. Figure 12-13 shows the options. You can also use group policies to specify which SUS server the workstations will connect to.

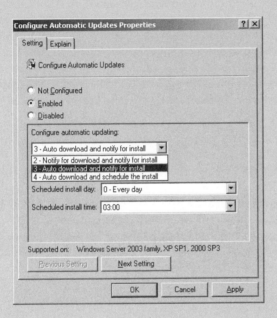

Figure 12-13. *Configuring the client component for automatic updates.*

For more details on using SUS and its integration with group policies, download the SUS white paper from the Microsoft Web site at *http://www.microsoft.com/windows2000 /windowsupdate/sus/susoverview.asp.*

Limitations to Using Group Policies to Manage Software

Although group policies provide powerful tools for managing software on client computers, there are still some limitations with the technology. These limitations are particularly apparent when comparing group policies to software management tools such as Microsoft Systems Management Server (SMS) or Intel LANDesk.

One of the most important limitations for many companies is that group policies can be used only to distribute software to Windows 2000 or Windows XP Professional client computers. Although this limitation is becoming less significant as more companies move to these latest operating systems, many large corporations still have Windows NT Workstation, Windows 95, or Windows 98 clients. If companies with these client computers want to use group policies to distribute software to newer clients, they must still maintain an alternative method for older clients.

A more significant limitation for companies that have the required clients is the lack of flexibility in group policies for scheduling a software installation. Applications are not advertised to the workstation until the user logs on again or until the computer reboots. The full-featured software distribution tools such as SMS provide other options. For example, you can configure SMS or LANDesk to start up a computer during the night using wake-on-LAN technology, install the software, and shut the computer down again. Or the software distribution can be scheduled at any time during the day and the user does not need to log off or necessarily even be aware that the software distribution is occurring.

Another limitation with using a group policy to distribute software is that it does not support the network's multicasting capabilities. Most network traffic is unicast traffic, that is, traffic that flows between two specific computers. With multicasting, a server can send out one stream of network traffic and multiple client computers can receive the same data. Because each software distribution is initiated by a client action, software distribution using a group policy cannot use multicasting. Using multicasting can save a great deal of bandwidth. For example, if you have several thousand clients in your company and you must distribute an urgent antivirus update, you will use up all the bandwidth on even the fastest network if you use a unicast solution. With multicasting, the software package is sent out only once and all the clients on the network will receive the update.

Yet another limitation with using group policies to distribute software is the lack of reporting features. Active Directory does not have any way to determine whether a piece of software was successfully installed on a workstation, and it has no way of reporting the success or failure of the installation.

Using a group policy to distribute software also has a limitation in that it cannot discriminate which clients should receive a software package other than through the assignment of the GPO at the container level or through filtering based on groups. More full-featured software distribution tools such as SMS and LANDesk create an inventory of all client computers. This inventory includes computer attributes such as hard disk space, CPUs, and RAM, as well as software installed on the computers. You can then use this inventory to discriminate which client computers will get a specific software package. For example, you might choose to install the latest version of Office only on the workstations that have adequate hard disk space and RAM.

Another important software distribution issue for some companies is dealing with disconnected clients. Some companies have large numbers of client computers that connect to the corporate network only occasionally and then only through a dial-up or VPN connection. A full-featured software distribution tool can deal with these clients in a number of ways. One option is to provide a Web site that can be used to install the software and manage the software after installation. Another option is to provide very intelligent management of the software distribution when the client is connected. For example, you can distribute software to all dial-up clients but strictly limit the amount of bandwidth the software distribution process can use. The software distribution process can also detect when the network connection is broken and restart the software distribution at the point where the connection was broken the next time the user connects to the network.

As can be seen from this list of limitations, using group policies to manage software does not provide all the functionality that you might want in a software distribution tool. However, for a small- to medium-sized company that is running Windows 2000 or Windows XP Professional on most desktops, group policies can solve many software distribution issues. For many companies, the price of using group policies is certainly right—especially when compared to the fairly expensive client licensing costs of using one of the other tools.

Summary

Group policies in Windows Server 2003 Active Directory provide powerful tools for deploying and managing software on workstations. Using group policies and Windows Installer technology, you can deploy software to workstations and then manage that software throughout the software life cycle. This chapter provided details on how to use group policies to deploy and manage software.

Chapter 13
Using Group Policies to Manage Computers

Chapter 12, "Using Group Policies to Manage Software," described one of the ways you can use group policies in Microsoft Windows Server 2003 Active Directory directory service to manage your network—using group policies to manage the software that gets installed on the workstations on your network. Using a centralized tool to manage client software provides a significant benefit for an organization. However, there are also many other concerns around managing client computers, including securing desktop computers, managing user profiles and data, and locking down user desktops to reduce the number of changes the users can make to their computers. This chapter explains how you can also use group policies to manage just about every other component of the client computer desktops.

In large organizations, managing client computers is one of the biggest tasks in administering the network. Just installing and deploying the computers is a major effort, but often managing the workstations after the deployment is a much greater task. Most large companies have an entire service desk dedicated to solving problems that users have with their computers. Often, this service desk is supported by a workstation support team that can visit client computers if the problem cannot be solved over the telephone.

Often, the service desk calls are needed because the user has done something that causes a problem. The user might have modified some system setting and now cannot connect to the network. Other calls are related to workstation configurations that were not correct when the workstation or applications were installed, and the settings might need to be modified after installation. Group policies can be used to reduce these service desk calls by allowing you to centrally manage the computers in your company. You can use group policies to prevent users from making changes to their workstations that will interfere with the correct functioning of the workstation. You can also use group policies to centrally configure many of the settings on the workstations in your company.

Real World **Individual Preferences vs. Centralized Control of Computer Desktops**

In most cases, managing user desktops requires a critical balance between strict centralized control of computers while dealing with users who want complete control of their own desktop. If you were to implement all the management options discussed in this chapter, you could lock down user desktops very tightly and ensure that users do not make any unauthorized changes that might create problems. Many administrators think that providing users with any ability to modify settings only means that they will configure things incorrectly, leading to more work for the administrators. Many users, on the other hand, see any attempt to control their desktops as an invasion of their space. From the user's point of view, the workstation is part of one's individual work environment, and any attempt to manage that work environment is strongly resisted.

Deciding the right balance between centralized desktop control and end-user control is different for all companies. Some companies already have a history of using system policies in Microsoft Windows NT 4 or group policies in Microsoft Windows 2000 Active Directory, where the end users are already accustomed to some level of desktop lockdown. In these companies, you might be able to implement new restrictions without too much concern. However, many companies have not implemented any restrictions. In these companies, the first attempt at implementing restrictions might be met with a great deal of resistance.

For most companies, the best approach to implementing desktop control is to start slowly and create a positive first impression. Creating a positive first impression usually means that you use group policies to resolve issues that are irritating to end users. If you can show the end users that desktop management will actually make their jobs easier, they are much more likely to accept additional management. On the other hand, if you try to implement desktop control and the first attempt results in hundreds of service desk calls, you will lose all support for implementing any desktop management. Another important ingredient to a successful implementation of group policies is support from management. In most companies, management will support any effort that will decrease the cost of managing workstations. If you can show that decreased cost is the end result of implementing desktop management, you are almost certain to have management support in dealing with the complaints from those end users who don't want you managing their desktops.

Desktop Management Using Group Policies

Windows Server 2003 Active Directory provides many group policy options that can be used to configure computers. In some cases, the settings are located in more than one location in the Group Policy structure. So, before going into the detailed descriptions of some of the settings, this section provides an overview of the settings that are available. Figure 13-1 shows an expanded view of the desktop management options within a single Group Policy Object (GPO). Table 13-1 briefly explains the top-level containers.

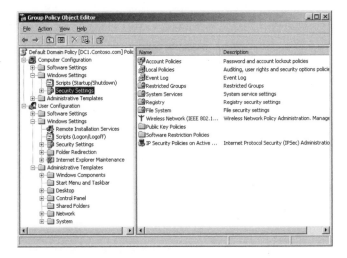

Figure 13-1. *The top-level containers under Default Domain Policy.*

Table 13-1.   Top-Level Containers in Default Domain Policy

Top-level container	Child containers	Contents
Computer Configuration and User Configuration	Software Settings	Contains the settings for the software packages used for software distribution.
Computer Configuration and User Configuration	Windows Settings\Scripts	Contains the startup and shutdown scripts for computers and the logon and logoff scripts for users.
Computer Configuration and User Configuration	Windows Settings \Security Settings	Contains the settings used to configure computer security. Some settings are specific to the domain level, and some can be set at the container level. Most security settings are configured under Computer Configuration.
User Configuration	Windows Settings \Folder Redirection	Contains settings that redirect user folders, such as the My Documents folder, to a network share.
User Configuration	Windows Settings\Remote Installation Services	Contains a single configuration option for Remote Installation Services (RIS).
User Configuration	Windows Settings\Internet Explorer Maintenance	Contains settings for managing the Microsoft Internet Explorer configuration on user desktops.
Computer Configuration and User Configuration	Administrative Templates	Contains a large number of configuration settings that can be used to configure the computer registry.

The rest of this chapter provides details on many of these high-level containers.

Managing User Data and Profile Settings

One of the challenges facing a network administrator is managing user data and user profiles. The data that users work with is often business-critical, so it must be properly secured and managed. In most cases, the data should be centrally stored and regularly backed up. Companies have many ways of dealing with this data. In most cases, the data is stored on a network share and all users are required to store all company data on that share. However, many users also store some data on their desktop computers, especially those who use portable computers, who might need the data when they are not connected to the network.

Another aspect of managing desktop computers is the management of user profiles, which is often of more concern to the end users than it is to the administrators. Some users spend a considerable amount of time configuring their applications and desktop to suit their own preferences. For these users, this desktop configuration is important and they want that desktop to appear regardless of which computer they log on to.

Before Active Directory was available, the primary means for managing user data and settings was the implementation of user profiles. Some companies have implemented roaming user profiles, in which the user profile is stored on a network share where it is accessible by the user from any workstation in the organization. Some companies impose restrictions on their user profiles by implementing mandatory profiles. With mandatory profiles, an administrator can create a standard profile for a user or a group of users, and then configure the profile so that users cannot change it.

Roaming and mandatory user profiles can be implemented using Active Directory, and some of the settings for controlling roaming and mandatory user profiles can be configured through group policies. In addition to user profiles, however, Active Directory also provides folder redirection to manage user data and settings. In fact, folder redirection provides some significant benefits for user profiles.

Managing User Profiles

A user profile contains all the configuration information for the user's desktop. This information includes the contents of the HKEY_CURRENT_USER subtree in the registry (stored as the Ntuser.dat file), which includes application and desktop configuration settings. Also, the profile contains folders such as My Documents, Start Menu, Desktop, and Application Data. Figure 13-2 shows the contents of a user profile on a server running Windows Server 2003.

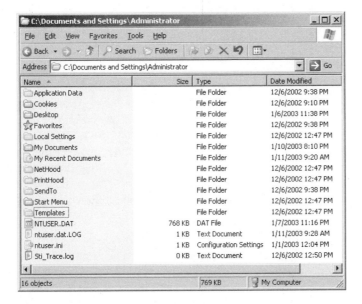

Figure 13-2. *The user profile contains all user desktop settings and folders for user data.*

By default, a user profile is created on each computer the first time that a user logs on to the computer. The initial profile is based on the default user profile, which is stored under the %systemdrive%\Documents And Settings folder. When the user logs off, the user's profile, including any changes the user has made to the default profile, is saved in a folder with the same name as the user's logon name in the Documents And Settings folder. When the user logs on again to the same computer, the user's profile is retrieved to present the user with the same desktop that the user had when he or she logged off.

Some companies have implemented roaming user profiles. Roaming user profiles are stored on a network share so that the profile is available to the user as he or she moves between computers. When a user who is configured for a roaming user profile logs on to a computer for the first time, the roaming profile is downloaded from the network share and applied to the computer. When the user logs off, the changes made to the user profile are copied back to the network share. A copy of the profile is also cached on the local workstation. If a user has logged on to a workstation before, the timestamp for the profile on the local workstation is compared to the timestamp for the profile stored on the network share. With Windows 2000 and Windows XP Professional, the timestamp on individual files is used to determine which files in the profile are newer. If the profile on the server is newer than the local profile, the entire profile is copied from the server to the local workstation. You can enable a roaming user profile by configuring the profile path on the Profile tab on the user's account Properties sheet in the Active Directory Users And Computers administrative tool.

Some companies have also implemented mandatory profiles. In most cases, mandatory profiles are used in combination with roaming profiles to create a standard desktop configuration for a group of users. For example, you might have a group of users who all perform the same functions and require a very limited desktop configuration. If you are a member of the Account Operators group, the Domain Admins group, or the Enterprise Admins group, you can create one standard desktop for this group of users and use mandatory profiles to prevent the users from changing the configuration. To enable mandatory profiles, you must first create the desired standard desktop configuration. Then save the entire contents of the user profile to a network share, and rename the Ntuser.dat file to Ntuser.man. Then configure all the required users to this profile as their roaming user profile. When the users log on to the network, they will be presented with the standard profile, and because it is mandatory, they will not be able to save any changes to the profile.

Roaming user profiles are still a useful option on a Windows Server 2003 network. If you have implemented roaming or mandatory user profiles, you can continue to use those profiles. You can even use group policies to manage user profiles. Most of the user profile settings are located in the Computer Configuration\Administrative Templates \System\User Profiles folder. A few additional settings are located in the subfolder of the same name under the User Configuration setting. Table 13-2 explains the configuration options.

Table 13-2. Configuring User Profiles Using the Group Policy Object Editor

Configuration option	Explanation
Do Not Check For User Ownership Of Roaming Profile Folders	Use this option to configure what to do if a roaming user profile folder already exists and the workstations have been upgraded to Microsoft Windows 2000 Service Pack 4 or Microsoft Windows XP Professional Service Pack 1. These recent service packs increase the default security on the user profiles. Enabling this option means that the earlier security is maintained.
Delete Cached Copies Of Roaming Profiles	Enable this option to delete the locally cached copy of the roaming user profile when the user logs off. Do not enable this option if you are using the slow link detection feature of Windows 2000 or Windows XP Professional because that feature requires a locally cached copy of the user profile.
Do Not Detect Slow Network Connections	Enable this option to prevent the computer from using slow link detection to configure how to manage roaming user profiles. If you enable this option, roaming user profiles will always be downloaded, regardless of network speed.
Slow Network Connection Timeout For User Profiles	Enable this option to define a slow network connection. If you enable this option, the default definition of a slow network connection is less than 500 Kbps, or—for non-IP computers—if the server takes more than 120 milliseconds to respond.

Configuration option	Explanation
Wait For Remote User Profile	Enable this option to always load the roaming user profile from the server. If you enable this option, the workstation will load the user profile even if a slow network connection is detected.
Prompt User When Slow Link Is Detected	Enable this option to provide the user with a prompt indicating that a slow network connection has been detected and providing the user with a choice about whether to load the local profile or the server profile. If you do not enable this option, the local profile is loaded without advising the user.
Timeout For Dialog Boxes	Use this option to configure how long the system will wait after prompting the user that a slow network connection has been detected. If the timeout is allowed to expire, the dialog box's default value or action is applied.
Log Users Off When Roaming Profile Fails	Enable this option to prevent users from logging on if the roaming user profile is not available. If you do not enable this option, the locally cached profile is loaded, if available. (Otherwise, the local default user profile is loaded.)
Maximum Retries To Unload And Update User Profile	Use this setting to configure how many times the system tries to update the Ntuser.dat file when the user logs off and the update fails. By default, the system will try to update the file once per second for 60 seconds.
Add The Administrators Security Group To Roaming User Profiles	Use this option to configure administrative access to user profiles. By default, with Windows 2000 and Windows XP Professional, the user account is given full control of the profile and the administrators are given no access.
Prevent Roaming Profile Changes From Propagating To The Server	Use this option to configure what happens when the user logs off the computer. If this option is enabled, the roaming profile on the server is not updated when the user logs off.
Only Allow Local User Profiles	Enable this option to configure whether roaming user profiles are copied from the server. If you enable this option, the roaming user profile will not be applied.
Connect Home Directory To Root Of The Share (under User Configuration)	Enable this option to configure the home drive mapping as it was configured in Windows NT. If you enable this option, the home drive for all users will be the network share where the user home folders are located. If you disable this option (the default), the home drives are mapped to the user-specific folder rather than to the higher-level share.
Limit Profile Size (under User Configuration)	Use this option to limit how large a user's roaming profile can be. You can also use this option to configure how the user will be prompted if his or her profile space is exceeded.
Exclude Directories In Roaming Profile (under User Configuration)	Use this option to prevent specified user directories from being included in the roaming user profile.

As you can see from Table 13-2, Windows Server 2003 Active Directory provides some powerful options for managing roaming user profiles. You can use these options to design very specific configurations for the users in your company. For example, for most of the people in your company who log on to the domain across a fast network connection, you might want to modify some roaming user profile settings, such as limiting the profile size but accepting all other defaults. For users who require special desktop configurations, you might require some of the other settings, such as not loading the roaming user profile or always loading the profile. For users who log on to the network across a slow network connection, you might need to configure the slow network connection parameters. By creating an organizational unit (OU) structure that matches the user profile requirements, you can implement very specific roaming user profile configurations.

Roaming user profiles can be very useful in companies where users do not use the same computer all the time. With the roaming profile enabled, the user's work environment is the same regardless of where the user logs on. However, roaming user profiles also have some limitations. In most cases, the biggest problem is that the user profile can become very large. For example, the user might store most of his or her documents in the My Documents folder. The user might also store large files on the desktop. Often, temporary Internet files can grow to be many megabytes in size. All of these files are stored in the user profile. The problem with roaming profiles when the profile is large is that the entire profile must be copied to the local workstation whenever the user logs on and the computer detects that the profile on the server is newer than the profile on the local workstation. If the user makes changes to any of the profile data, when the user logs off, the profile must be copied back to the server. This process can create a significant amount of network traffic.

Folder Redirection

Windows Server 2003 Active Directory provides folder redirection as a way to get some of the benefits of using roaming profiles while minimizing network bandwidth concerns. When you enable folder redirection, folders that are normally part of the local user profile are moved from the local profile and stored on a network share. For example, one of the most common folders that is configured for folder redirection is the My Documents folder. In many companies, this is a logical folder to redirect because it is the default location where users save files. When you configure this folder with folder redirection, you store the My Documents folder on a network share where it can be centrally backed up. At the same time, the end-user environment is maintained. This folder redirection is almost completely transparent to the end-user—the only way you can tell that the folder has been redirected is by looking at the properties of the My Documents folder.

Another reason to use folder redirection is that you can use this option to deploy a standard desktop environment rather than use mandatory user profiles. For example, you can redirect folders such as the Start Menu and Desktop folders to a network share. Then you can configure a group of users to all use the same folder. By giving all the users Read permissions to these folders but not Write permissions, you can configure a standard desktop for a group of users.

You can redirect four different folders in Windows Server 2003 Active Directory: the Application Data, Desktop, My Documents, and Start Menu folders. Folder redirection is configured in the Group Policy Object Editor by selecting User Configuration, then Windows Settings, and then Folder Redirection. Each of the four folders that can be redirected is listed so that you can configure each folder separately.

To configure the My Documents folder for redirection, locate the My Documents object in the Folder Redirection folder, right-click it, and then select Properties. The first tab of the object's Properties sheet is the Target tab, which is illustrated in Figure 13-3.

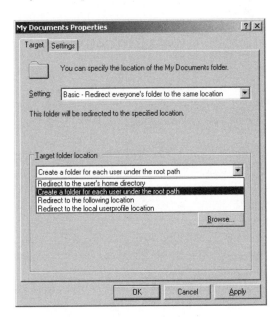

Figure 13-3. *Configuring the target folder location for folder redirection.*

You have three configuration options on this tab. By default, the Setting option is set to Not Configured, which means that the folder is not redirected to a network share. You have two other options for this setting:

- **Basic - Redirect Everyone's Folder To The Same Location** This setting is used if you want to create one location where all folders will be redirected. For example, you might want the folders for all users affected by this policy to be located on a *servername**sharename* network share.

- **Advanced - Specify Locations For Various User Groups** This setting is used to configure alternate locations for the redirected folder depending on which Active Directory group the user belongs to. If you choose this option, you can assign an alternate target folder location for each group.

Tip You cannot use the Advanced option to assign alternate locations for individual user accounts. Also, remember that this group policy applies only to user accounts that are in the container in which you are configuring the group policy. If you configure the Advanced option to redirect folders for a group to a specific location, the setting will be applied only to those user accounts in the group who are located in the container. If the group contains users from other containers, the folder redirection is not applied to those users.

Once you have chosen the setting for redirecting folders, you can then configure the target folder location. Again, you have several options for where you can store the folder:

- **Redirect To The User's Home Directory** This setting is used to redirect the My Documents folder to the user's home directory as specified on the user account properties. Use this option only if you have already created the home directory. If the home directory has not been created, configuring this option will not create the home directory. This option is only available for the My Documents folder.

- **Create a Folder For Each User Under The Root Path** This setting is used to specify a root path where the folders will be stored. When you choose this option, a folder will be created under the root path for each user. The folder name is based on the %username% logon variable.

- **Redirect To The Following Location** This setting is used to specify a root path and folder location for each user. You can use a Universal Naming Convention (UNC) path or a local drive location. You can use the %username% variable to create individual folders. This option can also be used to redirect several users to the same folder. For example, if you wanted to configure a standard Start Menu for a group of users, you would point them all to the same file.

- **Redirect To The Local Userprofile Location** This setting is the default configuration if no policies are enabled. If you set this option, the folders are not redirected to a network share.

In addition to configuring the target location for the redirected folders, you can also configure other settings for the redirected folders. To do so, click the Settings tab on the object's Properties sheet. Figure 13-4 shows the interface.

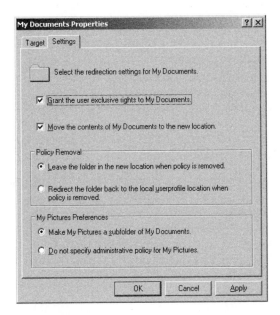

Figure 13-4. *Configuring folder redirection settings.*

The Settings tab provides several configuration options:

- **Grant The User Exclusive Rights To *foldername*** This setting grants the user and the system account full permission to the folder. Administrator accounts will not have any access. If you clear the check box, the folder permissions will be configured based on the inherited permissions.

- **Move The Contents Of *foldername* To The New Location** This setting moves the current contents of the redirected folder to the target location. If you do not select this option, the current folder contents will not be copied to the target location.

- **Policy Removal** This setting is used to define what should happen if the policy is removed. If you accept the Leave The Folder In The New Location When Policy Is Removed default setting, the redirected folder contents will not be moved to the local user profile if the policy is removed. Choosing the Redirect The Folder Back To The Local Userprofile Location When Policy Is Removed option will move the folder contents when the policy is removed.

- **My Pictures Preferences** This setting is used to configure whether the My Pictures folder is included in the My Documents folder redirection.

When you use folder redirection to redirect the My Documents folder, the folder contents are not copied back and forth from the server as they are with roaming user profiles. The folder contents are located on the server, just like any other data on a network share. Therefore, the only time any part of the contents of the folder cross the network is when a user opens a file in the folder. The same is true for the Desktop folder. If a large file is stored on the desktop, the file is stored on the network share and copied to the client computer only when the user opens the file. The fact that the data crosses the network only on demand can significantly improve logon performance, particularly if you have a large number of users all downloading their roaming user profiles at the same time.

One of the advantages of user profiles for storing folders such as My Documents, rather than using folder redirection, is that after the initial logon on a workstation, a copy of the user profile is always stored locally, which means that if the profile server is not available or if the workstation is disconnected from the network, the profile, complete with the My Documents folder, is still accessible on the workstation. When the workstation is reconnected to the network, the changes made to the user profile are copied to the server.

You can achieve the same functionality with folder redirection by combining folder redirection with offline files. Offline files are available on Windows 2000 or later workstations and can be used to maintain a synchronized copy of a shared folder between a local workstation and a network share. By default, the redirected folders are configured for offline use with Windows XP Professional clients. If you have Windows 2000 clients, you can right-click the My Documents folder on the desktop and select Make Available Offline. Enabling offline files means that the redirected folder will be copied to the client, making the folder available even if the network location where the folder has been redirected is not available.

Configuring Security Settings with Group Policies

One of the critical components to managing user desktops is configuring security on those desktops. Maintaining a consistent security configuration across thousands of desktops is almost impossible without some type of central management. Group policies can be used to provide that central management. Some of the security settings configured with group policies can be implemented only at the domain level. Other settings can be configured at any container level.

Configuring Domain-Level Security Policies

The Account Policies located in the Computer Configuration\Windows Settings\Security Settings container are security settings that can be configured only at the domain level. The Account Policies, as shown in Figure 13-5, include three groups of policies: Password Policy, Account Lockout Policy, and Kerberos Policy. These policies, with the exception of the Kerberos policies, apply to all users in the domain, regardless of what type of workstation the users are logging on from. Kerberos policies are applied only to those computers in the domain that are running Windows 2000, Windows XP Professional, or Windows Server 2003.

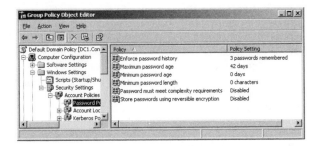

Figure 13-5. *Viewing the domain-level security policies.*

Password Policy

The Password Policy configuration options contain settings for password history, length, and complexity. Table 13-3 describes each setting.

Table 13-3.   Password Policies

Configuration setting	Description	Default
Enforce Password History	Defines the number of new passwords that have to be unique before a user can reuse an old password. Possible values: *0* to *24*	*24* passwords remembered for domain controllers and domain-member computers; *0* for stand-alone servers.
Maximum Password Age	Defines the number of days that a password can be used before the user is required to change it. To configure passwords to never expire, set the number of days to *0*. Possible values: *0* to *999*	*42* days.
Minimum Password Age	Defines the number of days that a password *must* be used before a user is allowed to change it. To allow immediate changes, set to *0*. Possible values: *0* to *998*	*1* day for domain controllers and domain-member computers; *0* for stand-alone servers.

(continued)

Table 13-3. *(continued)*

Configuration setting	Description	Default
Minimum Password Length	Defines the least number of characters required in a password. If no password is required, set the value to *0*. Possible values: *0* to *14*	7 characters for domain controllers and domain-member computers; *0* for stand-alone servers.
Passwords Must Meet Complexity Requirements	Increases password complexity by enforcing that passwords do not contain any part of the user's account name, are at least 6 characters in length, contain characters from three of the four following categories: English uppercase letters, English lowercase letters, Base-10 digits, special characters (such as !, $, #).	Enabled for domain controllers and domain-member computers; Disabled for stand-alone servers.
Store Password Using Reversible Encryption	Using this setting is the same as storing passwords in clear text. This policy provides support for applications that require access to the passwords for authentication.	Disabled.

Account Lockout Policy

The Account Lockout Policy configuration options contain settings for the password lockout threshold and duration, as well as for password reset. Table 13-4 describes each setting.

Table 13-4. Account Lockout Policies

Configuration setting	Explanation	Default
Account Lockout Duration	Defines the number of minutes that a locked out account remains locked out. After the specified number of minutes, the account will automatically become unlocked. To specify that an administrator must unlock the account, set the value to *0*. Any non-zero value should be equal to, or greater than, the value for Reset Account Lockout Counter After. Possible values: *0* to *99,999*	None. Set to *30* minutes if Account Lockout Threshold is set to *1* or greater.

Configuration setting	Explanation	Default
Account Lockout Threshold	Determines the number of failed logon attempts allowed before a user account will be locked out. A value of *0* means that the account will never be locked out. Possible values: *0* to *999*	*0* invalid logon attempts.
Reset Account Lockout Counter After	Determines the number of minutes that must elapse after a failed logon attempt before the bad logon counter is reset to *0*. Any non-zero value should be equal to, or less than, the value for Account Lockout Duration. Possible values: *1* to *99,999*	None. Set to *30* minutes if Account Lockout Threshold is set to *1* or greater.

Kerberos Policy

The Kerberos Policy configuration options contain settings for the Kerberos Ticket-Granting Ticket (TGT) and session ticket lifetimes and time-stamp settings. Table 13-5 describes each setting.

Table 13-5. Kerberos Policies

Configuration setting	Explanation	Default
Enforce User Logon Restrictions	Requires the Key Distribution Center (KDC) to validate every request for a session ticket against the User Rights policy of the target computer.	Enabled
Maximum Lifetime For Service Ticket	Determines the maximum amount of time, in minutes, that a service ticket is valid to access a resource. Possible values: *10*, up to a value less than or equal to the value (expressed in minutes) of the Maximum Lifetime For User Ticket setting, but not exceeding *99,999*. A value of *0* can be set and will cause the ticket to never expire, the Maximum Lifetime For User Ticket value to be set to *1*, and the Maximum Lifetime For User Ticket Renewal to be set to *23*.	*600* minutes (10 hours)

(continued)

Table 13-5 *(continued)*

Configuration setting	Explanation	Default
Maximum Lifetime For User Ticket	Determines the maximum amount of time, in hours, that a TGT can be used. When this expires, the workstation must obtain a new TGT. Possible values: *0* to *99,999*. A value of *0* indicates that the ticket will not expire and sets Maximum Lifetime For User Ticket Renewal to Not Defined.	*10* hours
Maximum Lifetime For User Ticket Renewal	Determines the amount of time, in days, that a user's TGT can be renewed. During this time period, a TGT can be renewed rather than requiring a new ticket. A value of *0* indicates that ticket renewal is disabled.	7 days
Maximum Tolerance For Computer Clock Synchronization	Determines the amount of time difference, in minutes, that Kerberos will tolerate between the client computer's clock and the time on the server's clock. Note that this setting is reset to the default value each time the computer is restarted.	*5* minutes

Account Polices must be set at the Domain Security Policy level on a domain controller. These settings affect all users and computers in the domain. Although these policies can be configured at the OU level, the policies will not affect anyone logging on to the domain. If you do set the policies for an OU, they will affect only the local security database for the computers in the OU. When these policies are configured at an OU level, they are applied only when users log on locally. When the users log on to the domain, the domain policies always override the local policies.

Configuring Other Security Settings

In addition to the domain-level security policies, group policies provide a large number of other security-related settings. As with Account Policies, many of these settings are configured by selecting Computer Configuration\Windows Settings\Security Settings. Some additional settings are configured by selecting User Configuration\Windows Settings\Security Settings. Figure 13-6 illustrates the options under each of the Security Settings folders. Table 13-6 summarizes the configuration options under each heading.

Figure 13-6. *Additional policies available in Security Settings.*

Using group policies to enforce the security settings for the computers on your network makes it much easier to create and maintain a secure networking environment. It is much easier to configure security using group policies than to deal with each workstation individually. All you have to do is create the central security policies, configure them in a GPO, and link it to an Active Directory container object. The next time the GPO is applied, the security will be configured on all the computers in the container. The use of group policies also makes it easy to continually manage the security settings for your computers. The security settings from the policy are continuously refreshed. Even if a user could modify the security configuration on a workstation, the policy would be reapplied at the next refresh cycle. It is also easy to modify the security settings because you can modify the policy and have the settings applied to all computers affected by the policy.

Table 13-6. Security Settings in Group Policies

Configuration option	Explanation
Local Policies\Audit Policy	Used to configure audit settings. You can set audit policies for options such as account management activities, logon events, policy changes, privilege use, and system events.
Local Policies\User Rights Assignment	Used to configure the rights that users will have on computers affected by this policy. You can set a variety of policies, including configuring who can perform actions such as logging on locally, accessing the computer from the network, backing up files and folders, logging on as a service, and so on.
Local Policies\Security Options	Used to configure security options for computers affected by this policy. You can configure options such as renaming the local Administrator account, managing who can install printers, controlling whether unsigned drivers can be installed, controlling whether a Microsoft .NET Passport can be stored on the workstations, and so on.
Event Log	Used to configure event log settings for all computers affected by the policy. You can configure options such as the maximum size for the event logs, who has permission to view the event logs, and whether to retain all event logs.
Restricted Groups	Used to limit the membership of local groups on computers affected by the policy. This is most commonly used to configure the membership of the local Administrators account on computers running Windows 2000 or later. If you use this option to configure the local group membership, all users or groups that are part of the local group but not on this policy's Members list will be removed the next time the policy is refreshed.
System Services	Used to manage services on computers. You can use this policy to define which services will automatically start on the computers or to disable services.
Registry	Used to configure security on registry keys. You can add any registry key to the policy and then apply specific security to that key.
File System	Used to configure security on files and folders. You can add any files or folders to the policy and then apply access control and auditing for those file system objects.
Wireless Network (IEEE 802.11) Policies	Used to create wireless network policies. The policies can then be used to control the security requirements for computers using wireless network connections.
Public Key Policies (This setting is included in both Computer Configuration and User Configuration. The User Configuration includes only the Enterprise Trust option.)	Used to configure several policies related to digital certificates and certificate management. You can also use these policies to create data recovery agents for recovering files that have been encrypted on local workstations using Encrypting File System (EFS).
IP Security Policies On Active Directory (*domainname*)	Used to configure IP Security (IPSec) policies. You can configure policies that define precisely what type of network traffic must be protected with IPSec, as well as which computers must have the policy enforced.

Note   Software Restriction Policies are also included in the Security Settings for both the User Configuration and the Computer Configuration settings. These policies will be covered in more detail in the next section.

Software Restriction Policies

One special type of security configuration available in Active Directory for Windows Server 2003 that was not available in Windows 2000 Active Directory is Software Restriction Policies. One of the biggest security concerns in recent years has been users running unknown or untrusted software. In many cases, the users are running the potentially unsafe software inadvertently. For example, millions of users have launched viruses or installed Trojan horse applications without any intent to run unsafe software. The software restriction policies are designed to prevent this from happening.

Software restriction policies protect your users from running unsafe software by defining which applications are allowed to run or not allowed to run. When you set up a software restriction policy, you can define a policy that allows all software to run, except for software that you specifically block. Or you can define the software restriction policy to allow no software to run, except for software that you explicitly allow to run. Although the second option is more secure, the effort required to define all the applications that should be allowed to run in a complex enterprise environment might be too high. Most companies will opt for the less secure but more manageable option of allowing all software to run and blocking only selected software. However, if you are deploying a set of workstations in an environment that requires high security, you might want to deploy the more secure option.

When you create a software restriction policy, you can configure five types of rules that specify the applications affected by the policy. The five types of rules are:

- **Hash rules**   A *hash rule* is a cryptographic identifier that uniquely identifies a specific application file regardless of the file name or location. If the Unrestricted object has been selected in the Security Levels folder and you want to restrict a particular application from running, you can create a hash rule using the software restriction policy. When a user tries to run the application, the workstation will check the hash and stop the application from running. If you have configured the software restriction policy to block all applications from running, you can use the hash rule to enable a specific application.

- **Certificate rules**   You can also create *certificate rules* so that the application selection criteria are based on the software publisher certificate. For example, if you have a custom application that you have developed, you can assign a certificate to that application and then configure the software restriction rule to trust the appropriate certificate.

- **Path rules**   You can also create *rules based on the path* where the application executable is located. If you choose a folder, all the applications in the folder are affected by the rule. You can also use environmental variables (such as %systemroot%) to specify paths. You can also use wildcards in the path rule (such as *.vbs).

- **Registry path rules** You can also create *rules based on the registry locations* that the application uses. Almost every application has a default location within the registry where it stores application-specific information that allows you to create a rule that blocks or enables an application based on these registry keys. No registry-specific option appears on the menu for creating registry path rules, but the New Path Rule option also allows you to create this unique set of rules. When you create a new software restriction policy, four default registry path rules are created. These rules configure an unrestricted software policy for applications in the system root folder and the default program files directory.

- **Internet zone rules** The final rule type is based on the *Internet zone from which the software was downloaded*. For example, you might want to configure a rule to allow all applications downloaded from the Trusted Sites zone to run or a rule that prevents all software downloaded from the Restricted Sites zone from running.

If you configure your default software restriction so that all applications should run except for specified applications, these rules define which applications will *not* run. If you have specified the more restrictive rule of disabling all applications, these rules specify which applications are allowed to run.

Software restriction policies can be defined for computers by selecting Computer Configuration\Windows Settings\Security Settings. For users, select User Configuration\Windows Settings\Security Settings. By default, no software restriction policies are installed with Active Directory. To create a policy, right-click the Software Restrictions Policies folder and select New Software Restrictions Policy. When you do, a default policy is created. Figure 13-7 shows the objects that are created.

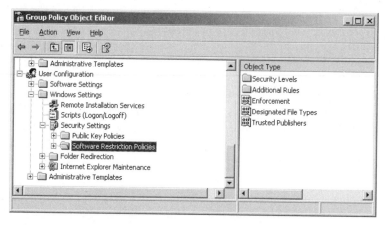

Figure 13-7. *Creating a new software restriction policy.*

The Security Levels folder is used to define the default security level. Inside the folder are two objects, *Disallowed* and *Unrestricted*. If you want to configure the security so that all applications can run except for the specified application, right-click the *Unrestricted* object and click Set As Default. If you want to set the more restrictive setting, right-click Disallowed and set it as the default.

The Additional Rules folder is used to configure the software restrictions rules. To configure a rule, right-click the Additional Rules folder and select the type of rule you want to create. For example, if you want to create a new hash rule, select New Hash Rule. To create the new hash rule, click Browse and locate the file that you want to identify with the hash. When you select the file, the file hash is automatically created. Then you can configure whether this application will be allowed or disallowed. The interface for reconfiguring an existing hash rule is shown in Figure 13-8.

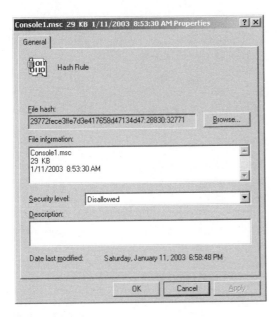

Figure 13-8. *Configuring a hash rule.*

The *Enforcement* object is used to define more specifically which applications are affected. You can configure the rules to apply to all applications or all applications except DLLs. You can also configure that the rules will apply to all users or all users except local administrators.

The *Designated File Types* object defines all the file extensions that are considered executable and therefore managed under this policy. You can add or remove file extensions from the list.

The *Trusted Publishers* object is used to define who can select whether a publisher is trusted or not. You can choose all users, only local administrators, or only enterprise administrators. You can also configure whether the workstation should check to see if an offered certificate has been revoked before running the application.

Security Templates

As shown in the previous sections, there are hundreds of options for configuring security using group policies on a Windows Server 2003 network. At first glance, the options can appear overwhelming; there are so many options that it is hard to know where to even start configuring the security options. Fortunately, Microsoft has provided security templates to make this task a little more manageable.

Security templates are predefined sets of security configurations that you can apply to computers on your network. Rather than having to go through every security setting discussed earlier in this chapter, you can choose a security template that is compatible with what you are trying to accomplish and then apply that template by using group policies. For example, if you are deploying workstations in an environment where you want to set strict security settings, you can choose one of the high-security templates. If you are deploying workstations that need less security, you can choose another template for those workstations. The security templates can also be modified. If you do not find a security template that exactly meets your needs, you can take one of the predefined templates and then modify a few settings.

Almost all the security settings configured by group policies can be configured using a security template. (The only exceptions are the IPSec and public key policies, which cannot be defined with a security template.) You can create your own security template, or use one of the predefined templates. If you modify the template, you can save it so that it will be accessible for other GPOs. When you save a template, it is saved as a text-based .inf file.

Predefined Security Templates

To make the application of security easier, Microsoft has created a variety of predefined security templates. These templates are configured by security categories such as default, secure, and high security. The templates are stored in the %systemroot%\security\templates folder.

When you install Windows Server 2003 or Windows XP Professional on a computer, the Setup Security.inf template is applied to the computer. This template is different for workstations and servers, and it is also different depending on whether your operating system was installed as an upgrade or as a clean installation. You can reapply this security template at any time after the initial installation. For example, if you have modified the security settings on a computer and want to return the computer to the default setting, you can reapply this template. This template is created during setup for each computer, and it should be applied only locally. This template contains many settings that are not configured as part of any other template. Therefore, you should not use group policies to deploy the default template. You can use group policies to deploy alternate security templates that might modify some of the settings in the default template.

If you install Windows Server 2003 or Windows XP Professional on a computer as an upgrade of a previous operating system, no default templates are applied to the computer. Not applying default templates ensures that any previous security configurations are still maintained after the upgrade.

If the default security settings do not meet your security needs, you can apply a variety of other security configurations using security templates. These templates are designed to be applied to computers already running the default security template. In addition to the default template, Microsoft has included the following templates with Windows Server 2003:

- **Compatws.inf** This template can be applied to workstations or servers. Windows Server 2003 is configured to be more secure than previous versions of Windows. In some cases, this increased security means that some applications that ran on previous operating systems will not run on Windows Server 2003 or Windows XP Professional. This is especially true for noncertified applications that require user access to the registry. One way to run these applications is to make the user a member of the Power Users group, which has a higher level of permissions than a normal user. Another option is to reduce the security settings on selected files and registry keys so that the Users group has more permissions. The Compatws.inf template can be used to apply the second option. Applying this template modifies the default file and registry permissions so that members of the Users group can run most applications.

- **Securews.inf and Securedc.inf** These templates provide increased security for areas such as account policy, auditing, and registry permissions. These templates also increase network security by restricting the use of NTLM authentication and enabling the use of Server Message Block (SMB) packet signing on servers. The Securews.inf template is for any workstation or server, but the Securedc.inf template should be applied only to domain controllers.

- **Hisecws.inf and Hisecdc.inf** These templates incrementally increase the security provided by the other templates. Security is increased primarily in the areas that affect network communication protocols. These templates should only be used on networks that include only computers running Windows Server 2003, Windows 2000, or Windows XP and should be tested and applied to all computers to make sure that each one is operating at the same security level. The Hisecws.inf template is for any workstation or server, while the Hisecdc.inf template should only be applied to domain controllers.

- **DC security.inf** This template is applied automatically whenever a Windows Server 2003 member server is promoted to a domain controller. It is available to give the administrator the option to reapply the initial domain controller security if the need arises.

- **Notssid.inf** This template removes the Terminal Users security group security identifier (SID) from all discretionary access control lists (DACLs) on the server. This template is used to make terminal servers more secure because applying this template means that all terminal server users will have their permissions applied through individual user and group memberships rather than the more generic Terminal Users security group. This template is included only on Windows Server 2003 servers that are configured as terminal servers in application mode.

- **Rootsec.inf** This template resets the default permissions of the system root folder, and it also propagates inherited permissions to all subfolders and files in the root folder. Applying this template does not modify explicit permissions assigned to files.

After you have decided which security template to use, you can manage the security templates through the Group Policy Object Editor. If you want to install one of the customized templates, right-click the Security Settings folder and select Import Policy. By default, the dialog box opens the %systemroot%\Security\Templates folder, where the predefined security templates are located. When you select one of the templates, it is loaded into the Group Policy Object Editor. You can then apply this group policy to the selected container object. You can also modify the imported security template so that it exactly matches your requirements. Once you have done this, you can export the template so that it is available for importing into other group policies.

Additional Security Configuration and Analysis Tools

Windows Server 2003 provides two more tools that can be used to manage security templates and apply the templates to computers. One of these tools is the Security Configuration And Analysis snap-in. This snap-in can be used to create or modify existing security templates. The template can then be loaded into the Security Configuration And Analysis snap-in and used to analyze specific computers. For example, you can load a high-security template and then analyze a computer to see what the difference is between the template and the current computer configuration. Figure 13-9 shows an example of the result of this analysis.

You can also use this tool to apply the security template to the computer. If you decide that you want to apply the high-security template to the computer, you can right-click Security Configuration And Analysis and select Configure Computer Now. All the security settings on the computer will then be modified to match the security template.

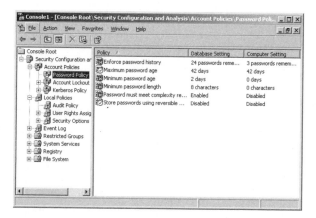

Figure 13-9. *Analyzing a computer security configuration using the Security Configuration And Analysis snap-in.*

The Security Configuration And Analysis snap-in is not intended to be used with group policies. This tool can use the same predefined security templates as the Group Policy Object Editor, but it provides an alternative means to deploy the template. This tool is designed primarily to be used with stand-alone computers.

The Secedit command-line tool provides functionality similar to the Security Configuration And Analysis snap-in. With Secedit, you can analyze the computer settings based on a template and then apply the settings. One of the useful features of the Secedit command-line tool is that you can use it to generate a rollback configuration before you apply a security template. This option provides an easy backout plan if the security template you apply is not appropriate.

Administrative Templates

One of the most powerful options for managing user desktops with group policies is to use administrative templates. Administrative templates are used to configure registry settings on computers running Windows 2000 Server, Windows 2000 Professional, Windows XP Professional, or Windows Server 2003. Administrative templates can be used to configure a great variety of settings—there are over 700 different settings available.

Because so many configuration options are available with group policies, this section cannot possibly cover all of them. Table 13-7 provides an overview of just a few administrative template selections to give you an idea of the power of group policies.

Administrative templates are also available in Windows 2000 Active Directory, but there are about 150 new settings available in Windows Server 2003. Table 13-7 also lists some of the new features that are available in Windows Server 2003 Active Directory with Windows XP Professional clients.

Table 13-7. An Administrative Templates Sampler

Administrative template location	Explanation
Computer Configuration \Administrative Templates \System\Net Logon	Provides a variety of settings controlling client computer locating and caching of DNS domain controller records.
Computer Configuration \Administrative Templates \System\Remote Assistance	Provides settings for the Remote Assistance feature available on Windows XP Professional.
Computer Configuration \Administrative Templates \Windows Components \Terminal Services	Provides settings that can be used to configure Terminal Services on a server and for configuring the Terminal Services client-experience.
User Configuration\ Administrative Templates \Network\Network Connections	Provides a wide variety of settings for managing network connections and limiting user access to network connections.
User Configuration\Administrative Templates\Control Panel	Provides for configuration of parts of the control panel and the user's ability to modify settings through the control panel.
User Configuration\ Administrative Templates \Windows Components \Internet Explorer	Provides a variety of settings to control the configuration of Internet Explorer. Requires Internet Explorer 5.01 or later.

 More Info   For a complete listing of all the Group Policy settings, see *http:// www.microsoft.com/windowsxp/pro/techinfo/administration/policy/winxpgpset.xls*.

One of the enhancements available in Windows Server 2003 Active Directory is much better help for Administrative Templates. Active Directory now comes with complete help files detailing each Administrative Template selection. To access the advanced help on Administrative Templates, right-click the Administrative Templates folder in Group Policy Object Editor and select Help. Then select the appropriate Administrative Template category. Figure 13-10 shows the details on the System category.

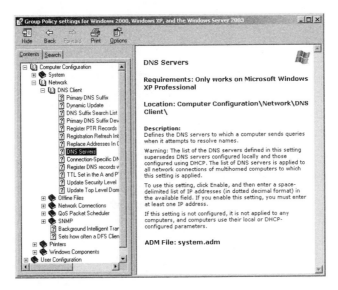

Figure 13-10. *Help And Support Center provides detailed descriptions of each Administrative Template option.*

System policies in Windows NT provide functionality similar to the administrative templates in Windows Server 2003 Active Directory. Both tools enable you to make registry changes on a client to modify the workstation configuration. However, administrative templates provide some very significant advantages over system policies. One of the biggest advantages of administrative templates in Active Directory over system policies in Windows NT 4 is that administrative templates do not brand the registry the way system policies do. When you implement a change using system policies, the change is written into the registry, and the only way to change this setting is to manually change it or use the system policy. If you just remove the system policy, the changes to the registry are not removed.

In Active Directory, the registry changes made by the administrative templates are written into special subkeys in the registry. Any changes made to the User Configuration are written to HKEY_CURRENT_USER and saved under either \Software\Policies or \Software\Microsoft\Windows\CurrentVersion\Policies. Changes made to the Computer Configuration are saved under the same subkeys under HKEY_LOCAL_MACHINE. When the computer boots up or the user logs on, all the normal registry settings are loaded and these keys are then examined for any additional settings. If these locations contain additional settings, they are loaded into the registry, overwriting existing entries, if applicable. If the administrative template is removed or if the computer or user is moved to another container where the template does not apply, the information in the Policies keys is deleted. This removal of the Policies key information means that the administrative templates are not applied anymore, but the normal registry settings still apply.

Administrative templates are stored in several .adm text files. By default, these files are located in the %systemroot%\Inf folder. Table 13-8 lists the administrative template files that are installed by default with Windows Server 2003.

Table 13-8.   Default Templates Loaded in Windows Server 2003

Administrative template	Configuration settings
System.adm	System settings
Inetres.adm	Internet Explorer settings
Wmplayer.adm	Microsoft Windows Media Player settings
Conf.adm	Microsoft NetMeeting settings
Wuau.adm	Windows Update settings

The administrative template files are made up of a series of entries defining the options available through the template. Each entry in the .adm file looks similar to the example shown in Figure 13-11. Table 13-9 explains the entries in the template entry.

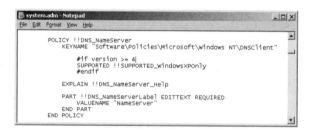

Figure 13-11. *One of the entries in the System.adm file.*

The administrative templates for each group policy are stored in the Sysvol folder on the domain controller and replicated to all other domain controllers in the domain. The templates are stored as a Registry.pol file located in the %systemroot%\SYSVOL\sysvol *domainname*\Policies*GroupPolicyGUID*\Machine folder for the Computer Configuration or in the %systemroot%\SYSVOL\sysvol*domainname*\Policies*GroupPolicyGUID* \\User folder for the User Configuration.

Table 13-9. Components of a Template Option

Template Component	Explanation
Policy	Identifies the policy name.
Keyname	Identifies the registry key modified by this setting.
Supported	Identifies the supported workstations, or the required software version, for this setting. Examples include Windows XP Professional, Windows 2000, or Windows 2000 with a specified service pack, Microsoft Windows Media Player version 9.
Explain	Identifies the text that explains the policy setting. The actual text is listed later in the .adm file.
Part	Identifies the entries that can be configured for this policy.
Valuename	Identifies the registry value that will be populated with the information from this setting.

Administrative templates provide a large number of administrative options. Just analyzing all the policies and determining which ones are needed for your organization can be a daunting task. In most cases, the best way to approach the use of administrative templates is to start slowly. There may be some basic settings that you want to configure, such as preventing users from using registry-editing tools and preventing users from modifying the system through most of the control panel. Another way to determine which settings might be most critical in your organization is to track service desk calls. By tracking these calls, you might be able to identify the configuration issues that result in the most service calls. Then you can see if there is an administrative template that you can use to modify that setting or to prevent users from changing a setting after you have configured it. In this way, you should be able to slowly implement an administrative template policy that can deal with the most critical desktop issues on your network.

Using Scripts to Manage the User Environment

Another tool that you can use to manage user desktops is scripts. The most common use for scripts is to create a simpler work environment for the user. Most commonly, logon scripts are used to map network drives or to map printers. They help to simplify the end user's environment. User logon scripts were available with Windows NT. However, the use of scripts in Windows Server 2003 Active Directory provides a number of significant advantages when compared to Windows NT 4, including:

- **Ability to assign startup and shutdown scripts** With Active Directory, you can assign scripts to run when computers start up and shut down. With Windows NT, this was very difficult. These scripts run in the security context of the LocalSystem account.

- **Ability to assign user logon and logoff scripts** Windows NT provided only logon scripts. With Active Directory, you can also run logoff scripts.

- **Ability to assign scripts to containers rather than to individuals** One of the biggest advantages of using Active Directory to assign scripts is that you can assign a script to a container object. In Windows NT, the only option for running scripts was to assign individual logon scripts to user accounts. When you assign a script to a container in Active Directory, the script applies to all users or computers inside the container.

- **Availability of native support for Windows Script Host scripts** In Windows NT, most clients are limited to running only MS-DOS batch files for logon scripts. In Windows Server 2003, Windows XP and Windows 2000, the clients provide native support for Windows Script Host (WSH) scripts. WSH scripts are much more flexible and powerful for configuring user desktops through scripts. With WSH, the scripts can be used for much more than just mapping network drives.

Windows Server 2003 Active Directory still supports the personal logon scripts that are assigned to the individual user accounts in Active Directory. If you have Windows NT Workstation clients on your network, you must use these logon scripts. Windows 2000 and Windows XP Professional clients will also process the individual logon scripts. If you still have individual logon scripts assigned to user accounts, they are run after the computer startup scripts and the user logon scripts assigned by group policies.

To configure the scripts for Active Directory, you must create the scripts and then copy the scripts to the domain controllers. You can store the scripts in any location on the server as long as they are accessible to the clients. A common place to store a script is in the %systemroot%\SYSVOL\sysvol*domainname*\scripts folder. This folder is shared with a share name of NETLOGON, which is the default location where down-level clients search for logon scripts. You can also store the logon scripts in the %systemroot%\SYSVOL\sysvol*domainname**GlobalPolicyGUID*\Machine\Scripts folder or the %systemroot%\SYSVOL\sysvol*domainname**GlobalPolicyGUID*\User\Scripts folder. After copying the script files to the server, open the GPO and locate the Scripts (Startup/Shutdown) folder under the Computer Configuration\Windows Settings folder or the Scripts (Logon/Logoff) folder under the User Configuration\Windows Settings folder. For example, to create an entry for a startup script, expand the Scripts (Startup /Shutdown) folder and double-click Startup. You can then add any startup scripts to the GPO.

Windows Server 2003 Active Directory provides a number of administrative templates that can be used to configure how the scripts will be processed on client workstations. Most of these settings are located by selecting Computer Configuration\Administrative Templates\System\Scripts, and a few are accessible also by selecting User Configuration\Administrative Templates\System\Scripts. The configuration options include whether to run the startup scripts asynchronously. If you choose this option, multiple startup scripts can run at one time. You can also choose to run logon scripts synchronously, which means that all the startup scripts must complete before the Windows desktop will appear for the user. You can also configure a maximum wait time for all the scripts to finish running. And finally, you can configure whether the scripts will run in the background and be invisible or whether the scripts should be visible when they run.

Summary

Windows Server 2003 Active Directory provides many tools and options for managing user desktops. Group policies can be used to manage user data and profiles to provide users with a familiar work environment while still centrally managing some of the data. Group policies can be used to configure security settings so that all computers affected by a group policy will have a standard and persistent security configuration. Group policies are also used to define administrative templates, which can configure registry settings to manage user desktops. This chapter provided an overview of how you can implement all these options to manage user desktops.

Part IV
Maintaining Windows Server 2003 Active Directory

Parts I, II, and III of this book have prepared you to understand the basic concepts and components, design and implement Active Directory directory service in Microsoft Windows Server 2003, and manage users and computers on your network using Active Directory. This last part of the book prepares you to maintain your Active Directory infrastructure after you deploy it. Chapter 14, "Monitoring and Maintaining Active Directory," details how to monitor Active Directory and includes information on monitoring the performance of Active Directory and Active Directory replication. Chapter 14 also discusses how to manage the Active Directory database. Chapter 15, "Disaster Recovery," discusses how to back up and restore Active Directory.
Active Directory is a critical service on your network, and you must be able to recover from any kind of disaster that may impact your implementation.

Chapter 14
Monitoring and Maintaining Active Directory

Even the best designed, planned, and implemented Active Directory infrastructures will not remain in optimum performing condition without routine monitoring and maintenance. The Active Directory directory service is a complex distributed network service and, particularly in larger organizations, will be subject to thousands of changes every day (such as created or deleted user accounts and their attributes, group membership, and permissions). To ensure that these changes and the ever-changing network and server environment on which the service is hosted do not negatively affect the performance of Active Directory, you must take proactive measures daily. This chapter examines the two fundamental elements of supporting your Active Directory infrastructure: monitoring domain controllers and maintaining the Active Directory database.

Monitoring Active Directory

Monitoring the health of Active Directory is essential to maintaining a reliable level of directory service for your organization. Your users rely on, and take for granted, the efficient running of the directory service—to log on to the network, to access shared resources, and to retrieve and send e-mail. The activities your user community would rank as critical all depend on the health and availability of Active Directory.

There is no single tool or package of programs for monitoring Active Directory. Rather, monitoring Active Directory health is a combination of tasks—all with the common goal of measuring the current performance of some key indicator (disk capacity, processor utilization, service uptime, and so on) against a known good state (the baseline). Therefore, your "monitoring solution" will consist of various tasks and tools. (Tool sets are available that can bring the monitoring of these key indicators together in an easy-to-manage interface, and for large organizations, these tool sets might be essential, but they are also expensive, resource-hungry, and complex.) This chapter discusses what you should be monitoring and examines some tools that are available in Microsoft Windows Server 2003 to do so. You can decide for yourself which Active Directory management tools are appropriate for your needs.

To understand Active Directory monitoring, you must know *why* to monitor Active Directory, *how* to monitor it, and exactly *what* within the Active Directory environment to monitor. To keep your directory service running at peak performance, you also need to know what to do in response to your monitoring efforts. For the purpose of this chapter, do whatever it takes to bring the service within the normal operating parameters that you have established. For example, if performance monitoring indicates that the drive on which the Active Directory database is located is fragmented, you should defragment it.

Why Monitor Active Directory?

The conventional reason given to monitor Active Directory is that monitoring identifies potential problems *before* they occur and result in long periods of service downtime. A more progressive reason is that monitoring enables you to maintain your service-level agreement (SLA) to your customer (the network user). In either case, you should monitor the health of Active Directory to catch problems as soon as possible—before an interruption of service occurs.

Note An SLA is a contract between a service provider (you) and the user community that defines the responsibilities of each party and constitutes a commitment to provide a particular level of service to a specified degree of quality and quantity. In the context of Active Directory, an SLA between the Information Technology (IT) department and the user community would contain the maximum level of acceptable system downtime as well as other performance metrics, such as logon time and response time for support requests. In exchange for the service provider's commitment to meet certain performance and operational standards, the user community commits to a certain volume of usage, for example, having 10,000 or fewer users in the Active Directory forest.

Another reason to monitor the system health of Active Directory is to track changes to the infrastructure. Has the size of your Active Directory database grown since last year? Are all of your global catalog (GC) servers online? How long does it take for changes made on a domain controller in France to replicate to a domain controller in Australia? Knowing any of this information might not prevent an error from occurring today, but it will provide you with valuable data with which you can plan for the future.

Benefits of Monitoring Active Directory

There are several benefits to monitoring Active Directory, including:

- Ability to maintain SLAs with users by avoiding service downtime
- Higher performance of Active Directory by eliminating otherwise undetected service bottlenecks
- Lower administrative costs through proactive system maintenance

- Increased ability to scale and plan for future infrastructure changes through in-depth knowledge of Active Directory components, capacity, and utilization
- Increased goodwill for the IT department through customer satisfaction

Costs of Active Directory Monitoring

Monitoring your Active Directory infrastructure is not without its costs. The following are a few of the costs required to implement an effective monitoring solution:

- Man-hours are required to design, deploy, and manage a monitoring solution.
- Sufficient funds are required to acquire the necessary management tools, training, and hardware required to implement service monitoring.
- A portion of your network bandwidth will be utilized to monitor the health of Active Directory on all the domain controllers in the enterprise.
- Memory and processor resources are used for running agent applications on target servers and on the central monitoring console computer.

It is worth noting that the cost of monitoring goes up quickly when you move to an enterprise-wide monitoring platform, such as Microsoft Operations Manager (MOM). Tools such as MOM are expensive, require operator training, and use up more system resources than many Windows Server 2003–native monitoring solutions, but they are proven, integrated, and supported products.

The level of monitoring you select will depend on your cost-benefit analysis. In all cases, the amount of resources you dedicate to your monitoring solution should not exceed the projected costs you will save through monitoring. For this reason, larger organizations find it cost-effective to invest in enterprise management solutions. Smaller organizations, more often, can justify using the monitoring tools built into Windows Server 2003.

More Info   MOM incorporates event management, service monitoring and alerting, report generation, and trend analysis. It does so through a central console in which agents running on the *managed nodes* (monitored servers) send data to be analyzed, tracked, and displayed in a single management console. This centralization enables the network administrator to manage a large and disparate collection of servers from a single location, with powerful management tools to remotely administer the server. MOM uses management packs to extend the knowledge base of data for specific network services, as well as server-based applications. The Base Management Pack contains knowledge data for all Windows Server 2003 services, including Active Directory, Domain Name System (DNS), and Microsoft Internet Information Services (IIS). The Application Management Pack includes knowledge data for Microsoft .NET Enterprise Servers, such as Microsoft Exchange 2000 Server and Microsoft SQL Server 2000. For more information on MOM, see *http://www.microsoft.com/mom*.

How to Monitor Active Directory

To monitor Active Directory, you will track key performance indicators and compare them to a baseline condition that represents the service operating within normal parameters. When a performance indicator exceeds a specified performance threshold, an alert occurs, notifying the network administration (or the *monitoring operator*, in the case of large organizations) of the condition. An alert can also initiate an automatic action to remedy the problem or to minimize any further deterioration of performance, system health, and so on.

The following is a high-level outline of the Active Directory monitoring process:

1. Determine what performance indicators you need to monitor. (Start by reviewing your SLAs.)

2. Monitor performance indicators to establish and document your baseline performance level.

3. Determine your thresholds for these performance indicators. (In other words, determine at what level you will need to take action to prevent a disruption of service.)

4. Design the necessary alert system to process a threshold hit. Your alert system should include

   - Operator notifications.

   - Automatic actions, if appropriate.

   - Operator-initiated actions.

5. Design a reporting system to capture historical data on Active Directory system health.

6. Implement your monitoring solution to measure performance of these key indicators on a schedule that reflects the variability of these indicators and the impact that each indicator has on Active Directory health.

The rest of this section examines each of these monitoring activities. Identifying the performance indicators is covered later in this chapter in the section "What to Monitor."

Establishing the Baselines and Thresholds

After you have identified what performance indicators you need to monitor, you should gather baseline data for these indicators. The baseline represents the performance indicator within normal limits of operation. The "normal limits" should include both the low and high values that are expected for a particular performance counter. To capture the most accurate baseline data, you should collect performance information over a sufficient period of time to reflect the range of values for a particular parameter during high and low activity. For example, if you are establishing the baseline for authentication request performance, be sure to monitor that indicator during the period when most of your users are logging on.

As you determine your baseline values, document this information and date the version of the document you create. In addition to being used for setting thresholds, these values will be useful for identifying performance trends over time. A spreadsheet formatted with columns for low, average, and high values for each counter, as well as thresholds for alerts, is well-suited for this purpose.

Tip   When your Active Directory environment changes (for example, if the number of users increases or hardware changes are made to domain controllers), reestablish your baselines. The baseline should always reflect the most current snapshot of Active Directory running within normal performance limits. An outdated baseline is not useful for analyzing current performance data.

After you have determined the baseline, next determine the threshold values that should generate an alert. Apart from the recommendations made by Microsoft, there is no magic formula for determining threshold values. You will need to determine, based on your network infrastructure, what performance level indicates that a performance counter is trending toward service interruption. In establishing your thresholds, start conservatively. (Use either values recommended by Microsoft or even lower values.) As a result, you will process a large number of alerts. As you gather more data about the counter, you can raise the threshold to reduce the number of alerts. This process might take several months, but it will eventually be fine-tuned for your particular implementation of Active Directory.

Performance Counters and Thresholds

The following tables list key performance counters and threshold values that are helpful for monitoring Active Directory, as recommended by Microsoft. Keep in mind that every enterprise environment will have unique characteristics that will affect the applicability of these values. Consider these thresholds as a starting point, and through the monitoring described earlier, refine these values to reflect your environment.

Active Directory Performance

The performance counters listed in Table 14-1 monitor the core Active Directory functions and services. Thresholds are determined by baseline monitoring unless otherwise indicated. To access these counters, open Start>Administrative Tools>Performance, and then click the Add button above the graph. Sections following this table describe how to set counter properties.

Table 14-1. Core Active Directory Functions and Services

Object	Counter	Interval	Why counter is important
NTDS	DS Search sub-operations / sec	Every 15 minutes	Subtree search requests are very system-resource intensive. Any significant increase can indicate domain controller performance problems. Check to see if applications are incorrectly targeting this domain controller.
Process	% Processor Time (Instance=lsass)	Every 1 minute	This counter indicates the percentage of CPU time being used by the Active Directory service.
NTDS	LDAP Searches / sec	Every 15 minutes	This counter is a good indicator for the amount of overall use a domain controller is getting. Ideally, this counter should be fairly uniform across the domain controllers. An increase in this counter might indicate that a new application is targeting this domain controller or that more clients were added to the network.
NTDS	LDAP Client Sessions	Every 5 minutes	This counter indicates the number of clients currently connected to the domain controller. A significant increase might indicate that other machines are failing-over to this domain controller. Trending this counter can also provide useful information as to what time of day people are connecting and the maximum number of clients connected per day.
Process	Private Bytes (Instance=lsass)	Every 15 minutes	This counter is good for trending memory needs by domain controllers. A continuously growing counter indicates either increased workstation demand, applications misbehaving (not closing handles), or increased number of workstations targeting this domain controller. When this counter significantly deviates from the normal value of other peer domain controllers, you should investigate the source of this demand.

Object	Counter	Interval	Why counter is important
Process	Handle Count (Instance=lsass)	Every 15 minutes	This trending statistic is useful for seeing if applications are misbehaving and not closing handles properly. This counter will increase linearly as client workstations are added.
Process	Virtual Bytes (Instance=lsass)	Every 15 minutes	This counter can be used to determine if Active Directory is running low on virtual memory address space, which might indicate a memory leak. Verify that you are running the latest service pack, and schedule a reboot during off hours to avoid a system outage. This counter can be used to determine if less than 2 gigabytes (GB) of virtual memory remains available.

Replication Performance Counters

The performance counters discussed in Table 14-2 monitor the quantity of replicated data. Thresholds are determined by the baselines you established earlier, unless otherwise indicated.

Table 14-2. Replication Performance Counters

Object	Counter	Recommended interval	Why counter is important
NTDS	DRA Inbound Bytes Compressed (Between Sites, After Compression) / sec	Every 15 minutes	Indicates the amount of replication data flowing to this site. A significant change in the counter indicates a replication topology change or that significant data was added or changed in Active Directory.
NTDS	DRA Outbound Bytes Compressed (Between Sites, After Compression) / sec	Every 15 minutes	Indicates the amount of replication data flowing out of this site. A significant change in the counter indicates a replication topology change or that significant data was added or changed in Active Directory.
NTDS	DRA Outbound Bytes Not Compressed	Every 15 minutes	Indicates the amount of replication data outbound from this domain controller, but to targets within the site.
NTDS	DRA Outbound Bytes Total / sec	Every 15 minutes	Indicates the amount of replication data outbound from this domain controller. A significant change in the counter indicates a replication topology change or that significant data was added or changed in Active Directory. This is a very important performance counter to watch.

Security Subsystem Performance

The performance counters listed in Table 14-3 monitor key security volumes. Thresholds are determined by baseline monitoring unless otherwise indicated.

Table 14-3. Key Security Volumes

Object	Counter	Recommended interval	Why counter is important
NTDS	NTLM Authentications	Every 15 minutes	Indicates the number of clients per second authenticating against the domain controller using NTLM instead of Kerberos (pre–Windows 2000 clients or interforest authentications).
NTDS	KDC AS Requests	Every 15 minutes	Indicates the number of session tickets per second being issued by the Key Distribution Center (KDC). This is a good indicator to use to observe the impact of changing the ticket lifetime.
NTDS	Kerberos Authentications	Every 15 minutes	Indicates the amount of authentication load being put on the KDC. This is a very good indicator to use for trending purposes.
NTDS	KDC TGS Requests	Every 15 minutes	Indicates the number of Ticket-Granting Tickets (TGTs) being issued by the KDC. This is a good indicator to use to observe the impact of changing the ticket lifetime.

Core Operating System Performance

The performance counters listed in Table 14-4 monitor core operating system indicators and have a direct impact on Active Directory performance.

Table 14-4. Core Operating System Indicators

Object	Counter	Interval	Threshold	Significance when the threshold value is exceeded
Memory	Page Faults / sec	Every 5 minutes	700 / second	High rate of page faults indicates insufficient physical memory.
PhysicalDisk	Current Disk Queue Length	Every 1 minute	2 Averaged over 3 intervals	Monitor volumes containing the Ntds.dit file and the .log files. This counter indicates that there is a backlog of disk I/O requests. Consider increasing disk and controller throughput.
Processor	% DPC Time (Instance=_Total)	Every 15 minutes	10	Indicates work that was deferred because the domain controller was too busy. Exceeding the threshold value indicates a possible processor congestion.

Object	Counter	Interval	Threshold	Significance when the threshold value is exceeded
System	Processor Queue Length	Every 1 minute	6 Averaged over 5 intervals	The CPU is not fast enough to process requests as they occur. If the replication topology is correct and the condition is not caused by failover from another domain controller, consider upgrading CPU.
Memory	Available MBytes	Every 15 minutes	4 megabytes (MB)	Indicates system has run out of available memory. Imminent service failure is likely.
Processor	% Processor Time (Instance=_Total)	Every 1 minute	85% Averaged over 3 intervals	Indicates CPU is overloaded. Determine if CPU load is being caused by Active Directory by examining the Process object, % Processor Time counter, lsass instance.
System	Context Switches / sec	Every 15 minutes	70,000	Indicates excessive transitions. There might be too many applications or services running, or their load on the system is too high. Consider offloading a portion of this demand.
System	System Up Time	Every 15 minutes		Essential counter for measuring domain controller reliability.

Caution   The values above are based upon the Microsoft-recommended threshold values that were available at the time of this printing and should be considered preliminary content. This information will be contained in the Directory Services Guide of the *Microsoft Windows Server 2003 Resource Kit*. For up-to-date information about the release of the resource kit, see *http://www.microsoft.com /windowsserver2003/techinfo/reskit/resourcekit.mspx*.

Designing Alerts

An *alert* is defined as a notification that is automatically triggered when a threshold value is met. Using the Performance administrative tool in Windows Server 2003, you can configure alerts for any available performance counter.

Note   When the Active Directory Installation Wizard installs Active Directory, the Wizard configures performance counters in the NTDS Performance Object that provide statistics about directory service activity. These counters apply to the entire directory, including GCs.

However, the Active Directory database performance counters for the ESENT database (Ntds.dit) are not installed during Active Directory installation. You have to add these counters manually. For an automated script that installs the Active Directory database performance counters, see the Install Active Directory Database Performance Counters article in the Microsoft Script Center at *http: //www.microsoft.com/technet/treeview/default.asp?url=/technet/scriptcenter /monitor/ScrMon08.asp*. You can copy this script to a text file, name the file with a .vbs extension, then run the file to install the ESENT database performance counters.

⊃ **For example, to create an alert for exceeding 20 Kerberos authentication requests per second on a domain controller, perform the following steps:**

1. Open Performance from the Administrative Tools folder.

2. Double-click Performance Logs And Alerts, and then click Alerts.

3. From the Action menu, select New Alert Settings.

4. In Name, type the name of the alert, and then click OK. This is the name that will show up in the Performance Logs And Alerts container, so use a name that identifies the counter you are monitoring.

5. On the General tab, define a comment for your alert, and then click ADD to add the necessary Performance Object and counters. See Figure 14-1 for an example.

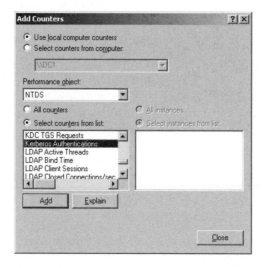

Figure 14-1. *Adding a counter to a new alert.*

6.   After you add the counter, enter the threshold limit used to trigger the alert. Also set the time interval for sampling the performance data. See Figure 14-2.

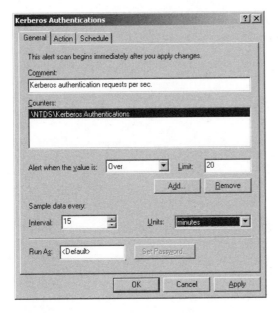

Figure 14-2. *Setting the threshold limit and the sample interval.*

7.   On the Action tab, define the events that should occur when the threshold value is met. To define when the service should begin scanning for alerts, use the Schedule tab. The Action tab shows that an alert can trigger several actions, including:

- Creating an entry in the application event log.
- Generating a notification message. This message can be sent either to an Internet Protocol (IP) address or to a computer name.
- Starting a performance log.
- Running a program.

See Figure 14-3 for an example.

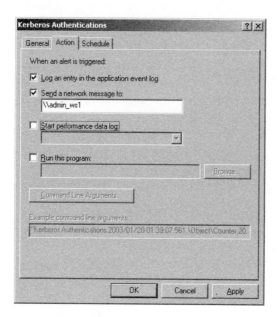

Figure 14-3. *Defining the actions for a new alert.*

In addition to the options specified in the Actions tab, it is essential for effective monitoring that you have a game plan in place for how you will respond to an alert. As you define your counters, baseline, and threshold values, be sure to document the remedial action you will perform to bring the indicator back within normal limits. This action might involve troubleshooting an error condition (for example, bringing a domain controller back online) or transferring an operations master role. If your system has reached its maximum capacity, you might have to add disk space or memory to correct the condition. Other alerts will trigger you to perform Active Directory maintenance, such as defragmenting the Active Directory database file. Such situations are discussed later in this chapter, in the section "Offline Defragmentation of the Active Directory Database."

Monitoring Server Health with System Monitor

Also included in the Performance administrative tool is the System Monitor tool. Using this tool, you can collect and view real-time performance data of a local computer or several remote computers. System Monitor provides a graphical representation of the same performance data you can monitor with Performance Logs And Alerts. This tool makes identifying performance trends a much easier task.

The following are the three default performance counters in System Monitor:

- Memory\Pages/sec
- PhysicalDisk (_Total)\Avg. Disk Queue Length
- Processor (_Total)\%Processor Time

> **Note**   The term to the left of the backslash is the performance object, with the instance in parentheses (if any). The counter is the term to the right of the backslash.

Each of these counters is tracked on a time/performance axis by a separately colored line. These counters are very useful for monitoring server (specifically, domain controller) system health. Figure 14-4 illustrates the default view of System Monitor.

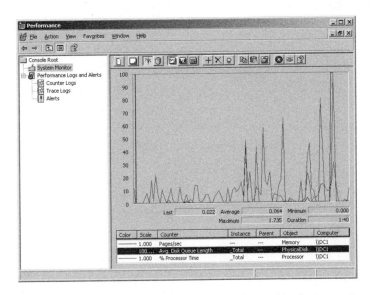

Figure 14-4. *The default performance counters in System Monitor.*

You can configure several useful options for System Monitor.

- To optimize the view of a particular counter, select the counter description at the bottom of the window and select the Highlight button on the toolbar. Doing so will change the selected counter graph line to bold white, where it is easily viewed against the graph.

- You can switch between the graph, histogram, and report view by selecting the appropriate button on the toolbar.

- You can save System Monitor graph settings as an HTML page. To do so, configure a graph with the necessary counters, right-click the graph, and select Save As. The graph will be saved as an HTML file that you can open in a browser. When you open the HTML version of the graph, the display is frozen. In the browser, click the Freeze Display button on the Performance toolbar to restart the monitoring.

- You can import a saved graph back into System Monitor by dragging the HTML file onto the System Monitor window, which is a convenient way to save and reload frequently used performance graphs.

- There are two new security groups in Windows Server 2003 that ensure that only trusted users can access and manipulate sensitive performance data: the Performance Log Users group and the Performance Monitor Users group.

➲ **To add additional counters to System Monitor, perform the following steps:**

1. Right-click the System Monitor details pane, and click Add Counters.

2. In the Add Counters dialog box, click Use Local Computer Counters to monitor the computer on which the monitoring console is run. To monitor a specific computer regardless of where the monitoring console is run, click Select Counters From Computer and specify a computer name or an IP address.

3. Select the desired Performance Object, and then click the counter you want to add. This interface is the same as the one used for adding counters to a new alert, as described earlier.

4. Click Add, and then click Close.

Monitoring Active Directory with Event Viewer

In addition to using the Performance administrative tool to monitor Active Directory, you should also periodically review the contents of the event logs by using the Event Viewer administrative tool. By default, the Event Viewer displays the following three logs:

- **Application log** Contains events logged by applications or programs
- **System log** Contains events such as valid and invalid logon attempts, as well as events related to resource use such as creating, opening, or deleting files or other objects
- **Security log** Contains events logged by Windows system components

In addition, for servers running Windows Server 2003 configured as domain controllers, the following event logs will be displayed:

- **Directory Service log** Contains events logged by Active Directory
- **File Replication Service log** Contains events logged by the File Replication Service

If the Windows Server 2003 domain controller is a DNS server as well, the following log will also be displayed:

- **DNS Server log** Contains events logged by the DNS Server service.

To view the event logs, select the Event Viewer from the Administrative Tools folder. Select the event log for the service you want to monitor. The left pane of Figure 14-5 shows all the event logs for a domain controller running Windows Server 2003 that is also a DNS server.

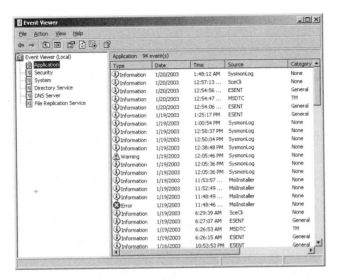

Figure 14-5. *The Event Viewer administrative tool with event logs.*

From the event log, review the event types for Errors and Warnings. To display the details of an event in the log, double-click the event. Figure 14-6 shows the details of a Warning event (Event ID 13562) from the File Replication Service log.

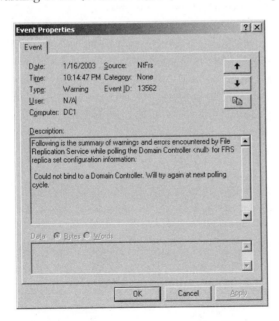

Figure 14-6. *The Event Properties sheet for an event log entry.*

What to Monitor

For monitoring the overall system health of Active Directory, you should monitor service-related performance and server-related performance indicators as well as events. You must ensure that Active Directory and the domain controllers on which it is running are performing optimally. When designing your monitoring solution, plan to monitor the following performance areas:

- **Active Directory replication** Replication performance is essential to ensuring that data integrity across the domain is being maintained.

- **Active Directory service** These performance indicators are monitored using the NTDS counters in the Performance administrative tool.

- **Active Directory database storage** The disk volumes that contain the Active Directory database file Ntds.dit and the .log files must have enough free space to allow normal growth and operation..

- **DNS performance and server health** Because Active Directory relies on DNS as a service locator, the DNS server and service must be operating within normal limits for Active Directory to meet its service-level requirements.

- **File Replication Service (FRS)** The FRS must be running within normal limits to ensure that the shared system volume (Sysvol) is replicating throughout the domain.

- **Domain controller system health** Monitoring for this area should cover overall server health, including memory counters, processor utilization, and paging.

- **Forest health** This area should be monitored to verify trusts and site availability.

- **Operations masters** For each Flexible Single-Master Operations (FSMO), monitor to ensure server health. Also monitor to ensure GC availability to enable user logon and universal group-membership enumeration.

Monitoring Replication

One of the critical components of Active Directory that you should monitor is replication. Unlike domain controller monitoring, which uses Performance Monitor, replication between domain controllers is most commonly monitored with tools from the Windows Server 2003 Support Tools collection: Repadmin.exe, Dcdiag.exe, and the Directory Service log (described earlier with the Event Viewer).

Repadmin is a command-line tool that reports failures on a replication link between two replication partners. The following command displays the replication partners and any replication link failures for the DC1 domain controller in the Contoso.com domain:

```
repadmin /showreps dc1.contoso.com
```

Dcdiag is a command-line tool that can check the DNS registration of a domain controller, check to see that the security identifiers (SIDs) on the naming context (NC) heads have appropriate permissions for replication, analyze the state of domain controllers in a forest or enterprise, and more. For a complete list of Dcdiag options, type *dcdiag /?*. The following command checks for any replication errors between domain controllers:

```
dcdiag /test:replications
```

Finally, the Directory Service log reports replication errors that occur after a replication link has been established. In particular, you should review the Directory Service log for any replication event where the event type is an Error or a Warning. The following are two examples of common replication errors as they are displayed in the Directory Service log:

- **Event ID 1311** The replication configuration information in the Active Directory Sites And Services administrative tool does not accurately reflect the physical topology of the network. This error indicates that either one or more domain controllers or bridgehead servers are offline or that the bridgehead servers do not host the required NCs.

- **Event ID 1265 (Access denied)** This error can occur if the local domain controller failed to authenticate against its replication partner when creating the replication link or when trying to replicate over an existing link. This error typically happens when the domain controller has been disconnected from the rest of the network for a long time and its computer account password is not synchronized with the computer account password stored in the directory of its replication partner.

Active Directory Database Maintenance

One of the important components of managing Active Directory is maintaining the Active Directory database. Under normal circumstances, you will rarely manage the Active Directory database directly because regular automatic database management will maintain the health of your database in all but exceptional situations. These automatic processes include an online defragmentation of the Active Directory database as well as a garbage collection process to clean up deleted items. For those rare occasions when you do need to directly manage the Active Directory database, Windows Server 2003 includes the Ntdsutil tool.

Garbage Collection

One of the automatic processes used to maintain the Active Directory database is *garbage collection*. Garbage collection is a process that runs on every domain controller every 12 hours. During the garbage collection process, free space within the Active Directory database is reclaimed.

The garbage collection process starts by first removing *tombstones* from the database. Tombstones are the remains of objects that have been deleted from Active Directory. When an object such as a user account is deleted, the object is not immediately deleted. Rather, the *isDeleted* attribute on the object is set to *true*, the object is marked as a tombstone, and most of the attributes for the object are removed from the object. Only a few attributes required to identify the object are retained, such as the globally unique identifier (GUID), the SID, the update sequence number (USN), and the distinguished name. This tombstone is then replicated to other domain controllers in the domain. Each domain controller maintains a copy of the tombstoned object until the *tombstone lifetime* expires. By default, the tombstone lifetime is set to 60 days. The next time the garbage collection process runs after the tombstone has expired, the object is deleted from the database.

After deleting the tombstones, the garbage collection process deletes any unnecessary transaction log files. Whenever a change is made to the Active Directory database, it is first written to a transaction log and then committed to the database. The garbage collection process removes all transaction logs that do not contain any uncommitted transactions.

As mentioned, the garbage collection process runs on every domain controller at 12-hour intervals. You can modify this interval by changing the *garbageCollPeriod* attribute in the enterprise-wide DS configuration object (NTDS). To modify this setting you can use a tool like Adsiedit.msc. Open ADSI Edit from the Run dialog box, and select the CN=Directory Service,CN=Windows NT,CN=Services,CN=Configuration,DC=*forestname* object. Then locate the *garbageCollPeriod* attribute and configure the value to meet your requirements. In most cases, you should not have to modify this setting. Figure 14-7 shows this attribute in ADSI Edit.

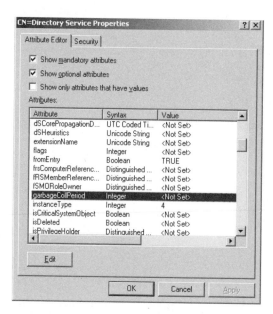

Figure 14-7. *The* garbageCollPeriod *attribute in ADSI Edit.*

Online Defragmentation

The final step in the garbage collection process is an online defragmentation of the Active Directory database. This online defragmentation frees up space within the database and rearranges the storage of Active Directory objects within the database to improve the efficiency of the database. The online defragmentation is necessary because of the process Active Directory uses when manipulating objects in the database.

During normal operation, the database system for Active Directory is optimized to be able to make changes to the Active Directory database as quickly as possible. When an object is deleted from Active Directory, the database page where the object is stored is loaded into the computer memory and the object is deleted from the page. As objects are added to Active Directory, they are written to database pages without consideration for optimizing the storage of that information for later retrieval. After several hours of committing changes to the database as fast as possible, the storage of the data in the database might not be optimized. For example, the database might contain empty pages where objects have been deleted, there might be many pages with some deleted items, or Active Directory objects that should logically be stored together might be stored on many different pages throughout the database.

The online defragmentation process cleans up the database and returns the database to a more optimized state. If some of the entries on a database page have been deleted, entries from other pages might be moved onto the page to optimize the storage and retrieval of information. Objects that should logically be stored together because they will be displayed together are moved onto the same database page or onto adjacent pages. One of the limitations of the online defragmentation process is that it does not shrink the size of the Active Directory database. If you have deleted a large number of objects from Active Directory, the online defragmentation process might create many empty pages in the database as it moves objects around in the database. However, the online defragmentation process cannot remove these empty pages from the database. To remove these pages, you must use an offline defragmentation process.

The online defragmentation process runs every 12 hours as part of the garbage collection process. When the online defragmentation process is complete, an event is written into the Directory Service log indicating that the process has completed successfully. Figure 14-8 shows an example of this event log message.

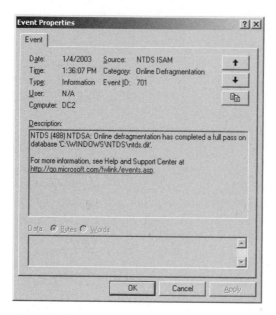

Figure 14-8. *A Directory Service log message indicating a successful online defragmentation.*

Offline Defragmentation of the Active Directory Database

As mentioned earlier, the online defragmentation process cannot shrink the size of the Active Directory database. Under normal circumstances, this is not a problem because the database pages that are cleaned up during the online defragmentation are just reused as new objects are added to Active Directory. However, in some cases, you might want to use offline defragmentation to shrink the overall size of the database. For example, if you remove the GC from a domain controller, you should run an offline defragmentation on the database to clean up the space used in the database to store the GC information. This need for an offline defragmentation is especially true in a multiple-domain environment where the GC can become very large. You might also want to use offline defragmentation if you have removed a large number of objects from the Active Directory domain.

➲ **To run offline defragmentation, perform the following steps:**

1. Back up the Active Directory information on the domain controller. This process is described in Chapter 15, "Disaster Recovery."

2. Reboot the domain controller. As the server boots, press F8 to display the Windows Advanced Options Menu. Choose Directory Services Restore Mode (Windows Domain Controllers Only).

3. Log on using the Administrator account. Use the password that you entered as the Directory Services Restore Mode password when you promoted the domain controller.

4. Open a command prompt, and type *ntdsutil*.

5. From the Ntdsutil prompt, type *files*.

6. From the File Maintenance prompt, type *info*. This option displays current information about the path and size of the Active Directory database and its log files.

7. Type *compact to **drive:\directory***. Select a drive and directory that have enough space to store the entire database. If the directory path name contains any spaces, the path must be enclosed by quotation marks.

8. The offline defragmentation process creates a new database named Ntds.dit in the path you specified. As the database is copied to the new location, it is defragmented.

9. When the defragmentation is done, type *quit* twice to return to the command prompt.

10. Copy the defragmented Ntds.dit file over the old Ntds.dit file in the Active Directory database path.

11. Restart the domain controller.

Note   If you are defragmenting the database because you have deleted a large number of objects from Active Directory, you must repeat this procedure on all domain controllers.

Managing the Active Directory Database Using Ntdsutil

In addition to using Ntdsutil to defragment your Active Directory database while offline, you can use it to manage the Active Directory database in several other ways. The Ntdsutil tool can be used to perform several low-level Active Directory database recovery tasks. The database recovery options are all nondestructive—that is, the recovery tools will try to correct a problem with the Active Directory database, but they will never do so at the expense of deleting data.

Recovering the Transaction Logs

Recovering the transaction logs means forcing the domain controller to re-run the transaction logs. This option is automatically performed by the domain controller when the domain controller restarts from a forced shutdown. You can also force the soft recovery using the Ntdsutil tool.

Note   Chapter 15 describes in detail how transaction logs are used in Active Directory.

➲ **To perform a recovery of the transaction logs, perform the following steps:**

1. Reboot the server, and select the option to boot into Directory Services Restore Mode. All the Ntdsutil database operations require that the domain controller be in this mode.

2. Open a command prompt, and type *ntdsutil.*

3. From the Ntdsutil prompt, type *files.*

4. From the File Maintenance prompt, type *recover.*

The recover option should always be the first step in any database recovery because it ensures that the database is consistent with the transaction logs. Once this is complete, you can run the other database options if needed.

Checking the Database for Integrity

Checking the database for integrity means that the database is checked at a low (binary) level to check for database corruption. The process also checks the database headers and checks all the tables for consistency. Because every byte of the database is checked during this process, it will take a long time to run on a large database. To run the integrity check, type *integrity* at the File Maintenance prompt in Ntdsutil.

Semantic Database Analysis

The semantic database analysis is different from the integrity check in that it does not examine the database at a binary level. Rather, the semantic analysis checks the database consistency against the Active Directory semantics. The semantic database analysis examines each object in the database to ensure that each object has a GUID, a proper SID, and the correct replication metadata.

➲ **To perform the semantic database analysis, perform the following steps:**

1. Open a command prompt, and type *ntdsutil.*

2. At the Ntdsutil prompt, type *semantic database analysis.*

3. At the Semantic Checker prompt, type *verbose on.* This setting configures Ntdsutil to write additional information to the screen when the semantic checker is running.

4. At the Semantic Checker prompt, type *go.*

Note   If you have used Active Directory in Windows 2000, you might have seen that Windows 2000 included a Repair option. This option, which performs a potentially destructive repair of the Active Directory database, is not available in Windows Server 2003.

Moving Database and Transaction Log Locations

The Ntdsutil tool can also be used to move the Active Directory database and transaction logs. For example, if the transaction logs and the database are all on the same hard disk you might want to move one of the components to a different hard disk. If the hard disk containing the database file fills up, you will have to move the database.

◑ **To move the database and transaction log to new locations with the server in Directory Services Restore Mode, perform the following steps:**

1. Open a command prompt, and type *ntdsutil*.

2. From the Ntdsutil prompt, type *files*.

3. To see where the files are currently located, at the Ntdsutil prompt, type *info*. This command lists the file locations for the database and all logs.

4. To move the database file, at the File Maintenance prompt, type *move db to* **directory**, where *directory* is the destination location for the files. This command moves the database to the specified location and reconfigures the registry to access the file in the correct location.

5. To move the transaction logs, at the File Maintenance prompt, type *move logs to* **directory**.

Summary

This chapter introduced the processes and some of the tools necessary to monitor Active Directory and the system health of the domain controllers on which it runs. By putting in place a regular monitoring solution, you will be able to identify potentially disruptive and costly system bottlenecks and other performance issues before they occur. Effective monitoring of Active Directory will also provide you with valuable performance trend data so that you can prepare for future system improvements. Monitoring is one way to trigger the necessary support tasks you must perform to keep your Active Directory infrastructure running in top condition. In the absence of event log errors and alert notifications, you must still implement a regular database maintenance program to keep the Active Directory database functioning efficiently. This chapter described the online and offline defragmentation process as well as the garbage collection process for removing deleted (tombstoned) Active Directory objects.

Chapter 15
Disaster Recovery

Active Directory directory service is perhaps the most critical network service that you will deploy on your network. If the Active Directory infrastructure fails, the users on your network will be extremely limited in what they can do. Almost all network services on a Microsoft Windows Server 2003 network depend on users authenticating to Active Directory before they access any network resource. Because Active Directory is critical, you must apply at least the same level of preparation to Active Directory disaster prevention and recovery as you do to any other network resources. It is essential when you deploy Windows Server 2003 Active Directory that you prepare for the protection of the Active Directory database and put into place a plan for recovering the database in the event of a critical failure.

This chapter begins by discussing some basic practices that you can implement to provide redundancy and protection for Active Directory. It then discusses the components of the Active Directory database and the optimal configuration of these components to ensure disaster recovery functionality. The main part of this chapter discusses options and procedures for backing up and restoring the Active Directory database.

Note This chapter deals with disaster recovery as it relates to Active Directory only. It does not address the issues of rebuilding servers running Windows Server 2003; it only addresses restoring Active Directory after you have restored the server.

Planning for a Disaster

The first steps in disaster recovery must take place long before the disaster strikes. In fact, if you haven't done the proper planning for a potential disaster, a problem such as a hardware component failure on a domain controller might turn into a real catastrophe rather than just a minor inconvenience.

Planning for disaster includes considering all the elements that make up the normal network infrastructure, as well as some Active Directory–specific planning. The procedures on the following page are critical.

- Develop a consistent backup and restore regimen for the domain controllers. The first step in any recovery plan is to install the appropriate backup hardware and software to back up the domain controllers. You should then create and test a backup and restore plan.

- Test your backup plan before you deploy Active Directory and frequently after you deploy. Once you have deployed Active Directory, your users will require that it be available all the time. You should also repeatedly test the restore plan. Many of the best-managed network environments have a consistent restore testing procedure, in which every week some component of the restore procedure is tested. If you actually have a disaster, you will be under a great deal of pressure to get Active Directory back up and running as quickly as possible—that should not be the first time that you are using the Active Directory restore procedure.

- Deploy Active Directory domain controllers with hardware redundancy. Most servers can be ordered with some level of hardware redundancy at little additional cost. For example, a server with dual power supplies, redundant network cards, and a hardware-based redundant hard disk system should be standard equipment for the domain controllers. If this redundancy saves you even one all-night effort restoring a domain controller, it will have been one of the best investments you have ever made. In many large environments, this hardware redundancy is taken to another level, where each domain controller is connected to a different power circuit and connected to a different Ethernet switch or network segment.

- In all but the smallest networks, you should deploy at least two domain controllers. Active Directory uses circular logging for its log files, and this default cannot be modified. This circular logging means that with a single domain controller, you might lose Active Directory data if the domain controller crashes and you have to restore from backup. Even in a small company, multiple domain controllers are critical. If you want all the users to use one domain controller most of the time, you can modify the Domain Name System (DNS) records by adjusting the priority for each domain controller. The second domain controller can then serve another function and be used only for backup when the first domain controller fails.

Active Directory Data Storage

As mentioned in Chapter 2, " Active Directory Components," the Active Directory database is stored in a file called Ntds.dit, which is located in the %systemroot%\NTDS folder by default. This folder also contains the following files:

- **Edb.chk** This file is a checkpoint file that indicates which transactions from the log files have been written to the Active Directory database.

- **Edb.log** This file is the current transaction log. This log file is a fixed-length file exactly 10 megabytes (MB) in size.

- **Edb*xxxxx*.log** After Active Directory has been running for a while, there might be one or more log files with the *xxxxx* filename portion being a value that is incremented in hexadecimal numbers. These log files are previous log files; whenever the current log file is filled up, the current log file is renamed to the next previous log file and a new Edb.log file is created. The old log files are automatically deleted as the changes in the log files are made to the Active Directory database. Each of these log files is also 10 MB in size.

- **Edbtemp.log** This log is a temporary log that is used as the current log file (Edb.log) fills up. A new file named Edbtemp.log is created to store any transactions, and the Edb.log file is renamed to the next previous log file. Then the Edbtemp.log file is renamed to Edb.log.

- **Res1.log and Res2.log** These files are reserved log files that are used only when the hard disk that contains the log files runs out of space. If the current log file fills up and the server cannot create a new log file because there is no hard disk space left, the server will flush any Active Directory transactions currently in memory to the two reserved log files and then shut down Active Directory. Each of these log files is also 10 MB in size.

Tip If you have worked with any of the recent versions of Microsoft Exchange Server, this discussion of Active Directory database components and processes will sound very familiar. The Active Directory database is the same database that is deployed with servers running Exchange Server 4 or later.

Every modification to the Active Directory database is called a *transaction*. A transaction can consist of several steps. For example, when a user is moved from one organizational unit (OU) to another, the object must be created in the destination OU and deleted from the source OU. For the transaction to be complete, both steps must be completed, and if one of the steps fails, the transaction should be rolled back so that neither step is completed. When all the steps in a transaction are complete, the transaction is *committed*, or completed. By using a transaction-based model, Windows Server 2003 ensures that the database remains in a consistent state at all times.

Whenever any change is made to the Active Directory database (for example, the telephone number for a user is changed), the change is first written to a transaction log file. Because a transaction log file is essentially a text file where the changes are written sequentially, writing to a transaction log is much quicker than writing to a database. Therefore, the use of transaction logs improves the performance of the domain controller.

Once the transaction has been written to the transaction log, the domain controller loads the database page containing the user object into memory (if it is not already in memory). All changes to the Active Directory database are made in the memory of the domain controller. The domain controller will use as much memory and retain as much of the Active Directory database in memory as possible. The domain controller flushes database pages from memory only when available free memory becomes limited or when the domain controller is being shut down. The changes to the database pages are written to the database during low server-utilization periods or at server shutdown.

The transaction logs not only improve the performance of the domain controller by providing a place to rapidly write changes, but also they provide some recoverability in the event of a server failure. For example, if a change is made to Active Directory, the change is written to the transaction logs and then to the database page in the server memory. If the server shuts down unexpectedly at this point, the changes in the server memory will not have been committed to the database. When the domain controller restarts, it checks the transaction logs for any transactions that have not yet been committed to the database These changes are applied to the database as the domain controller service restarts. The *checkpoint file* is used during this recovery process. The checkpoint file is a pointer that indicates which transactions in the transaction logs have been written to the database. During the recovery process, the domain controller reads the checkpoint file to determine which transactions have been committed to the database, and it then applies all the changes that have not been committed.

Planning The use of transaction logs enhances the performance of the domain controllers and improves the recovery of data in the event of an unexpected shutdown. These advantages are maximized when the transaction logs and the database are located on separate hard disks.

Active Directory in Windows Server 2003 is configured for circular logging, and this configuration cannot be changed. With circular logging, only previous log files containing transactions that have not been written to the database are retained. As the information in the previous log file is committed to the database, the log file is deleted. The circular logging creates the potential for data loss if your domain controller hard disk fails and you have to restore the database from a backup. For example, suppose that you back up Active Directory every night, but your domain controller hard disk crashes at 5 P.M. after you have made several hundred changes to the database over the course of the day. As you made the changes, the previous transaction logs were deleted as the information in the logs was committed to the Active Directory database. When you restore the database to the previous night's backup, all the changes that you made to the directory are lost.

The only way to prevent this data loss is to deploy at least two domain controllers that replicate to each other during the day. If one of your domain controllers fails, you can restore the database on that domain controller and all the changes you made during the day will be replicated to the restored server.

Backing Up Active Directory

The Active Directory design puts some important restrictions on Active Directory backups. The most important of these is that Active Directory can be backed up only as part of the System State data on the domain controller. The System State data on a domain controller includes:

- The Active Directory database and transaction logs
- The system and startup files under Windows File Protection
- The domain controller's registry
- All Active Directory–integrated DNS zone information
- The Sysvol folder
- The COM+ Class Registration database
- The Certificate Services database (if the domain controller is also a Certificate Services server)
- Cluster service information
- The Microsoft Internet Information Services (IIS) metadirectory (if IIS is installed on the computer)

All these components must be backed up and restored as a whole because of their tight integration. For example, if a certificate has been created in the Certificate Services server and that certificate has been assigned to an Active Directory object, the Certificate Services database (which contains the record of the certificate creation) and the Active Directory object (which contains the record of the certificate mapping) must be retained. If one of these components is restored without the other, you will have inconsistent information.

Almost all backup programs can perform different types of backups, including normal, incremental, differential, and so on. The System State backup on a domain controller is always a normal backup where all the files in the System State are backed up and marked as backed up.

Note   By default, only members of the Administrators group and the Backup Operators group have permission to back up domain controllers.

Which domain controllers should you back up? As a general practice, all your domain controllers should be part of the regular backup cycle. The one possible exception to this rule is if you have multiple domain controllers in one office. In this case, you can implement a disaster recovery procedure for domain controllers in which you will always restore domain controllers by installing a new domain controller and populating the directory on that domain controller through replication. However, even in this scenario, at least some of the domain controllers should be backed up in case of a catastrophic event that destroys all the domain controllers in the office. You should also back up at least the operations masters in all cases.

Another issue to consider with domain controller backups is the frequency of backups. Active Directory imposes a definite limit to the backup frequency, in that the *backup age* cannot be older than the tombstone lifetime configured for your domain. By default, the tombstone lifetime is 60 days. The reason the backup cannot be older than the tombstone age is because of the way Active Directory uses tombstones. When an object is deleted, the object is not actually removed from the directory until the tombstone expires. Instead, the object is marked as tombstoned and most of the object attributes are removed. Then the tombstoned object is replicated to all the other domain controllers. At the end of the tombstone lifetime, the tombstoned object is finally deleted from the directory on each domain controller. If you could restore a domain controller from a backup tape that was older than the tombstone, you could find inconsistent directory information between domain controllers. For example, if a user was deleted from the directory the day after backup, the tombstoned object would remain in the directory for 60 days and then be deleted. If the backup was restored to a domain controller more than 60 days after the object was tombstoned, the restored domain controller would have the user object, and because the tombstone object no longer existed, it would not delete the object. In this scenario, the domain controller would have a copy of an object that did not exist anywhere else in the directory. For this reason, the system backup and restore program prevents you from restoring the directory from a backup that is older than the tombstone period.

Although the tombstone lifetime places a hard limit on the frequency of backups, you should obviously back up the domain controllers much more frequently than every 60 days. There are many issues in addition to the tombstone problem that you need to think about if you are trying to restore the domain controller from a backup that is more than a couple of days old. Because the restore of Active Directory includes all the System State information, that information will be restored to a previous state. If the server is a Certificate Services server, any certificates that you issued since the backup will not be included in the Certificate Services database. If you have updated drivers or installed any new applications, they might not work because the registry has been rolled back to a previous state. Almost all companies use a backup regimen in which at least some servers are backed up every night. The domain controllers should be part of the nightly backup.

Restoring Active Directory

There are two reasons you might need to restore Active Directory. The first reason is if your database is unusable—perhaps because one of your domain controllers has experienced a hard disk failure or because the database has been corrupted to the point where it cannot be loaded. The second reason is if human error has created a problem with the directory information. For example, if someone has deleted an OU containing several hundred user and group accounts, you will want to restore the information rather than reenter all the information.

If you are restoring Active Directory because the database on one of your domain controllers is not usable, you have two options. The first option is to not restore Active Directory to the failed server at all, but rather to create another domain controller by promoting another server running Windows Server 2003 to become a domain controller. This way, you are restoring the domain controller functionality rather than restoring Active Directory on a specific domain controller. The second recovery option is to repair the server that failed and to then restore the Active Directory database on that server. In this case, you will perform a nonauthoritative restore. A nonauthoritative restore restores the Active Directory database on the domain controller, and then all the changes made to Active Directory since the backup are replicated to the restored domain controller.

If you are restoring Active Directory because someone deleted a large number of objects in the directory, you only have one way to restore the information. You will restore the Active Directory database on one of the domain controllers using a backup that contains the deleted objects. Then you will perform an authoritative restore. During the authoritative restore, the restored data is marked so that it is replicated to all other domain controllers, overwriting the deletion of the information.

Restoring Active Directory by Creating a New Domain Controller

One of the options for restoring Active Directory functionality is to build a new domain controller to replace a failed domain controller. If one domain controller fails, you can build another server running Windows Server 2003 and Active Directory, or you can use an existing server and promote that server to be a domain controller. Then you can use normal Active Directory replication to populate the Active Directory database on the new domain controller. Creating a new domain controller is the best solution in the following situations:

- You have an available domain controller in addition to the failed server. This is an absolute requirement. If you do not have another domain controller that is available to be used as a replication partner, your only option is to restore the Active Directory database on a new or repaired domain controller.

- The time required to build the new domain controller and replicate the information from another domain controller is significantly less than the time needed to repair the failed domain controller and restore the database. This calculation depends on the size of the Active Directory database, the network connection speed between your domain controllers, and the speed with which you can rebuild and restore a domain controller. If you have a relatively small Active Directory database (less than 100 MB) and another domain controller is on the same local area network (LAN), creating another domain controller and replicating the database will be faster than repairing and restoring the failed domain controller. If you have a large database or the only available replication partner is across a slow wide area network (WAN) connection, repairing the failed domain controller and restoring the database will usually be the quicker option.

- You cannot repair the failed domain controller. Although it is possible to re-store Windows Server 2003 and the Active Directory database onto a server with different hardware from the original domain controller, this process is usually difficult and can be very time-consuming. If you cannot rebuild the failed server with similar hardware, building another domain controller will usually be quicker.

Planning The recovery options listed are not needed if you can repair a failed domain controller without having to rebuild and restore. Windows Server 2003 provides several advanced troubleshooting options, such as the Recovery Console, and various boot options, such as Last Known Good Configuration and Safe Mode. Use these tools to try to recover the domain controller before you perform a complete restore.

To build an additional domain controller to replace the failed server, use an existing server running Windows Server 2003 (or build a new server) and promote it to be a domain controller. During the promotion process, the directory will be replicated from one of the other domain controllers. If the failed domain controller was a global catalog (GC) server or the holder of one of the operations master roles, you will need to consider how to restore this functionality. Recovering GC servers and operations master servers is covered in detail in the section "Restoring Operations Masters and Global Catalog Servers" later in this chapter.

As discussed in Chapter 6, "Installing Active Directory," Windows Server 2003 provides the option of installing a new domain controller and loading the Active Directory database from a restored backup rather than through the normal process of replication. This option is very useful when creating a domain controller in a remote office connected to the central office across a slow network connection because the bulk of the initial replication does not have to cross the WAN link. If you have a good backup of the failed domain controller in the remote office, you can use this same technique to build a new domain controller.

If you do choose to restore Active Directory functionality by creating a new domain controller, you still need to remove the old domain controller from the directory and from DNS. If you are planning to use the failed domain controller's name for the restored domain controller, you need to clean up the directory before starting the recovery. If you are using a different name for the new domain controller, you can clean up the directory after installation.

⮕ **To clean up the directory, perform the following steps on any Windows 2000 workstation or server, Windows XP Professional workstation, or server running Windows Server 2003 that is a member of the domain:**

1. Open a command prompt and type *ntdsutil*.
2. At the Ntdsutil prompt, type *metadata cleanup*.

3. At the Metadata Cleanup prompt, type *connections*. This command is used to connect to a current domain controller to remove the failed domain controller.

4. At the Server Connections prompt, type *connect to server **servername***, where *servername* is the name of an available on domain controller. If you are logged in with an account that has administrative rights in Active Directory, you will be connected to that domain controller. If you do not have administrative rights, you can use the *set creds **domain username password*** command to enter the credentials of a user with domain-level permissions. (If you type *help* at the Server Connections prompt, you will see one of your command options is *connect to server %s*. The *%s* variable must always be replaced by a character string value. In this case, the string is either the DNS name of the domain controller or the server's IP address.)

5. At the Server Connections prompt, type *quit*, which will return you to the Metadata Cleanup prompt.

6. Type *select operation target*. This command is used to select the domain, site, and domain controller so that you can remove the domain controller.

7. At the Select Operation Target prompt, type *list domains*. All the domains in your forest are listed with a number assigned to each.

8. Type *select domain **number**,* where *number* is the domain containing the failed domain controller. (If you type *help* before you type *select domain **number***, you will notice one of the command options is *select domain %d*. The *%d* variable must always be replaced by a number.)

9. Type *list sites*. All the sites in the forest are listed.

10. Type *select site **number*** to select the site containing the domain controller that you need to delete.

11. Type *list servers in site*. All the domain controllers in the selected site are listed. Use the *select server **number*** command to select the domain controller that you need to delete. Ntdsutil then lists the selected domain, site, and domain controller. (See Figure 15-1.)

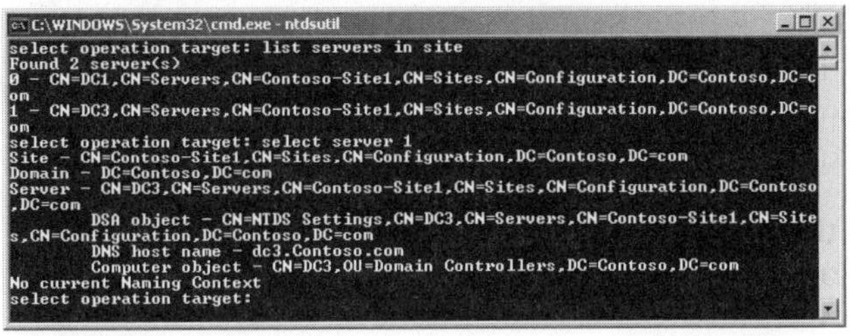

Figure 15-1. *Listing the selected domain, site, and domain controller in Ntdsutil.*

12. Type *quit*. You are returned to the Metadata Cleanup prompt.

13. Type *remove selected server*. You are asked to confirm that you want to remove the server from the directory. Click Yes.

14. To exit Ntdsutil, type *quit* at each command prompt until you exit the program.

The Ntdsutil Tool

Chapter 14, "Monitoring and Maintaining Active Directory," provides several examples of how Ntdsutil can be used to manage the Active Directory database. Ntdsutil is a command-line tool that can be used to manage some components of Active Directory as well as the Active Directory database. Ntdsutil is a powerful tool and should be used with caution.

Start the Ntdsutil tool by opening a command prompt and typing *ntdsutil*. The tool then shows the Ntdsutil prompt. From there you can enter a variety of commands, depending on what you want to do. If you type *help* at any command, you are given a list of all the commands that you can use at that point. For example, Figure 15-2 shows the list of menu commands available from the Ntdsutil prompt.

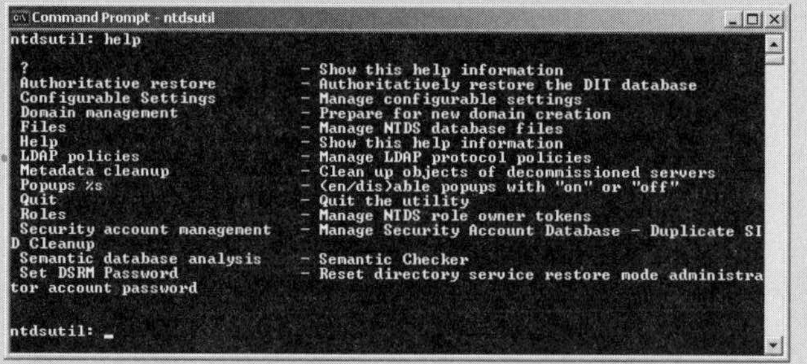

Figure 15-2. *List of available commands at the Ntdsutil command prompt.*

The rest of this chapter provides several more examples of using Ntdsutil to manage Active Directory. For more detailed directions on using Ntdsutil, see the Help And Support Center.

In addition to cleaning up the directory object using Ntdsutil, you should clean up the DNS records for the failed domain controller. Remove all DNS records from DNS, including all domain controller records, GC server records, and primary domain controller (PDC) emulator records. (The last two will exist only if the domain controller was configured with these roles.) If you do not clean up the DNS records, clients will continue to receive the DNS information and try to connect to the domain controller.

You should also remove the failed domain controller from the domain and site. To remove the domain controller from the domain, use the Active Directory Users And Computers administrative tool and delete the object associated with this computer from the Domain Controllers OU. In the Active Directory Sites And Services administrative tool, remove the object associated with this computer from the Servers container for the site where the domain controller was located.

Performing a Nonauthoritative Restore

The second option for restoring the Active Directory database is to repair the domain controller that has failed and then restore the database. Instead of repairing the failed domain controller, you might choose to restore the database to a new server. Restoring the database on a new or repaired server is the best choice under the following circumstances:

- The server is the only domain controller in the domain. If this is the case, you do not have any option as to how you will restore the Active Directory service. You will need to restore the database on a new or repaired server.

- Replicating the information from another domain controller will take too long. In some cases, you might be able to repair the failed domain controller and restore the database more rapidly than you would be able to install a new domain controller and build the database through replication. This will almost always be the case if the failed domain controller is across a slow network connection from any other domain controller. Even if your domain controller is connected to other domain controllers with faster network connections, you might still choose to restore the database.

Planning Without testing the options in your particular environment, it is difficult to say whether it is quicker to restore a domain controller from backup tape or restore Active Directory by creating an additional domain controller. In some cases, it will clearly take less time to create a new domain controller—for example, if you already have a server running Windows Server 2003 installed on the same fast network segment that you can promote to be a domain controller and the Active Directory database is less than 100 MB in size. In other cases, it will clearly take less time to repair the failed domain controller and restore the domain information from backup tape—for example, if your database is several hundred megabytes in size and all other domain controllers are across a slow network connection. However, most network scenarios fall somewhere between these extremes. The only way to know which option is quicker in your environment is to test both options, long before you need to choose.

To restore the Active Directory database, you must have a good backup of the domain controller. If the hard disk containing only the Active Directory database crashes, you will be able to boot directly into Active Directory Restore Mode and restore the System State data. If the system disk crashes as well, you will need to repair the hardware and then rebuild the server.

In some cases, you might need to restore the domain controller on a server that uses different hardware than was available on the original server. Although it is possible to restore Windows Server 2003 on hardware that is different from the hardware on the server that produced the backup, this process is often fraught with problems. If you try to restore Windows Server 2003 on a server with different hardware, try to choose hardware that is as compatible as possible. In particular, ensure that the hardware abstraction layer (HAL), video cards, and network cards are identical. Also ensure that the hard disk configuration on the new server is the same as it was on the failed server. Even if you take these precautions, restoring Windows Server 2003 to a server with different hardware is difficult, with no guarantee of success. A possible alternative is to use the option to create the domain controller from a backup set. In this case, you can take advantage of performing a clean installation of Windows Server 2003, while at the same time being able to create the initial copy of the database from a backup rather than through replication.

Automated System Recovery

One of the backup and restore options provided with Windows Server 2003 is the Automated System Recovery (ASR). This option simplifies the process of restoring the System State data. Before you can use the ASR, you must create the ASR backup, which consists of using the Backup tool to back up the System State data and create an ASR boot disk. The boot disk contains the files needed to boot the server, as well as information about the hard disk configuration on the server and the System State backup. If the server fails, this ASR backup can be used to partially automate the restoration of the server.

If you have made any changes to Active Directory since the backup, the backup tape will not contain those changes. However, the other domain controllers in the domain will have the most recent information. If you are rebuilding the domain controller because the server failed, the domain controller should get the changes from its replication partners after the restore is complete. For this to happen, you must perform a nonauthoritative restore.

➲ **To perform a nonauthoritative restore, follow these steps:**

1. Repair the failed domain controller, and reinstall Windows Server 2003 on the server. After the server has been rebuilt, restart the server and press F8 to boot into the Windows Advanced Options Menu.

2. Choose to boot the domain controller into Directory Services Restore Mode (Windows Domain Controllers Only). If you choose this option, the domain controller will start in safe mode and not load any Active Directory components.

3. Select the operating system you want to start.

4. Log on to the server using the Administrator account with the Directory Services Restore password that was configured on the domain controller when Active Directory was installed.

5. Use the system backup and restore program to restore the System State information on the server.

6. After the data is restored, reboot the domain controller.

After the domain controller reboots, it will connect to its replication partners and begin updating its own database to reflect any domain information modified since the backup.

Note Only the local Administrator can restore Active Directory information. This account is created when Active Directory is installed on the domain controller. The password for the account is also configured during the promotion. The password can be reset only through the Ntdsutil utility.

Performing an Authoritative Restore

In some cases, the nonauthoritative restore does not address the issue that you are dealing with. For example, if someone has just deleted an OU that contains several hundred users, you do not want the domain controller simply to reboot after performing the restore and then begin replication with other domain controllers. If you do, the domain controller will receive the information that the OU has been deleted from its replication partners, and by the time you open the Active Directory Users And Computers administrative tool, the OU will be deleted again.

In this scenario, you must use an authoritative restore to ensure that the restoration of the OU is replicated to the other domain controllers. When you perform an authoritative restore, you restore a backup copy of the Active Directory that was made before the data was deleted and then force that data to be replicated to all the other domain controllers. Forced replication is done by manipulating the update sequence number (USN) for the restored information. By default, when you perform an authoritative restore, the USN on the restored objects is incremented by 100,000 so that the restored object becomes the authoritative copy for the entire domain.

Authoritative Restore Issues

There are several significant issues related to authoritative restores. The most important has to do with group memberships. In some cases, the authoritative restore could result in incorrect group memberships on the domain controllers that are not authoritatively restored. Incorrect memberships can arise when the authoritatively restored object (for example, an OU) contains user and group accounts. When the OU is authoritatively restored, the OU object and the user and group objects are replicated to all the other domain controllers. This happens when the restored group information replicates to a destination domain controller before the user information replicates. When the destination domain controller receives a group, it notices that one or more user accounts listed in the group do not have valid user accounts, and it deletes the users from the group. When the user account is replicated to the destination domain controller, it is not added back to the group. If the user information replicates before the group information, the group memberships will be assigned correctly. Unfortunately, there is no way to control which objects will get replicated first.

The only way to correct this potential error is to create a temporary account and add it to each group that is affected by the authoritative restore. You should do this after the domain controller has rebooted and the initial authoritative replication has completed. Adding the member to the group forces the domain controller to replicate the group membership list to all the other domain controllers. If those domain controllers have deleted the user account, they will restore the user account to the group when they receive the updated group membership list.

Another potential issue dealing with group memberships occurs if a group membership has been changed on another domain controller before or during the authoritative restore. In this case, the group membership on the originating domain controller is modified and might be replicated to all the domain controllers except the domain controller used to perform the authoritative restore. However, the authoritative restore sets the USN for the restored objects much higher than the USN on the group membership change. So, the domain controller used to perform the authoritative restore will never receive the modified group membership information, and the directory information will be inconsistent between the different domain controllers. This inconsistency can be detected only by viewing the group membership list for each group. The easiest option to repair this problem is to update the group membership lists manually.

A third issue with the authoritative restore has to do with domain and computer trusts. When a computer running Microsoft Windows NT, Windows 2000, Windows XP Professional, or Windows Server 2003 is added to the domain, a password known only to the domain controllers and the member computer is created. This password is used to maintain the trust relationship between the computer and the domain. However, by default, the password is also changed every seven days. If you perform an authoritative restore, it will restore the trust passwords that were in use when the backup was made. If the member computer has negotiated a different password for the trust, the trust relationship between the domain and the member computer might fail. NTLM trusts between Active Directory domains and Windows NT domains use a similar process to maintain the trust; these trusts can also fail if the older password is restored. In either case, the trust must be rebuilt. A domain trust can be rebuilt by deleting the domain trust and re-creating it. Workstation trusts with the domain can be rebuilt by using the NetDom command-line tool or by removing the workstation from the domain and then adding it back.

> **Caution**   The issues that arise from using an authoritative restore suggest that the authoritative restore must be used with caution. These issues also illustrate the importance of consistently backing up your domain controllers. The older the backup of the directory is, the more likely you are to run into these problems. Also, you should have a well-designed and practiced disaster recovery program for authoritative restores. The more quickly you can restore the directory, the fewer problems you are likely to have.

Authoritative Restore Procedure

The most common type of authoritative restore is likely to be one in which you need to authoritatively restore only part of the directory. For example, if someone accidentally deletes an OU, you should authoritatively restore only that OU, not the entire directory.

◗   **To perform an authoritative restore, perform the following steps:**

1.   Follow steps 1 through 5 in the nonauthoritative restore procedure; do not reboot the server when the restore is complete.

2.   Open a command prompt, and type *ntdsutil.*

3.   At the Ntdsutil prompt, type *authoritative restore.*

4.   At the Authoritative Restore prompt, type *restore subtree **objectname***. For example, to restore the Managers OU in the NWTraders.com domain, you would type *restore subtree ou=managers ou,dc=nwtraders,dc=com*. You can restore individual group or user accounts (for example, *restore subtree cn=manager1,ou=managers ou,dc=nwtraders,dc=com*). You can also use this command to restore application partitions.

5.   To authoritatively restore the entire directory, type *restore database* at the Authoritative Restore prompt.

6.   Exit Ntdsutil, and reboot the server.

> **Caution**   In some cases, you might want to restore the entire Active Directory database using the authoritative restore. Authoritatively restoring the whole directory is a significant operation and should be done only in cases where the database has been corrupted or some other very serious error has occurred. The authoritative restore of the entire directory increments the USN on every object in the domain and configuration directory partitions by 100,000. The schema partition cannot be authoritatively restored.

Restoring Sysvol Information

So far, the focus of this chapter has been restoring the Active Directory database—that is, the database of accounts and settings for the domain or forest. However, the Sysvol folder on each domain controller also contains critical domain information, such as the group policy templates and scripts used by computers or users on the network. Therefore, restoration of the Sysvol information can be as critical as restoration of the Active Directory database.

The Sysvol folder is backed up as part of the System State information on the domain controller, which means that if a domain controller fails, the Sysvol information can be restored as part of the normal domain controller restoration process. Also, if you choose not to rebuild a domain controller but to restore the functionality by creating another domain controller in the domain, the Sysvol information will be replicated from any existing domain controllers. This information is replicated using the File Replication Service (FRS) rather than the normal Active Directory replication process.

One potential complicating factor could be if you need to perform a restore that is authoritative for the Sysvol container. For example, if someone deleted all the logon scripts in the Sysvol folder, you might want to restore the scripts rather than rebuild them all. The problem is that if the deletions have replicated to all the other domain controllers, the deletion has a more recent replication value than the restored domain controller. So, if you just perform a normal restore on a domain controller, it will replicate the deletion from another domain controller. The solution is to perform a primary restore of the Sysvol information. If you are using the Windows Server 2003 system backup and restore program, you will perform the normal nonauthoritative restore, but when you run the restore program, you should not accept the default restoration settings. Instead, on the Advanced Restore Options page of the Restore Wizard, you should select the When Restoring Replicated Data Sets, Mark The Restored Data As The Primary Data For All Replicas option, as shown in Figure 15-3. Selecting this option marks the Sysvol folder on this domain controller as the primary container for Sysvol replication.

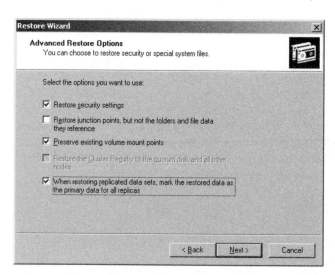

Figure 15-3. *Performing a primary restore for the Sysvol information.*

Restoring Operations Masters and Global Catalog Servers

The operations master server roles require extra consideration when planning for disaster recovery. The operations master roles can be distributed across multiple domain controllers, but each role can be held by only one domain controller in a domain or forest at a point in time. So, restoring these roles is different from restoration for domain controllers that do not hold these roles. The actual procedures for restoring the domain controllers are essentially the same as restoring any other domain controller; the difference is the planning that must go into the disaster recovery. For example, because only one domain controller can hold a particular role, you must determine how long the network will be able to operate without that operations master. In some cases, the absence of the operations master might not cause any problems for several days; in other cases, the failure might have an almost immediate effect. If you can restore the domain controller before the operations master role is needed, you can repair the domain controller and perform a nonauthoritative restore of the server. The operations master will be restored when the server is restored.

In some cases, you might decide that rebuilding the failed domain controller will take longer than your network can operate without that operations master. Or you might decide that you do not want to restore that domain controller at all but would rather create a new domain controller and transfer the operations master role to the new domain controller. Transferring the operations master role is easy if both domain controllers are online because the domain controllers can ensure that they have completed replication before the role is transferred. However, if the operations master has failed and you need to move the role to another domain controller, you will need to seize the role.

Planning   Because of the important roles that the operations master servers play on the network, you should plan the placement and management of these roles carefully. The operations master should always be included in a regular backup regimen. Also, the operations masters should be located in the same site as at least one other domain controller to ensure that at least one other domain controller contains the same information as the operations master.

For example, if a user has just changed his or her password using a down-level client, the change was made on the PDC emulator. The PDC emulator will replicate that change to a replication partner in the same site within 15 seconds. If there is no replication partner in the same site, the password replication will not occur until the next scheduled intersite replication. If the domain controller fails before this scheduled time, the password change will not be replicated to other sites. If a domain controller is in the same site as the operations master server, the chance of incomplete replication is much less. The domain controller that is in the same site as the operations master is also the best choice for seizing the operations master role because it will have the most current information from the operations master. If you have more than one additional domain controller in the same site as the failed operations master, you can use the *repadmin /showvector namingcontext* command to determine which domain controller has the most recent updates from the failed domain controller.

To seize the operations master roles, you can use either the Ntdsutil tool or the Active Directory Users And Computers administrative tool (to seize the PDC emulator and infrastructure roles). The RID Master, Schema Master, and Domain Naming Master can be seized only using the Ntdsutil tool.

To seize operations master roles using Ntdsutil, follow these steps:

1. Open a command prompt, and type *ntdsutil.*

2. At the Ntdsutil prompt, type *roles.*

3. At the Fsmo Maintenance prompt, type *connections.*

4. At the Server Connections prompt, type *connect to server* **servername.domainname**. The *servername* is the domain controller to which you want to seize the operations master role. Type *quit* to return to the Fsmo Maintenance prompt.

5. At the Fsmo Maintenance prompt, type *seize **operations_master_role***. The *operations_master_role* is the role you want to seize and can be *schema master, domain naming master, infrastructure master, RID master,* or *PDC.*

6. Accept the warning statement. The server will first try to perform a normal transfer of the operations master role. When that fails because the failed domain controller cannot be contacted, the role will be seized. See Figure 15-4 for an example of the output when you seize a RID master role.

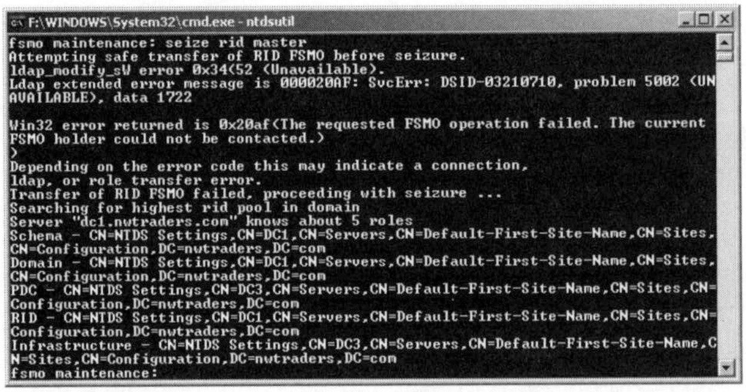

Figure 15-4. *The output from seizing a RID master role through Ntdsutil.*

7. Type *quit* at each command prompt until you exit Ntdsutil.

The PDC emulator and infrastructure master roles can also be seized through the Active Directory Users And Computers administrative tool. To seize these roles, open the Active Directory Users And Computers administrative tool and use the Connect To Domain Controller option to make sure that it is connected to the domain controller to which you want to seize the role. Then right-click the domain name and select Operations Masters. If you do try to seize the role, you will receive the warning message shown in Figure 15-5. If you choose to force the transfer, the operations master role will be seized. Only the PDC emulator and infrastructure master roles can be seized in this way—trying to transfer any other operations master using anything other than Ntdsutil fails.

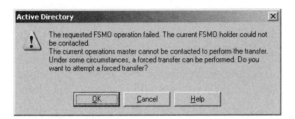

Figure 15-5. *The warning message received when seizing an operations master role through the Active Directory Users And Computers administrative tool.*

PDC Emulator

On most networks, the failure of the PDC emulator usually has a greater immediate effect than the failure of any other operations master. In a domain that is operating at the Windows 2000 mixed functional level or the Windows Server 2003 interim functional level, the PDC emulator is the primary replication partner for all the Windows NT backup domain controllers (BDCs). So, until the PDC emulator is restored, the BDCs will not receive updated information. Also, down-level clients such as Windows NT, Windows 95, and Windows 98 (without the Directory Services client) must connect to the PDC emulator for a user to be able to change his or her password. Even in a domain operating in Windows 2000 native functional level or higher, the PDC emulator plays a role as the primary replication partner for password changes. The PDC emulator is also the preferred server for making any changes to group policies. If the PDC emulator is not available when you try to view a group policy, you will receive a warning message indicating that the PDC emulator is not available. Because the PDC emulator provides all these services, restoring the PDC emulator role on the network must take a high priority.

Although the PDC emulator plays a critical role in the domain, seizing the role to another domain controller while the original PDC emulator is unavailable also has limited implications. In fact, seizing the role is similar to seizing the PDC role in a Windows NT domain. If the PDC ever failed in a Windows NT domain, you could choose another domain controller and configure it to be the PDC. The same functionality exists in Windows Server 2003. If the PDC emulator fails, you should move the role to another domain controller. Even if the domain controller will be unavailable for only a couple of hours, you should transfer the role. When the original PDC emulator is restored and connected to the network again, it will detect the presence of the new PDC emulator and give up the PDC emulator role.

Schema Master

The schema master plays an essential role in a Windows Server 2003 domain, but it is also a role that is used very infrequently. The schema master is the only domain controller in which the schema can be changed. If this server fails, you will not be able to make changes to the schema until the server is restored or until the role has been seized to another domain controller.

The schema master functionality is rarely used because the schema will rarely be modified on most networks. The testing that is required to ensure that the schema change is compatible with the current schema usually means that the schema change has been planned for some time, and in most cases, delaying the deployment of the schema change until the schema master has been restored should not be a problem. However, if you are not planning on restoring the schema master, you can seize the role to another domain controller using Ntdsutil. If you do seize the schema master role to another domain controller, the original schema master should never be restored on the network.

Tip   For all the operations master roles other than the PDC emulator and infrastructure master, it is recommended that if you seize the role to another domain controller, you should not restore the original operations master to the network. This recommendation is because there is a risk of incompatible changes on the network. For example, if you seize the schema master role and then make changes to the schema, the original schema master will not have those changes. If you do not make any changes to the schema, this will not be a problem. However, if you do not plan on making any changes to the schema while the schema master is offline, there is really no need to seize the role.

Domain Naming Master

The domain naming master is another role that is infrequently used. This operations master is required only when adding or removing domains. If this domain controller is not available for a short period of time, there will be few repercussions in a stable production environment. However, if you must add or remove a domain and you do not have time to restore the domain naming master, you can seize the role. Just like the schema master role, if you do seize the domain naming master role to another domain controller, the original operations master should never be brought back online unless the operating system is reinstalled on the server, eliminating the domain naming master role on that server.

Note On most networks, the schema master and domain naming master roles are used so rarely that if these domain controllers fail you do not have to seize the role to another server. However, these domain controllers are normally located in the forest root domain, and the forest root domain controllers do play essential roles. If you have only a single forest root domain controller and it fails, the network will certainly be affected. Any type of cross-domain activity, such as logging on to a domain other than your home domain or accessing a resource in another domain, will fail if there are no root domain controllers (unless there is a trust path between the domains that does not include the root domain). So, although the schema master and domain naming master don't always have to be available, at least one domain controller in your root domain must be available at all times.

Infrastructure Master

The infrastructure master's role is perhaps the least significant from a disaster recovery perspective. The infrastructure master monitors display-name changes for user and group accounts across multiple domains. This activity is transparent to the normal user and is an issue only when administrators are viewing group memberships. Therefore, seizing the infrastructure master role is a fairly low priority because it does not disrupt any network services.

If you decide to seize an infrastructure role to another domain controller in a multiple-domain environment, you should ensure that the destination domain controller is not a GC server. If you do seize the role, you can subsequently restore the original infrastructure master.

RID Master

The RID master is a domain-level operations master that assigns RID pools to other domain controllers as new security principals are created. If the RID master is not available for an extended period, the domain controllers might run out of RIDs to assign to new security principals. Each time a domain controller runs out of RIDs, it requests an additional RID pool from the RID master. The RID master then assigns an additional RID pool of 512 RIDs. If the RID master is not available, the domain controller will not allow any more security principals to be created until it can get additional RIDs from the RID master. The RID master is also important if you are moving security principals between domains. In this case, if the RID master is not available, moving the accounts will fail immediately.

If your RID master domain controller fails, you will need to decide whether you should seize the role to another server. If you need to create a large number of security principals or move users between domains before the RID master can be restored, you will need to seize the role. Also, if you are not planning on restoring the original RID master, you will have to seize the role. If you choose to seize the role, the original RID master should not be brought back online because of the potential for duplicate security identifiers (SIDs).

GC Servers

The GC servers also require some additional planning for disaster recovery, despite the fact that the GC servers do not have any special requirements when backing up or restoring. The only issue that you will need to plan for is that if you have multiple domains in your forest, the directory database on the GC server will be considerably larger than the database on the other domain controllers. If you choose to restore a GC server by restoring the database on the domain controller, the server will automatically be configured as a GC server. If you choose to restore Active Directory functionality by promoting another server to become a domain controller, you will need to configure that server as a GC server.

The GC server is critical on the network for client logons in a domain operating at a Windows 2000 native or higher functional level or when using user principal names (UPNs). The GC is also critical if you have deployed Microsoft Exchange Server 2000. In this case, you might need to configure additional GC servers in the location while you rebuild the failed domain controller. For example, if the only GC server in a site where you have a server running Exchange Server 2000 fails, you will probably need to configure one of the other domain controllers in the site as a GC server and restore the functionality as quickly as possible.

Summary

This chapter covered the essential topic of disaster recovery in Windows Server 2003 Active Directory. Disaster recovery is one of the network administration tasks that you hope you will never need to use. However, as any experienced administrator knows, you will almost certainly need to use the disaster recovery procedures at some time. This chapter began by discussing the basic data elements in Active Directory. It then discussed the practices for backing up Active Directory. The majority of this chapter explained the procedures for restoring Active Directory in both authoritative and nonauthoritative modes. One of the issues that must be dealt with in a disaster recovery scenario is the management of the operations master roles and the special planning issues involved in restoring these roles on the network.

Index

Stan Reimer is a Corporate Technology Specialist with Great West Life Assurance Company. He brings the perspective of an enterprise infrastructure architect and directory specialist to this book. Working primarily with Active Directory, Stan designs and deploys directory services for eBusiness solutions. Before joining Great West Life Assurance Company, Stan worked as a consultant to enterprise clients designing and implementing Microsoft technologies including Microsoft Windows NT, Windows 2000 Active Directory, and Microsoft Exchange Server. Stan has also written courseware on Windows 2000 for IBM Learning Services, and he is the author of *Migrating to Microsoft Exchange 2000*.

Mike Mulcare is a subject matter expert and an instructional designer in the Training and Certification division of the Microsoft Corporation, where he develops courseware for Active Directory and Microsoft Windows Server 2003. Prior to joining Microsoft, Mike created Windows 2000 courseware for IBM Learning Services and worked as a technology consultant specializing in system deployment and migration. He has been a Microsoft Certified Trainer since 1997.

At Microsoft Press, we use tools to illustrate our books for software developers and IT professionals. Tools very simply and powerfully symbolize human inventiveness. They're a metaphor for people extending their capabilities, precision, and reach. From simple calipers and pliers to digital micrometers and lasers, these stylized illustrations give each book a visual identity, and a personality to the series. With tools and knowledge, there's no limit to creativity and innovation. Our tag line says it all: *the tools you need to put technology to work*.

The manuscript for this book was prepared and galleyed using Microsoft Word 2002. Pages were composed by Microsoft Press using Adobe PageMaker 6.52 for Windows, with text in Garamond and display type in Franklin Gothic. Composed pages were delivered to the printer as electronic prepress files.

Cover Designer:	Methodologie, Inc.
Interior Graphic Designer:	James D. Kramer
Interior Graphic Artists:	David Holter and Joel Panchot
Project Manager:	J&L Publishing
Principal Compositor:	Dan Latimer
Copyeditor:	Uma Kukathas
Proofreaders:	Brenda Denzler and nSight, Inc.
Indexer:	Julie Kawabata

Get a **Free**
e-mail newsletter, updates,
special offers, links to related books,
and more when you

register on line!

Register your Microsoft Press® title on our Web site and you'll get a FREE subscription to our e-mail newsletter, *Microsoft Press Book Connections.* You'll find out about newly released and upcoming books and learning tools, online events, software downloads, special offers and coupons for Microsoft Press customers, and information about major Microsoft® product releases. You can also read useful additional information about all the titles we publish, such as detailed book descriptions, tables of contents and indexes, sample chapters, links to related books and book series, author biographies, and reviews by other customers.

Registration is easy. Just visit this Web page and fill in your information:

http://www.microsoft.com/mspress/register

Microsoft®

Proof of Purchase

Use this page as proof of purchase if participating in a promotion or rebate offer on this title. Proof of purchase must be used in conjunction with other proof(s) of payment such as your dated sales receipt—see offer details.

Active Directory® for Microsoft® Windows® Server 2003 Technical Reference

0-7356-1577-2

CUSTOMER NAME

Microsoft Press, PO Box 97017, Redmond, WA 98073-9830